Full-Spectrum Strategic Leadership

*Being on the Cutting Edge
through Innovative Solutions, Integrated Systems,
and Enduring Relationships*

Full-Spectrum Strategic Leadership

*Being on the Cutting Edge
through Innovative Solutions, Integrated Systems,
and Enduring Relationships*

David L. Rainey
Rensselaer Polytechnic Institute

INFORMATION AGE PUBLISHING, INC.
Charlotte, NC • www.infoagepub.com

Library of Congress Cataloging-in-Publication Data

A CIP record for this book is available from the Library of Congress
http://www.loc.gov

ISBN: 978-1-62396-649-2 (Paperback)
      978-1-62396-650-8 (Hardcover)
      978-1-62396-651-5 (ebook)

Copyright © 2014 Information Age Publishing Inc.

All rights reserved. No part of this publication may be reproduced, stored in a retrieval system, or transmitted, in any form or by any means, electronic, mechanical, photocopying, microfilming, recording or otherwise, without written permission from the publisher.

Printed in the United States of America

Dedication

I would like to dedicate this book to Richard Huskes, Gene Avery, Ronald Bancroft, and Robert Scott, the officers of A Battery, 3rd Missile Battalion, 7th Artillery, and all of the U.S Army officers who served with me in Schweinfurt and Bamberg, Germany during 1969, 1970, and 1971. They taught me the fundamentals of leadership through their insights and actions. I was fortunate to have such wonderful colleagues to show me the ways of authentic leadership during my first experiences as a leader.

I would also like to dedicate the book to Colonel James Harrover, Colonel Clive Goodyear, and Major Edward Langston who as the senior leaders of the battalion provided incredible guidance and support of the young officers under their charge. They gave me the wonderful opportunity to be a leader at a young age. Through their leadership and inspiration, I learned the awesome responsibilities of leadership that provided the seeds for lifelong learning.

Contents

List of Figures xi

List of Tables xiii

Introduction xv

1 **Full-Spectrum Strategic Leadership** 1
    Introduction 1
    Perspectives on Leadership and Management Constructs 3
        A brief evolutionary tract highlighting select management constructs 3
        Contemporary views about holistic management systems and business models 8
        Perspectives on leadership and management constructs 11
    Full-Spectrum Strategic Leadership 18
        The meaning and implications of full-spectrum strategic leadership 18
        Dual-sided perspectives of FSL 20
        The implications of multifaceted leadership perspectives 22
        FSL and multifaceted leadership perspectives 24
    Reflections 28
    Notes 29
    References 30

2 **The Driving Forces of Change and the Influences of the Business Environment** ... 31
    Introduction 31
    The Critical Driving Forces 32
        The expansion of market spaces 32
        Cultural and ethnic imperatives 34
        The intensity of competition in terms of costs and quality 37
        The expanding role of technology 39
        The ubiquitous Internet 43

The Dynamics of the Business Environment 45
    General perspectives 45
    Market spaces 46
    Social dimension... 47
    Political dimension 51
    Ethical dimension 52
    Economic dimension 53
Reflections 59
Notes 60
References 62

3 Leading Change through Insightfulness 63
Introduction 63
General Concepts and Implications Pertaining to Leading Change 64
    The dynamics of globalization 64
    The acceleration of change... 68
    The enormity of change 69
Technological and Environmental Dimensions Pertaining to Change................... 71
    Implications of technological change.. 71
    Technology developments... 74
    Environmental concerns and responses 76
Selected Perspective about Insightfulness 78
    Academic insights about leading change 78
    Insights of strategic leaders and professionals about leading change............. 80
General Model for Leading Change 82
Reflections 86
Notes 86
References 87

4 Crafting Solutions through Innovativeness 89
Introduction 89
General Perspectives Pertaining to Solutions 91
    The solution set and its primary elements... 91
    Value creation and the solution set... 95
The Solution Development Process 100
    Perspectives about the process and the key elements 100
    The design and development of the solution 108
    Solution in the context of the development of the value system and the enterprise........ 110
    Deployment of the solution... 113
Reflections 115
Notes 115
References 116

5 Shaping Systems through Inclusiveness 119

Introduction 119

Cutting-Edge Leadership and Management Constructs 120

The embedded management system 120

The essential constructs pertaining to systems thinking 123

Framing the Management Systems 128

Holistic perspectives in system design and development 128

Forming the management systems 132

Process design and development 134

Reflections 136

Notes 136

References 137

6 Building Relationships through Connectedness 139

Introduction 139

The Critical Underpinnings in Building Relationships 142

General perspectives about relationships 142

Narrow versus broad-based relationships 144

Building Mutually Beneficial External Relationships 147

High-level external relationships 147

Relationships with upstream entities and people 149

Relationships with downstream entities and people 152

Reinforcing Internal Relationships 153

Overarching perspectives and themes pertaining to internal relationships ... 153

The increasing importance of internal connections 156

Sustaining Relationships through Connectedness 159

Reflections 163

Notes 163

References 164

7 High-Level Strategic Innovations 165

Introduction 165

Critical Factors Involving Strategic Innovations 167

Overview 167

Theoretical considerations pertaining to strategic innovations 170

The strategic logic for leading change through strategic innovations 173

The Main Elements of Strategic Innovation 178

Value innovation: the underpinning of strategic innovation 178

Corporate research and development and corporate entrepreneurship 180

Radical innovation 181

Reflections 184

Notes 184

References 185

8 Business Model Innovation ... 187
Introduction ... 187
Business Model Innovation ... 188
Underpinnings ... 188
A skeleton of a business model framework ... 191
The Main Elements of the Enterprise-Wide Business Model Framework ... 197
Value drivers ... 197
Value proposition ... 199
Values ... 203
Vision ... 204
Value configuration ... 204
Value innovation ... 206
Value creation ... 206
Value development ... 206
Value chain ... 209
Value system ... 210
Value networks ... 213
Value deployment ... 214
Reflections ... 215
Notes ... 217
References ... 217

9 Sustainable Success and Concluding Comments ... 219
Introduction ... 219
Sustainable Success and FSL as the Means and the Ends ... 221
Exciting opportunities and challenges for sustainable success ... 221
FSL: The means and mechanisms for personal and organizational development ... 225
Concluding Comments ... 227

Glossary ... 233

About the Author ... 245

List of Figures

Figure 1.1	A simple characterization of the hierarchical model	4
Figure 1.2	Porter's Value Chain	5
Figure 1.3	Simple characterization of the value system (customer-driven perspective)	6
Figure 1.4	Hamel's unpacking of the business model	8
Figure 1.5	The elements of the enterprise-wide strategic management system	10
Figure 1.6	A mapping of selected management constructs	14
Figure 1.7	Full-spectrum strategic leadership	18
Figure 1.8	A simplified depiction of the matrix of key dimensions pertaining to FSL	26
Figure 2.1	The dimensions of the business environment	45
Figure 3.1	General model for leading change	83
Figure 3.2	Leading change and sustaining success	85
Figure 4.1	The solution set for a sustainable solution	92
Figure 4.2	Key elements of the solution development process	104
Figure 5.1	Cutting-edge leadership and management constructs for systems integration	124
Figure 5.2	Framework of a business unit's system based on an external perspective	129
Figure 6.1	Conventional relationship protocol based on single point of contact	145
Figure 6.2	Enhanced relationship protocol based on multiple points of contacts	146
Figure 6.3	Critical factors affecting internal relationships	158
Figure 7.1	The hierarchy of organic strategic innovations	167
Figure 7.2	Theoretical view of incremental and radical innovations	172
Figure 7.3	The front-end of the radical innovation framework	183
Figure 8.1	Enterprise-wide business model framework	194

Figure 8.2	Value equation of the value proposition	200
Figure 8.3	Value chain example: Siemens Automation and Drives	209
Figure 8.4	Porter's value system	210
Figure 8.5	Connections of the value system based on ESM	212
Figure 8.6	Value deployment	214
Figure 9.1	Theoretical levels of sophistication of companies/business units	223

List of Tables

Table 1.1	List of Leadership Perspectives: Narrow and Broad	25
Table 3.1	The Stages of Environmental Perspectives and Management Considerations	78
Table 4.1	Selected Elements and Aspects of the Solution Set	98
Table 4.2	Hypothetical Example of the Results of Two Different Growth Rates	106
Table 4.3	Hypothetical Example of the Results Based on Ten-Year Life	107
Table 6.1	Categories of Short- and Long-Term Effects (attributes and impacts)	160
Table 8.1	Selected Sub-Elements of Value Configuration	205
Table 8.2	Key Considerations in Value Development	208
Table 8.3	Selected Elements Linking Strategies, Solutions, Systems, and Structures	216

Introduction

Overview

Leadership and management are two of the most discussed and written about subjects pertaining to business organizations. Exceptional strategic leadership and effective senior management are critical for achieving sustainable success and ensuring that the organization is heading in the right direction. But what are strategic leadership and senior management? They are often viewed in terms of positions of the incumbents and/or one's status in an organization. The members of senior management are often perceived to provide leadership and management because of their positions, power, and authority. Corporate executives, strategic leaders, senior managers, and general managers of companies, business units, subsidiaries, divisions, and joint ventures among many other forms of high-level positions have specific roles, responsibilities, and duties that give them the legitimate authority to lead and manage their organizations. However, such lofty positions do not automatically mean that the incumbents have the capacity to lead and manage. Strategic leadership is more than just being the incumbent in a senior position within an organization. It implies leading people and achieving success, not just managing operations, activities, resources or things.

Leadership and management positions, especially strategic ones, run the gamut from static designations that may be inherited by birthright or bestowed by superiors through political processes to more open-ended situations in which the incumbent earns the respect of the people across the organization and the business environment. The former involves individuals who are given or granted high-level positions because of their heritage, family background, political connections, and/or linkages within the hierarchy of the organization. Obvious examples include family members who are selected to head family-owned or family-controlled businesses and individuals who are selected because they know the right people or are in the right places. Examples also include organizations that have autocratic or dictatorial executives at the top in which future strategic leaders are selected on the basis of their support of and acquiescence to the prevailing senior management. While not everyone who inherits or is selected to a senior position in these ways is a static leader or manager, being a strategic leader or senior manager implies more than just occupying important positions within an organization; true strategic leaders exhibit leadership qualities and take full responsibilities for what happens or fails to happen.

High-level strategic positions and the roles, responsibilities and duties thereof are obtained, enhanced, and demonstrated through the incumbent's knowledge, abilities, competencies, performance, experiences, and positive outcomes. Such leadership perspectives should be the case regardless of the situations or circumstances. True strategic leaders know the meaning of leadership and act for the benefit of the whole organization and enterprise. They are aware of the awesome obligations and actions that require the incumbents to subordinate their personal goals and rewards in deference to those of the organizations and the people that they are responsible for. True strategic leaders are neither superior nor subservient to the organization, but are individuals with special duties to ensure the success of the whole business enterprise and all that it touches.

Senior management involves being a senior manager or general manager in some part of the organization, having a strategic management position, engaging in governance, providing guidance, managing organizational units or business units, and achieving desired outcomes through strategies, solutions, and actions. However, many of today's senior managers and general managers concentrate their efforts on the short-term aspects of satisfying customers, beating competitors, and making money. Their efforts focus on providing acceptable product-market attributes, complying with laws and regulations, meeting the industry standards and norms, and beating the financial expectations. While such actions are usually proper and appropriate, they are often narrow with limited perspectives in terms of scope and time. There may be little lasting value in just satisfying customers and stakeholders and complying with the existing rules and regulations in a quest to make larger profits in the short term, if success cannot be sustained in the long term. In simple terms, short-term efforts and results on a narrow front (the economic and legal aspects only) may not be good enough. Over the last several decades, many companies and their strategic leaders achieved excellent market success and great profitability in the short term only to lose market share and money in the long term because of unsustainable positions and poor strategic leadership. For example, Lucent Technologies was one of the most successful companies in the late 1990s as it exploited the demand for Y2K (year 2000) solutions, but the company was unable to sustain its strategic positions after the concerns about potential Y2K problems were alleviated. Moreover, long-term success does not just happen; it takes exceptional strategic leadership to realize it.

In today's rapidly changing and turbulent business world, sustainable success depends more and more on the qualities, capabilities, knowledge, and perspectives of the strategic leaders and senior managers of the company and its enterprises and their abilities and willingness to lead and inspire people and achieve extraordinary performance in both the short term and in the long term. Strategic leaders and managers have to have courage and confidence to lead change, craft and implement proactive strategies, create innovative solutions, establish integrated systems and organizational structures, and build solid relationships with people across the business environment. Outstanding strategic leaders and senior managers are those enlightened individuals who achieve the desired strategic outcomes and sustain success while at the same time contributing to the social and economic well-being of the people they affect and to the preservation of the natural world.

Astute strategic leaders and senior managers take broad perspectives of all the critical dimensions of the business environment and market spaces, connect with external customers, stakeholders and constituents, and transition and transform their organizations and enterprises to higher levels of sophistication. They translate objectives, strategies, analysis, actions, and relationships into beneficial outcomes. They achieve extraordinary performance from the positive conversions of inputs to outputs, efforts into realities, knowledge into intellectual capital, and experiences into valuable contributions and real-world solutions. This kind of leadership and management exemplifies a commitment to making the business world richer by "walking the talk."[1]

Today, strategic leaders and senior managers have to craft and implement strategies, create *innovative solutions,* develop *integrated systems,* and build *enduring relationships* based on all of the external and internal considerations and connections, not just on what their products and services are. Solutions have to be supported by the management systems across the entire business enterprise and all of the capabilities and resources of the key contributors. The management systems and their connections with the business world must be based on the solid foundations of the relationships with the people involved. People make the difference between success and failure.

Strategic leaders have to embrace the entire business enterprise when developing strategies, solutions, systems and structures, and building relationships. Strategic leaders must continuously demonstrate their commitment to the organization and reinforce their dedication to the people across the enterprise through interactions based on respect and recognition. This kind of strategic leadership is referred to in this book as *full-spectrum strategic leadership* (FSL) as introduced herein and discussed in more detail in Chapter 1.

A Turbulent and Rapidly Changing Business World

Many strategic leaders of the twentieth century learned their management theories and techniques and developed their know-how and skills based on narrow perspectives and concepts like profit maximization, production and consumption, supply and demand, vertical integration, single-sided marketing (just communicating the positive aspects) and the hierarchical organizational structure. However, the business world has changed dramatically over the last decade. Leadership and management constructs of today have to be more holistic and comprehensive in scope and reach to ensure that all significant forces and factors are considered when leading change, making strategic decisions and taking decisive actions. Strategic leaders have to be on the ***cutting edge***.

The so-called "Great Recession" is clearly not a normal economic downturn that periodically occurs to correct some of the excesses in the business environment. The depth and length of the Great Recession are staggering when using traditional measures. Unemployment in the U.S. exceeded ten percent in 2009 and lingered at nine percent for most of 2010 and 2011. Business failures cut across most sectors and some of the largest companies like Bear Stearns, Lehman Brothers, Circuit City, and Merrill Lynch went bankrupt. Whole industries like insurance and banking suffered catastrophic losses. The resulting financial meltdown and its disruptive effects and impacts were felt by consumers, investors, retirees, and governments; few were immune. The U.S. government spent hundreds of billions of dollars to bail out banks and insurance companies, including AIG, Citigroup, and Wells Fargo. Manufacturers like General Motors (GM) and Chrysler received billions as well. Moreover, some companies like GM were converted to government-owned enterprises. Still others like Merrill Lynch had to be acquired by a more solvent companies.

The economic crisis provides evidence that the business world has significantly changed and that most of the old-line business approaches are no longer suitable for sustaining success in a more complicated business world. It can be argued that many of the failures were due to strategic leaders of many of the largest corporations simply following industry norms that are outdated and too simplistic. The old view of "business as usual" is no longer adequate for obtaining even modest results. The current realities provide evidence that the business paradigm of the last century has to be modified to be in synch with the social, ethical, economic, technological, and environmental shifts of the business environment as globalization matures and the positive and negative aspects of a more global economy take hold. Moreover, the business world has changed dramatically since the collapse of the Soviet Union, the integration of the European Union (EU), the expansion of the global economy, and the explosive growth of the internet. The enormity of these changes is evident as business leaders around the world respond to the challenges of a more intense, interconnected, fast-paced, and global business world. With the rapid industrialization of China, India, and Brazil and the expansion of international trade, the business environment is now more exciting, complicated and turbulent. However, there are no guarantees that the rapid expansion in these countries will continue. There are signs China, India, and Brazil may be slowing down as other developing counties assume the role of low-cost producers.

The human population has more than doubled over the last half century from about 2.5 billion people circa 1950 to approximately 6.1 billion in 2000.[2] And the global population is expected to increase from 7 billion in 2012 to over 9 billion by 2050.

These changes have had profound effects on the social, ethical, economic, technological, and environmental underpinnings of the business world and the underlying social world and natural environment. Such effects have radically changed the ways in which business is conducted and how strategic leaders set strategic direction, make decisions, and take actions. Strategic leaders have to rethink their basic perspectives, philosophies, principles, strategies, and actions and establish new leadership and management constructs that allow them to lead change and achieve sustainable success. Strategic leaders and senior managers have to be much more sophisticated, have broader perspectives of the business environment, and use cutting-edge theories and practices. Without a doubt, there are incredible opportunities for astute strategic leaders and senior managers to create exciting new solutions and enjoy success. For instance, new technologies such as biotechnology, nanotechnologies, and digital technologies provide opportunities for creating new solutions to social, economic, and environmental challenges. In particular, digital technologies have made many old analog technologies outmoded; the related technologies have created numerous new products like liquid crystal display (LCD) televisions, digital cameras, and smart cell phones. These technological changes and the underlying economic and social forces have turned many mature markets into exciting growth opportunities and have produced new ways for providing innovative solutions for people in thw developed and developing countries.

While a popular perception adheres to the view that the world is shrinking due to reduced trade restrictions, the improved interconnectedness between companies, countries, and economies, the expansion of information and communications technologies, and the enhancements in global logistics, in reality the business world has expanded dramatically over the last twenty years. It is true that communications, transportation, and freer trade have made the world much smaller on a geographic basis; however, in terms of market economies, social interconnections, the exchanges of goods and services, and the number of potential customers, the global economy and its market implications are significantly larger and more varied than a generation ago. From the perspectives of strategic leaders, the business world today includes potentially every country and every person. Market potential on a global basis has more than quadrupled from the so-called elites numbering about one billion people in the developed countries before the end of the Cold War to essentially the entire global population. In approximately twenty years, the global business landscape has radically changed from a narrow market space of providing products and services to the richest people to a broader scope of meeting the needs and requirements of billions of people living in varied and often desperate situations. Cutting-edge leadership and management perspectives have to consider all facets of the human condition across the world and determine how to provide solutions that fit the prevailing realities and exciting possibilities. While the changes are enormous and the challenges are great, the prospects arising from a more inclusive business world are incredible.

The business world today is not only more exciting, fast-paced, and technologically sophisticated, it is subject to disruptions and dislocations and fraught with difficulties, uncertainties, and risks. For many strategic leaders around the world, it is akin to sailing in uncharted waters and travelling in new territories without proven theories, methods, and practices. The flux is enormous as old-line companies like GM and Ford Motor Company reinvent themselves at the same time innovative start-ups like Facebook and Google, Inc. quickly became star performers. Moreover, some of the high-flyers of the previous decade or two like Cisco Systems, Home Depot, and Sony find it challenging to sustain their performance as market conditions and trends change and new competitors enter the fray. Even some of the most well-endowed and successful companies like Nestlé, Unilever, and Proctor & Gamble (P&G) have to create new solutions, develop strategic innovations, and/or orchestrate dramatic mergers and acquisitions in their efforts to stay ahead of the incredible changes. For example, P&G merged with Gillette to preempt the power of Walmart and other retailers whose size and financial power give them enormous clout in consumer markets. And even the most innovative and dynamic companies or the newest stars are not immune to the challenges of change and staying on the cutting edge. For example, Facebook, founded in 2004, quickly became the cutting-edge leader in social networking. The previously leader, MySpace, was quickly replaced as the market share leader in 2008.

Today, the business world is more diverse, multifaceted, and complicated. Strategic leaders and senior managers of today have to direct and manage their own businesses, operations, capabilities, and resources as well as orchestrate the efforts of their key contributors across the broad horizons of the global business environment. They have to provide great solutions for customers and stakeholders and ensure success for shareholders, employees, suppliers, and other contributors. The opportunities are great and the challenges are daunting, but strategic leaders and senior managers with comprehensive understanding of the realities and possibilities can achieve great outcomes. To do so, astute strategic leaders have to develop new perspectives, concepts, theories, and practices for leading and managing their business enterprises in more innovative, inclusive, integrated and interconnected ways. Leadership and management constructs using narrow perspectives, especially those based on just doing business in developed countries, have to evolve into multidimensional constructs that are underpinned by broad, multicultural, and multifaceted approaches based on the realities and expectations of the global business environment.

Full-Spectrum Strategic Leadership

FSL is a dynamic and broad-based strategic leadership construct for leading change and sustaining success in complex business situations. FSL implies having and using a broad array of qualities, capabilities, values, attitudes, duties, roles, and responsibilities. These include having the knowledge, capability, confidence, and courage to lead change, being broad-minded and selfless, practicing self-discipline, respecting and inspiring people, upholding the highest ethical standards, and being the architect of the organization's future. FSL involves creating extraordinary value, making people successful, and achieving outstanding business performance. It necessitates having broad social, economic, ethical, market, technological, environmental, and organizational perspectives, crafting proactive strategies, and taking positive actions that are based on a holistic framework for understanding global realities and opportunities, for orchestrating strategic direction, and for achieving the desired outcomes. It goes beyond the traditional leadership and management philosophies and approaches of the last century that focused on growing businesses, making money, satisfying customers, and motivating employees. FSL involves discovering the underlying forces that provide new opportunities, developing insights about what can be done, creating innovative solutions, and deploying the solutions to ensure that everyone in the organization and across the enterprise is successful. It also involves designing and establishing the systems and structures, building relationships within and across the enterprise(s), and engaging people to sustain success from one generation to the next. It requires being on the cutting edge.

People generally perform well when they are excited about their aspirations and the contributions they make. For sustainable success, the challenges, the work, and the results have to be stimulating and satisfying so that people enjoy what they are doing on a day-to-day, month-to-month and year-to-year basis. If it takes years or decades to accomplish the desired outcomes, the processes for getting there have to be fulfilling and the contributors must be encouraged, recognized, and rewarded along the way. FSL involves inspiring people to be the best they can be.

FSL involves being creative and providing the best solutions possible. For instance, every product or service has both positive and negative attributes. Great solutions maximize the positives and minimize the negatives. Providing great solutions involves improving all of the possible benefits, positive effects, and contributions made, and similarly, reducing all of the costs, defects, burdens, and impacts associated with the negative side. Great strategic leaders ensure that the value created is the best possible given the realities of the business environment and that every effort is made for maximizing the positives and minimizing the negatives. This perspective is dual-sided. It means considering the full spectrum of possibilities from the origin of the raw materials to the end of the useful lives of the solutions and engaging both the positives and the negatives.

FSL has to be ever-present and always fully energized. While perfection is a distance dream, FSL involves the pursuit of perfection. It is truly the overarching element of effective strategic management and organizational management.

Single-Sided and Dual-Sided/Multi-Sided Perspectives

A perspective is the mental view of the relationships between given subjects (to each other and to the whole) and the ability of the individual(s) to perceive the interrelationships and their comparative importance and usefulness. Many of the traditional management theories, approaches, practices, and business models of the last century were single-sided. *Single-sided perspectives* are usually narrow and generally concentrate on the positive aspects. The notions of profit maximization and relying on core competencies are among the best known single-sided perspectives that are still widely-used management theories. Profit maximization suggests that strategic leaders do everything possible to make the most profits and obtain outstanding financial performance. It is a good example of a conventional single-sided perspective that assumes the primary responsibility of strategic leaders is to provide the maximum return on shareholders' investments. It contends that business leadership is rightly guided by the economic self-interest of capitalism; i.e., the purpose and primary objectives of corporations are to maximize profits and shareholder wealth. While making money is crucial, strategic and financial success is usually achieved by engaging in all facets of a business enterprise, providing complete solutions, and having integrated systems and solid relationships; not just by generating profits. Strategic leaders who engage in profit maximization may do well in the short term, but they often lose in the long term as the other key considerations like customer success and product liabilities turn negative and wipe out the gains.

The concept of focusing on core competencies was one of the most pervasive theories of the 1990s. Core competencies are the critical capabilities of an organization that it uniquely possesses; they provide competitive advantages and are difficult for others to emulate. C.K. Prahalad and Gary Hamel define them as "the collective learning in organization, especially how to coordinate diverse production skills and integrate multiple streams of technologies."[3] Prahalad and Hamel view core competencies as relatively rare. The theory suggests that strategic leaders should focus on their core competencies and invest into businesses, technologies, products, and operations they support. While having core competencies is critical for achieving business success, the belief that one's existing core competencies are the most important elements for achieving success can also lead to problems and difficulties in the long term. As the business environment changes over time, new competencies in the forms of radical technologies, innovative methods, and new ventures may undercut the power, importance, and value of many of the existing competencies and capabilities of an organization. Such changes make the company vulnerable if strategic leaders are narrowly focused on the prevailing core competencies. Moreover, focusing on existing core competencies and capabilities is single-sided. Strategic leaders who concentrate primarily on core competencies often skew their business strategies and decision making toward those areas that are supported by the core competencies. Such strategic thinking may limit the perspectives about opportunities to those related to the core competencies instead of what is appropriate and necessary in terms of the business environment and market spaces. A related theory suggests that strategic leaders follow the strengths of the organization and exploit them, and minimize, if not outsource, areas of weaknesses. Many such conventional theories are generally too simplistic in a fast paced business world that is interconnected and global. For example, Kodak was a market leader that focused on its competencies in chemical-based photography and fell behind in the development of digital technologies. Such companies and their leaders often fail to take a holistic approach in creating the best solutions possible. The business world is multifaceted and there are many critical factors necessary for achieving success.

Dual-sided (multi-sided) *perspectives* involve broader insights and understandings that include satisfying customers and making them successful, having an effective and integrated business enterprise, achieving success, providing positives outcomes for all contributors and recipients, and gaining new knowledge and capabilities through learning and experience. Dual-sided perspectives are holistic and multifaceted. The notion of a dual-sided perspective is based on the concept that strategic leaders have to manage all aspects of every situation and circumstance. A dual-sided perspective does not imply that there are just two parts or two opposing sides. A dual-sided perspective involves enhancing the positives and eliminating the negative effects and impacts to the largest extent possible. It also involves achieving success in the short term and in the long term. It suggests that there are multiple perspectives that can be characterized based on two or more aspects, some of which may be opposites. It means informing customers, stakeholders, and society about all of the great things the company does and how wonderful its solutions and systems are, while telling people about the negative aspects as well.

Dual-sided perspectives offer numerous counterpoints to the older theories and popular views on leadership and management constructs. They take on a more balanced view of strategic leadership by focusing on both theoretical and practical aspects. Dual-sided perspectives examine the opportunities and threats; the strengths and the weaknesses; the positives and the negatives; the known and the unknown; the upstream and downstream aspects of the value system; the good and the bad; the rich and the poor; the north and the south; the east and the west; and the short term and the long term. For instance, while focusing on one's strengths is generally viewed as good, the lack of attention to weaknesses and other negative aspects may become detrimental to long-term success. Weaknesses often beget more weaknesses that can cause the management systems and organizational structures to become overwhelmed by problems and difficulties. For example, during the 1960s and 1970s GM failed to effectively handle many of its issues with work rules and employee benefits. Such problems increased GM's costs structures in the long term, thus making it less competitive. The results of such weaknesses often do not manifest themselves in the short term, but become significant limitations to sustainable success.

Dual-sided perspectives imply that profits are derivatives of great achievements and outcomes pertaining to the business environment and market spaces. They also imply that strategic leaders maximize financial rewards by maximizing the value created and ensuring that all contributors and recipients are duly supported and rewarded. Dual-sided perspectives involve using core competencies whenever appropriate and developing new ones on a concurrent basis to stay ahead of changes. They also involve continuously improving existing products and services and using strategic innovations to create exciting new solutions.

Philosophical Perspectives and the Purpose of This Book

Based on the prevailing realities and exciting possibilities of today's global economy, strategic leaders, business professionals, academic researchers, and management students have to reflect on the prevailing business paradigm and examine what is appropriate and what is not. A valid paradigm should present a good picture of reality and provide strategic leaders and decision-makers with theories, management constructs, models, methods, and practices that produce excellent performance, above-average results, and sustainable success. While it is always difficult to make exact judgments about the appropriateness and effectiveness of the existing business paradigm and the related management constructs, it is clear to most business leaders, practitioners, and observers that the old system is broken and that there are many failures, deficiencies, defects and problems among numerous other concerns in today's business environment. In this context, strategic leaders have to be more sophisticated and capable in leading change and managing their business enterprises.

This book articulates how strategic leaders, senior managers, business professionals, aspiring young business leaders, and management students can make dramatic improvements in their endeavors, enrich their knowledge and capabilities, and learn the essential perspectives of strategic leadership and general management. In today's world, strategic leaders regardless of venue have to be aggressive in their aspirations, holistic in their perspectives, proactive in their strategies and actions, and lead change ahead of the prevailing driving forces. FSL and being on the cutting edge are about leading from the front and being ahead of changes in the market spaces and business environment, seeking new opportunities, creating unique solutions, embracing innovations, and building relationships before others are even aware of the underlying changes.

The book examines cutting-edge leadership and management constructs and practices. It describes how to create value across space and time and how to sustain success in a more turbulent and global business world. It explores how to lead change through insights and imagination. It describes what a solution is and how strategic innovations play significant roles in creating success and valuable outcomes. It also discusses how to establish integrated value systems that are inclusive and how to build enduring relationships.

The book describes theories, constructs, models, insights, guidelines, and practices based on the principles and philosophies of FSL and dual-sided (multifaceted) perspectives. Given the current level of sophistication in theories and practices in today's business world, the discussions represent the beginning of a dialogue on cutting-edge leadership and management. The book provides food for thought and perspectives about actions. It implies that innovative strategic leaders have to have holistic perspectives and be proactive. In today's business realities, strategic leaders are creating, innovating, developing, improving, growing and sustaining success; or they are falling behind and moving toward oblivion.

The following provides a general flow of the essential topics:

Chapter 1: Full-spectrum Strategic Leadership
☐ External and internal perspectives ☐ Full-spectrum strategic leadership

Chapter 2: The Driving Forces of Change and the Influences of the Business Environment
☐ Critical driving forces ☐ Market spaces ☐ Social and economic dimensions
☐ Ethical aspects

Chapter 3: Leading Change through Insightfulness
☐ Implications of change ☐ Environmental aspects ☐ Insightfulness
☐ General model

Chapter 4: Crafting Solutions through Innovativeness
☐ Solutions ☐ Solution set ☐ Value creation ☐ Development process
☐ Deployment

Chapter 5: Shaping Systems through Inclusiveness
☐ Cutting-edge management systems ☐ Management constructs ☐ Value systems
☐ Processes

Chapter 6: Building Relationships through Connectedness
☐ High-level connections ☐ External relationships ☐ Interfaces

Chapter 7: High-level Strategic Innovations
☐ Hierarchy of innovation ☐ Value innovation ☐ Research & development
☐ Radical innovation

Chapter 8: Business Model Innovation
☐ The underpinnings ☐ The framework ☐ The elements ☐ Value systems and networks

Chapter 9: Sustaining Success and Concluding Comments
☐ The means ☐ The ends ☐ The mechanisms ☐ Challenges ☐ Dynamics of leadership

Notes

1. Charles O. Holliday, Jr., Stephan Schmidheiny, and Philip Watts, *Walking the Talk* (London, UK: Greenleaf Publishing Limited, 2002). The book is an official publication of the World Business Council for Sustainable Development. It provides case examples of corporations that walking the road to sustainable development.
2. United Nations Human Settlements Programme, *The State of the World's Cities 2004/2005: Globalization and Urban Culture* (London, UK: Earthscan, 2004, p23).
3. C.K. Prahalad and G. Hamel, "The Core Competencies of the Corporation", *Harvard Business Review,* May-June 1990, p 79-91.

References

Holliday, Jr., Charles O. Stephan Schmidheiny, and Philip Watts (2002) *Walking the Talk.* London, UK: Greenleaf Publishing Limited.

United Nations Human Settlements Programme, (2004) *The State of the World's Cities 2004/2005: Globalization and Urban Culture.* London, UK: Earthscan.

1

Full-Spectrum Strategic Leadership

Introduction

For most of the 20th century, strategic leaders used relatively simple concepts and methods for organizing and managing their businesses. The general organizational approach employed a hierarchical structure. The erstwhile hierarchal pyramid linked strategic direction, decision making, and actions in a vertical structure. It was a simple construct that made command and control down the organizational structure relatively easy, but made bottom-up and lateral communications difficult. The basic structure of authority between layers of management were seemingly adequate, but in general the required decisions and information flows were usually slow and consumed enormous amounts of time and resources. It necessitated many interactions between layers of leadership and management up, down, and across the chain of command. The strength of the hierarchical structure was the ability to focus on the specific elements within the organizational structure, facilitate strategic decision making, and accomplish near-term outcomes. The main weaknesses were the lack of integration, poor cohesion, limited interactions, and ineffective communications; the vertical structure incorporated many distinctive parts that were effective in downward connections and upward reporting, but allowed only limited feedback to the higher strategic levels and inadequate integration across the functional areas.

Management constructs were likewise straightforward. Senior management established the strategic direction, crafted and implemented strategies, orchestrated organizational structure, allocated resources, and monitored the expected results. They specified the objectives, determined the missions of the business units, and developed action programs that guided business unit and functional managers. General managers provided the leadership and management of the strategic business units (SBUs), divisions, and subsidiaries. Functional managers focused on strategic implementation of action plans, operations, and processes. They were the tacticians and practitioners responsible for managing, doing, supervising, and accomplishing outcomes.

Using such approaches, senior managers and other corporate leaders were effective in formulating strategies and planning actions, but they often had difficulties with implementation and execution because of the limited dialogue and the slowness of the connections across the organization and within the operating systems. Functional managers were typically effective in day-to-day operations, but they often lacked the information, knowledge, and time to engage fully in strategic actions and high-level programs. Typically, certain parts of the organizational structure were developed and optimized as if they were semi-independent entities. While examining and exploiting the parts separately facilitated analysis, decision-making, and the execution of the activities within the prevailing context, the integration of the parts into a cohesive management system became more challenging as an organization grew and expanded. Due to the lack of integration across the SBUs and operating levels, senior managers and strategic leaders had to play significant roles in resolving difficulties within the organizational structure. While this is a broad-brush illustration of the historical situation, it is clear that most businesses optimized the individual functional areas and specific processes, but had difficulties integrating the business units and the functional areas into truly effective organizations.

Full-spectrum strategic leadership (FSL) is the term introduced and used in this book to discuss cutting-edge strategic leadership perspectives, methods, and practices; ones focusing on the full extent of duties, roles, and responsibilities of corporate leaders, high-level strategic leaders, and other leaders. At the SBU level and higher, strategic leadership and strategic management constructs in sophisticated corporations and small and medium size enterprises (SMEs) tend to merge into cohesive, integrated, and fully-articulated constructs that are holistic, all-encompassing, and dynamic. This chapter highlights leadership and management constructs and discusses the main elements of FSL. Subsequent chapters provide specific details about the most critical elements, especially those pertaining to leading change, crafting solutions, developing systems, building relationships, developing strategic innovations, designing business models, and sustaining success.

This chapter includes the following main topics:

- Perspectives on leadership and management constructs
- The critical elements and implications of FSL

Perspectives on Leadership and Management Constructs

A brief evolutionary tract highlighting select management constructs

During the nineteenth century and early twentieth century, the centralized organizational structure was the predominant framework for strategic leadership, business management, and administration. Most companies were functional organizations that were managed and controlled using narrowly defined roles and responsibilities and hands-on management through mostly face-to-face contacts. As companies enjoyed spectacular growth during the mid-twentieth century, many of the largest corporations changed their organizational designs to more decentralized organizational forms based on lines of businesses, divisions, and/or SBUs. While there was still a hierarchical structure with functional departments within the divisions and business units, decentralization allowed corporate leaders and general managers to manage more effectively and efficiently the many elements, functions, departments, divisions, and SBUs of their far-flung businesses.[1]

Historically, the organizational structure defined the lines of authority and the management roles and responsibilities. It also defined the reporting relationships, the scope of activities, and the work processes. The management perspectives were typically hierarchical, focusing on the objectives and requirements of the corporation and the operations. From an external perspective, the organizational structure generally linked the transactional activities of the internal operations with the direct external entities. In many situations, exchanges and economic activities were based on us versus them thinking. For instance, suppliers were neither considered to be part of the business enterprise nor partners, but rather necessary support entities that had to be carefully controlled and even exploited. Likewise, customers were viewed as buyers and users of products and services and the sources of revenues and cash flow, but their total satisfaction was not viewed to be critical as long as they continued to buy the company's products and services. While there were many exceptions, most corporations and SMEs had limited scopes and were organized according to the views of explicit roles and responsibilities and internal reporting relationships. Such thinking may have worked reasonably well during the early years of the 20th century, when most business leaders had similar approaches and customers had few options. Moreover, most customers and stakeholders had limited access to information and data. Today, it is just the opposite; people have access to enormous amounts of information and data via the Internet.

Senior management (corporate leaders and possibly SBU strategic leaders) and the board of directors were the prime authorities and key decisions makers. They focused extensively on internal perspectives, external demand, and what made the company successful. However, the focus was not necessarily on what made the company more sustainable, but what the profits and shareholder returns were and how strategic leaders could improve financial results. While there were many variations to the theme, most strategic leaders exploited the hierarchical structure to reinforce their authority and power and used the organization to achieve financial goals for shareholders and

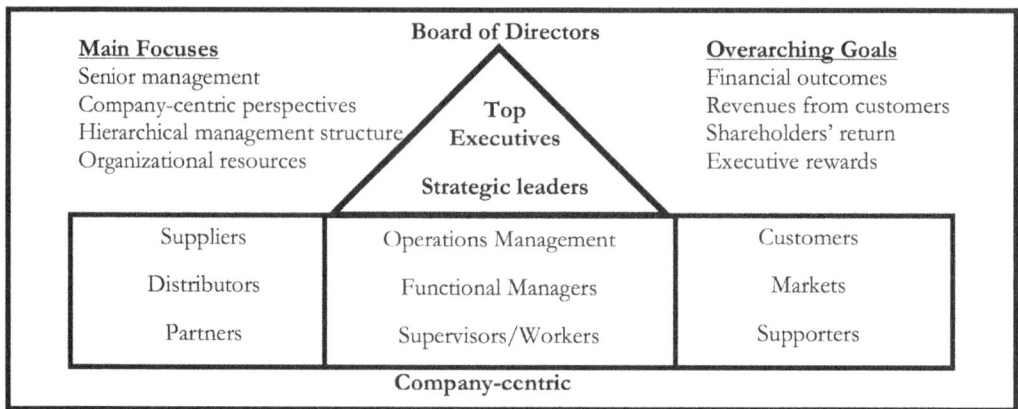

Figure 1.1 A simple characterization of the hierarchical model.

high-level strategic leaders. Figure 1.1 provides a characterization of the hierarchical structure which could as be called a company-centric model.

Corporate executives and strategic leaders generally had the power and they used it. People within the organization were viewed as resources that were necessary for achieving the desired ends, but in many cases they were neither viewed as critical ingredients for success nor as the intellectual capital of the company. The organization's capabilities and resources and those of suppliers, distributors, and other upstream partners were deployed to further the goals of the company. On the downstream side, customers and markets were deemed to be important in the sense that they were the main sources of revenues and profits, but making money and financial rewards were often the primary considerations. Money was the overarching form of capital and its importance was foremost in strategic thinking and management.

During the early 1980s, Michael Porter, renowned professor at Harvard Business School, developed his well-regarded models of the value chain and the value system. His management constructs dramatically shifted the mainstream management perspectives and the associated framework(s) from vertical organizational structures to horizontal management systems.[2] The value chain involves the "collection of activities [and processes] that are preformed to design, produce, market, deliver, and support its [the company or SBU] products."[3] The value chain includes the internal processes necessary to satisfy customer needs and expectations. Porter's generic value chain includes the primary flow of inbound logistics, operations, outbound logistics, marketing and sales, and service; the support elements include the firm's infrastructure, human resource management, technology development, and procurements.[4] The actual value chain of an organization depends on the company's scope of its strategies, decisions, actions and activities, and what it chooses to do and what it wants others to do.

Porter's construct of the generic value chain was instrumental in establishing process management as the main construct for managing the operational and functional aspects of an organization. It linked the flow of activities within the operations and started the transition to a more horizontal perspective on value creation within the firm. Porter articulated the primary activities from the flow of materials and parts into the operations via inbound logistics to the actual in-house operations involving production and assembly of products or operational elements for services. He linked the marketing and sales efforts with the upstream elements of operations and the downstream aspects of services and customer support. Porter suggested that the successful integration and execution of the activities created margins and financial rewards. The shift involved new strategic thinking about the importance of the management system and a new realization that financial outcomes were derivatives of strategic thinking, business integration, and well-honed execution. Figure 1.2 depicts Porter's value chain.

Porter identified the requisite internal support activities that reinforced achievements and provided for ongoing success. The support activities include procurement, technology development, human resource management, and firm infrastructure. Procurement is often referred to as supply chain management in today's terminology. It involves managing and assuring that inputs are available as required and that they are of the kind and quality necessary for the production and delivery of high-quality goods. Technology development involves the means and mechanisms for creating, developing, and implementing innovations within the firm. It includes developing new products, inventing new-to-the-world technologies, and managing strategic innovations. Technological development requires a different mindset than just satisfying current business and customer needs. It focuses outside the domain of existing positions and the established knowledge of value networks and current customers' expectations. Human resource management (HRM) pertains to the policies, processes, and

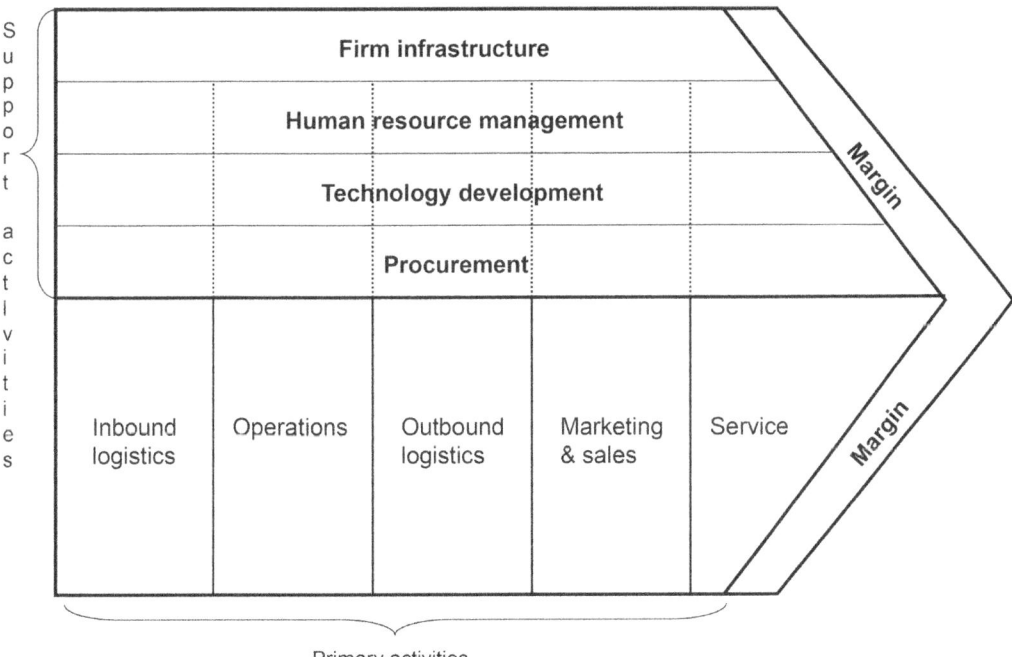

Figure 1.2 Porter's Value Chain

activities for maintaining effective management, administration, and control of the people within the organization. HRM is somewhat of a misnomer in the sense that people are the essence of the organization and not resources at all. People are unique and should be valued for that quality. People make success possible; it is only through people that success is achieved. Resources on the other hand are things that can be created, substituted, and replaced fairly easily. The firm infrastructure includes the plant and equipment, facilities, and the support mechanisms.

The management construct of the value system is possibly one of Porter's most significant and valuable contributions. It includes the value chains of upstream supply networks and other contributors to value creation and delivery, and the downstream aspects related to customers and their applications. The upstream elements include parts and materials flow from raw material extraction, materials refinement, energy providers, parts fabrication, production of end products, and the requisite support services. The downstream aspects include customer buying patterns and applications, reuse and end-of-life considerations. The value system typically involves the core operating level focusing on value creation and value delivery. It concentrates on existing conditions and meeting the market, production, technical, and financial requirements of the organization. It is supported by product and process innovations and the related organizational capabilities for updating, improving and achieving superior performance. The focus is on inputs, outputs, production, marketing and outcomes. The elements of the value system focus on producing results through well-defined processes. Figure 1.3 provides a characterization of the value system, which is based on a market-driven perspective.

The focus of the model is on how to create value for the participants in the value systems (herein called contributors), and for the customers (herein called recipients) of the company's products and services, the related benefits, and the complementary products and services (solutions). Porter's construct of the value system shifted the emphasis from company-centric thinking to market-centric perspectives and to customers' needs and expectations. Moreover, overall management perspectives shifted from

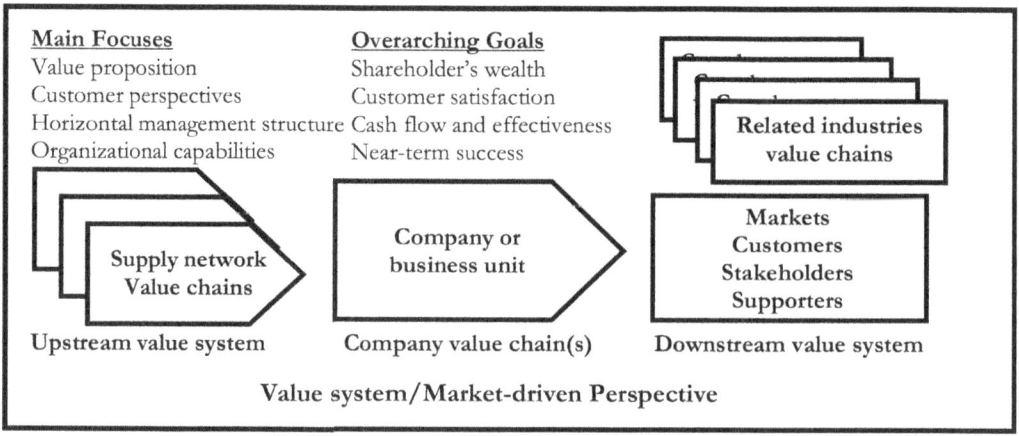

Figure 1.3 Simple characterization of the value system (customer-driven perspective).

internal operations and functional aspects to a horizontal management structure that concentrated on the flow of activities from the upstream value system to customers and markets. The overarching goals became customer satisfaction and shareholders' wealth creation. The financial aspects were still very important, but the objectives and measures changed to cash flow and near-term financial success.

During the 1980s total quality management (TQM) became important in the U.S. TQM was developed in Japan during the 1950s and 1960s by management gurus like W. Edwards Deming. Deming developed fourteen total quality principles focusing on management commitment and involvement, employee training, and continuous improvement.[5] He believed that invoking these principles would lead to the desired results. His principles focused on understanding customer needs and expectations, establishing objectives, setting priorities, developing quality plans, assuring quality, and improving the management system. They also focused on managing the ongoing changes necessary to achieve superior and sustainable outcomes. Deming's work and that of the other TQM gurus spawned the six-sigma quality approaches that many global corporations use today. Things that were unthinkable in 1980 have become the prevailing capabilities thirty years later.

During the late 1980s, additional management constructs were developed for integrating functional management activities within the strategic management structure. Henry Mintzberg developed an organizational construct consisting of "six basic parts of the organization."[6] The six parts included the primary level of the operating core, the middle line, the strategic apex, the support structure of the supporting staff, the techno-structure, and the ideology. The strategic apex is comprised of strategic management and the strategic direction of the organization. It is the domain of strategic leaders. Middle line connects the higher levels of strategic management with the lower levels of functional management. It provides stability and control and facilitates the flow of information and decision making. The operating core involves the basic operations, functions, processes, and activities of the organization. It involves the design, development, production, marketing, distribution, and delivery of the products and services. Techno-structure is the technical expertise, especially the professionals who design the systems and processes and provide the technical support and control mechanisms. The supporting staff includes the specialists in data management, accounting, HRM, and numerous others who support the middle line and the core. The ideology includes the beliefs, values, philosophies, and culture of the organization.

With the rise of globalization, the intensity of competition and the importance of strategic innovations during the early 1990s, the company-centric and simple customer-driven models used by corporations and their SBUs became less adequate for understanding and managing the complexities of the business environment. A higher level of management sophistication evolved for incorporating all of the forces relevant to the organization and its linkages, partners, stakeholders, and customers. Over the last ten years the dependence on external value networks has become pivotal as more corporations depend on supply networks, strategic alliances and external relationships for sustaining their vision, mission, strategies, actions and activities. This is especially true as more corporations and SMEs outsourced operations, processes and activities.

Contemporary views about holistic management systems and business models

In *Leading the Revolution*, Gary Hamel proposes that the contemporary business environment is undergoing the 'age of revolution'. He states that, "it is not knowledge that produces wealth, but insight—insight into opportunities for discontinuous innovation."[7] Knowledge and information are important, but it takes true strategic leaders to translate them into new perspectives and innovative business models for achieving success. Hamel's model includes "four major components: core strategy, strategic resources, customer interfaces, and value networks."[8] He incorporates the concept of innovative solutions and focuses on innovation as an essential component in the model.[9] Figure 1.4 presents Hamel's unpacking of the business model and the main components described.

Hamel refers to the four major components as unpacking the business model. He shows customer interfaces as the initial component. The focus of his business model is on fulfillment of customer expectations and providing ongoing support to customers. This is accomplished through information and insights about what is critical and necessary. Most importantly, building relationships is pivotal for success, as is fair and appropriate pricing. The benefits that customers obtain are linked to the core strategies of the businesses. The core strategies include the mission and the scope of the product/market offerings. The core strategy relate to how strategic leaders obtain differential positions.

Core strategies are linked to strategic resources that are necessary for realizing success. The linkage involves the configuration of how the business develops and deploys its resources and capabilities and how it defines its strategic positions. The strategic resources are the core competencies [capabilities], assets, and core processes. These are connected to external value networks that complete the package of essential requirements and provide proper outcomes for people. The internal resources and the value networks help define the company boundaries or scope of interactions. The value networks include supply networks, partners and coalitions.

Understanding a business model is critical for strategic leaders who are the architects of their business enterprises. Hamel's model shows some of the essential components

Customer benefits	Configuration		Company boundaries
Customer interfaces	**Core strategy**	**Strategic resources**	**Value networks**
-Fulfillment & support -Information & insights -Relationship dynamics -Pricing structure	-Business mission -Product-market scope -Basis for differentiation	-Core competencies -Strategic Assets -Core processes	-Suppliers -Partners -Coalitions
Efficient/Unique/Fit/Profit boosters			

Figure 1.4 Hamel's unpacking of the business model[10]

for creating success. He suggests that the key factors are efficiency of the system and the uniqueness of the solutions. Effective strategic leaders do not defeat their competitors; rather, they find unique ways to fit into the business environment and market spaces and provide the best solutions and outcomes possible. Strategic leaders enjoy success when recipients (customers and stakeholders) and contributors (partners, allies and employees) are successful. Companies realize profits and other rewards due to their solutions and systems, the people involved, and the relationships thereof.

Hamel has it right; it is all about insights and innovation! It is about strategic leaders being innovative and proactive in leading change. Strategic leaders must employ FSL and strategic management to create new realities that are more exciting and full of innovative opportunities. They must inspire their organizations to become proactive in creating more productive solutions. The objective is to create a more fruitful future for the organization and for humankind.

An innovative management construct of today is the relatively new notion of *enterprise-wide strategic management* (ESM) that incorporates Porter's value system with the extended enterprise. It further defines main components of Hamel's view of unpacking the business model. The extended enterprise includes all of the suppliers and suppliers of suppliers and all of the downstream entities: customers, stakeholders, strategic partners, related industries, competition, and infrastructure. It incorporates the contributions of the value networks and what customers seek and expect, plus the full scope of all contributing and receiving entities. ESM involves creating, developing, and deploying unique solutions and systems that generate the maximum value possible. It suggests that strategic leaders have to incorporate external value networks as essential components as well as internal capabilities and resources in constructing a business model that focuses on the needs, requirements, mandates, and expectations of the markets.

From a high-level strategic perspective, FSL and ESM are cutting-edge strategic leadership constructs that incorporate the full integration of the strategic aspects of the organization and the internal functional areas with all of the external driving forces of change, critical factors influencing the business and the extended enterprise.[11] ESM encompass the whole, both internal and external, and the present and the future. The power of these constructs is that they are inclusive of all of the essential dimensions in managing and leading an organization and for achieving sustainable success.

Figure 1.5 shows the value chain, value systems and the essentials of the extended enterprise, all integrated into a comprehensive business model based on FSL and ESM. The purpose of showing the details is to provide a sense of the flow of the elements and the interconnections. As can be seen, it includes Porter's constructs of the value chain and value system. However, it goes beyond Porter by including stakeholders, related industries, the infrastructure, and competitors that operate in parallel with the company's or SBU's value system. It also extends the value system to include suppliers of suppliers all the way upstream to the origins of the raw materials and downstream to the secondary applications and end-of-life considerations. The upstream contributors provide the raw material, parts, components and logistics for developing and

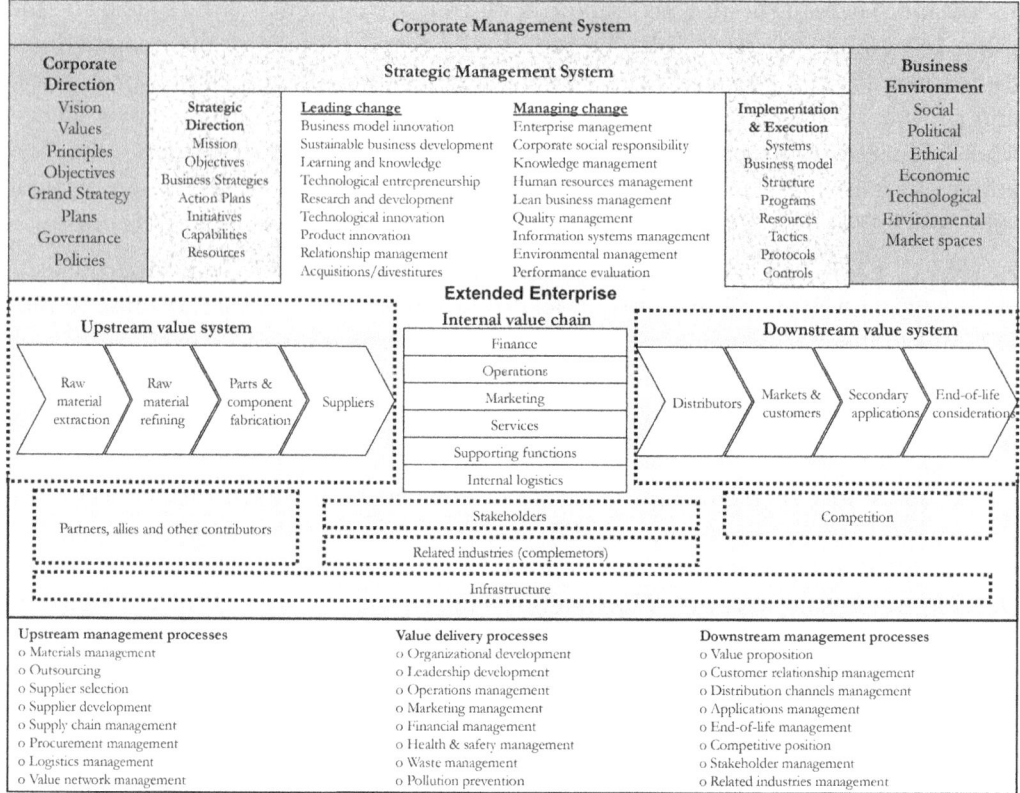

Figure 1.5 The elements of the enterprise-wide strategic management system[12]

deploying solutions. The internal value chain translates inputs into valuable outputs. The downstream recipients are the beneficiaries and the people that create the opportunities in the first place.

The extended enterprise is flanked with numerous entities and individuals that make solutions real and help determine what the solutions are. Complementors (related industries) provide complementary products and services that support the recipients with the additional benefits they require or desire. For example, the commercial media and artists in the music industry provide the content for iTunes and iPods that make those products popular and successful. Stakeholders provide feedback on critical social, ethical, economic, and environmental issues that allow strategic leaders to determine or fine-tune their solutions. The value networks of partners, allies, and other contributors enhance the solutions, making them more powerful, less costly and more effective, depending on the situations. For instance, significantly lower transportation and telecommunications costs over the last decade have opened up new avenues of sources of goods and services that would have been too expensive to obtain in previous generations. Outsourcing data processing to India is cost-effective because of the low wages of the professional workers there and the inexpensive communications linkages across the world. Even competitors may be viewed as contributors, because they often keep the power of the prevailing products and services at the forefront, rather than alternatives or substitutes. For example, it is difficult for outsiders to overcome the collective power of the existing automobile manufacturers, given the dominance of internal combustion engine technology and the support structures sustaining the current automobile types. Moreover, the infrastructure reinforces the power of the existing solutions. It ties the elements together and makes connectedness possible through logistics, communications or other mechanisms. Think about the effectiveness of globalization without telecommunications, global logistics, ships, roads, trucks, etc.

The totally integrated value system with the extended enterprise creates value and provides new opportunities for achieving sustainable success. Strategic leaders articulate, develop and deploy the system and processes used for producing and providing the solutions. It is the power of the solutions, the inclusiveness of the system(s), the interconnectedness of the entities and the relationships that result in positive gains and long-term success. These elements are defined and discussed in more detail in Chapters 3 through 6. Strategic innovations are discussed in Chapter 7. Business model innovation is discussed in Chapter 8. Remember, strategic leaders are the architects who devise the solutions, develop and deploy the systems, create the structures, build relationships, and articulate the management constructs used by the company and the extended enterprise to obtain results and achieve success.

Perspectives on leadership and management constructs

Socioeconomic and technological changes make the business environment today more complex and dynamic. Keeping ahead of turbulent changes is one of the most significant business challenges of the twenty-first century. Wide-spread use of the Internet, fourth generation digital telecommunications, advanced microprocessors, global positioning systems, information technology, biotechnology, and nanotechnology are just a few of the revolutionary technologies affecting almost every industry and corporation.

Strategic leadership and business management have evolved from the slow-paced constructs and techniques associated with managing production, operations, machines, and workers to focusing on broad horizons, including the natural environment, the social/human world, business environment and global markets. The realm of business has expanded from the narrow view of supply-and-demand economics to a much broader and richer context of social, ethical, economic, technological, and environmental driving forces and factors that are implicit in market spaces and business decisions. Market spaces and the needs and expectations of customers and stakeholders are highly dynamic and significantly more complex, and becoming more so every day. Such perspectives make the business world more exciting and full of opportunities and challenges.

Contemporary leadership and management constructs must provide outstanding performance in the short term and secure sustainable success for the long term. However, today's business world is full of challenges and pitfalls. Many of the time-proven practices established in the mainstream of business are no longer adequate. Likewise, average performance is insufficient for sustaining success. Indeed, following the pack, mimicking the majority, and concentrating only on one's core competencies are prescriptions for difficulties, since they are often duplicated by others and typically fail to be dynamic enough to obtain distinctiveness and uniqueness.

Effective senior managers and strategic leaders set themselves apart from the mainstream and develop leadership and management constructs and business models with unique characteristics that are difficult for others to copy, at least in the near term. For example, Microsoft's strategic leaders created not just products and services, but an integrated system for connecting people and making their lives more successful and rewarding. Microsoft set the standards, and it is difficult to emulate its success. eBay created unique interactive systems with individualized outcomes. Toyota integrated production from the far reaches of its supply networks to its just-in-time assembly. It instituted lean business practices via the Toyota Production System (TPS). Competitors might have copied Toyota's products, but it was much more difficult to copy all of the specific details of TPS. Any alternative has to be significantly superior, not just better.

In today's turbulent business world, strategic leaders must go beyond the mainstream and explore new theoretical constructs for achieving success. Using mainstream or popular leadership and management constructs may allow strategic leaders to quickly obtain a consensus within the company because managers and employees understand the methods and techniques, but such approaches may lead to inferior results because they are not exceptional, do not add new value, or lack uniqueness. They fail to provide sustainable advantages in the business environment and/or the markets and customers. Even in successful situations, the results may provide just average or short-term returns. Following the consensus approaches typically does little better than achieving parity with the mainstream. Moreover, most of the prevailing models of the past are out of sync with the realities of the present and the future trends. It is not that they were always bad, but that they were developed and used under significantly different circumstances, especially those in the U.S. following World War II, in which the gross domestic product (GDP) of the global economy was heavily skewed toward the U.S. For instance, Milton Friedman's view of maximizing profits was broadly accepted in the early 1960s, but it now often leads to inferior performance because the underlying perspectives are too narrow given the complexities of a global economy. Friedman's theory focuses on the internal goal of making money and the simple external exchanges involving supply and demand. Strategic leaders generally can achieve a simple goal like making money, but in doing so they often sub-optimize everything else and leave their organizations and enterprises vulnerable in the future. Today the business world is much more diverse and open-ended. While the U.S. still has the largest national economy, it is now only about twenty percent of the global GDP.

With all of the changes that occurred over the last fifty years, many strategic leaders and managers have yet to envision bold and innovative ways to lead change and manage their companies, SBUs, and extended enterprises. However, But, they must move from having narrow perspectives to developing broad ones; from thinking about the short-term to being future-oriented; and from being company-centric to market–centric or enterprise-centric, and beyond. Strategic leaders have to achieve all of the requisite objectives and outcomes, not just those that pertain to financial aspects or shareholder value in the short term. The financial and shareholder objectives are critical for sustainable success, but strategic leaders have to be careful not to make trade-offs in other essential areas in order to maximize financial rewards.

Developing more sophisticated leadership and management constructs that integrate the whole extended enterprise and focus on sustainable solutions and success presents exciting options for going beyond the norm and for exceeding expectations. ESM and Hamel's perspectives about the business model provide cutting-edge leadership and management perspectives for realizing more exciting solutions, sophisticated systems and business models. Moreover, the interconnections of the extended enterprise offer critical thinking and new ways about what strategic leadership and strategic management have to be in a more complex world. The long-term success of most organizations depends on multifaceted constructs, capabilities, and systems. Very little is simple in a complex and global business world. For instance, a company might be successful in the short term, but if strategic leaders fail to develop future leaders, the organization may become stymied in its ability to succeed and prosper. Such problems are usually not immediately apparent and the negative implications are manifested only in the out years, perhaps ten or more years in the future. By the time the strategic leaders recognize the difficulties, it may be too late to affect the required actions. For example, Blockbuster® provided videos for rent at thousands of stores across the U.S. Its success declined over the last decade, because it failed to make significant changes to its business model.[13] During the same time frame, Netflix gained market share leadership by offering customers low-hassle (convenient) solutions using online connections or U.S. mail linkages. Its business model was straightforward and cost effective. Netflix was able to find tremendous new opportunities when its competitors were experiencing declining demand and limited success. But a successful business model has to be assessed on an ongoing basis as new innovations take hold and replace even the most exciting models of the past. Moreover, in a complex business environment, strategic leaders have to be masters of their domains and not just generalists who have a sense of strategic management, finance, organizational behavior, marketing, operations management, and other standard management constructs. Such management knowledge and skills are good to know and are essential, but they may be insufficient for achieving success in dynamic markets and demanding business environments with many world-class companies having six sigma capabilities, excellent competencies, powerful brands, outstanding strategic resources and exceptional people.

Figure 1.6 provides some examples of leadership and management constructs and their perspectives (broad or narrow context) and the business management focus (company-centric or market-centric). The intent is to highlight some of the most salient constructs and their implications for business management. It provides a general overview of the prevailing leadership and management constructs, but it is not meant to be comprehensive. The mapping is not intended to be precise. Some of the constructs listed as near-term, like product innovation, might belong in the quadrant pertaining to long-term constructs, depending on the development cycle and product life cycle implications. The representation provides a relative sense of traditional, mainstream and cutting-edge leadership and management constructs.

		Time Horizon	
		Near term	Long term
P e r s p e c t i v e	Broad	**Mainstream** Corporate strategic leadership Operations management Lean business management Green management/marketing Product/technological innovations Ethical management	**Cutting edge** Full-spectrum strategic leadership Enterprise-wide strategic management Extended enterprise/business model Sustainable business development Strategic innovations Corporate social responsibility
	Narrow	**Traditional** Supply and demand economics Functional management Total quality management Core competencies Regulatory compliance Strengths and weaknesses analysis	**Mainstream** Product-market expectations Customer relationship management Six sigma quality Customer satisfaction Pollution prevention Integrated risk management
		Company-centric [internal]	**Market-centric [external]**
		Mindset [focus]	

Figure 1.6 A mapping of selected management constructs.

The traditional constructs include focusing on supply-and-demand economics, functional management, quality management, core competencies, regulatory compliance, and strengths and weaknesses analysis. The underpinnings of traditional management constructs or models like business economics are still important, but have to be expanded to address the rapidity of change and the vastness of the real world. While none of the traditional constructs may be exactly wrong or inappropriate, they are often limited in scope and company-focused and may result in short-term gains and long-term difficulties. They are often insufficient to provide good solutions and obtain sustainable advantages. For instance, focusing on core competencies tends to drive decision-making toward the current strengths of the organization, rather than toward opportunities in the market space or the changing technological underpinnings. It is important to recognize that the selected leadership and management constructs should not be "either–or" choices. Some of the traditional management constructs are absolutely critical and must be used to meet external mandates and requirements, but in many cases they have to be modified to be in concert with today's realities. For instance, regulatory compliance implies meeting the external government mandates, but simply meeting expectations is usually not good enough. TQM encourages making continuous improvements, but again, simply making incremental improvements may not lead to superior outcomes. TQM is a good concept, but it is usually internally focused, i.e., on products and processes. Enhancing functional management aspects may result in reasonable gains, and they are necessary for having effective and efficient processes. While it is useful to have solid functional capabilities, optimizing the functions may result in a sub-optimization of the whole system. Strategic leaders have to think about what the functional capabilities should be, not just what they are.

Today's strategic leaders must go beyond supply and demand economics and strengths and weaknesses analysis and include all of the entities and requisite actions of the value system and extended enterprise. Strategic leaders must also go beyond regulatory compliance and TQM methods and provide ways to eliminate the root causes of defects, environmental burdens, and the precursors to the government mandates. And core competencies may be the strengths of the organization, but they are not timeless. Today's core competencies may become irrelevant as the business world changes.

The good news is that strategic leaders are becoming more proactive and inclusive in their strategic thinking and actions. Many of the late twentieth century management perspectives have changed from company-centric to a more market-centric mindset, as shown in the lower right quadrant. Porter's value system has broadened management thinking and perspectives. In many corporations, TQM has been replaced by six-sigma quality thinking and management that go beyond products and processes and include customer relationships and linkages across the value networks. Regulatory compliance thinking has morphed into pollution prevention, green marketing, product stewardship, and sustainable business development (SBD). No longer are laws and regulations the only drivers of the social, political, ethical, and environmental considerations. Now, market and value-based initiatives prevail as well. In short, management constructs have evolved from the economic theories to the product-market and enterprise-wide theories of the value system, the extended enterprise, and business models. The focus has moved from the producer to the customer, from the internal to the external, from the organization to the enterprise, from the short term to the short and long term, and from management to leadership.

Internal constructs are also shifting to be more sophisticated, as shown in the upper left quadrant. Innovative management constructs incorporate lean business practices and green management approaches, like those developed by Toyota and Honda. They include management constructs, such as strategic innovation and integration. The world of lean business practices implies finding creative ways of managing operations and using every mechanism possible to improve the social, economic, technological, and environmental aspects of their processes and systems. Innovative lean business practices focus on minimizing inventory and other resources by producing exactly what is required by customers when they require it. They also attempt to minimize all residuals, including economic and environmental wastes. If businesses waste money on inferior products and services, they will have fewer resources and be less capable of sustaining the enterprise. Likewise, customers lose; indeed, everyone loses. Instead, successful outcomes produce improved customer value and benefits, enhanced customer and stakeholder relationships, better employee rewards and contractor opportunities, and increased shareholder wealth and value, all on a concomitant basis. Everyone wins. The successes of the microprocessor in general and Intel's contributions, in particular, over the last two decades demonstrate this phenomenon.

The dynamics continue. The most critical cutting-edge leadership and management constructs are the primacy of strategic leadership and strategic management, especially FSL, ESM, SBD, and corporate social responsibility (CSR). They concentrate on reaching across space and time to include all of the essential dimensions of the business environment, linking the players in the market spaces, and integrating entire extended enterprise(s) into holistic and innovative frameworks. Coupled with the increasing importance of business models, they form the basis of how global corporations and SMEs can achieve extraordinary outcomes and sustainable success.

ESM constructs have expanded the scope of the analysis and strategic formulation and implementation to include the extended enterprise, as presented in my book, *Enterprise-Wide Strategic Management: Achieving Sustainable Success through Leadership, Strategies, and Value Creation*.[14] ESM constructs not only have a broader context, but they involve a broader management mindset that realizes the critical importance of the external contributors and recipients as well as the participants (employees) within the company. This includes fundamental shifts in strategic thinking from more passive views like business ethics, environmental management and legal aspects based on being good and not breaking the laws to the more dynamic perspectives of SBD, CSR and strategic innovations for actively creating new value, solving problems and achieving appropriate outcomes.

SBD is a holistic management construct that includes the entire business system from the origins of the raw materials to production processes and the customer applications, and to the end-of-life solutions. SBD involves making dramatic improvements, and positive changes to the full scope of relationships and linkages of the supply networks, customers and stakeholders, and support service providers for handling wastes, residuals and impacts. It also involves life cycle thinking and management about all of the effects, impacts and consequences from cradle to grave. It involves achieving sustainable outcomes that balance the performance objectives of the present with the needs and expectations of the future.

Strategic innovations involve making dramatic changes, revolutionary developments, and significant improvements that have positive and typically clean outcome(s) with respect to customers, stakeholders, and the organization. FSL thinking implies that strategic leaders have an implicit duty to create the best solutions and mitigate negative aspects to the extent possible. Developing clean technologies and producing a lean business enterprise go a long way toward realizing these outcomes.

Strategic leaders must engage people and build relationships. The perceptions of employees and people in general have drastically changed in recent years. In the past, people assumed that strategic leaders would fulfill their duties and responsibilities. They also assumed that negative effects and impacts were part of the tradeoffs necessary for economic prosperity and employment opportunities. There are numerous examples of people living in risky environments (neighborhoods) near manufacturing plants because the residents depend on the corporations for their livelihood, and the people in the community do not have other options. In many situations, people do not even understand the risks they face. For instance, the people who lived near the Union Carbide plant in Bhopal, India may not have known about the risks involving toxic chemicals, and even if they knew about the dangers, they may have tolerated the risks because they needed jobs. Unfortunately, the plant was not fully safeguarded against fatal accidents. In 1984 the plant experienced what Union Carbide described as sabotage that resulted in a significant release of methyl isocyanides killing several thousand people in the local community.[15] The accident at Bhopal was one of the worst disasters at a production facility during the twentieth century. Today, with abundant accessible information provided by government agencies and non-governmental organizations (NGOs), people are better informed about the products, operations, activities, and impacts of companies and are better able to use their political and economic power to force improvements, if necessary.

Historically, the mindset of strategic leaders pertaining to CSR focused on making money, providing employment opportunities for employees, satisfying customers and building wealth for shareholders. This concept was reinforced by Friedman's view that the only responsibility of corporate leaders is to make as much money as possible for shareholders. But most companies now realize that while strategic leaders have a responsibility to produce revenues and profits, they also have fiduciary responsibilities to protect corporate assets, intellectual property, company resources, and the well-being of people. Such strategic thinking requires that the organization and its people, its reputation, and business prospects are safeguarded, sustained and improved over time and that strategic leaders fulfill their social, economic, and environmental responsibilities.

FSL involves getting results and achieving extraordinary financial performance in the short term and investing in innovations, developments and improvements, and sustaining success for the long term. A singular focus on maximizing profits assumes that achieving business objectives requires trade-offs between mutually exclusive outcomes; i.e., if the company spends time and money on initiatives pertaining to CSR or the like, it will reduce profits. However, investments that protect the reputation of the corporation, enhance its goodwill, mitigate the risks associated with stakeholders and communities, satisfy customers, and improve compliance with mandates help a corporation achieve the desired financial objectives. These kinds of measures are not to be viewed as expenses without benefits, but rather, as necessary and appropriate expenditures for achieving sustainable success. They provide the means and mechanisms to have effective risk management.

The most important changes in leadership and management thinking about FSL, ESM, SBD and CSR involve the realization that social, ethical, economic, technological, and environmental responsibilities and corporate profitability are not mutually exclusive. They are compatible and can be achieved on a concurrent basis. SBD and CSR actually contribute to reducing the costs of doing business by eliminating defects and burdens and mitigating risks and vulnerabilities that often create cost implications and threaten strategic, market and financial viabilities.

Specifically, the cutting-edge leadership and management constructs focus on creating frameworks that include and enhance the whole corporation and its management systems and secure ongoing success. They unify the entire scope of plans, programs, responsibilities, obligations, and actions, including every facet of the activities of every entity. Cutting-edge companies and their strategic leaders create fully integrated management systems that link internal operations with customers, stakeholders, supply networks and related industries, and that seamlessly provide the flow of products, services, and information from origin of materials to the application by customers and end-of-life considerations.

Full-Spectrum Strategic Leadership

The meaning and implications of full-spectrum strategic leadership

FSL encompasses the broad roles and responsibilities that cut across the whole organization and the entire extended enterprise from horizon to horizon. The underpinnings of FSL require senior managers and strategic leaders to play leading roles in dealing with critical issues affecting businesses and people; to help resolve the related problems and challenges; and to participate in the development and deployment of solutions based on the full spectrum of needs and expectations of the organization, market spaces, business environment and society. It also includes all of the organizational aspects for creating success.

FSL necessitates openness, insightfulness, inclusiveness, innovativeness, and fair-mindedness. It requires strategic leaders to create an extraordinary vision and to fulfill their missions to develop, support and promote the extended enterprises and the market spaces served by their businesses. Strategic leaders have duties to people to ensure that they are protected and not harmed.

Figure 1.7 depicts the horizon-to-horizon perspectives of FSL. The external perspectives (dimensions) are portrayed on the right side of the graphic. Strategic leaders have to concentrate on satisfying all of the needs, expectations, requirements and mandates of the external dimensions. The external dimensions include markets,

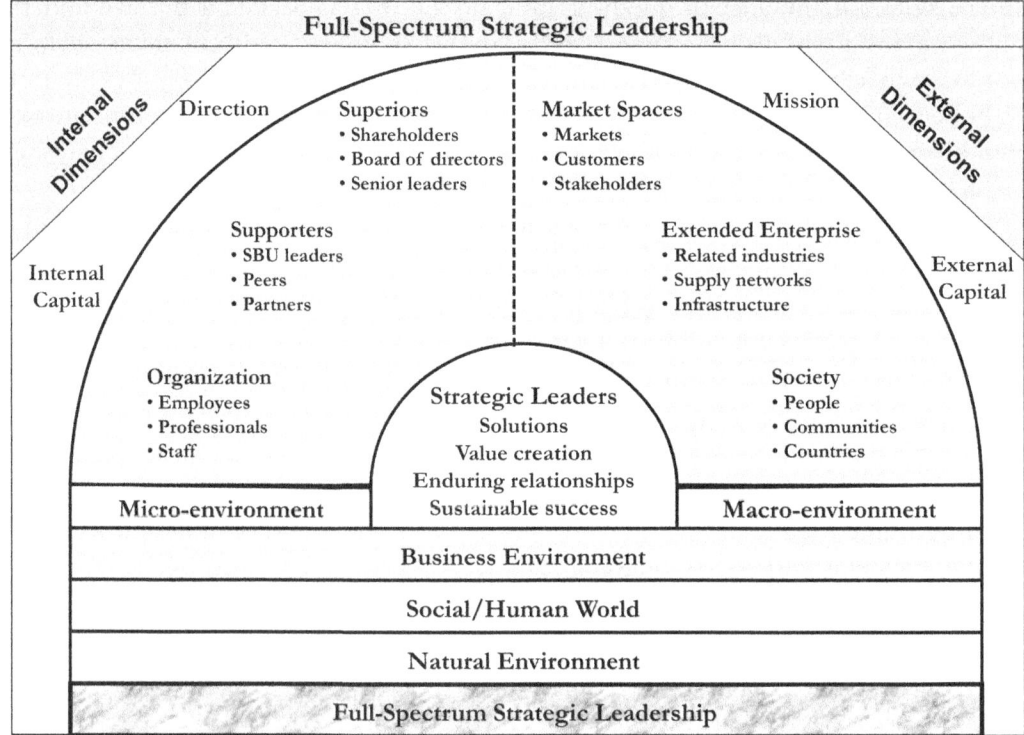

Figure 1.7 Full-spectrum strategic leadership.

customers, stakeholders, supply networks, related industries, infrastructure, and competition. In the graphic, the elements of market spaces are shown separately from those of the extended enterprise to focus on the importance of markets, customers, and stakeholders. They are the recipients of the economic mission(s) and outcomes of the organization and/or are impacted by them. They are the primary driving forces. The broadest perspectives involve the well-being of society and the general social, economic, and environmental good. Strategic leaders ensure that their organizations and enterprises are fully capable and that they serve and support markets, customers and stakeholders. Strategic leaders provide solutions and achieve successful outcomes. Also, strategic leaders fulfill their broad responsibilities to society through positive actions to improve the social and economic fabric of the human world and to mitigate the negative impacts.

The internal aspects are shown on the left side. Rather than portraying the traditional view of top down in which the strategic leaders report to the board of directors and shareholders through the executives of the corporation (corporate officers) with the rest of the organization depicted as subordinates, FSL advocates that everyone is important and each plays a critical role in achieving sustainable success. Strategic leaders interface with their board of directors to determine the vision and strategic direction and to obtain approvals for strategies, plans, programs, and actions. At the highest levels, the strategic leaders are the executives and senior managers.

Strategic leaders work with peers, high-level leaders in other organizations, and key contributors to ensure coordination and cooperation across the whole enterprise and connections with other entities. They also work with partners, allies, and collaborators who support the company and its strategies and action plans. Most importantly, they build consensus and willingness within the whole organization to achieve the desired outcomes and with strategic partners and allies.

FSL is about teamwork. Strategic leaders have multi-sided relationships with the internal players. They respond to the commands and requirements of the higher level authorities (board of directors & shareholders) and at the same time they expect that their superiors support them in their legitimate needs, actions and pursuits. Likewise, they expect employees to fulfill their directives and requests, and they have an obligation to support the employees through the appropriate means and mechanisms. Every role is multifaceted, i.e., a two-way street.

FSL is not a radical new concept or theory, but a logical extension of many modern leadership concepts and approaches. One is the notion of responsibility and accountability. Strategic leaders have to act as architects, innovators, integrators, supporters, and stewards. They are not just superiors that command the respect and loyalty of the organization, but they are ultimately the responsible individuals who inspire, develop, support, respect and reward people across the organization and the enterprise in their pursuit of extraordinary performance and positive outcomes. They are not at the top of an organizational pyramid, but they are at the pivotal hub of the connections, relationships and interactions, as well as the all-encompassing guiding energy and inspirational force. They link all elements of the organization and enterprise(s) together so that people move in a common direction guided by individuals who are leading and managing for the benefit of the whole and are taking care of everyone, regardless of rank, role or position. Strategic leaders have many obligations, including protecting the well-being of the organization and its intellectual capital and assets and ensuring that everyone is recognized, respected and appropriately rewarded, especially those making the significant contributions for achieving sustainable success.

FSL implies that all of the elements are essential for creating solutions and achieving success. Conventional theories often focused on making money and satisfying shareholders or customers as being the most important elements for realizing success, but strategic leaders of today cannot take such limited perspectives. However, shareholders are ill-served if strategic leaders concentrate just on customers or short-term objectives like maximizing profits and sub-optimize future successes due to a lack of long-term investments and strategic innovations or because customers, stakeholders, suppliers, distributors, employees, and other important contributors are not treated properly. The former may lead to near-term rewards, but produce long-term problems and failures, especially due to obsolescence. The latter may produce profits, but create disaffected relationships and long-term unhappiness, especially in the form of angry customers and incensed stakeholders.

Customers, in particular, are disadvantaged in the long term if strategic leaders concentrate on a narrow front and try to maximize a relatively small number of market-related aspects like providing inexpensive products or increasing market shares. Affordability is important to customers and inexpensive products may lead to customer satisfaction in the short term. While customers desire products and services that are affordable, reliable, and cost-effective to own and operate, they also want a plethora of other attributes that may be latent and not fully articulated, yet critical for obtaining satisfaction and customer success. In most of the developed countries customers want everything: high quality, ease of use, no burdens, defect-free products, reliability, and numerous others attributes. Success is achieved when total solutions are produced and delivered. Solutions are provided when the whole value delivery system is optimized and not just one or two facets of it.

FSL perspectives are multifaceted; they involve directing and listening; giving and receiving; supporting and being supported; and being respectful and being respected. For instance, strategic leaders engender contributions and hard work from the employees within the organization, and they have a duty to take appropriate care of them and the supporting entities. FSL perspectives replace the narrow notion of superior and subordinate with constructs that everyone has roles, responsibilities and duties to perform and that everyone has obligations to ensure equality, fairness, honesty, good will and positive outcomes.

Dual-sided perspectives of FSL

Most of the critical parameters of FSL and strategic decision making are multi-faceted, as discussed in the introduction and above. Many conventional management constructs recognize that there are at least two sides to most situations and choices; i.e., astute leaders have to examine both sides of their options and their decisions. One of the earliest management constructs is the analysis of strengths, weaknesses, opportunities and threats (SWOT). It is based on the realization that one has to assess and determine the strengths and the weaknesses of a product, service, organization, entity, or person to obtain a proper understanding of the advantages and disadvantages and value. SWOT is also based on understanding the external opportunities and threats and how to manage them. While assessing and understanding reality is critical for success, most situations and circumstances require more detailed analysis than just using a single construct like SWOT and the internal and external context thereof. SWOT may have merit for the prevailing factors and forces, except that it is backwards. Assessments should start with the external context first, i.e., the opportunities and threats, and then followed by the internal context—strengths and weaknesses. SWOT seems to make intuitive sense to most strategic leaders and professionals, but it has several significant flaws from a strategic perspective. It is generally viewed from a static perspective of what is instead of the dynamic view of what is expected to be, what could be or what ought to be. It may be adequate for operational aspects that are in play today like selling the existing product lines and managing operational capabilities. It may be useful for examining and determining the prevailing situation; however, it is rather limited in exploring the future prospects, especially in the long term. For instance, there are many experts on theoretical leadership constructs who advocate focusing on one's strengths and not being too concerned about one's weaknesses. Thus, a simple strengths and weaknesses analysis of an individual manager might indicate certain strengths in technical skills and a number of weaknesses in financial areas. The person involved might not be concerned about his weaknesses, because he is a project engineer who spends most of his time of dealing with the technical aspects and making technical decisions. Moreover, at his current level within the organization there may be scores of people who handle the financial details; he does not have to get involved with such matters. However, because of his aplomb, engineering talents, and recent successes he might be promoted to be a program manager in charge of all aspects of a strategic program. In his new capacity, he has to spend more than fifty percent of his time concerned about financial considerations and reporting. If he followed conventional theories and focused on his strengths, he would be unprepared to provide the management, direction, and oversight of the financial aspects that his new position requires. His technical strengths are still as powerful, but less relevant as the program manager. The good news of the promotion manifests his Achilles heel, which he could have prepared for but did not view as necessary given his previous situation. Unfortunately, such people learn too late that they have overinvested in their strengths and competencies and have underinvested in eliminating or neutralizing their weaknesses and limitations. Many people facing such situations are stymied by their failures to be proactive in improving the negative aspects (their limitations). As the hypothetical example suggests, one can be successful in the short term by focusing on strengths, but such actions might increase his or her vulnerabilities or limit one's potential by not rectifying weaknesses. The same kinds of situations occur in companies.

The concept of dual-sided (multifaceted) perspectives does not suggest that situations or decisions can always be separated into two categories, classifications, factors or aspects. To the contrary, it recognizes that most situations are complex and that there are usually many variables that have to be considered. It is based on the premise that in most situations the parameters and/or variables can be divided into two broad areas (positives and negatives; old and new; short term and long term, etc.) of consideration with many sub-elements in each, requiring a depth of analysis. For instance, when examining market spaces one can view them in terms of developed and emerging markets, i.e., the industrialized countries and newly industrializing ones or existing marketing and latent ones. Most importantly, every situation can be examined in terms of two categories; one having the element(s) and the other not having them. Obviously there are numerous sub-categories.

Dual-sided perspectives focus on insights based on the full spectrum of realities and possibilities, balanced strategic thinking, inclusiveness, innovativeness and thoroughness. They involve new ways of thinking and decision making, not just analyzing and strategizing. They explore variables and parameters to the fullest extent possible, and they are used in tandem within the constructs of FSL.

In the slow-paced world of the mid twentieth century, when organizations employed many specialists and administrators to handle the operational aspects and financial details, being a specialist was viable for achieving success. The same can be said of the pure generalist. Generalists understood the big picture and were generally not too concerned about being competent in the specific aspects or the related details. They had a myriad of middle and line managers who were trained in the specific disciplines to handle and manage the particulars. However, in a fast-paced world with ever-changing situations and positions, strategic leaders have to be multi-specialists as well as highly capable generalists. They have to be competent in many areas and have the ability to quickly learn the requisite aspects and become competent to the extent necessary. With the ongoing requirements for leading change, developing new ways of achieving success and obtaining results, there may not be enough time to depend on financial advisors.

Strategic leaders have to understand the big picture and many of the small details. They have to be competent strategists as well as capable administrators and selfless managers. They have to focus on the short term and the long term. They must be capable of building solid relationships with people and be technically proficient at managing many technical areas. Most importantly, they must continuously improve their strengths and capabilities and must eliminate or neutralize their weaknesses, especially ones related to future situations.

The implications of multifaceted leadership perspectives

The notion of multifaceted leadership perspectives is a new way of thinking and leading in a more complicated business world. It is conceptually simple, but it is more involved than many existing constructs. It involves examining decisions from more holistic perspectives. It does not guarantee success, but increases the probability of succeeding because more of the important elements that go into decision making are contemplated, considered, analyzed and understood before decisions are rendered.

Multifaceted leadership perspectives examine variables, parameters, phenomena, and circumstances from multiple sides or views. There are many perspectives that can be viewed as dichotomies, thus dual-sided. But one must examine every perspective from multiple points of view, especially when there are various counterpoints. The purpose is to avoid making decisions that are based on perspectives that support the prevailing views, are in keeping with mainstream thinking, or are simply based on long-standing assumptions of the organization and the business environment. For instance, many organizations have the tendency to select strategies, initiatives, programs, and projects that are in line with the core capabilities and strengths of the organization because such approaches are beneficial to most of the people involved. However, such thinking limits decision making within existing perspectives and/or prevailing situations. In reality, the organization may have greater opportunities that are not aligned with the core capabilities of the organization. But the organization may not take advantage of the opportunities because such perspectives require building new strengths and core capabilities, mitigating existing weaknesses, and/or investing into new ventures. If the strategic leaders are not careful with their views of the realities, decision making becomes skewed toward what is perceived to be favorable to the organization or aligned with the prevailing situation. While it is sensible to exploit the organization's strengths and core capabilities, strategic leaders have to ensure that all options are duly considered and are given appropriate treatment. They must ensure that situations, positions, options and/or approaches that are perceived to be unfavorable are not simply avoided or categorically eliminated before analyses are conducted.

Strategic leaders often try to keep things simple by avoiding complexities. Overcoming weaknesses or mitigating threats tends to be more complicated than reinforcing strengths and exploiting opportunities; therefore, under the banner of simplicity strategic leaders often bias decisions and actions toward the easier approaches and focus on what appears to be more predictable and more achievable. Again, such approaches are concerns since they are often single sided. Strategic leaders often favor the simple and avoid the complex; they improve strengths but fail to overcome weaknesses; they select related opportunities as a way to avoid dealing with threats.

Multifaceted leadership perspectives require strategic leaders to think beyond just generating revenues and making money. Strategic leaders have to be cognizant of all of the critical factors in the natural world and business environment and deal with all aspects, regardless of the complexities involved. They have an implicit, if not explicit, duty to assure that the broader social world and the natural environment are considered as well as the shareholders and the people of the organization and enterprise. Multifaceted leadership perspectives provide opportunities to fulfill those responsibilities and to make substantial gains regardless of the underlying social and economic situations. There are often tensions between people and groups holding different perspectives. Unresolved tensions often are the causes of difficulties and complications in the long term. The sooner strategic leaders manage the tensions in their business environment, the more likely they can create favorable outcomes and advantageous future possibilities.

FSL and multifaceted leadership perspectives

FSL involves multifaceted perspectives focused on all sides of opportunities, situations, positions and/or realities, as well as the methods, techniques and practices involving strategic leadership and management. They may require more time and effort in the present, but ultimately they provide better solutions and outcomes over time. They provide more holistic and inclusive perspectives for making decisions in the complex world of today. Multifaceted leadership perspectives, i.e., those of FSL, necessitate a "mindset shift" from conventional thinking about leadership and management of the company to one that embraces the full dimensions of the company and its enterprise(s). While the dimensions of a business can be articulated using many additional perspectives, the four primary aspects for strategic thinking and decision making are strategic direction, space, time, and people. The mindset shift involves a new view of what strategic leaders have to do to be successful. Unlike most conventional theories that focus on a single parameter or two, FSL involves developing strategies, solutions, systems, structures, relationships and business models that meet all of the requisite criteria and expectations of the entities and people involved. FSL avoids making tradeoffs and involves a fully-integrated approach for achieving and sustaining success. Moreover, the approach does not just balance perspectives, but has the potential to reach greater heights and more sophisticated capabilities and outcomes. The key elements are:

- *Strategic direction* includes the overarching principles, philosophies, values, constructs, models, and paradigm used to guide the organization in establishing the vision, specific objectives, strategies, action plans, and targets for achieving success and in making strategic decisions.
- *Time* includes the determination of the time horizon for analyzing external and internal contexts, the necessary rate of change, and the time frame for strategies and actions.
- *Space* includes the extent of the business environment and market spaces, the scope of the enterprise(s), the elements of the management systems, and the reach of the economic, ethical, social, technological, and environmental factors and considerations.
- *People/resources* include the capabilities, know-how, knowledge, resources, and contributions of the corporation and its enterprises. They also include building connections and relationships among contributors and recipients and ensuring the people are successful.

Table 1.1 provides a short list of narrow and broad leadership perspectives. Historically, many strategic leaders focused on limited perspectives. While such approaches are

TABLE 1.1 List of Leadership Perspectives: Narrow and Broad

Category	Perspective	Narrow (Conventional)	Broad (Multifaceted/FSL)
Direction	Vision	Improvements	Transformations and transitions
	Objectives	Profits and cash flow	Value creation/sustainable success
	Strategies	Products and services	Solutions/sustainability
	Targets	Money making	Long-term & short-term outcomes
Time	Time horizon	Near term	Long term
	Rate of change	Keeping pace with realities	Leading change/proactive
	Time frame	Short term and near term	Short term and long term
Space	Scope	Micro-view/components	Macro-view/the whole
	Market space	Existing markets	Existing and emerging markets
	Social	Needs, requirements/mandates	Ethics, duties, and expectations
	Economic	Cost-benefits	Value proposition/enduring benefits
People/ resources	Capabilities	Organization	Organization and enterprise(s)
	Know-how	Intellectual property (IP)	Intellectual capital and IP
	Knowledge	Known	Known and unknown
	Resources	Company's	Company's and enterprise's
	Connections	Organizational links	Personal relationships

not wrong per se, they are narrow and tend-to reduce the options because the choices available are constrained by the selected framework.

Multifaceted leadership perspectives in relation to the categories are portrayed in Figure 1.8 showing the implications of the narrow perspectives in the shaded box and those of the broader perspectives in the dashed lines of the outer box. While the graphic is a theoretical characterization of FSL that requires ongoing research to determine the actual aspects of the management constructs and how they play out over time, it makes intuitive sense that the broader perspectives provide more opportunities, options, and an improved sense of reality. It also makes sense that strategic leaders have to move beyond focusing on making incremental gains in the prevailing businesses and reach out for greater results and sustainable success.

Assuming that sustainable success can be achieved through the integration and deployment of all of the categories and the perspectives thereof, it follows that outcomes can be enriched by having both narrow and broad perspectives. For instance, the outer box has a volume that may be two to four times greater that the inner box. Obviously, potential outcomes may be increasing based on the powers of the space, time, and people dimensions. On the other hand, if the focus is just on one aspect or one category, even with great improvements, the results tend to increase proportionately. However, small increases in every category can lead to significant and extraordinary outcomes overall; ones that are nonlinear. Multifaceted leadership perspectives indicate that strategic leaders must take on all of the important categories and focus on both the narrow and broad perspectives. Broad-based outcomes are critical factors for success, but unless they are complemented by short-term outcomes as well, strategic leaders may be vulnerable to the prevailing realities and circumstances. It is not an "either-or" construct.

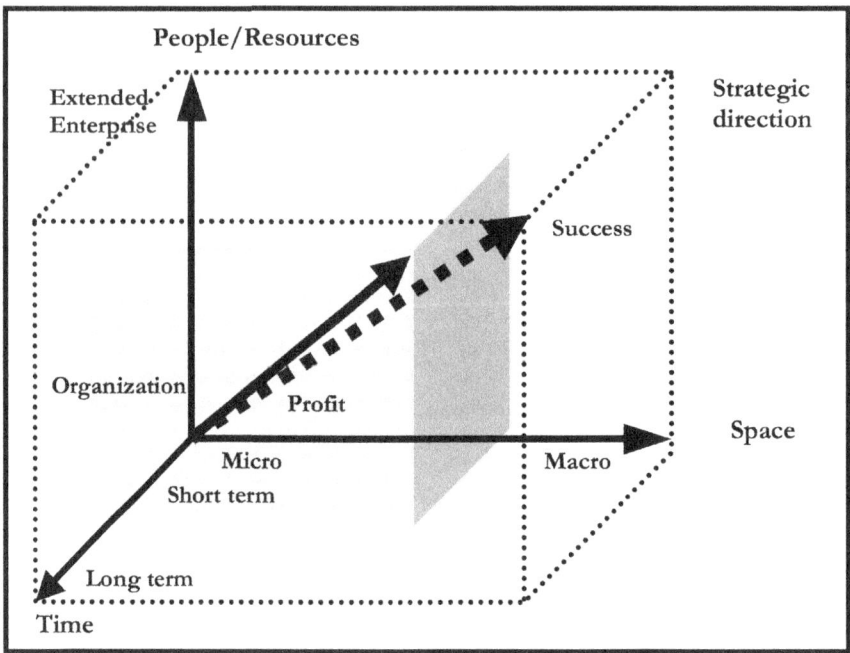

Figure 1.8 A simplified depiction of the matrix of key dimensions pertaining to FSL

As strategic leaders expand their horizons, they have to think about the strategic direction and select the approaches to use in determining how to craft strategic decisions and what has to be done. They must ensure continuous improvements through transitions to their management frameworks/constructs and strategic innovations related to new-to-the-world technologies, products, processes, and services. They also have to make transformations of higher levels of sophistication through embracing FSL, ESM, SBD and CSR.

Companies must generate profits and cash flow and ensure that they have the financial wherewithal to endure over the long term. But they must not sacrifice long-term strategic positions to maximize short-term gains. They must create sustainable success and duplicate it again and again. The most effective business strategies are crafted based on solutions that customers and stakeholders want and expect. Products and services may provide some of the key ingredients that make up the solutions, but success depends on creating and delivering internally- and externally-based solutions and outcomes, and not just on providing one's prescribed products. The purpose of business is to create value for people within and outside the company. Value creation drives money making. While money making is an important part of a business enterprise, profits are derivatives of value creation and value delivery. The ultimate broad-based target is sustainable success.

The time aspects are among the most complicated and difficult to orchestrate. While the vision that strategic leaders have for the future may not always be the most essential perspective, it does set the stage for many other time dependent aspects, including determining the time horizon and the rate of change. The time horizon should have elements that can be realized in the short term, such as enhancing the realities of the corporation or making dramatic improvements to a prevailing situation. And the time horizon should map out what has to be accomplished in the long term. The rate of change that strategic leaders select must keep pace with changes in the business world, and preferably lead changes across the enterprise. Leading change through FSL focuses on exceeding expectations and employing strategic innovations that outpace the prevailing rate of change, i.e., being proactive. For instance, if all of the leading companies are improving their businesses by five percent per year on average, then strategic leaders must improve their businesses by a rate significantly higher than the rate achieved by the most successful companies if they want to realize real gains and competitive advantages. This implies that companies achieving the five percent improvements are not making gains at all, but are just staying abreast of the pack and maintaining parity. It also implies that the measure is not just competitors, but all successful companies in related endeavors. This is a critical factor because if a company has poor competitors, strategic leaders may become complacent, believing that they are superior when they are really not keeping up with the most sophisticated companies, especially on a global basis. The effects of compounding improvements are profound. A five percent rate on average compounded over time results in doubling in fourteen years; a relatively small increase to seven percent provides a doubling in ten years. The former can be expected to double twice in thirty years, whereas the latter can be expected to double three times.

Selecting the spatial dimensions of the business framework is a critical decision that strategic leaders have to make whether implicitly or explicitly. Many strategic leaders select a framework that is relatively small; one that includes mostly the direct connections and the related elements. This usually includes the company itself and its value systems: the micro-view. The broader perspectives also include the micro-view and the macro-view of the whole business environment with all of the entities of the extended enterprise. This provides a richer array of possibilities and alternatives for decision making. It is more complex because of the large number of variables, but offers many more options for achieving success. Strategic leaders can expand their spatial horizons by addressing emerging markets as well as exploiting existing markets. They can enhance success by determining the value propositions for creating solutions and systems, not just using cost-benefit analysis. They can exceed external mandates and requirements, not just trying to comply with them. This is especially powerful when accelerating one's positions beyond the prevailing situations to achieve sustainable advantages. As the business world becomes more complex over time and scope, every effort should be made to enhance strategic positions and to reduce vulnerabilities.

The last category is the most difficult to describe and truly ascertain. While it is identified as people/resources, it is really dominated by people and their contributions. The focus is on the core capabilities of the organization on the narrow side and those of the organization and its extended enterprises on the broad side. FSL involves achieving success through the specific capabilities of the employees of the corporations and its business units, and the beneficial relationships and capabilities of all of the key contributors from the initial tiers of the supply networks to end-of-life contributors. The narrow perspectives focus on the intellectual property (IP) of the organization and what is known and can be acted upon. The broader perspectives focus on all of the intellectual capital and IP available across the enterprise and what is known and unknown. Unknowns generate uncertainties and risks. The concept herein is to exploit what is known and to engage in uncovering the unknowns so the uncertainties and risks are reduced. Resources are the things that are employed to produce and deliver solutions. Resources can be internally owned or shared with external entities. The former requires investments and the latter requires having solid systems and great relationships.

Ultimately, strategic leaders have to decide on their view of FSL and select their own perspectives. Again, it is not an either-or decision or one that has to be purely one, the other, or both. The theoretical leadership perspectives suggest that there are great opportunities for achieving extraordinary outcomes and realizing sustainable success by being as broad as possible at the same time ensuring that narrow perspectives are not sacrificed.

Strategic leaders have huge challenges to exceed expectations and continue to be successful year after year. As corporations increase in size and complexity and enjoy success, it may become more difficult to keep pace with the realities of the business world. Therefore, it is imperative that successful strategic leaders reinvent what they are doing periodically and reach out for new and more effective ways of thinking, strategizing, and executing. Strategic approaches that worked well as a developing company may not be effective for a market share leader or a sophisticated corporation.

FSL indicates that small changes in multiple categories and perspectives can lead to incredible changes and improvements overall. The intangible elements can be just as powerful as the tangible ones. Being open and honest can encourage people across the enterprise to believe in the strategies and messages pertaining to positive change. Resistance to change is usually due to the lack of engagement and the failure to energize people.

Reflections

FSL combines holistic thinking and strategic assessments about the business environment and how strategic leaders can improve, develop, expand, transition, and transform their companies, business units, and extended enterprises to achieve sustainable success. Strategic leaders and other strategists apply experiences, knowledge, and insights about the use of strategic positions, intellectual capital, competencies, capabilities, and resources, and the potential to leverage and/or influence those same attributes of their strategic partners, allies, and value networks to create extraordinary opportunities and outcomes.

Cutting-edge companies need highly competent, innovative, and technologically sophisticated leaders who have the mindset, imagination, insights, and innovativeness to think broadly and to create new landscapes for meeting the needs and dreams of customers, stakeholders, employees, shareholders, and society. Moreover, such strategic leaders must extend their reach beyond the traditional perspectives of the corporation and take responsibility for the corporation's direct and indirect effects and impacts on the extended enterprise, market spaces and business environment.

Global corporations and SMEs depend on the competencies and intellectual capital of all of their contributors, both internal and external, and on the strengths and capabilities of the interconnected entities to realize the desired outcomes. The power, strategic position, and success of a company and its business units are determined by the contributions and performance of all of the players, direct and indirect. Outcomes are the sum of all of the contributions, from the conception and development of the technologies and products, the generation of new product ideas, the origin of the materials, and the conversion of inputs into outputs like products and services to the delivery of those outputs to customers, their applications and the final disposition of the residuals. Strategic leaders must ensure that the specialized capabilities, knowledge and advantages of the contributors are leveraged to produce the desired value-added outcomes. FSL involves both investing in creating a more sustainable future and in transforming positions, strategies, systems, operations, processes, and practices into value-added outcomes and more sophisticated realities.

Notes

1. Alfred Chandler, Jr., *Strategy and Structure: Chapters in the History of the American Industrial Enterprise* (Cambridge, MA: M.I.T. Press, 1962, pp52-113). Chandler maps out how DuPont created its autonomous divisions.
2. Michael Porter, *Competitive Advantage: Creating and Sustaining Superior Performance* (New York, NY: Free Press, 1985, p33-61).
3. Id, p36.
4. Id, p37.
5. W. Edwards Deming, *Out of The Crisis* (Cambridge, MA: MIT Press, 2000, pp23-24). Deming's 14 points are:
   1. Create constancy of purpose for the improvement of products and service, with the aim to become competitive and to stay in business, and to provide jobs.
   2. Adopt the new philosophy. We are in a new economic age. Western management must awaken to the challenge, must learn their responsibilities and take on leadership for change.
   3. Cease dependence on mass inspection to achieve quality. Eliminate the need for inspection on a mass basis by building quality into the products in the first place.
   4. End the practice of awarding business on the basis of the price tag. Instead, minimize total cost. Move toward a single supplier for any one item, on a long-term relationship of loyalty and trust.
   5. Improve constantly every process, whether planning, production or service.
   6. Institute training on the job.
   7. Institute leadership. The aim of supervision should be to help people and machines and gadgets to do a better job. Supervision of management is in need of overhaul, as well as supervision of production workers.
   8. Drive out fear, so that everyone may work effectively for the company.
   9. Break down barriers between departments. People in research, design, sales and production must work as a team, to foresee problems in production and in use that may be encountered with the product and service.

10. Eliminate slogans, exhortations and targets for the workforce asking for zero defects and new levels of productivity. Such exhortations only create adversarial relationships, as the bulk of the causes of low quality and low productivity belong to the system and thus lie beyond the power of the workforce.
11. Eliminate work standards on the factory floor. Substitute leadership. Eliminate management by objectives. Eliminate management by numbers, numerical goals. Substitute leadership.
12. Remove barriers that rob hourly worker of his right to pride of workmanship. The responsibility of supervisors must be changed from sheer numbers to quality. Remove barriers that rob people in management and in engineering of their right of pride of workmanship. This means *inter alia,* abolishment of annual merit rating and of management by objectives.
13. Institute a vigorous program of *education* and self-improvement.
14. Put everybody in the company to work to accomplish the transformation. Transformation is everyone's job.

6. James Brian Quinn, Henry Mintzberg and Robert M. James, *The Strategy Process: Concepts, Context and Cases* (New York, NY: Prentice Hall, 1988, p277-279.
7. Gary Hamel, *Leading the Revolution* (Boston, MA: Harvard Business School Press, 2000, p13). Hamel introduces the notion of business concept innovation. It focuses on changing the business model for true innovation and achieving competitive advantage.
8. Id, p70.
9. Id, p283 & 313.
10. Id, p94.
11. David L. Rainey, *Enterprise-Wide Strategic Management: Achieving Sustainable Success through Leadership, Strategies, and Value Creation* (Cambridge, UK: Cambridge University Press, 2010, pp16-64).
12. Id, p444.
13. http://www.blockbuster.com/corporate/investorRelations. In early 2011, Blockbuster was acquired by DISH Network Corporation.
14. Id.
15. Union Carbide Corporation's (UCC) plant in India was a joint venture between UCC and the government. Nevertheless, UCC has been held primarily responsible.

References

Chandler, Jr., Alfred (1962) *Strategy and Structure: Chapters in the History of the American Industrial Enterprise.* Cambridge, MA: M.I.T. Press.

Deming, W. Edwards (2000) *Out of The Crisis.* Cambridge, MA: MIT Press.

Hamel, Gary (2000) *Leading the Revolution.* Boston, MA: Harvard Business School Press.

Porter, Michael (1985) *Competitive Advantage: Creating and Sustaining Superior Performance.* New York, NY: Free Press.

Quinn, James Brian, Henry Mintzberg and Robert M. James (1988) *The Strategy Process: Concepts, Context and Cases.* New York, NY: Prentice Hall.

Rainey, David L. (2010) *Enterprise-wide Strategic Management: Achieving Sustainable Success through Leadership, Strategies, and Value Creation.* Cambridge, UK: Cambridge University Press.

2

The Driving Forces of Change and the Influences of the Business Environment

Introduction

Cutting-edge leadership and management involve discovering and dealing with opportunities, challenges, and risks based on far-reaching perspectives and insights; ones involving significant changes in the market spaces and the business environment. Effective strategic leaders seek to understand and determine the driving forces that shape the world of tomorrow and how they can take advantage of the changes. Their perspectives are based on strategic thinking about what is occurring, what is changing, what the expected consequences are, and how to position one's company and enterprise for success.

The business world of the early twenty-first century is far more demanding than what was the situation just twenty years ago. The global economy is changing at increasing rates as industrialization moves rapidly across the business world. Dramatically improved logistics, advances in information and communications technologies (ICT) and the ubiquitous Internet are among the many forces of change that have connected customers, businesses and societies on a global basis. For instance, ICT has made it possible to transact business from the U.S. or the European Union (EU) to Pacific Rim locations and vice versa at very low costs and incredible speeds. Products can be produced in China and shipped to consumers in the U.S. and the EU with small effect on the cost of goods and the quality of the outcomes.

The business world has expanded from the "economic elites" living in the developed countries to include the broader economic opportunities of people living in developing countries. Moreover, emerging companies in rapidly industrializing countries (RICs) like China, India, and Brazil are playing significant roles in producing goods and providing services. The world is shrinking in terms of geography, communications, logistics, and connectedness, but expanding in terms of potential demand, emerging markets, new customers, nascent competitors, service providers, and stakeholders. Competition is intensifying as emerging companies, especially from RICs, become significant players in their home markets and eventually powerful forces in the global economy.

Strategic leaders have to be on the cutting edge of proactive change addressing and resolving many of the social, ethical, economic, technological, environmental, and market-related problems and creating extraordinary value and outcomes for all of the contributors and recipients. The overarching aspirations are to ensure that natural, human, and economic capital and all of the related resources are used efficiently, effectively and appropriately. Strategic leaders have to engage in full-spectrum strategic leadership (FSL), improving the positive side of the value creation by developing and delivering sustainable solutions that maximize benefits and positive outcomes and minimize the adverse effects and negative impacts. FSL includes perspectives on reducing or eliminating resource depletion, environmental degradation, social and economic disruptions, and environmental wastes.

The chapter includes the following main topics:

- Exploring the major global forces of change that influence strategic decision-making and provide opportunities for companies, businesses and their extended enterprises
- Assessing the dynamics of the social, political, ethical, economic, and environmental dimensions and the ever-changing needs and expectations of markets, customers, stakeholders and society

The Critical Driving Forces

The expansion of market spaces

Globalization has become one of the most important phenomena of the last decade as the effects and impacts of many of the social, ethical, economic, technological, and environmental forces shifted from national and regional settings to a global landscape. Globalization is a complex term that has many meanings from narrow ones focusing on the economic aspects of a single global economy to the broader view of a totally interconnected, interrelated, and interactive business world.

The changes from a narrow perspective may be viewed as part of the ongoing evolution of economic and social exchanges and activities that have expanded dramatically since the beginning of the industrial revolution to include most countries and societies. While economic expansion has changed and expanded in recent years, the historical evidence suggests that for most of the previous two centuries, the industrial age was centered in the Western nations and most of the benefits were derived by people living in Western Europe, Canada, U.S., and Japan. During the early years the expansion of the economic benefits was relatively slow-paced. The early developments were centered in the United Kingdom (UK), Germany, and other European countries and subsequently moved to the U.S. and Japan. Not only was economic progress slow to migrate from country to country, but advancements in the broader underpinnings of the social, ethical, economic, and environmental forces only improved gradually in the industrialized countries, since the owners of capital generally enjoyed overwhelming advantages related to the driving forces and wealth creation. Customers and consumers eventually realized some economic gains, but at relatively steep purchase prices and high cost of ownership. Labor obtained some of the benefits of industrialization, but workers paid a heavy personal price in terms of poor working conditions and detrimental health and safety effects and impacts. Only during the latter part of the twentieth century did governments in the developed countries affect more balanced approaches by enacting laws and promulgating regulations to protect consumers and the health and safety of workers and to preserve the natural environment.

The broader perspectives may be perceived as a more recent phenomenon that has dramatically taken hold since the end of the Cold War with the acceleration of advanced ICTs and more cost effective means and mechanisms for producing and transporting goods, especially from distance locations. Whereas it is always difficult to identify the starting point of a paradigm shift during the early stages of the transformation, the most profound changes have occurred over the last twenty years. The demise of the Soviet Union and the end of its control over client states in Eastern Europe ultimately eradicated many of the old tensions between the First World, the economic and military powers of the G7 (UK, France, Germany, Italy, U.S., Canada, and Japan), the Second World, the Soviet Union and its Warsaw Pact allies. The post-World War II period ended in the early 1990s as the Second World evaporated into many independent countries vying for their own place in the world. The notion of the Third World, which included most of the other nations, was often used based on negative perspectives about being undeveloped or underdeveloped countries. They were often viewed during the Cold War period as pawns in the global "chess games" between the superpowers or seen as essential, but not coequal allies that provided critical resources like petroleum, metal ores, military bases, and/or other valuable tangibles and intangibles. Today, the First World countries are called the developed countries and the Third World countries are called developing countries.

The rise of the Internet has had possibly the most profound effects. Today, most large companies have excellent information and data about the markets that they serve. Such markets are examined on an ongoing basis by strategic leaders, strategic planners, economists, marketing professionals, and numerous others. The prevailing market situations are typically well understood and well articulated. However, the main concern is that most of the strategic analysis is done based on the existing conditions and trends, rather than what the situations could be if certain strategic decisions were made; i.e., if better solutions were available and more inclusive management systems were developed. It is always difficult to understand what could be instead of what is, but simply assessing just the prevailing situations can be misleading. For instance, why do people buy the products that are offered? Usually, the answer is because they want to satisfy their needs and expectations, but in certain situations they may really want products and services that are not available. They want something better, more affordable, more efficient, and more reliable, but those choices may not be available. Such people continue to seek such solutions, but they often keep on buying the existing products until they find the right solutions. The companies that can create such solutions often obtain first-mover advantages, such as Apple's success with the iPad and iPhone.

Large multinational corporations (MNCs) are usually well-positioned in the developed countries, but they have minuscule operations and market shares in the developing countries. While there are notable exceptions like Coca-Cola, Procter & Gamble, Nestlé, and Unilever, the market spaces in most of the developing countries are wide open for proactive companies to establish significant positions. If emerging competitors from the RICs can capture significant positions in the emerging markets, they may develop the size and scale to compete more effectively with the giant MNCs elsewhere. By achieving market successes in providing affordable products that meet the basic needs of people in China, India and other industrializing countries, emerging companies may obtain huge economies of scale and have the capacity to leverage such successes globally. Their products may become the global solutions of tomorrow. The Toyota story of the 1950s and 1960s exemplifies how innovative approaches like lean production and quality management developed for one's home market can be leveraged into strategic advantages across other markets, allowing the innovator to compete against the market leaders in their home markets as well as elsewhere.

Cultural and ethnic imperatives

Cultural and ethnic differences continue to play powerful roles in understanding and dealing with changes that cannot be overlooked as companies pursue more global perspectives. Each nation and ethnic group has its own unique mindset about how to solve problems and how life should be lived. It is imperative that strategic leaders understand these mindsets and include such considerations in both general and specific terms in their strategic thinking. It is also critical to contemplate the cultural context of stakeholders, supply networks, partners, and others, not just those of customers and markets. Dutch cultural expert, Fons Trompenaars, wrote in *Riding the Waves of Culture* that "culture can put the brakes on any movement to internationalize."[1] His research indicates that there is no single best approach for addressing cultural issues and that management has to think about intrinsic values, beliefs, and behaviors of the people involved. Some of his most poignant insights for dealing with international and transnational management are:[2]

> While you cannot give universal advice that will work regardless of culture and while general axioms of business administration turn out to be largely American cultural axioms, there are

universal dilemmas or problems of human existence. Every country and every organization in that country faces dilemmas:
- In relationships with people
- In relationships to time
- In relations between people and the natural environment

Business is about people, and people are prime considerations in determining strategic direction, positions, strategies, solutions, systems, and innovations. People everywhere have many commonalities in that they experience the human condition and have many similar human needs, wants, and desires. Still, people differ in cultural beliefs, values, norms, behaviors, and how they view the world and other people. Understanding cultural differences, respecting the differences, and working with people from various backgrounds are important elements in gaining a broader view of the business world. Creating relationships with people who think and live differently requires insightfulness and adaptability about what is necessary to forge and maintain common ground. How people perceive things and make strategic decisions are key factors. For instance, people in the U.S. typically value individual contributions and analytical reasoning, while people in many Asian countries value collaborative interactions and holistic reasoning. The former tend to make decisions based on what is rational, while the latter focus more on the relational and emotional reasons.

The way people view time is also an important variable. Different cultures often have their own views of the importance of time. People may have different perspectives on concepts like being on time and getting work done on schedule and in a timely manner. In Western thought, time is unidirectional and definitive. In other cultures, time is circular with reoccurring events. For instance, timeliness is important and an absolute in the U.S., but it may be relative in many Latin American countries. In Brazil there may be some fuzziness about what time a ten o'clock meeting means, while in the U.S. it means starting at exactly ten o'clock.

Views on nature also vary among people and cultures. Historically, most people had a strong connection with the natural world. Many of the technological developments and the spirituality of the ancient world were associated with cycles of the sun, the moon, the seasons, the weather, and nature in general. Even during the eighteenth and nineteenth centuries people were still keenly interested in the cycles of the moon, the tides, and rainy and dry seasons. Farmers, in particular, were concerned with nature and paid attention to the proper timing for planting and harvesting. The variety of farmer's almanacs, of which Ben Franklin's Poor Richard's Almanac was best known in the U.S., is a testament of the importance of understanding nature during previous centuries.

Today, most of the people in the developed countries, especially those living in the large metropolitan areas, generally have little direct connections with the natural environment and often view natural phenomenon such as hurricanes, typhoons, snow storms, volcanic eruptions, and other natural occurrences as inconveniences in their daily lives or travel plans. Moreover, many strategic leaders assume that the raw materials of nature like water, air, and natural resources, especially petroleum, metal ores and plants, are plentiful or that the current conditions can be expected to prevail for a long time. Additionally, many business people believe that modern technologies can control the effects of nature and that technological innovations can provide solutions to resource depletion and environmental degradation. Many of the business leaders believe that if negative social or environmental changes do occur, the governments would be responsible for managing the effects and implications of such phenomena, especially such phenomena as climate change and natural disasters. While such assumptions are often correct in the short term and validated by the prevailing experiences, the natural environment is ever changing. From a business point of view, most of the effects and impacts of changes in the natural environment may take decades to become apparent and to affect the fortunes of businesses. Unfortunately, in many situations there is usually no call to action until it is too late and many of the best options are no longer be available.

In many countries, people want to protect their national character and prevent outside influences from contaminating the native culture. For instance, the French have tried to keep foreign words out of their language and way of life, especially those originated by American corporations like McDonald's and Coca-Cola. Sometimes such efforts attempt to achieve a balance between globalization and the local or regional character. Other times, there is solid resistance to change and a desire to maintain the traditional ways. In Italy, food companies have coined the concept of "slow food" as a way to differentiate their approaches from those of the global giants in fast food businesses. Slow food means enjoying the whole experience as one consumes food and wine. It involves providing a solution (the experience) rather than just providing a product (the hamburger).

Similarly, the development of local, national, or regional standards that require special provisions for operating in a given market is perhaps the most significant countervailing force to open trade and the free exchange of goods. While most such standards are based on high principles and lofty goals, the effects in the short term and possibly the long term as well may be to limit competition, especially from companies outside the countries or regions that impose the standards. Examples include EU requirements for manufacturers to take back their products at the end of life and the restrictions placed on the use of hazardous substances.[3] In the EU and elsewhere, there are growing trends to hold producers to be more responsible for the products they design, produce, and market and for the decisions that they make in the process. This includes the decisions and actions of related external parties like suppliers and distributors. Such expectations include providing relevant information about the proper applications of products and ensuring that there is a total solution available for retiring the used products and residuals. On the positive side, there are economic opportunities in capturing the residual value in end-of-life products. On the negative side, the inability to manage end-of-life considerations may become a barrier to selling products in the EU and elsewhere. This may limit free trade and reduce open competition. While the requirements are complicated and take-back systems are implemented by individual countries within the EU, the implications are profound. It may make doing business in the EU more involved, costly, and difficult for producers and distributors, especially those using virtual methods of doing business who do not have direct access to the actual physical distribution channels. Corporations without a real presence in the EU may find it difficult to adhere to the provisions of the directive.

The intensity of competition in terms of costs and quality

The intensity of global competition has increased dramatically over the last three decades. According to the United Nations Conference on Trade and Development, World Investment Report 2001, the number of global corporation has increased from approximately 7,000 in 1970 to over 63,000 in 2000.[4] Today, the number is estimated to be over one hundred thousand. Competition amongst the most capable companies, typically MNCs, is increasingly waged on a regional and global landscape.[5] In addition, MNCs are becoming more sophisticated in their operations (production and marketing), management capabilities, market responsiveness, technological developments, strategic innovations, and global supply chain management. For example, many of the principal producers of cell phones like Nokia, Samsung, Ericsson, and Motorola claim to be six-sigma quality producers. Customers expect high-quality cell phones and they generally know that each of these companies provides world-class quality and reliability. The strategic leaders of such companies have to find even more innovative ways to differentiate their products and positions beyond just high-level product specifications and six-sigma manufacturing. They have to stay on the cutting edge before they are surpassed by even more capable producers like LG. They have to invent unique and enduring solutions and integrate their entire management system(s) and enterprise(s) using the most effective ways to gain every advantage. Customers expect everything from the best quality and lowest cost to cutting-edge technologies and complete solutions.

Exploiting global sourcing for reducing the cost structures of materials, parts, components, or even whole products is one of the major battlegrounds for this kind of competition. Most of the global corporations have formed relationships with suppliers and/or have outsourced production processes to supply networks in the Pacific Rim and elsewhere to increase gross margins and enhance market positions. In the short term, suppliers in China and India have low costs because they have access to low-wage labor that receives marginal benefits. These situations are often viewed to be critical requirements for commodity-type products that are sold predominately on the basis of price. While price does have a major influence on the value proposition, and producers usually make supply decisions based on costs, such tactics also drive down consumer prices as most of the major competitors achieve comparable low-cost structures in the same way. Customers do enjoy more affordable and cost-effective products. In the long term, gross margins are reduced for most of the competitors resulting in only short-term advantages in revenues and margins. This phenomenon has helped to keep inflation low and makes products available to a broader array of customers, especially those in demographic groups with low disposable incomes. However, competition becomes more intense over time and the success of many of the companies often declines.

While the social questions pertaining to the exploitation of labor are covered in the next section, the viability of many of the outsourcing tactics that rely on finding and producing low-cost goods based on low labor rates may eventually run their course over this decade. While there are millions of unemployed or underemployed people around the world, representing a large potential supply of low-paid labor, many stakeholder groups like the Fair Labor Association are increasing social and political pressures to improve working conditions and enhance the pay of people in the low-wage countries.[6] Social advocacy groups worldwide are increasingly demanding human rights protection and improved working conditions in the developing countries. They try to impose political and regulatory restrictions in the developed countries against trading with countries and/or companies that do not meet generally accepted social, economic, ethical, and environmental standards. Economic conditions within the RICs may also put pressure on indigenous companies to increase wages and benefits. For instance, in the U.S. during the 1950s and 1960s, many producers in the northern states moved their operations to southern states to take advantage of the lower pay scales. As more and more manufacturers moved south, wage rates increased substantially and the cost advantages dissipated. While the absolute value of the increased wages may not be significant, the percentage of increase is expected to put pressure on the profitability of commodity products from developing countries and make them less attractive.

Over the last twenty-five years, most global corporations have improved the quality and performance of their operations and processes. Improvements began through the Total Quality Management initiatives of the 1980s and continued in the early 1990s with dramatic improvements in the quality and value of products and services, and in innovative processes for creating new products and services. The three main approaches used for making improvements have focused on improving costs structures, quality improvements for existing products and services, and product and process innovations for new or redesigned products and services. Cost reduction efforts usually involve incremental product improvements that are often easily duplicated by competitors. Moreover, incremental improvements for existing products may not address and solve entrenched difficulties, thereby perpetuating fundamental weaknesses.

The same is often the case for most other incremental process improvements. While the improvements may be important and even significant, unless they are translated into sustainable competitive advantages, the results usually produce only marginal gains in the company's strategic positions. Moreover, incremental process improvements might be trumped by new technologies or radical innovations by one or more of the competitors or even companies outside the prevailing industry. For example, film-based photography companies like Kodak and Fuji were unable to improve film processing sufficiently to compete with the technological advantages of digital cameras. Kodak had to make significant investments into their digital camera businesses to stay competitive; in 2006 its Digital & Film Imaging Systems was transformed into Consumer Digital Imaging Group Segment and Film and Photofinishing Systems Group Segment.

Continuous improvement in quality has been the mantra for more than thirty years for most U.S. companies and twice as long in Japan. While improving quality inherently makes sense, the gains made by improving existing products and processes tend to diminish as further improvements are made. For instance, the quality differences between American and Japanese car companies were obvious to most American customers in the 1980s when the defect rate per hundred cars was approximately 400 for the American producers and 100 for the Japanese. Similarly, improvements from bad quality levels of 400 to 200 defects per hundred automobiles tend to be discernable. Today, given that defect rates are further improved (30 less than defects per 100 vehicles) a similar reduction rate may be undetectable by customers and not as effective in improving one's positions.

Product innovation has also become an important methodology for obtaining more enduring competitiveness. By the mid-1990s, most global corporations had adapted some form of integrated product development (IPD) to accelerate the processes for creating new products and processes. IPD is a powerful product innovation construct that systematically links the external business environment and its needs, wants, opportunities, and challenges with the internal dimensions of the organization and its capabilities and resources to create innovative solutions. It involves the concurrent development of new products using cross-functional teams that are aligned strategically and tactically. IPD is the prevailing form of product innovation today.[7] The total time to develop and introduce new products has been cut by a factor of two or more in many industries.

The expanding role of technology

The industrial revolution was based on innovative technologies derived from the steam engine and later driven by the railroads and telegraph. Many technologies that evolved from various steam engines were used to power ships, steamboat and locomotives and to mechanize steel production and other heavy industries. By the end of the nineteenth century, industrialization based on continued technological advancements in electricity, lighting, machinery, transportation and communications had significantly revolutionized the quality of life in the industrialized nations. Thomas Edison's light bulbs, Nikola Tesla's AC power dynamos, Alexander Graham Bell's telephone and Otto Benz's automobile, to name a few, shifted the attention of the commercial world and the business mindset from satisfying basic needs to creating new-to-the-world technologies.

Technological innovations in the early twentieth century focused extensively on social and economic dimensions to find new ways to expand business opportunities by improving lifestyles through cost-effective products and services. Henry Ford's Model T revolutionized the world of manufacturing and marketing by lowering the cost of production through the use of assembly lines and economies of scale, making low-end cars affordable for the average person. Ford used technological innovations to change the underlying mechanisms of production and increased market potential by integrating his business operation into new solutions for people to enjoy. His solutions increased mobility and social and economic freedom. Ford's greatest insight was to understand what markets could be, instead of focusing on what the markets were based on the existing demand, market structures, and production methods.

Companies have historically viewed technologies in terms of products and production processes. Some of the most significant technological advancements over the last fifty years have occurred in electronics and ICTs. From mainframe computers, transistors, calculators, microprocessors, personal computers, cell phones, software, plasma TVs, digital cameras, LCDs, the Internet, and digital technologies using virtual reality, companies have focused on the physical and commercial attributes of the technologies by decreasing size and material intensity, increasing power and performance, improving the value and usability, and reducing defects and negative impacts. As the rate of technological change accelerates, technology developments have become critical factors for success in many sectors, especially in electronics, computer-related hardware and software, ICT, and Internet technologies. During the late 1990s, many corporations made significant investments in replacing pre-Internet and pre-Y2K technologies with state-of-the-art technologies, making quantum leaps in their strategic positions. Moreover, the focus changed from just creating new products and processes to providing extraordinary value via new-to-the-world technologies.

The essence of strategic innovations has changed from mainly manipulating the physical, chemical, and biological dimensions to using intellectual capital for creating innovative solutions, developing sophisticated systems, and enriching reality for humankind. The Internet is an example of a dynamic system and new reality. In simple terms, the Internet provides connectivity to the multitudes around the world allowing them to share ICTs and enjoy the rewards of numerous innovations. Using resources that have already been developed, it expands the applications of those resources thousands, if not millions of times, from their initial contributions. While such expansions do require some additional resources and actions like new servers and maintenance personnel, the core resources and operations often require little added investments or efforts and can be used to serve millions of clients with marginal increases in costs. For example, providing annual financial reports of corporations historically involved the production, printing, handling, and distribution of the hard copies and expensive mailings. While such activities are usually still required for the shareholders, many more clients can receive a copy of an annual report via the Internet at no additional cost.

Twenty-first century strategic innovations involve leading and managing at the cutting edge of change. They are dominated by new sciences and technologies like biotechnology and nanotechnologies. While there will undoubtedly be many nuances among the technologies of the future, most innovative technologies are expected to exhibit several common characteristics. Some of the most salient aspects include:

- Enhanced value creation: The technologies must provide excellent returns and rewards to the corporations and their investors, customers, stakeholders, and society.
- Improved value propositions: The technologies must be the underpinnings of valuable solutions that eliminate problems and difficulties.

- Minimized resource depletion: The technologies must be efficient and effective in resource deployment and use only the minimum materials and energy necessary to achieve the desired solutions.
- Zero pollution and degradation: The technologies must be clean, avoid toxic substances, and produce only minimal waste streams and residuals that can be redeployed in other processes.
- Reduced negative impacts: The technologies must be balanced from economic, social, ethical, technological, and environmental considerations and have positive life cycle implications. Their impacts on the business environment must also be minimal.
- Reduced costs and time: The technologies must be efficient and effective with minimal costs and time requirements; i.e., they are easy to learn about and to use. They must be developed in a reasonable time frame so that they are economically feasible.

The list is not comprehensive. The criteria define some of the underlying requirements for cleaner technologies. The premise is that many of the technological advancements have to focus on being clean, lean, and ease to use. The notion of clean technology is an often used, but it is an ill-defined term that includes systems, processes, equipment, and know-how used to eliminate, reduce, and/or control pollution and waste streams and to minimize resource utilization better than alternatives. Clean technologies are advanced, state-of-the-art technologies designed and employed to maximize positive benefits and minimize negative aspects.

Many of today's technologies exist in virtual reality. Electronic purchase transactions for music, videos, books, and other types of documents often occur without any physical reality. For instance, e-books using Amazon's Kindle and Barnes and Noble's Nook allow customers to download books, magazines, and other documents in electronic form. This minimizes resource requirements and makes products available to millions at low costs and few impacts. Using electronic (paperless) transactions facilitates speed, cost-effectiveness, and quality outcomes and is a major trend in banking, finance, and stock trading. In fact, the whole phenomenon of e-business, with business to business (B2B), business to customer (B2C) and customer to business (C2B) transactions using the Internet is based on the concept of maximizing value creation (minimizing costs) by providing exact solutions for each customer (mass customization). Moreover, producers and marketers do not have to guess how many goods to inventory; everything is in virtual space.

Life science technologies provide opportunities to better understand the need side of the human condition and the social and economic implications so that there are more precise understandings of what the best solutions are and how to create them. The genomics project, the mapping of the human genome, provides a database about the mechanisms of life and how to improve the quality of life and prevent diseases and physical deterioration. Biotechnology promises to improve agriculture and the ability to reduce or eliminate the vast quantities of toxic chemicals used for growing food for humans and feed for animals.

Nanotechnology is the study and application of matter on a nanometer scale.[8] It allows the engineering of products and processes that use exactly what is necessary for producing the solution without residuals or wastes. While such outcomes are still in the developmental stages, the promise and potential of clean technologies using the concepts of nanotechnology are central to sustainable solutions and sustainable success.

The most important central characteristic of clean technologies may be the concept of the "*power factor.*" The power factor derives from the fact that a clean technology can be developed, produced, and deployed multiple times with little additional expense and relatively few impacts after the initial investment. The power factor is akin to the concept of leveraging physical resources and operations, especially those involving production. Leveraging usually means increasing capacity utilization by ten to twenty percent, such as using the existing but underutilized productive resources for counter-seasonal products, thereby improving many aspects of the operating system through more efficient deployment of resources. Leveraging involves arithmetic improvements. The power factor involves improvements of hundreds, thousands, or millions of times more than what the previous or alternate technology could do. The power factor involves geometric advancements, making it possible for investments in technology developments to produce incredible gains and long-term successes. While most business people measure gains in terms of economic or financial rewards, the power factor also involves social, ethical, political, and environmental considerations as well. For instance, digital photography enjoys a power factor, because it eliminates the requirements for toxic chemicals that result in hazardous wastes, which cost money to manage and eliminate and damage the natural environment. They have adverse effects on human health and well-being. Digital technology allows consumers to instantaneously determine whether the picture is good and worth keeping or to delete it without any cost or real effort. If the user prints the pictures, he or she prints only the pictures that are desired, avoiding making copies of unwanted ones. On the social side, wireless telephone technologies provide opportunities to not only reduce the unsightliness and resource deployment of wires, but they offer users mobility and the benefits of continuous access to telecommunications.

The power factor expresses unique benefits that new-to-the-world technologies and products bring to the business environment. For example, eBay is a company using the power factor to near perfection—at least during its first decade. The company's online auction business grew from approximately three hundred thousand auctions in 1996 to close to a billion by 2003. The number of registered users increased from forty-one thousand to nearly ninety-five million over the same time frame. The power of eBay is its software and management system that connects tens of millions of traders in a convenient and cost-effective business model that allows effective and efficient person-to-person exchanges of information, goods, and money. With safe and secure transactions supported by eBay's system and augmented by logistical support from United Parcel Service, U.S. Postal Service and other allies, clients, and entrepreneurs can leverage the benefits of eBay for achieving their objectives and making transactions that would be impossible on an individual basis. Many people have started their own businesses using eBay's system. For eBay, the power factor is based on a framework that can accommodate a significant increase in business transactions without a linear increase in investments.

Technology developments have provided great solutions; however, new strategic innovations across the world will have to achieve even higher levels of advancements and sophistication if the social, economic, and environmental objectives of an expanding world economy are to be realized. Given that the population estimates for the world of 2050 are based on sound data and adjusted for diseases like HIV/AIDS, and that the economies of China, India and other RICs are expected to grow dramatically, the technologies of the future have to be cleaner, leaner, and more effective for improving the quality of life for all people. Assuming the population of the world increases by 30 percent over the next 40 years (from 7 to 9 billion people) and the overall activities of all people increase by a factor of two, then in order to keep the total global environmental impacts at their current levels, technological advancements have to be improved and negative impacts have to be reduced by a factor close to three.[9] Technologies of the future have to use resources more efficiently, pollute less, carry significantly reduced burdens and harms, be more cost-effective, and offer more benefits. Clean technologies have to be more sustainable, create extraordinary value, minimize environmental impacts, and provide cost-effective and enduring solutions. While there are no perfect technologies and each technology has advantages and disadvantages, strategic innovations have to correct mistakes of the past and provide more sustainable solutions for the future.

The ubiquitous Internet

The Internet is the publicly accessible network of computers, servers, and software that by 2002 had linked the entire world together with constant flows and exchanges of information and data. It represents the fusion of many technologies, including telecommunications, computers, protocols, and electronic and digital products and processes that provide effective means and mechanisms for interactive exchanges on a global basis. The Internet has been one of the most revolutionary technologies to be developed in the last fifty years, and it is a critical force of change that must be considered and managed from broad perspectives. Today, the Internet connects people from the most advanced cities to some of the most remote regions. It is changing the way business is conducted and how people buy and use products and services. The e-business reality is a fast-paced world of B2B, B2C, and C2B interactions that provide new ways of satisfying the needs and expectations of a more complicated and often turbulent business world.

The Internet has grown exponentially from approximately 2 million hosts in 1995 to over 233 million at the beginning of 2004.[10] At the end of 2003, approximately 675 million people or 11.8 percent of the total population worldwide had access to the Internet.[11] As of 2009, there were approximately 650 million hosts.[12] The Internet epitomizes the fusion of technologies that eliminate time and distance barriers that once made global business difficult and expensive. Moreover, it allows newly industrialized countries and small companies to rapidly acquire advanced ICTs and to effectively and efficiently connect with the rest of the world. The Internet is now one of the primary means of quality, low-cost, and instantaneous communications between businesses, individuals, and every conceivable combination. It is the core of the information technology systems and operating systems of most global corporations. In addition, most companies use intranets—interconnected computers within the corporation and its organizational units that share information, manage data warehouses, and provide decision support systems. Extranets, in turn, link corporations with their suppliers, distributors, customers, and partners, among a myriad of other external entities.

Internet marketing allows companies to present information about themselves, their products, processes, and performance, providing both the salient points to those who wish a broad understanding and details for those who want to know more. Moreover, Internet technologies offer numerous ways to obtain feedback from customers concerning the corporations, their products, operations, and activities. Website activities (hits) and customer emails are rich sources of additional information that facilitates business knowledge and activities. The ability to track individual choices, preferences, and views provides marketers with the data necessary to customize solutions. The Internet also provides customers and stakeholders the ability to examine a corporation in greater detail. This is vividly portrayed by the numerous automobile-related web sites that compare and contrast customer options for purchasing a car. In addition, many global corporations have to contend with the web sites of non-governmental organizations (NGOs) like Greenpeace that provide opposing views to those of the corporations. These counter-company web sites are forcing corporations to be more open and direct in providing accurate and compelling information, not just to customers, but also to an array of stakeholders and constituencies around the world. It is becoming more and more difficult to keep secrets.

The implications of the Internet are pervasive. The Internet continues to change the world of ICTs with voice over Internet protocol (VoIP) platforms that offer telecom users low-cost, global communications. More and more employees telecommute using Internet connections and personal computers to perform their duties at home or in various settings from coffee shops to hotel rooms. E-business involves a vast array of electronic buying and selling using the Internet and e-businesses have been established in many industries and market sectors to improve linkages, cut costs and reduce the time factor in doing business. Some of the most famous new businesses and corporations are e-businesses like Amazon.com, eBay, Google, and Facebook. Strategic leaders of such companies look beyond the physical realities of conducting business and focus extensively on the essence of what is required to meet and fulfill customer expectations and achieve desired outcomes. Their new solutions have demonstrated how companies can satisfy customers within a virtual reality as well as through conventional ways. Likewise, global companies have set up e-alliances with supply networks to expedite the exchange of information and goods. Such alliances are a natural extension of the extended enterprise construct.

The Dynamics of the Business Environment

General perspectives

The business environment is the broad external context that includes the external forces impinging upon businesses and the market spaces providing opportunities for solutions. It involves the social, political, ethical, economic, technological, environmental, and market forces. The business environment is a more comprehensive perspective of the external dimensions than the more well-known, but less precise notion of the macro-environment. The macro-environment generally pertains to the broad aspects of economic forces and the market structures. Historically, business leaders were primarily interested in the economic drivers and their implications on markets and customers. However, in a fast paced business world, reality must be viewed broadly.

Figure 2.1 depicts the interrelationships between the natural environment, the social/human world, the business environment, and market spaces.[13] The first two may be viewed as general external considerations that business leaders should be aware of, while the latter two involve the more specific opportunities, challenges, concerns, issues, requirements, risks, and vulnerabilities that directly drive strategic direction and decision-making.

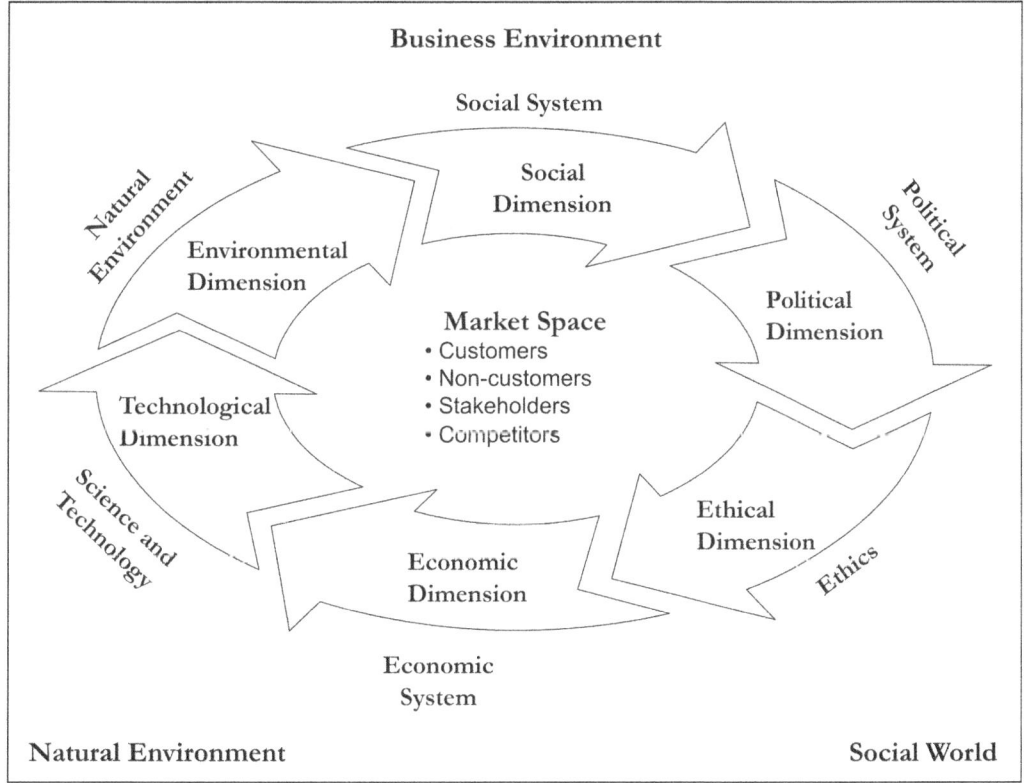

Figure 2.1 The dimensions of the business environment[14]

The business environment is dynamic. There are no starting or ending points. However, it is useful to think about the social dimension first, since business is about people and people drive markets and the associated opportunities and challenges. The social dimension covers a broad array of elements about how people live and behave. It might also include the political and ethical dimensions, since they relate to people as well. But, for the sake of thoroughness, the latter two are classified as separate dimensions. The political dimension involves political systems, governance, public policy, and laws and regulations. The ethical dimension includes non-traditional, more intangible forces that focus on the principles and universal standards of proper behaviors and practices across the business world, especially in countries that lack good governance or legal and regulatory mandates. The technological dimension involves all of the existing technologies, intellectual capital, innovations, and sources of knowledge and learning. The environmental dimension, also referred to as the ecological dimension, is possibly the broadest and most challenging to understand and deal with. It covers the critical elements of the natural environment that provide resources and ingredients, are affected and impacted by businesses, and are essential for life and nature.

In traditional management constructs, the natural environment and the social/human world are often viewed as subordinate to the market spaces and the other elements of the business environment because most of their main elements and important factors are not directly or even indirectly related to the company's strategies and actions. But great care has to be exercised when making such assumptions. What may be tangential to one's business interests today could be the most exciting opportunities tomorrow. For instance, digital technologies were seemingly irrelevant for companies like Fiji in the 1980s, but they have become the mainstream camera technologies of the twenty-first century.

Effective strategic leaders have the responsibilities to think broadly and examine the driving forces that affect and impact businesses. They have to extend their perspectives toward the indirect effects and impacts and beyond. The social, political, ethical and economic dimensions are discussed in the following sub-sections. The technological and environmental dimensions are discussed in the next chapter.

Market spaces

Market spaces may be viewed as subsets of the social and economic dimensions, since they involve people. However, they are the primary driving forces from a business point of view. Market spaces involve customers, non-customers, stakeholders, and competitors. They are the pivotal perspectives, since most businesses are market-oriented entities that produce and sell products and services for customers. While strategic leaders and operating management focus on existing customers, full-spectrum strategic leaders also pay attention to the realm of non-customers as well. Non-customers are people, especially those in less affluent countries and regions around the world who would like to buy certain products and services if the right solutions were available, i.e., ones that meet the requirements of the person's situations and circumstances, are affordable, and can function with the existing support mechanisms. Market spaces are the economic drivers with customers and stakeholders linked to the social, political, ethical, and economic dimensions. Market spaces also include the competitors who provide similar products and services. It is important to note that competitors are often viewed as adversaries, but they also support the industry's efforts and the products and services being provided.

Market spaces are critically important because companies and their business units are directly connected to them. Strategic leaders attempt to discover insights about how to create or improve unique solutions that make competition less relevant. Moreover, visionary strategic leaders explore the breadth and depth of market spaces and the business environment to explore the less obvious possibilities that could lead to significant innovative outcomes and to uncover unknowns that could be barriers to success or great opportunities for future developments.

Social dimension

The social dimension encompasses all of the social factors pertaining to people, their human rights, and the prevailing conditions and trends. It includes demographics, people's economic circumstances, cultures, lifestyles, the makeup of local, regional and global communities, and the concerns and perceptions of stakeholders and people in general.[15] Most business opportunities depend on the social factors and characteristics pertaining to people, i.e., who they are, where they live, what they need and want, what perceptions they have, how they behave, and how they change. Without connections to people, businesses and their solutions are irrelevant.

The social factors pertain to civil society and the characteristics of populations and people. The information and data about the social factors are generally available in most countries and easy to obtain, especially in the developed countries. The challenges involve making determinations about the realities and the ongoing changes that are not always apparent. For instance, the demographics of the local, national, regional, and global populations are shifting in profound ways; the richest countries are getting older and the poorest countries are getting younger. Demographics typically involve segmenting the overall population according to age, geographic distribution, ethnic mix, and income levels. In the U.S. for example, the baby boomers historically have had dramatic effects on the economy in general and specific product categories like education, housing, luxury goods, and retirement-oriented products and services.

Cultural aspects are important ingredients in determining social factors and how people live. Everyone has his or her own cultural background and experiences, and it is impossible to truly think or walk in someone else's shoes. Astute strategic leaders have empathy for other people and recognize and respect the cultural differences among people. Cultural differences and requirements are often difficult for strategic leaders to completely understand and appreciate. Strategic leaders formulate solutions based on what people desire, not just what businesses have to sell. They are not mystics, but decision makers that have the wisdom to engage people in determining what they really want and need, as opposed to taking "the all-knowing view" based on their own perceptions. The arrogant "know it all" types usually fail to understand how to create effective solutions; they simple offer products and services that meet their objectives, not the objectives of customers and stakeholders.

Strategic leaders examine the social dimension to ascertain the underlying dynamics of how people live and the salient aspects of civil society, its institutions, the cultural aspects, the communities, and social organizations. They examine the critical social factors to determine what may lead to opportunities and challenges and how they may be interrelated with the other dimensions. It is crucial to understand whether the general conditions and trends are moving in positive directions and if human development in a given country is improving or not. Such perspectives can be determined on a national, regional, and/or an international basis. It depends on the reach of the company and the willingness of strategic leaders to engage in the requisite research.

Understanding the breadth and depth of the social dimension allows strategic leaders to develop a more comprehensive strategic framework for linking their businesses with the market spaces and the business opportunities, especially in developing strategic innovations. It gives them insights about reality and expected changes that may reinforce the strategic direction or cause corporate leaders to reexamine their visions and grand strategies. Strategic leaders not only have to track the needs and expectations of their target groups, but they have to envision what the expected requirements are for all of the groups impacting the company.

Strategic leaders use statistical data about population(s) to understand what the opportunities are or might be. For instance, families in societies and/or countries with large portions of poor people with many youngsters, as in the case of many developing countries, usually devote a large portion of their meager incomes to the basic necessities of life: food, water, shelter, clothing, and caring for the young. Because they usually do not have discretionary income, it is difficult for such people to break the cycle of poverty. Children receive little formal education and they are typically caught in the web of survival activities like getting fire wood or drinking water.

The typical strategic leader might determine that there are limited business opportunities because the people lack financial resources, i.e., money. On the other hand, visionary strategic leaders who focus on the needs of such people and figure out ways to create solutions for them may open the door to many potentially great opportunities. As an aside, Sam Walton during the early days of the development of Walmart understood that poor people living in the rural areas of the U.S. represented huge opportunities for making money by satisfying the basic needs of people (perspective customers) at the low end of the economic pyramid. Rather than taking the mainstream approach and building fancy department stores for the middle class, Walton's insight inspired him to create an efficient and cost-effective enterprise of discount stores with a wide variety of high quality, branded products, selling them at modest gross margins (30%). Walton understood that success depended on having an integrated system, serving the majority, keeping the unit costs low, and achieving high turnover and rapid inventory flow. While today's Walmart may be significantly different from the original construct of Walton, such visionary strategic thinking can be used to help people with marginal incomes and at the same time create huge opportunities for realizing above average profits.

People in low income countries are generally concerned about basic living conditions and meeting the fundamental requirements for survival. Again, there are business-related opportunities for improving the prevailing situations from just subsistence to making substantial progress and helping people escape from poverty. Strategic leaders might make credit available so that such people can buy more cost-effective products rather than the relatively expensive short-term products they often have to buy. For instance, a poor family might buy one candle at a time for its lighting needs, because it never has enough money to purchase the more cost-effective solution, a light emitting diode (LED) lantern. Over the course of time, say a year, the LED device is more economical and superior in lumens, but a poor family usually cannot find the means to make the original investment in the better solution. Think about how many people in the U.S. or EU who can buy products like automobiles or kitchen appliances with cash in comparison to those using financial instruments like car loans and credit cards. Such business transactions without the availability of credit would be a fraction of what they are, as evidenced during the credit crunch of 2008 and 2009.

Conversely, for affluent societies and countries with a significant elderly population like those in the EU and Japan, strategic leaders might concentrate on undiscovered opportunities to fill the needs and expectations in the expanding market segments of the elderly. While the most obvious needs include products and services for health care and assisted living accommodations, there are numerous other possibilities. Assuming that many of the retired people may have a life expectancy of twenty to thirty years after they retire, there are many products and services like video games and travel arrangements that retired people would want, but the products and services have to be tailored to the market and customer needs. Such products and services have to enhance lifestyle and make living more enjoyable. And they are now much more feasible and profitable given the significantly larger numbers of people over sixty-five.

Lifestyle is a complicated notion used to characterize how people live. It pertains to all people, but it is significantly more in line with people living in the high-income countries (incomes over US$20,000 per capita). People with high levels of disposable income have many more choices in what they decide to buy and what they do. Lifestyle describes the general patterns of people's behavior, their day-to-day activities, and their attitudes about living. While lifestyle includes a wide range of social and cultural considerations, it typically involves one's decisions and actions pertaining to education, employment, leisure time, household formation, living arrangements and numerous other elements of life. Appreciating lifestyle considerations means understanding the patterns of living and the underlying business opportunities that they create.

Historically, strategic leaders viewed the sale and consumption of goods and services as the critical factors for business success. Thus, they focused on the demand for more elaborate products and services, especially ones with high margins. This thinking skewed decision making toward people in high income countries that have high consumption levels and high levels of disposable incomes. But trying to encourage even higher levels of consumption has positive and negative implications in today's business world. The positive aspects include known market demand, excellent turnover, and good cash flow. The negative aspects involve saturated markets, low growth rates, depletion of resources, and the possible decline in overall personal wealth as people convert their incomes and savings into short-term pleasures. The ability of people to continue high rates of consumption is a major concern, especially if income levels decline due to the outsourcing of jobs.

During most of the twentieth century, one of the most important megatrends in the developed countries was businesses reaching out and including more and more people in economic activities through the availability of more affordable products and higher levels of income. For example, Henry Ford created an inexpensive automobile for the masses; however, his success would have been limited if he did not introduce the five dollar work day, which essentially doubled the wages of his employees. Ford's genius was not just based on developing the Model T and mass production; it was his use of an early form of FSL that envisioned a rich mosaic of roles and responsibilities, from creating great products to making sure that people had the money to buy the products. While Ford was not perfect and he had many detractors, he did avoid many of the traps of either-or thinking, which permeates a lot of strategic thinking today. Strategic leaders today often think that low cost is so critical for making profits that they fail to ensure that other crucial factors like employee and customer success are duly considered. Many strategic leaders are willing to sacrifice the success of their employees or customers to make extra profits in the short term. Such actions often make everyone more vulnerable and possibly less successful in the long term.

Many strategic leaders may have forgotten that their prosperity is directly linked to the overall prosperity of the people they serve and the successes of the exchanges. Low-cost products are inconsequential if potential customers do not have the income levels to purchase the goods. This line of strategic thinking fits both the developed countries and the developing ones. In both situations, people need the means and mechanisms to buy and enjoy the solutions and benefits provided by businesses. Affordability is the primary factor, not costs or margins. Astute strategic leaders are insightful strategists who have the intellectual capital to figure out how to make products and services better and more affordable while at the same time ensuring that people have sufficient incomes to buy those products. Strategic leaders have multifaceted responsibilities to ensure that the social and economic factors are stable and that people can sustain success.

Strategic leaders can improve their standing in society by ensuring that they deal fairly with people across the spectrum of the social dimension based on the perceptions and cultural aspects of the people. They must understand and reflect on a broad range of social factors as they create win-win solutions. Visionary strategic leaders must eschew exploiting disadvantaged people and view their challenges as opportunities to enrich the social aspects and business outcomes.

Political dimension

The political dimension is extremely complex, as there are many forms of national governments, political subdivisions, and political structures. It is theoretically about the proper governance of civil society and the common good. The political dimension deals with governance of people, the affairs of governments and political leaders, and public policy. Governance in this context is about the systems, structures, and management of government and public affairs. It involves making good policy decisions for the greater good of society and ensuring balance and fair treatment for all. It especially involves enacting laws and promulgating regulations to protect the well-being of people, to control and punish deviant actions and behaviors, and to provide fairness and a level playing field for individuals and entities. It also includes providing input and stability to economic, social, and environmental dimensions. However, these aspects and the interactions thereof are complex and vary considerably in the real world, from basic oversight to various forms of command and control.

Political leaders have roles and responsibilities that are different than business leaders. They include administering the government(s) (local, state, provincial, and national, or regional), providing good governance, determining public policy, and managing and enforcing the public good. While it is the duty of political leaders to be impartial, open, and honest, they often take the opposite road; they are not always focused on the common good. Some politicians, like many business leaders, are arrogant and self-serving. They use flowery rhetoric when making speeches, but their words ring hollow. They do not govern for civil society or the greater good, but for their own self-interests or for a small clique of powerful people. They fail to initiate fair public policy, but rather they often create privileges for their friends, financial contributors, or those that support their political agendas.

Astute strategic leaders realize that businesses have self-interests in having fair and stable laws and appropriate and unbiased regulations. Strategic leaders help promote the common good and engage in dialogue with political leaders to orchestrate proper public policy. While there are numerous theories about how business leaders work with political leaders to provide for the proper functioning governments, in simple terms business leaders have a duty to be ethical and just in dealing with government leaders. A primary duty is to help develop public policies for industry and business in general, to set standards for proper performance and generally acceptable behaviors and mechanisms, and to determine appropriate reporting requirements and information disclosures. Good public policy seeks a balance between incentives for businesses and needs for society. For instance, government agencies provide protocols for determining the acceptability of products like airplanes, automobiles, electrical devices, pharmaceuticals and a myriad of others. In some cases, it articulates disincentives in the form of fees and penalties.

Business leaders often view regulations as having negative effects or involving adverse controls on their companies. While there are situations in which regulations make doing business more costly, and some regulations are overly broad and poorly articulated, appropriate regulations may also stabilize the business environment and make it easier for well-intentioned, honest companies to deal with not-so-honest and ill-behaving businesses. Regulations raise the standards of acceptable practices and behaviors and make it more difficult for negative elements to survive. They provide control mechanisms for certain business operations and assure health and safety of the public and workers.

Ethical dimension

The ethical dimension focuses on adhering to proper principles, standards, codes of conduct, and practices. The ethical dimension is based on universal principles, underlying human rights, and the generally accepted practices and behaviors that most people, cultures, and societies adhere to. For instance, most countries and people accept the concepts of ontological good and the sanctity of human rights. The Principles of the UN Global Compact spell out standards of conduct that most business leaders and people generally agree with.[16] The ethical dimension is especially important in those countries with weak or poorly enforced laws and regulations. It involves principles and standards of corporate behaviors that transcend laws and regulations when those laws and regulations do not adequately provide for proper behaviors and safeguards. It establishes a basis for doing business that is respectful of the people, cultural aspects, and the natural environment.

The ethical dimension is a critical consideration for strategic leaders since they are engaged in inventing solutions, building relationships, and satisfying people. Ethical business aspects and practices have to be constructed on a solid foundation of truth, honesty, integrity, and right behaviors. A corporation's reputation and strategic positions take years to build but an instant to destroy if generally accepted principles and right behaviors are not engrained into the corporate culture, articulated properly, and followed precisely. However, the ethical dimension is difficult to truly articulate and ensure its full implementation because the standards, requirements, and norms tend to be more open-ended than those pertaining to legal or regulatory mandates. Not everyone agrees with what the universal standards and norms are. Strategic leaders have to be careful not to be ethnocentric or too narrow in their perspectives. With that said, most business leaders do have a sense of what is right and acceptable. They know that fundamental human rights are inalienable and that all people deserve respect, recognition, and fair treatment. They also recognize that the natural environment is precious and it must be protected and preserved.

Effective strategic leaders help to formulate such ethical principles and standards if government officials or social institutions fail to do so. Great strategic leaders realize that a small minority of unethical business leaders can cause a maelstrom that the other leaders have to deal with and in many cases cause all business entities to suffer. For example, the effects and impacts of the illegal and unethical behaviors of certain corporate leaders at Enron and WorldCom have casted a shadow across many businesses in the U.S. and even across the entire business world. Indeed, governments set new mandates that make doing business more costly.

Astute strategic leaders can take the lead by setting the highest standards possible, forcing other business leader to follow suit. If they take the high road and institute the highest ethical standards in their own organizations and enterprises, it makes deviant behaviors more obvious and less tolerable. Moreover, as the gap between the best and the worst increases, it becomes even more obvious when certain companies are acting in unethical and unacceptable ways.

Economic dimension

The economic dimension includes the economic forces and factors and the market conditions and trends of the global economy and the national economies. It includes economic activities in general. The economy, whether national, global, or subsets thereof, consists of the aggregation of the exchange of goods and services, the availability and use of resources, and the applications of labor and intellectual capital, land, and rents, among numerous other considerations. The economic dimension is the traditional domain taken by most strategic leaders of business transactions and exchanges. The perspective is generally on markets and customers and their needs, wants, and expectations. Historically, the key determinants were supply and demand, production and consumption, and revenues and profits. Market structures, cost structures and competition were also primary considerations.

The concept of supply and demand and the interrelationship between them has been central to economic theory for centuries. It derives from the principle of resource scarcity and examines how businesses make decisions when confronted with scarce resources and limited choices, especially insufficient time, capital, energy or natural resources to meet economic requirements. The theories pertaining to supply and demand involve determining the pricing and cost structures that establish equilibrium between production and consumption. While traditional economics is much more comprehensive and involved than just resources, pricing, and costs, the focus generally was on inputs, outputs, and conversion processes. Moreover, it assumes that decisions reflect trade-offs on either a micro or macro scale. It also assumes that the trade-offs are best resolved using cost-benefit analysis. In reality, cost-benefit analysis is better conveyed as benefit-to-cost, since the critical factors really depends on what the benefits are. Benefit-to-cost (B/C) analysis, using a B/C equation, depicts the sum of the benefits of a course of action (product) relative to the sum of the costs. It is a ratio of expected beneficial outcomes to expected costs (investments). The equation can be expressed as: $B/C = \Sigma$ benefits (B) $\div \Sigma$ costs (C) or as $B - C = \Sigma$ benefits (B) $- \Sigma$ costs (C).

Traditional economics also focused on the principle of comparative advantage. Individuals, companies groups (clusters), and countries supposedly do well when they concentrate on activities, in which they have inherent advantages over others, either in costs, benefits or other factors.[17] For instance, the Province of Quebec, Canada has an overwhelming comparative advantage in North America in aluminum production because it has extremely low electricity costs due to the large number of hydroelectric power plants. Given that electricity requirements account for approximately thirty to forty percent of the cost of primary (virgin, not recycled) aluminum, having a ready supply of low-cost electricity provides an incredible competitive advantage. Supply and demand considerations are pivotal in decision-making based on traditional economics. If the demand is high and the supply is low, prices increase until an equilibrium point is reached. However, actual supply and demand phenomena are more complicated due to the power of producers or owners of capital and land, the knowledge of consumers, costs paid by society (externalities), the elasticity of demand, and the many distortions in the markets around the world that are created by governments that provide subsidies, imposed taxes, and engage in other forms intervention. Moreover, there are numerous other factors like managing wastes, dealing with pollution, and managing end-of-life considerations that have to be factored in real world situations.

The economic dimension also involves other factors like the state of the economy, economic growth, interest rates, cost of capital, living standards, people's income and savings, international trade, foreign exchange, concentration of wealth, land ownership, the availability of capital and labor, and applications of investments. The state of a given economy depends on these factors and many others; indeed, it is one of the most critical considerations relating to the economic dimension. Recessions and expansions are part of the normal cycles of macroeconomic conditions. Improved productivity, higher levels of investments, and economic developments generally contribute to stability and growth that help reduce unemployment and lower inflation. Improved standards of living and human happiness are also important factors.

The main purpose of economic activities is to satisfy the needs and wants of humankind. While some producers may believe that the primary purpose is to make profits and consumers may think in terms of consumption, the economic dimension is really a complex array of transactions, interactions, and relationships aimed at producing the means and mechanisms for people to satisfy their needs, to create an acceptable standard of living, and to provide investors and shareholders with rewards that compensate them for their contributions and risks. In advanced economies, customers and employees seek a reasonable degree of economic stability. Owners of financial capital, land, resources, and manufacturing capacity seek an adequate return on their investments.

In the developed countries, consumers generally drive the economy through the choices they make as they seek to satisfy their needs and expectations and their lifestyle requirements. Needs for food, shelter, and clothing involve both required expenditures and some discretionary spending as well. Discretionary spending is a function of the disposable income that people have and their desire to gain satisfaction from the benefits they seek. Consumer confidence and perceptions about reality and the prospects for the future are important factors in having positive economic conditions. If economic conditions are positive, people tend to increase spending on goods and services, especially on discretionary goods. On the other hand, if there are significant concerns and a lack of confidence about the state of the economy, people generally become more conservative in their expectations and spending. For instance, automobile purchases are typically cyclical with higher demand during good economic times and lower demand during recessions.

In the developing countries, economic conditions usually revolve around fundamental human needs and the supply and demand of basic goods. Traditional economies in many of the least developed countries often depend on non-monetary exchanges of the basic requirements for subsistence. People try to meet their basic needs through barter systems that have elaborate methods for establishing fair value. While approximately 2.6 billion people earn less than PPP$ (purchasing power parity in U.S. dollars) $5 per day and that 3.5 billion people in low-income countries earn less than 20 percent of the world's income. In many such countries a majority of the economic activities may not be accounted for in the gross domestic product (GDP).[18] GDP measures the value of all of the goods and services produced by an economy, including the contributions of government. Making comparisons becomes more difficult where barter systems are predominant, since not all exchanges and activities are measured. There are billions of people living at the margins, who may not even be counted. Moreover, it is difficult to make good comparisons because the exchange rates between the currencies of the world are not very accurate.

Whether developed or developing countries, economic growth is fundamental to positive market conditions and stability. It is often measured in terms of the increase in GDP. However, GDP is an imprecise measure, since it does not discern the quality of the outcomes. For instance, when the Exxon Valdez spilled 10.8 million gallons of crude oil into Prudhoe Bay, Alaska, it created employment opportunities for thousands of people. While the people who earned the money were positive contributors and their incomes and purchases added to the GDP of the U.S. at the time (1989), it is ludicrous to say that such events or situations are desirable and really improve the economic conditions of a country.

Still, despite the difficulties in measuring it, economic growth provides the means for human development and improved living standards. In the developed countries, a significant portion of the economic improvements depends on growth-related activities like construction, new housing, infrastructure improvements, and capital development projects. Businesses, such as those in the construction industries, producers of capital equipment, architectural firms, and land developers, are usually greatly affected by the economic conditions and often suffer severely during recessions. If there isn't any growth over long periods, as in some of the least developed countries, growth-dependent companies like those in building construction and related products go out of business.

Economic growth also depends on population growth and on increasing affluence, which trigger more demand and consumption. In high-income countries, population growth has been low over the last quarter century (0.7 percent), and it is expected to actually decline 0.4 percent through 2015.[19] Therefore, economic growth has come to depend more on consumption growth and less on population growth. With greater affluence, people buy more, consume more, and seek more convenience and time saving products and services. The economies of the high-income countries of Europe, Japan, Canada and the U.S. have shifted from production-oriented to consumption-based economies. Overall, consumers and producers have shifted toward using greater quantities of short-life products that result in high levels of resource utilization and waste generation. While there have been significant debates about the limits to such growth and the sustainability of the business world, the central challenge may be the viability of the economic systems, specifically how business leaders, political and social leaders, and economists deal with value creation and how well they are able to develop more sophisticated ways to measure progress.

At least from the perspectives of the developed countries, improved economic models are necessary to provide a better balance of the economic benefits of providing more goods and services and contributing to human development and well-being. The new models also have to ensure that resources are used wisely and that wastes are eliminated to the extent possible from every point in the product life cycle, i.e., from supply and production though consumption to the end-of-life. The new economic models have to be integrated with the social and political systems to create more comprehensive solutions that address social problems, environmental pollution, educational imbalances, social injustice, and other challenges in the path toward broader, sustainable social and economic progress. The greatest challenge may be providing the proper distribution of economic outcomes and ensuring that the underclass and the unemployed in a society are treated appropriately and that such people have opportunities to improve their lifestyles. This may become an absolute necessity for the continuation of affluence, as the rich in the developed countries get older and the young become poorer. Currently, the lack of education (knowledge and learning) limits the potential of young people in both the developed and the developing countries, leaving them unable to understand and work with sophisticated technologies and advanced business practices. In the developed countries especially, opportunities for entry-level employment continue to decline as automation, technological advancements, outsourcing, and a myriad of other changes reduce the number of unskilled and manual labor positions.

Economic growth in developing countries derives from providing the basic requirements of life and improving human development. Human development is critical for developing countries to make their way in a complex world of powerful economic forces. Ending hunger and poverty, building adequate housing, providing proper health care, preventing and curing diseases, finding solutions to educational problems, providing good public transportation, and creating political stability are fundamental requirements for improving the underlying economic systems. For instance, it is difficult for people in developing countries, especially people in Sub-Saharan Africa (SSA), to concentrate on moving toward an income-based economic system given the significant number of social, political, and economic barriers to progress. They need support from global corporations and NGOs in the global business environment if they are to participate effectively in the global economy. Such support includes foreign direct investment, advanced technologies, know-how, education and training assistance, and support for producing and distributing goods and services. They need multifaceted support, not just financial aid or philanthropy.

Regardless of location, in-country production and distribution requires labor, thus employment opportunities, which, in turn, generate income for the people. Income allows people to enjoy a better standard of living and to improve their quality of life. The economic system links producers and consumers and provides a sense of equilibrium as production of goods provides more income for people to buy more goods. While this view is a basic perspective, it does indicate that such approaches generally work to benefit producers, consumers and workers alike. However, a perfect balance is rarely achieved. And, while distortions like subsidies and protectionism muddle the picture, economic growth over the last fifty years in the high-income countries has been based (in both theory and practice) on the creation of more value and wealth for most people. The earnings provide employees with the monetary resources to afford the products and services they need and desire. Producers need adequate numbers of customers to buy their products and services that allow for the recovery of their invested capital with a reasonable return. This kind of stability is critical for the proper functioning of the economic system and for economic growth. Capital is rewarded when the economic systems are in balance; i.e., when producers make money and people earn money and spend some of it.

The expansion of international trade has been a boon to most of the developed countries and RICs like China and India. In 2002, the total value of exports for all countries was $6.4 trillion in goods and $1.6 trillion in services (US dollars).[20] There has been a threefold increase since 1980, with a 6.8 percent and 8.1 percent rate of growth for goods and services, respectively.[21] However, the rate of growth in world exports was at a high in 2005 at 11.2% and declined to only 4.3% in 2008 due to the global economic slowdown.[22]

International trade and its implications have dominated the economic dimension over the last decade or so. The developed countries currently account for 65 percent of exports measured in U.S. dollars. However, the share of exports deriving from developing countries is growing. The production of commodities is shifting from the high-wage, industrialized (developed) countries to low-wage, developing countries. In particular, China and India have benefited significantly as global corporations seemingly attempt to exploit the comparative advantages of low wages, marginal benefits, and the lack of stringent regulations. With the reduction in costs, consumers in the developed countries can theoretically purchase more goods at a lower price and consume more because products are more affordable. Prices are established on the basis of global economics. The people in the developing countries, in turn, obtain employment opportunities based on production of large quantities of goods, most of which are for export. Most of these workers would not earn the same level of income if the production was based on product demand in their home country because there is insufficient means (disposable income) for people to buy the products. Therefore, the theory suggests that exports (international trade) make the development of manufacturing capacity and industrial output in a country like China possible. While such an economic model seems to be a sensible approach for making global corporations more cost-competitive, the ramifications are far-reaching and more complex than the simple economic construct of supply and demand suggests. There are many concerns. As employment opportunities for manufacturing and certain service jobs shift to the developing countries, this may leave more people in the developed countries looking for employment. The unemployment rate in the U.S. was more than 9% for most of 2010 and 2011. Moreover, if the aggregate net income available to households in the developed countries declines in real terms, it is not clear that the disposable income of people in the developing countries will increase quickly enough to continue to drive the global economy. The low wages paid to people in countries like China and India may be insufficient to provide the economic development necessary to sustain their economies. The loss of jobs in the U.S. and the EU may cause a long-term economic decline across the business world. Many of the existing problems in the U.S., like funding Social Security and government pension programs, may become even more difficult to manage if overall employment is insufficient to provide requisite tax revenues. Moreover, there may not be enough people to buy the available products regardless of the low prices (costs) due to the reduction in disposable income on a global scale. In addition to these economic concerns, there are many underlying social and human rights issues about the fairness of the low wages and benefits paid to many of the workers in RICs and developing countries. While low wages are not always considered to be exploitation by many business leaders in those countries, it is clear that such conditions would not be tolerated by the national governments, NGOs, and labor unions in the EU, U.S. or Japan. Moreover, various interest groups and communities would object if such conditions were prevalent in the developed countries. For example, Walmart is the largest private employer in the U.S. with many low-wage employees by American standards. While it generally pays above the federal and state governments' minimum wage standards, there are still numerous advocacy groups questioning the fairness of the wages and benefits that Walmart provides its employees. Several states (Maryland, in particular) considered legislation imposing requirements for companies with more than 10,000 employees to provide health care programs for their employees or contribute to the programs run by the state government. If sub-par employment conditions are not acceptable in the developed countries, one must wonder why or how long they would be acceptable elsewhere.

Foreign exchange problems and currency valuation are huge concerns as certain countries try to maintain economic advantages by artificially keeping their currencies undervalued in world markets. These mechanisms distort the economic analysis done by corporate leaders who believe that the low-cost structures in countries like China and India will continue for the long term. Currency values affect the balance of payment between countries like the U.S. and China. Any adjustments in exchange rates could have severe consequences on the ongoing exchange of goods and services.

Another critical issue is the concentration of economic power and wealth across the world in the hands of the wealthiest corporations and individuals. In many countries, wealth, land ownership, and economic and political control are held by a minority of the people, making it difficult for the poor to improve their economic status due to a lack of tangible assets and freedom. This inequality of income and assets translates into tension between the rich and poor and between countries. For instance, per capita income measured in PPP$ was 33,082 in 2005 for high-income countries and only 7,416 and 2,531 for middle-income and low-income countries, respectively.[23] This situation requires additional study to determine the global trends and whether people are becoming more affluent or if only certain individuals are.

The long-term implications of international trade, outsourcing, and global economics are mega-issues of the early 21st century as corporations and countries try to find new comparative advantages in a more complex world. Great care has to be exhibited to discern the economic conditions and trends and to ensure the pathways taken are sustainable and meet the standards of human rights and the global community. Finally, the availability and effectiveness of capital and labor are critical for long-term development. Capital usually chases the highest returns. While trying to achieve the highest returns is seemingly a sensible criterion for making investment, the underlying social, political, and economic aspects and their stability are also important in determining whether or not to invest in a country or company.

Reflections

Today, as the rate of change accelerates and the interconnectivity of the natural, social, and business worlds increases, astute strategic leaders have to be mindful of all of the forces of change affecting the global landscape. As globalization expands and the impacts of business decisions increase across many spheres, distinguishing between what is business related and what is not becomes more difficult to determine. Moreover, indirect forces that seemingly have little impact on business activities today may quickly (in just a few years) become critical concerns affecting economics, market viability, resource availability, and the strategic direction and sustainable success of corporations. For example, in the wake of hurricane Katrina in 2005, weather-related phenomena are now much greater concerns. Katrina shut down the city of New Orleans and caused billions of dollars of economic and personal losses; and it impacted businesses across the region and country. It also caused global impacts as the loss of 3 million barrels per day of Gulf Coast production sent oil prices on world commodity markets soaring. The earthquake in Japan on March 11, 2011 and the tsunami that severely damaged the nuclear reactors at Fukushima Dai-ichi quickly affected the global nuclear power industry just when many countries were reconsidering the nuclear power option. Italy stopped its renewed interest in nuclear power and the German government voted to phase out of nuclear power.

As the world changes and businesses respond to those changes, it is imperative that strategic leaders think in broader terms and keep pace with changes in the business environment. Prudent strategic leaders should consider making this perspective a priority in deciding appropriate approaches based on the perceived opportunities, challenges, risks, and vulnerabilities affecting the company's positions and situations. The perspectives on the natural environment and social world are also critical. They include identifying, quantifying, and evaluating the driving forces of change and how they might influence and impact the corporation. It requires understanding the current situation and exploring the potential opportunities, challenges, risks, and vulnerabilities associated with the most critical phenomena. The overall objective is to discover opportunities or difficulties as soon as possible and to take whatever actions necessary to exploit or mitigate them.

Corporations have to develop their own strategies, approaches, methods, and techniques for dealing with the realities of the broader context of the business environment. The approaches have to be tailored to the strategic direction of the corporation and its extended enterprise and the realities of the business world. The analysis should be based on providing tangible benefits to the corporation and insights for its strategic leaders—insights that can be used to more accurately define the business environment and the extended enterprise.

In a world that is more interconnected and interactive because of social institutions, global economics, communications, etc., outside-the-box thinking about the roles and responsibilities of strategic leaders and the scope of their strategies and actions is critical for developing innovative ways for exceeding expectations and building more vibrant businesses and sustainable success. Great strategic leaders are respectful of people and the world in which they live and work. They are mindful of their broad responsibilities to their corporations, the extended enterprise, civil society, employees, people and the common good. Ultimately, they seek to create a better world for everyone.

Notes

1. Fons Trompenaars, *Riding the Waves of Culture: Understanding the Deive3rsity in Global Business* (Chicago, Il: Irwin Professional Publishing, 1993, p190).
2. Id, p180.
3. Official Journal of the European Union, February 13, 2003, Directive 2002/96/EC of the European Parliament and of the Council dated January 27, 2002 on waste electrical and electronic equipment, p L 37/24-38. Directive 2002/96/EC of the European Parliament and of the Council dated January 27, 2003 specifies take-back requirements on waste electrical and electronic equipment (WEEE) and initiates directives that national government in the EU have to impose on producers and distributors. The WEEE directive involves a legal framework that requires producers to create a system they own alone or in partnership with others that will collect, process, recycle, recover, and/or dispose of the products they market. The EU also initiated Directive 2002/95/EC of the European Parliament and of the Council dated January 27, 2003 pertaining to restrictions on the use and shipping of certain hazardous substances (RoHS) in electrical and electronic equipment. It also includes restrictions or prohibitions on the use of certain heavy metals such as mercury, cadmium, lead, chromium and bromine flame retardants.
4. United Nations Conference on Trade and Development, *World Investment Report 2001* (New York, NY: United Nations, 2001, p9).
5. Multinational corporations are generally defined as those that operate internationally through subsidiaries, offices and/or manufacturing plants in a number of countries, but such companies usually target opportunities where their strengths provide a competitive advantage. Global corporations are usually defined as international corporations that have a presence (sales, marketing and operations) in most of countries of the world and their product and services are available to broad market sectors around the world and are recognized by diverse populations. Coca-Cola is the best example of a truly global corporation. It obtains more than 72% of its revenues outside its home country. The concept of a global corporation is more difficult to define precisely because of a lack of criteria.
6. http://www. fairlabor.org. FLA's workplace code of conduct requires that employers recognize that wages are essential to meeting employees' basic needs. It prescribes that "employers shall

pay employees, as a floor, at least the minimum wage required by local law or the prevailing industry wage, whichever is higher, and shall provide legally mandated benefits."
7. David L. Rainey, *Product Innovation: Leading Change through Integrated Product Development* (Cambridge, UK: Cambridge University Press, 2005, pp21-27).
8. A nanometer is one billionth of a meter.
9. Barry Commoner, *The Closing Circle: Nature, Man & Technology* (New York, NY: Alfred A. Knopf, 1971, pp140-177) and Paul R. Ehrlich, *The Population Bomb* (New York, NY: Ballantine Books, 1968, pp15-35). Commoner argued that technology was the significant contributor to environmental problems and social difficulties. On the other hand, Ehrlich argued that population growth was the main culprit in the degradation of the natural environment and stresses in the social world. Both authors used the simple formula I = PAT to provide evidence pertaining to their arguments. In the formula, 'I' represents impacts, 'P' is population, 'A' is activities, and 'T' is technology. The equation suggests that relationships are linear and that each contributes directly to impacts. Commoner argued that "the predominant factor in industrial society's increased environmental degradation is neither population (people) nor affluence (more activities), but increasing environmental impact per unit of production due to technological change." Whereas antagonists can provide compelling evidence about technology's contributions to environmental impacts, technology and innovation are also clearly precursors to improvements and a cleaner environment. The formula itself demonstrates how technology can enhance solutions; cleaner technologies reduce the 'T' component, thereby reducing impacts. For instance, if the world population increases by 30% and global activities (uses) double, then technologies in the future have to be about three times better than they are today to keep total impacts about the same as today. Obviously, this is a simplistic view of what has to be accomplished to manage impacts on a global scale.
10. UNCTAD Secretariat, *E-Commerce and Development Report 2004* (New York and Geneva: United Nations, 2004, p4).
11. Id, p1.
12. http://www.photius.com/ranking/communications/internet_hosts_2010_0.html
13. David L. Rainey, *Enterprise-wide Strategic Management: Achieving Sustainable Success through Leadership, Strategies and Value Creation* (Cambridge UK: Cambridge University Press, 2010, p159).
14. Id.
15. Id, pp161-169.
16. www.un.org/Depts/ptd/global.htm. The Principles of the Global Compact are:
    Human Rights
    - Principle 1: The support of and respect for the protection of international human rights;
    - Principle 2: The refusal to participate or condone human rights abuses.
    Labour
    - Principle 3: The support of freedom of association and the recognition of the right to collective bargaining;
    - Principle 4: The abolition of compulsory labor;
    - Principle 5: The abolition of child labor;
    - Principle 6: The elimination of discrimination in employment and occupation.
    Environment
    - Principle 7: The implementation of a precautionary and effective program to address environmental issues;
    - Principle 8: Initiatives that demonstrate environmental responsibility;
    - Principle 9: The promotion of the diffusion of environmentally friendly technologies.
    Anti-Corruption
    - Principle 10: The promotion and adoption of initiatives to counter all forms of corruption, including extortion and bribery.
17. Industry clusters are agglomerations of competing, complementary and collaborative industry, government, university, research and support participants in a region networked into verti-

cal and horizontal relationships involving strong common linkages, and relying on shared information and activities of specialized economic institutions. Clusters combine all of the key resources and capabilities necessary to achieve sustainable enterprise success. They help create new wealth in a region and drive economic growth.

18. United Nations Environmental Programme, *Global Environmental Outlook 3* (London, UK: Earthscan Publications Ltd., 2005, pp35, 222, 235). In 2003, low income countries had a population of 2.6 billion people who had an average per capita income of PPPUS$ 2,168.
19. Kevin Watkins, *Human Development Report 2005, International cooperation at the crossroads: Aid, trade and security in an unequal world* (New York, NY: United Nations Development Programme, 2005, p235).
20. United Nations Conference on Trade and Development, *Development and Globalization 2004: Facts and Figures* (New York, NY: United Nations Publications, 2004, pp48-49).
21. Id.
22. United Nations Conference on Trade and Development, *Trade and Development Report 2009* (New York, NY: United Nations Publications, 2010, p3).
23. Kevin Watkins, *Human Development Report 2007/2008, Fighting climate change: Human solidarity in a divided world* (New York, NY: Palgrave Macmillan, 2007, p280).

References

Commoner, Barry (1971) *The Closing Circle: Nature, Man & Technology*. New York, NY: Alfred A. Knopf.

Ehrlich, Paul R. (1968) *The Population Bomb*. New York, NY: Ballantine Books.

Rainey, David L. (2010) *Enterprise-wide Strategic Management: Achieving Sustainable Success through Leadership, Strategies and Value Creation*. Cambridge UK: Cambridge University Press.

Rainey, David L. (2005) *Product Innovation: Leading Change through Integrated Product Development*. Cambridge, UK: Cambridge University Press.

Trompenaars, Fons (1993) *Riding the Waves of Culture: Understanding the Deive3rsity in Global Business*. Chicago, Il: Irwin Professional Publishing.

UNCTAD Secretariat (2004) *E-Commerce and Development Report 2004*. New York and Geneva: United Nations.

United Nations Conference on Trade and Development (2010) *Trade and Development Report 2009*. New York, NY: United Nations Publications.

United Nations Conference on Trade and Development (2004) *Development and Globalization 2004: Facts and Figures*. New York, NY: United Nations Publications.

United Nations Conference on Trade and Development (2001) *World Investment Report 2001*. New York, NY: United Nations.

United Nations Environmental Programme (2005) *Global Environmental Outlook 3*. London, UK: Earthscan Publications Ltd.

Watkins, Kevin (2007) *Human Development Report 2007/2008, Fighting climate change: Human solidarity in a divided world*. New York, NY: Palgrave Macmillan.

Watkins, Kevin (2005) *Human Development Report 2005, International cooperation at the crossroads: Aid, trade and security in an unequal world*. New York, NY: United Nations Development Programme.

3

Leading Change through Insightfulness

Introduction

Leading change is dynamic, interactive, demanding, and essential. It implies thinking about how to take advantage of the existing opportunities and how to create a more exciting future. It necessitates going beyond managing the strategic and operational aspects of the prevailing business situations. Leading change examines how to stretch beyond the limits of the present possibilities and transform current strategic positions into more powerful and beneficial realities. It involves the never-ending quest for excellence from every vantage point and for realizing extraordinary performance with enduring outcomes. It includes developing more favorable solutions and propositions, succeeding through cooperation and collaboration, and building the best possible systems, structures, and relationships.

Leading change is based on the theory that the best approach for meeting the needs, wants, expectations, and mandates of the market spaces and business environment is to leap ahead of the prevailing and expected requirements and to exceed the desires and expectations of the people and entities involved. It requires selecting the best options and making good decisions for developing innovative ways of achieving success. While there are numerous means and mechanisms to put such thinking into effect, the primary focus herein is on how strategic leaders use insightfulness, imagination, and innovativeness to create and journey along the pathways to success. The key to success is to employ full-spectrum strategic leadership (FSL) and strategic innovations.

Strategic leaders set the tone for their organizations through strategic direction, enterprise-wide strategic management (ESM), strategic innovations, and business integration. Insightful, creative, confident, and courageous strategic leaders are the architects who discover, develop, and produce more advantageous and fruitful ways to achieve successful outcomes for customers, stakeholders, shareholders, employees, contributors, and society.

This chapter focuses on how strategic leaders use insightfulness to achieve their goals and desired ends. *Insightfulness* involves understanding the true nature of the underlying forces of change and how to successfully engage them. It involves discerning the most appropriate innovative solutions that provide customers, stakeholders, and all related contributors and recipients with extraordinary outcomes. Insightfulness also involves how strategic leaders can explore, develop, improve, and expand their strategic and operational positions through knowledge, intellectual capital, competencies, capabilities, and resources, and how to leverage those of their strategic partners, allies, and value networks. Insightfulness is an essential element for leading change, inventing solutions, making investments, managing risks and creating business value.

This chapter includes the following main topics:

- General concepts and implications pertaining to change
- Technological and environmental dimensions pertaining to change
- Selected perspectives about leading change through insightfulness
- General model for leading change

General Concepts and Implications Pertaining to Leading Change

The dynamics of globalization

As discussed in the previous chapter, the spread of the Internet during the last two decades is one of the most powerful forces in the global business environment. It provides low cost and rapid communications and information and data transfer. With millions of web sites and billions of hits, people and businesses have access to details that would have been impossible to obtain without the ubiquitous Internet. Internet communications has become a critical factor in conveying messages to existing and potential customers and invoking them to take actions. Businesses are able to provide massive amounts of information about themselves, their products, processes, and performance. They are able provide both the salient points of their messages and details in great depth, if someone is interested. They can cost-effectively submit annual reports, product brochures, sustainability documents, and more. Moreover, the Internet gives people options for offering feedback about products and services and for sharing information with other customers.

The Internet provides customers and stakeholders with the means and mechanisms to examine businesses from a broad array of inputs that are both positive and negative;

they can obtain counterpoints from many sources, including stakeholder organizations. Many companies have to contend with the web sites of non-governmental organizations (NGOs) and other stakeholder groups that provide information and data pertaining to corporate performance, which force corporations to provide accurate and compelling information not just to customers, but also to a broad array of stakeholders and constituents around the world. It is becoming more difficult to keep secrets or to just send out flowery messages and marketing campaigns that are single-sided.

The rapid industrialization and the rise of emerging markets in China, India, Brazil and certain developing countries are powerful forces that have the potential to increase the well-being of people in those countries and improve the global economy. While the forces of change have many positive aspects as multinational corporations (MNCs) and small and medium size enterprises (SMEs) use supply networks in China, India, and elsewhere to reduce the costs of their products and their investments in plants and equipment and to enhance the national economies of certain developing countries, there are concerns about the lack of controls, especially those pertaining to meeting global standards, managing environmental wastes, and ensuring proper resource utilization. Given the size and scope of the economic and environmental impacts, sustainability of the present and long-term situations and circumstances is critically important. To sustain the global economy, existing and emerging companies have to use resources wisely and have to acquire effective pollution abatement technologies to control and eliminate waste streams to the extent possible.

Strategic leaders who outsource production have to think about the basic assumptions they make when engaging in outsourcing and sending production to distance locations. First, the economic benefits may be short-term as the costs of production and logistics are expected to increase in the future due to rising wages, adverse exchange rates, and/or increased logistics costs. For instance, transportation is assumed to have a relatively low effect on the overall costs of products, but with rising energy costs such assumptions may be faulty in the long term. Second, rapid economic growth and uncontrolled raw material and commodity costs in the developing countries may lead to economic instability and severe competition for resources. While marketplace competition was a critical factor in the twentieth century, obtaining resources may be the major form of competition in this century. Third, today's economic partners, i.e., one's suppliers, may become tomorrow's competitors as they learn the requisite know-how for designing, producing, and marketing the final products. Indeed, emerging competitors may usurp all of the competitive advantages of the MNCs except for their brand names and other intangibles. Furthermore, if emerging competitors have overwhelming cost advantages, they may be able to overcome the benefits of well-established market positions in the developed countries by having extremely cost-effective solutions. Fourth, the mistakes and miscues of suppliers and their lack of compliance with laws, regulations, and international product standards may do more harm to the branded products and their companies than to the actual culprits (the suppliers) in the developing country. Consumers often only have knowledge about the large global corporations and not the suppliers and manufacturers in obscure locations. Finally, the extended enterprise is now a more critical part of the overall value delivery system(s) as MNCs and SMEs expanded internationally. Strategic leaders need the capability to develop extensive and unique business models based on the concepts of sustainable business development (SBD), and companies have to become sustainable enterprises. They have to be more sophisticated and deploy integrated management constructs if they are to enjoy success in a more complex and turbulent business world. They must engage FSL and strategic innovations to stay ahead of their competitors and ahead of the great expectations in the market spaces.

On the macro-environment side, global concerns, risks, and vulnerabilities are becoming even more compelling. In the new industrializing countries and other developing countries, rapid economic growth may outpace the ability of the political and social systems and structures to incorporate the required changes. For instance, difficulties or failures to create effective solutions to the underlying social problems and needs and/or to provide economic and political freedoms for the whole population may lead to instability and economic problems in many of the developing countries. It is relatively easy to grow and develop an emerging economy during the early years, but often such expansions cannot be sustained over the long term due to the lack of attention to the negative effects like pollution, unsafe or inadequate working conditions, the exploitation of workers and the population, political strife, and economic instability. Moreover, such problems in the new industrialized countries, in particular, may have huge economic consequences on the developed nations as the seemingly high-growth economics like China become anchors on the global economy. The threat of nationalization is an old one, but one that is ever-present. This is particularly worrisome if the foreign direct investments (FDIs) by MNCs over the last several decades are usurped by the political powers in some of the developing countries. In the long term, the emerging competitors in the rapidly industrializing countries (RICs) may be the beneficiaries of globalization and the FDIs of the MNCs as the new competitors obtain the requisite know-how to play on the world stage.

High growth rates in the emerging economies are generally positive, but there are potential difficulties if the economies continue to expand without due consideration for dealing with all of the social, economic, and environmental effects. Certain metropolitan areas like greater Shanghai and Mumbai may become unsustainable as they reach expected populations circa 2025 of over 50 million people.[1] Government officials may find it increasing more difficult to provide the support systems and structures for such densely populated locations. Moreover, if the political regimes continue to be controlled by small cliques of party leaders and bureaucrats, investments by MNCs may become less tenable and fruitful as further government restrictions make the MNCs' positions less attractive. Authoritarian control by government officials over the economic and political structures may sway the competitive advantages to the ingenious companies in countries like China, India and Russia. Indigenous companies may be granted special considerations or waivers in providing goods for the home market. They may be exempt from some of the regulations pertaining to economic and environmental mandates. Even more challenging, the governments may not enforce regulations on indigenous companies and at the same time redouble their efforts on the strict enforcements of foreign corporations. The investments and market positions of foreign companies may become irrelevant as the indigenous companies are allowed to dominate the local markets. Moreover, many of the foreign companies may find that they are no longer necessary once they have transferred their proprietary technologies to the joint venture (JV) companies that they established with national companies in countries like China and India. Once one's technologies and intellectual capital have been transferred, control is most likely lost. The overwhelming concern about FDIs and JVs in China and elsewhere over the next decade is that the political or economic elites like the Chinese Communist Party (CCP) still control almost everything. Whereas CCP may have relaxed certain economic and social control mechanisms, there are no constitutional guarantees that the prevailing situation will continue or that the government may reverse its policies on economic liberalization. Most importantly, the lack of economic and political freedoms may cause the indigenous population to rise up against the political elites and try to gain their fair share of the political and economic benefits. The numerous examples of uprising in the Middle East, particularly in Egypt, Syria and Libya, during 2011 are possible precursors of political changes elsewhere in the future. While the implications of such possibilities may be positive, strategic leaders have to be careful about making too many assumptions pertaining to the current situations. In an era of globalization, strategic leaders have to expect dramatic changes with unexpected outcomes.

Globalization generally means that more of the economic activities are played out on the world stage. The positive effects include low-cost structures and more affordable products. People are more receptive to buying goods from remote locations and foreign producers. However, there is a growing disconnect between the income people obtain from producing the products and the consumers' ability to buy the products. While improved cost structures on a global basis have made many products more affordability, affordability is a relative term. Most people in the new industrialized countries, except for the elites and the new upper middle class, may not have sufficient wages to buy the products produced. And, with high unemployment rates in many of the developed countries, fewer people are able to buy the low-cost products because they do not have sufficient incomes. MNCs may find that their affordable products are not selling because people are wary of their financial situations. The underlying problem is that there is a growing disconnect between earning income in the production of products and people having money to buy the products.

There are many other significant concerns and problems. While there are usually adequate protections for people using end products produced in the developed countries, the situation is less clear for goods produced in countries without adequate laws and regulations. Many of the developing countries do not have stringent controls over what is used in the products and how products are made. Governments in the developed countries are less effective in scrutinizing the health, safety, and quality aspects of products produced in remote locations. For example, Mattel, a producer of toys, had to recall millions of toys because a few Chinese suppliers used lead paint on some of their components. While the actual number of defective items in a given product may be small, the negatives effects are large. It is very costly to recall products and sort out the deficiencies.

The most significant changes are expected to be in the emerging markets, with billions of people needing products that fit their circumstances, not ones that have been designed and developed for the more affluent people living in the developed countries. Some of the most profound trends are expected to be the growth of emerging markets and the opportunities to provide new products that are affordable and fit the specific needs of the people at the bottom of the economic pyramid. According to the concept of the *bottom of the pyramid* (BOP), most of the economic benefits in the world are enjoyed by the elites living in the developed countries, but there are enormous opportunities to provide solutions for people living in the developing countries. C. K. Prahalad argued that business leaders must change their strategic thinking and focus more of their attention on serving the more than 5 billion people at the BOP.[2]

In *The Next 4 Billion*, a publication of the World Resources Institute and International Finance Corporation, the authors map out the enormous opportunities for developing market-based solutions for meeting the needs of people at the BOP.[3] Stuart Hart, Chair of Cornell University's Sustainable Global Enterprise and an advocate for making "the great leap downward," describes how business leaders can develop new opportunities by "driving innovation from the BOP [potential customers with low incomes]."[4] He suggests that strategic leaders should concentrate on what can be done instead of just thinking about the limitations, i.e., the lack of disposable income, market demand, and infrastructure. He suggests that business leaders have to provide the right choices for people based on their situations.

The acceleration of change

Since the beginning of the industrial revolution change has been ever present and relentless. In the nineteenth century, it was manifested as steady change. For instance, the railroads and the telegraph companies dramatically increased the ability for people to travel and communicate. At the beginning of the last century, the exciting new sciences and technologies of the previous century morphed into the speed of change. The speed of change was typified by riding in a Model T at fifty miles per hour—breathtaking, yet within the norms of the person's reality; fifty years later it was typified by flying in a Boeing 707 at five hundred miles per hour—exhilarating, but still explicable.

Today, the business perspectives are not only affected by the speed of change, but by the acceleration of change. It is akin to traveling along a Formula One race track at two hundred miles per hour (320 kilometers per hour), and in the next moment the reality shifts to a new venue on the digital highway travelling at the speed of electrons. For instance, a person can get money twenty-four hours a day from an ATM, while others wire money countless times around the world each day to obtain the best interest rates, take advantage of exchange rates, or fund actual projects. Reality has moved beyond the speed of physical objects to a virtual world of digital technologies.

Whereas the first mechanical steam engine (the Newcomb engine of 1712) was fundamentally unchanged for fifty years until James Watt invented his breakthrough technologies for controlling the outputs of the machines, modern technologies are radically changed or improved in cycles measured in months. Change is the norm, but it is a new type of normalcy; highly dynamic and unpredictable. It is fraught with huge uncertainties and incredible impacts, but there are enormous opportunities and awesome possibilities. Today, the challenges are great and the rewards may be even greater. Strategic leaders have to use all of their insights and innovativeness to keep ahead of change and ensure that outcomes are positive. If one tries to stand still in an accelerating reality, the most likely result is to be ejected from the future possibilities and to become inconsequential in the long term, i.e., to fade into oblivion without regard. Many of the great companies simply failed to meet the challenges of change. For example, few people remember and even fewer care about some of the great companies of the last century like RCA, Digital Equipment Corporation (DEC), and NCR that faded away. Moreover, many of the market share leaders like Pan Am and A&P stores have come and gone. It is difficult to stay on the cutting edge.

Strategic leaders and successful investors are not concerned about the great achievements of the past; they want to know what the future holds. Just as General Motors' (GM) preemptive position in the automobile industry withered away during fifty years of slow reactions and incremental improvements, industry leaders of today face similar fates if they rest on their laurels or are slow in leading their enterprises. Strategic leaders have to think about the acceleration of change and stay ahead of its implications and impacts. In the context of dynamic change, continuous improvements may not be good enough.

Not only do strategic leaders have to expect everything to change, they should expect it to change even more rapidly as time marches on. Dramatic change is the one aspect that strategic leaders may assume to be predictable. Leading change implies that the best way to run a business is to tackle change head on and to become the architect of change. Being on the cutting edge implies that following the pack or just keeping pace with the changes in the business environment are usually insufficient and ineffective. Following the pack of competitors or peers often results in huge business problems and financial difficulties. Mainstream approaches are often rooted in the past. Business history is replete with stories of foolish business leaders chasing the dreams of incredible profitability with exuberance based on faulty assumptions and a lack of understanding about the prevailing conditions and trends. The debacles of many savings banks in the late 1980s and the sub-prime mortgage disaster of 2007 and 2008 in the U.S. are just two examples of strategic leaders following the ill-fated strategies of the supposed industry leaders. More importantly, simply maintaining the prevailing positions is possibly the worst strategic decision.

The enormity of change

In the developed countries, businesses depend on customers to shape the domain of what is needed and expected and to purchase products and services. Businesses are usually driven by what their customers demand. Most good strategic leaders try to ensure that their customers are well satisfied. Positive economic and social outcomes reinforce the prevailing business climate that seems to support the sense of normalcy.

Moreover, political forces play a key role in maintaining economic and social stability and ensuring that there are rules and regulations to provide a fair and predictable playing field. When examining change, the key driving forces are usually analyzed and determinations are made about the prevailing conditions. Without frequently delving into the depths of reality, strategic leaders may perceive a steady state of supply and demand. Products are made and sold. Customers purchase products and services and are seemingly satisfied. Economic outcomes are stable and can be expected to continue unabated. Of course, there are always the possibilities of recessions like the Great Recession in which demand drops dramatically and production has to be reduced significantly. And, there may be occasional radical innovations in the underlying technologies that change the industry structures and the dominant forms of the products offered. For instance, early cell phones were based on analog technologies that have been replaced by digital technologies. The external forces of change shape what companies need to do and the choices that strategic leaders have. It is the external context that drives change and how quickly the changes affect ongoing changes. Moreover, the broad driving forces of change are derived from the broader context of social world and the natural environment.

Determining reality is challenging because the driving forces are often interrelated. For instance, some experts argue that examining political forces apart from social forces is an arbitrary distinction and a sociopolitical perspective is a more accurate characterization. While the separation of the political forces from the social ones may be useful for focusing attention on specific issues and concerns, the piecemeal approach may not get to the root cause of the difficulties or what people really want and expect. People affect the political world; at least in the democracies. Politics is often a reflection of social pressures and public opinions that shape and prescribe the realm of acceptable solutions. From a business perspective, public policy and the social and political agendas represent opportunities for business leaders to determine acceptable solutions to problems and to lead change by developing and delivering new solutions. Strategic leaders need to understand the whole as well as the specifics. A simple example is the ongoing debate about climate change. Climate is often thought to be immutable from a business leader's perspective. Whereas most people have a sense of what the normal patterns are, in reality weather and climate are always changing, whether due to cyclical factors or long-term variations. Likewise, the social patterns are also constantly changing, as the social world evolves due to lifestyle considerations, demographics, economic conditions, etc. In the developed countries, people are living longer and are generally more affluent. They have more information and data and can exert more pressure on businesses and governments. Moreover, the time lag between events and changes and the realizations of the outcomes and implications by the average citizen and the public in most of the developed countries has been reduced to a very small interval (weeks and in some cases days). Moreover, people get their information from multiple sources and have access to many alternatives that allow them to discern the truth, if they wish to do so. People have their own views of reality and they are less likely to be swayed by the mainstream media, advertisements and general propaganda promoted by anyone or any entity. And, there are incalculable other changes.

People expect everything; they want better and more affordable products and services with higher quality and enhanced benefits. People may tolerate certain adverse situations only for so long before they want actions and demand new solutions. They want products and services without negative aspects. They want the best solutions possible and the whole truth about the negative effects and impacts, if there are any. The whole story eventually becomes available as the dissemination of information is a constant force. Given the prevailing situations, strategic leaders can gain positive positions by simply giving people what they want; taking proactive approaches, telling the whole story and leading change.

Economic well-being is tied to social, political, and economic agendas. The global economic environment is extremely dynamic as financial and trade transactions impact businesses and consumers. It is imperative that the analyses of the driving forces take a long-term view. Social and economic forces are usually considered to be the most important ones affecting businesses; however, other forces like environmental impacts may become just as critical and can cause turbulence that leads to restrictions or even new ways of thinking. For instance, post-consumer wastes were big problems in many of the developed countries until they became so overwhelming as to stretch the resources of governments to keep pace with the messes. Government leaders passed the problems back onto businesses. Businesses then initiated actions to reduce the waste streams and to make certain products more recyclable and reusable or ones made from recycled materials. This is particularly the case in the European Union (EU) mandated take-back systems.

Technological changes drive the social and economic forces. New technologies are being developed at rapid rates. The life cycles of technologies and products continue to shrink, making keeping up difficult and getting ahead of competitors even harder. But, new technologies can also present opportunities to correct or eliminate many of the social, economic and environmental problems of the past and create a more sustainable future. Rapid technological change also makes obtaining an adequate return on investment more difficult as changes beget changes. Clean technologies afford people in the both the developed and developing countries opportunities to improve their life styles or living conditions and do so at a significantly lower cost in terms of resource usages and environmental impacts. These technological changes will ultimately replace the inefficient and polluting technologies of today and yesterday. They will also begin to alter the very nature of business, extending solutions to multitudes of people in emerging markets who have not been able to afford the expensive products and services developed with conventional technologies.

Technological and Environmental Dimensions Pertaining to Change

Implications of technological change

The patterns of technological change are difficult to precisely identify and characterize. Truly large-scale revolutionary changes occur only every generation or so, but when they do, they have profound effects on the whole social-economic-technological structure of the business environment. Such changes are often described as new techno-economic paradigms, also referred to as paradigm shifts. Some examples of paradigm shifts include: the mass production of automobiles, especially due to the innovations of Henry Ford and his Model T; the downsizing of computer-related technologies, especially the development of Intel's microprocessors and the personal computer (PC); and, the virtual reality of the Internet and its effects on the interconnectedness of the modern world. The automobile provided mobility, reduced the barriers of geography for the average person, and made people more independent. The PC individualized the work environment and decentralized the means and mechanisms for obtaining outcomes, particularly in the professional ranks. The Internet linked individuals and whole societies into a massive "information and communications system" that provided speed, low costs, and access to humankind's knowledge. In simple terms, the automobile linked people with their neighbors, the PC linked them with far-flung colleagues, and the Internet connected humankind. Each in its own way changed the nature of business, how innovative strategic leaders found incredible new opportunities to achieve success and how the laggards failed to cope with change.

Joseph Alois Schumpeter, the great Austrian-American techno-economist of the 1930s and 1940s, became famous for his concept of "creative destruction."[5] He suggested that there were long waves of technological change that transformed the whole business environment and the underlying technological and economic systems. He viewed radical technological innovations as significant driving forces of change and major contributors to new opportunities that changed many of the fundamental aspects of business. Moreover, according to his concept each technological wave had both positive and negative sides that would inundate many of the existing ways and means for developing, producing, and delivering the outcomes to customers. For instance, the massive conversion of chemical-based (film-based) photography to digital technologies over the last decade fits Schumpeter's concept. The old assets and resources became less valuable, if not worthless, as the new digital technologies become dominant. In some cases, the old competitors fade away and new ones emerge as the market leaders. For example, Kodak and Fuji were the dominant players in chemical-based technologies, but they are less powerful in the new digital world of photography.

N. D. Kondratiev, a Russian economist, was also a proponent of similar ideas, noting that long "K-waves" lasted approximately fifty years.[6] K-waves represent distinct technological patterns that follow the life cycle of a "technological-economic system" from the creative-destruction stage of transforming a business reality into the new paradigm and replacing the old technologies with the richer ones, to the subsequent stages of the development and deployment of the new systems. Eventually, the new phenomenon leads to another decline and replacement by the subsequent paradigm fifty or so years later. During the height of the wave, there is prosperity and enormous economic and social benefits and gains. Not everything is always positive, however, and the model(s) suggests that there can be recessions and possible depressions, especially during the declining stages. Automobile technologies, their effects, and their consequences exemplify the theory. Initially the automobile provided huge economic benefits, mobility, and a sense of economic freedom. By the middle of the 20th century, it had influenced almost everything from highway systems, motels and drive through fast-food restaurants like MacDonald's to the growth of suburbia and large centralized shopping centers (malls) in every conceivable variation. Later in the cycle, these influences waned and other phenomena like computers and microprocessors took primacy.

Whether or not one accepts the K-wave theory, it is clear that technological change is a significant contributor to socioeconomic changes.[7] Moreover, technological shifts are more profound than just the underlying technological aspects. For instance, Guglielmo Marconi (1874–1937) invented wireless radio for communicating across the continents, which he proved in 1901 with his famous trans-Atlantic radio signals.[8] Yet, he did not envision the broader applications that include the use of radio for entertainment, local news, and much more. In most situations, it is virtually impossible to contemplate all of the possible implications of new technologies, both the positives and the negatives. In many situations, the positives tend to lead and the negative tend to lag. For instance, chlorofluorocarbons (CFCs) were invented in 1929 by the DuPont Company. They were viewed to be a safe and powerful medium for refrigeration. People were able to enjoy having refrigerators in the homes to keep perishable foods for many days. The benefits were great, including the development of supermarkets. Then, more than sixty years later, CFCs were phased out because they were destroying the ozone layer that protects life from solar radiation.

Technological change is driven by investments made by MNCs, SMEs, governments, private research organizations, universities, entrepreneurs, and individuals. Many of the technological developments of the mid-twentieth century were outgrowths of World War II (WWII), the Cold War and the space programs. Many of the most important technological innovations were the result of high-level strategic programs at large research and development (R&D) laboratories funded by governments and/or large corporations. This was especially true in the U.S. For example, the U.S. government during WWII supported the development of ENIAC at the University of Pennsylvania. ENIAC was one of the first electronic computers. After WWII, IBM and several other companies developed binary computers to improve and expand processing power and reliability. Their efforts were dramatically enhanced with the use of the newly invented transistors and later by integrated circuits. The government not only supported the early research, it played a pivotal role in the commercialization process by purchasing a majority of the early computers (before 1962) for Department of Defense purposes. The advancements in computer technologies have influenced many other industrial sectors including electronics, electrical devices, automobiles, aircraft, etc. The technological trends include making devices smaller, more robust, less expensive, highly reliable and easier to use; ones that provide real time solutions for producers and users. Computer technologies have evolved from IBM's expensive mainframes in the 1960s and the more flexible minicomputers of DEC in the 1970s to the PC revolution of the 1980s and 1990s. While the early computers were almost exclusively the purview of big business and big government, PC technologies and products opened the door for

SMEs, entrepreneurs, and the average person to take advantage of what the computer could do for them and what they can do with computers.

Technology developments

Global corporations play many significant roles in technological change. Corporations and governments in the developed countries account for approximately ninety percent of R&D spending around the world. However, more and more R&D programs have become collaborative efforts between global corporations, their supply networks, governments and other partners. Moreover, the actual programs cut across the borders of many countries. For example, Siemens, a German technology-rich company, has R&D facilities in Singapore, Munich, and Princeton, New Jersey with researchers working on joint programs that share cultural, intellectual and technical skills and know-how for creating new solutions based on multifaceted perspectives. These global collaborative and multi-cultural arrangements allow Siemens to develop certain R&D projects on twenty-four hour per day efforts that cut development cycles in less than half. Siemens also obtains insights from different cultures and geographical locations that help to broaden the considerations and final outcomes.

The rapid transfer of technology, knowledge, and talent from corporation to corporation and country to country is one of the key drivers of technological developments. In a digital world of fast-paced change and mobility, it is difficult to keep secrets and to protect intellectual property (IP). Patents, trademarks, and copyright laws in the developed countries and many of the developing countries provide a reasonable level of protection for IP. However, there are wide disparities among nations in the actual governance of such protections. Many abuses exist on a global basis. Moreover, as corporations become more dependent on their suppliers, distributors, and partners for materials, parts, components, products, and knowledge, there is an increasing sharing of technology and related know-how with the participants of the extended enterprises. For instance, as global corporations and SMEs outsource their production to companies in China, India and elsewhere, they are enriching the organizations therein with the ability to manufacture some, if not all, of the technologies and products. The implications of such technology transfer may change the competitive scene as suppliers in China and India strive to ascend to the world stage.

The story of digital computer technologies reveals the forces driving technological developments. Speed, processing power, affordability, decreasing size, enhanced compatibility, and ease of use are some of the essential attributes provided by computer makers and related suppliers across many industries. New technological developments are accelerating as underlying needs, expectations, and mandates affect competition across the business world. Bigger does not always relate to better. For instance, one of the most critical potential PC product-market might be for a small, cost-effective product that people in developing countries need for enhancing their economic opportunities. The solution might be a fully functioning PC that provides the basics of computing and having Internet connections in a downsized version with a price of $50.

As big businesses, especially MNCs, gain more influence on social, economic, political, and technological developments, they have to assume greater responsibility for solving problems and providing better solutions. Civil society and governments expect future technologies to be cleaner and eliminate many of the problems of the past. New technologies must reflect the conditions and trends in the natural and the social worlds and provide enhanced value. Clean technologies have to evolve into even cleaner technologies until the ideal solution is closer at hand. While it is difficult to obtain perfection, the quest toward perfection is one of the ultimate objectives of technological development. As in J.R.R. Tolkien's *Lord of the Rings,* the quest was not for riches and rewards, but the elimination of the negative side; the objective for the ring was characterized accordingly.[9]

> In discussing how to get rid of the ring, Glorfindel [an elf] suggests 'let us cast it into the deeps...in the sea it would be safe.' 'Not safe forever,' said Gandalf [the wizard]. "There are many things in the deep waters; and seas and lands may change. And it is not our part here to take thoughts only for a season, or for a few lives of Men, or for a passing age of the world. We should seek a final end of this menace, even if we do not hope to make one [even if the quest is impossible]."

The unique aspect of the quest in *Lord of the Rings* was to get rid of something, the ring (the menace), instead of the normal quest to find something (riches). It is philosophically the opposite of the archetypal stories about the search for positive outcomes. Literature is replete with stories about the search for wonderful tangible outcomes like King Solomon's gold mines, intangible ones like Ponce De Leone's quest for the fountain of youth, or even ill-defined effects as in Sir Thomas Malory's *Morte d'Arthur,* in which Sir Galahad and the other knights seek the Holy Grail for its own sake. Likewise, clean technologies and sustainable solutions focus on creating positive benefits and getting rid of the negatives of toxic substances, waste generation, air and water pollution, habitat destruction, resource depletion, adverse effects on the human condition, and degradation of the natural world. These things menace humankind and the sustainability of the world. Clean technologies and SBD can provide the means and mechanisms for a safer and brighter future for humankind.[10] From the broadest perspective, technological developments can move the business world toward a more ideal future; one that addresses the full scope of needs, expectations and mandates and reflects both philosophical concepts of leading change: eliminating the negatives and revealing more positives. To get there, global corporations and SMEs will have to ensure that their technologies and contributions and those of their support entities do just that: create more positives and fewer negatives. The good news is that many of the new digital technologies and potential nanotechnologies are in synch with these perspectives. They have significantly fewer deleterious impacts than the older technologies.

Environmental concerns and responses

Environmental issues and problems have changed dramatically over the last forty plus years, from seemingly operational requirements that lower-level managers and professionals took care of to mainstream considerations that are critical for the success of business enterprises. During the 1970s, companies in many of the developed countries desperately tried to stay abreast of the new laws and regulations pertaining to pollution and wastes. Governments promulgated numerous regulations that forced strategic leaders to take actions in reducing air emissions, improving water effluents, managing and reducing hazardous waste, preventing spills and accidents, affecting cleanups, and dealing with the legacy problems of improperly disposed wastes. These challenges required significant investments into improved practices, pollution abatement devices and remediation programs.[11] However, some companies resisted government encroachment into their domain or others simply followed the laws and regulations, while trying to minimize the implications on their operations and businesses. Changes were made to accommodate the requirements, but there were few attempts to make fundamental changes to the manufacturing, operations and processes.

During the late 1970s and early 1980s, strategic leaders experienced many pitfalls, barriers, and problems as their organizations learned how to respond to the ever-changing landscape of environmental laws and regulations. The prevailing methodology was to manage the compliance aspects and keep the business out of trouble with the regulatory agencies. Business leaders often did not view environmental issues and problems as critical considerations of strategic management. Environmental concerns and responses were usually viewed as tangential requirements that had to be dealt with, but were not deemed to be mainstream nor ones that offered opportunities. They were generally perceived to be important asides that cost money to manage.

During the 1990s, market-driven mandates became key drivers. Customers and stakeholders began to demand better solutions and expected business leaders to respond accordingly. Pollution prevention (P2) rather than just relying on compliance and waste management became the prevailing methodology for solving environmental problems. While strategic leaders still had to comply with the laws and regulation, they embraced P2 as a way to minimize the costs and negative effects of government mandates. The emphasis changed from responding to problems and issues to creating environmental management systems (EMSs) for systematically reducing the effects and impacts.

Environmental management has evolved significantly since those days. The history of EMSs and environmental responses provides a good example of how to manage change. The early perspectives was to keep the problems and issues separate from the strategic management considerations and to comply with government requirements, but do little more than what was specified. During this initial stage, strategic leaders focused on compliance and legacy problems and typically dealt with environmental issues and difficulties after producing them. The mainstream philosophy was to keep it simple and do just what was necessary. However, the related approaches turned out to be expensive propositions, since once the waste streams were generated engineering professionals and operating personnel had to spend money on waste management and remediation projects. Strategic leaders often had to engage lawyers to defend their companies from litigation for non-compliance or from people claiming injury, damage, and losses through tort.

To mitigate the rising costs and to reduce impacts and their consequences, many astute strategic leaders shifted their thinking toward preventing problems instead of managing the effects and impacts. This second stage focused on pollution prevention and waste minimization as strategic leaders attempted to prevent difficulties and adverse situations by improving products and processes. Mitigating and/or eliminating environmental concerns are important agenda items for cutting-edge businesses because environmental problems have direct and indirect impacts on economic activities, social stability, and the health, safety and security of people and the business world. However, with all of the improvements many environmental problems still persist.

Over the last ten years, many strategic leaders recognized that they have to lead, not just respond. The green movement in many of the developed countries changed many people's views about what was acceptable. Customers and stakeholders demanded better solutions. Strategic leaders had to find ways to make dramatic improvements. This changing philosophical perspective resulted in strategic leaders in many corporations taking a proactive role in creating better solutions. The paradigm change is toward SBD and corporate social responsibility (CSR). Now, many strategic leaders focus on creating new technologies, products, and processes that have environmental solutions built in. SBD moves the solution space from the present to the future through FSL and strategic innovations. It moves the solution from fixing problems to avoiding or eliminating them.

Today, strategic leaders of cutting-edge corporations are now focusing on integrated approaches for managing social, ethical, economic, technological, and environmental considerations. Such changes have had a profound impact on the landscape of Corporate America and the European and Japanese giants. Many of the largest corporations have reduced their waste streams by 90% or more since 1990. Yet with such success, customers and stakeholders are demanding even greater successes over the next ten years.

FSL involves even more creative methods and innovations for solving existing problems and managing emerging issues. Such leadership and management means being on the cutting edge of proactive changes of EMSs, dealing with the environmental consequences of every product and process from cradle to grave, and obtaining significant environmental improvements from every facet of the enterprise. Solutions have to emanate from upstream processes such as product development and shop floor operations as well as downstream activities such as customer use and end-of-life considerations.

Table 3.1 provides a summary of some of the salient aspects pertaining to the changes in environment management.

Of all of the critical issues that strategic leaders have to understand and manage, climate change is among the most complicated. Climate change is a hot topic. Whether caused by humans or not, the issues and the potential deleterious effects are broadly discussed among business leaders, politicians, government officials, leaders of NGOs, and academics. The biggest concern is the production of greenhouse gases. Greenhouse gases reduce the amount of heat radiating from the Earth back into space,

TABLE 3.1 The Stages of Environmental Perspectives and Management Considerations

Stages	Focus	Driving force	Key Internal Participants
1st Stage *Compliance*	Past and Present (Legacy problems)	Laws & regulations Compliance	Lawyers and engineers Operations personnel
2nd Stage *Pollution Prevention*	Near term (Existing issues)	Market factors Customer satisfaction Stakeholder satisfaction	Engineers Operations personnel Environmental professionals
3rd Stage *Sustainable Enterprise* (Social, economic and environmental integration)	Short term & Long term (Opportunities and challenges)	Business environment Markets and customers Stakeholder groups Governments Society Extended enterprise	Strategic leaders Marketing personnel R&D professionals Product designers Operations personnel EHS professionals
4th Stage *Sustainable Development*	Sustainable success Zero wastes Zero defects	The quest toward perfection; the pursuit of sustainability	Everyone

thereby increasing the ambient temperature. While natural causes contribute significantly to the increase in greenhouse gases, certain scientists and many environmental organizations believe that industrial activities and processes are also responsible and that business leaders must take actions to reduce greenhouse gases. The challenge is that most industrial processes require energy in the forms of heat and electricity that are a result of combustion processes, which produce carbon dioxide, a greenhouse gas. Moreover, energy is critical to economic development, social well-being, and a country's gross domestic product. Regardless of one's views about its criticality and causes, there appears to be a consensus that it is worrisome and specific actions have to be contemplated and initiated.

International conferences pertaining to climate change, including the Kyoto Protocol in 1997 and the Copenhagen Conference in December 2009, indicate that there are serious concerns in the global community. Some of the anticipated consequences of unchecked climate change include dramatic loss in the productivity of agriculture, increased sea levels and coastal flooding, extreme weather conditions, and negative impacts on human health and well-being. Climate changes are expected to have negative impacts on people, businesses, agriculture and the natural world. The difficulty for strategists is that the implications and consequences of climate change are almost impossible to predict and map out.

Selected Perspective about Insightfulness

Academic insights about leading change

An all-encompassing definition or perspective of leading change is difficult to exactly specify. It generally involves using cutting-edge leadership and management thinking and approaches to achieve extraordinary value and to produce exceptional outcomes and sustainable success before anyone else. It is based on the concept of being ahead of the pack and proactively staying ahead over time. From a FSL perspective, it means formulating and implementing proactive strategies and actions to preempt the driving forces of change: to lead rather than follow! It involves creating new-to-the-world solutions through strategic innovations and delivering the solution through integrated systems. Leading change is a compelling topic in the realms of academic scholars, business schools, and high-level business leaders. Given the trends in the global economy and the incredible changes that have occurred over the last decade, business scholars and astute strategic leaders recognize that leading change is an essential ingredient for realizing success and achieving business objectives. The discussions no longer centered on whether it fits in the grand scheme of business, but on what needs to be done, how to do it, and what are the necessary ingredients to achieve the desired outcomes.

Christopher Meyer, author of *Fast Cycle Time* and *Blur*, stated that there is only one rule of business and that rule is:[12] "Rule 1: The competitor who consistently, reliably, and profitably provides the greatest value to the customer first wins... There are no other rules."[13] Meyer's rule about leading change fits the general perspectives even though he is thinking in terms of competition and not market realities and the business environment.

Daryl R. Conner, author of *Managing at the Speed of Change*, discussed a fundamental axiom of change: "Our lives are most effective and efficient when we are moving at the speed that allows us to appropriately assimilate the changes we face."[14] Moreover, he suggested that "As the world grows more complex, the pressures mount for us to manage more change at increasing speed."[15]

John P. Kotter of the Harvard Business School is one of the most renowned advocates for leading change. His "eight-stage process of creating major change" provides strategic leaders, professionals, and functional managers with the fundamentals for leading change and transitioning and transforming their organizations. In his book, *Leading Change*, Kotter outlines the stages:[16]

1. Establishing a sense of urgency
2. Creating a guiding coalition
3. Developing a strategic vision
4. Communicating the change vision
5. Empowering broad-based action
6. Generating short-term wins
7. Consolidating gains and producing more change
8. Anchoring new approaches in the culture

Kotter views leading change as a process rather than an overarching perspective. However, his stages fit the elements of FSL fairly well. The perspectives are different, but the implications are similar. For instance, his first stage, a sense of urgency, is really the ongoing necessity and never-ending reality of leading change. Change is not a choice but an imperative. Likewise, creating guiding coalitions involves one of the most critical factors of FSL, i.e., building enduring relationships: ones that are mutually beneficial to the parties, as discussed in Chapter 6. Developing a vision and communicating it are also essential aspects involved in the quest for sustainable success. Strategic leaders provide people with the vision for what can be or must be done; however, visions are worthless unless strategic leaders can implement their strategies and action plans. They have to inspire people to become part of the solution and avoid resistance to change.

Strategic leaders produce results not just visions, objectives, and strategies. Moreover, results and outcomes have to be realized in the short term and in the long term. Gains have to be made over time, and contributors need inputs, guidance, and recognition. Most people may not be willing to make huge investments of time and energy without obtaining some feedback indicating that they are on the pathway to success and that their performance is appropriate and appreciated. Short-term successes in particular give people the courage and conviction to continue to contribute because they understand the benefits. Consolidating gains and anchoring them with the corporate culture makes leading change a reality.

Whether leading change is an overarching perspective or a process is not the critical discernment. The most important questions relate to how quickly strategic leaders engage change, i.e., the rate of change and the rate of learning, and what are the requisite means and mechanisms to be successful, i.e., the types of transitions and transformations. Most importantly, empowering the people of the organization builds awareness, acceptance, and trust. It also provides them with a sense of what has to be done and how quickly. People usually want to perform well, but they have to be encouraged and given the knowledge and resources they need to execute. They have to be trained and educated in the accepted ways of carrying out the changes. If new means and mechanisms are used, then success depends on making everyone aware of how to do their job and contribute.

Insights of strategic leaders and professionals about leading change

Strategic leaders and management professionals have to become comfortable with leading change and thinking in terms of the future and not just the present or near term. As the father of Wayne Gretzky, the great hockey star, told him: "skate to where the puck is going, not where it's at." Leading change from a practitioner's perspective means being accustomed to thinking from the future and becoming comfortable in orchestrating change and making decisions based on the possibilities and uncertainties involved.

Most strategic leaders and professionals are taught to use strategic analysis of the markets, competition, and business environment to determine the realities and possibilities and to formulate and implement strategies and action plans. Understanding the prevailing market and socioeconomic aspects makes good business sense and helps strategic leaders to understand consumers and public perceptions so that their products and services are acceptable social and economic solutions. Such approaches are often successful for senior professionals and lower-level managers, but they may not be sufficient for the high-level strategic leaders who are or should be the visionary strategic leaders of their business enterprise. Such strategic leaders have to go beyond just understanding reality and finding opportunities within it. They are or should be proactive change agents who are pioneers and innovators, not just the interpreters of reality. They set the stage and determine how they can be proactive in leading change. Leading change is more than just having a vision for what the organization and its enterprise should become, it is creating the landscape and trajectories for realizing the aspirations for the future and energizing the organization to make them real. Successful strategic leaders exhibit the relentless pursuit of excellence, innovativeness, connectedness and sustainable success. While such concepts are easy to understand, they require dedicated, committed and knowledgeable strategic leaders who are willing to take on challenges.

The late Ken Iverson, the former chief executive officer (CEO) of Nucor Steel, was one of the most innovative strategic leaders of the last half century. When he assumed the leadership of Nucor in 1965, the company was a small specialty manufacturer of parts for the nuclear industry. It was an insignificant dot in the grand scheme of the steel industry. Under his leadership Nucor steadily changed from a producer of parts to a manufacture of steel and steel shapes. During the 1970s, Nucor concentrated on technologies to produce steel from scrap using electric-arc furnaces and mini-mills. The company focused on the low end of the product specifications making rebar and channels. Its products were commodities with low margins and little distinction. Very few of the major competitors in the steel industry paid any attention to Nucor at the time. Undaunted, Iverson continued to lead change by aggressively investing into more sophisticated technologies with significantly improved cost structures and very efficient and effective processes. Still under the radar of most of its competitors, Nucor elevated its capabilities and strategic positions from the marginal to the high end. In 1989 Nucor opened its state-of-the-art flat roll, continuous strip steel plant in Crawfordsville, Indiana. The plant had the capability to produce high-quality, high-value coil steel for the automobile industry using electric arc furnaces with continuous processing that were more cost-effective than the processes of the competitors. Iverson improved his relationships with customers by providing them with better solutions and better support. He took market share from the main competitors like US Steel and Nippon Steel and made them irrelevant from his perspective. And, he shared the economic benefits with the employees. Most employees were rewarded with bonuses every two weeks if their production team exceeded production quotas and other metrics. Iverson encouraged people to perform, and they did. His philosophy is typified in the following:[17]

> "We can make a pretty strong case, incidentally, for the idea that working people are the real geniuses. A well-run integrated steel mill might produce about 700 tons of steel per employee each year, at a labor cost of $100 per ton. Nucor's min mills annually produce about 2,000 tons of steel per employee, at a labor cost of roughly $40 per ton. Our experience strongly suggests that when you ask employees to make most of the decisions, they can be more productive."

Iverson invested the company's money and resources only on productive activities and expenditures. Corporate staff was minimal and there were few perks for executives. He was driven by fundamental economics and sought to obtain the best results in every endeavor.

Another recently retired strategic leader that advocated leading change during his business career is John Pepper, the former CEO of Proctor & Gamble (P&G). His leadership of P&G for sixteen years was based on respecting the core values of P&G and being willing to change everything else.[18] In his book, *What really Matters: Service Leadership, People and Values,* Pepper suggests that P&G's brand leadership is based upon: (1) being first and better; (2) continual holistic innovation; (3) value via cost discipline; and (4) continuity of expertise.[19] Pepper continued P&G's long tradition of leading change and recognizing that good is never good enough. Moreover, he advocated that being innovative and enhancing organizational capabilities ahead of the competition were essential ingredients for reinventing the corporation generation after generation. P&G was founded in 1837 by William Procter, a candle maker, and James Gamble, a soap maker. Although P&G is well-known for high performance products, its main strategic asset may be the company's outstanding reputation. The reputation was built on its insightfulness, innovativeness, and creative employees who are encouraged to be in-touch with reality. Many of its policies, principles, and core values date back to its inception. They have evolved into a corporate culture that guides strategic direction and decision-making. Over the years, P&G's strategic leaders have invested heavily in strategic innovations to stay on the cutting edge with superior products and processes. It has also supported extensive marketing research to identify new consumer trends and used in-depth product and market testing to avoid making big marketing mistakes. The primary focus has been on the long-term viability of its products and their systematic, ongoing development to maintain profitability, consumer preference, confidence, and safety. In 1999, under Pepper's leadership, sustainability became the mantra. The company created a Corporate Sustainable Development Organization. One of its most important initiatives was the conversion of the annual Environmental Progress Report to the P&G Sustainability Report. The strategic focus shifted from quality management to sustainable development and ethical behaviors.

In a Fortune Magazine article on the "Leader Machine," Geoff Colvin states that "Your competition can copy every advantage you've got except one. That's why the world's best companies are realizing that no matter what business they are in, their real business is building leaders."[20] Fortune Magazine ranked P&G number two in the top companies for strategic leaders in 2007.[21] General Electric and Nokia were ranked number one and three, respectively.

General Model for Leading Change

FSL involves a complex array of integrated and interactive capabilities, skills, knowledge, and experiential aspects in leading change, crafting solutions, establishing systems, building relationships, and sustaining success. There are great opportunities for strategic leaders who have the proper insights and imaginations about what reality can be instead of simply thinking about what reality is. As discussed earlier, Henry

Ford realized that there was a huge market for an affordable car if he could produce a cost-effective vehicle with the functional necessities. His great solution, the Model T, reached out to the millions of people who wanted and needed an automobile but lacked the means to buy the available products that were very expensive. Moreover, his value creation included developing a new operating system, i.e., mass production, and new ways of distributing products to the markets. Ford was a preeminent entrepreneur who looked beyond accepted reality to find exciting opportunities. He created success for previously non-engaged people (potential customers), farmers and rural residents. These people were previously non-customers. Non-customers are people who would like to enjoy the products or services but do not or cannot due to barriers such as high costs/prices and the lack of infrastructure. Generally, the lack of affordability, as in the case prior to Ford's Model T, is a key reason why people are not participating in the market spaces or buying the products. Products are there, but the solutions are missing. Ford's great insight was to understand that the market potential required a better solution than the expensive automobiles that existed prior to his innovations. Ford's insights created numerous other opportunities for scores of other strategic leaders and entrepreneurs in related and unrelated industries. The examples are too numerous to cite completely, but they include motels, drive-in movie theaters and shopping malls.

FSL is the never-ending commitment, devotion, and involvement to achieve outstanding business performance and to make the world a better place. It embraces people through crafting and implementing the best possible strategies and actions plans. It focuses on strategic innovations and crafting the best possible solutions. Solutions are the total package necessary for achieving success. Solutions include products and services, but they go beyond just what is being developed, produced, and sold. Solutions encompass the whole enterprise and all of the systems and processes that make the solutions possible. They also depend on enduring relationships among people across the business environment and the market spaces.

Leading change involves an ongoing self-reinforcing continuum that creates social, economic, ethical, technological, and environmental outcomes that are beneficial for the corporation, its business units, extended enterprises, markets, business environment and people in general. Figure 3.1 depicts a general model for leading change.

Sustaining Success			
Strategizing	Crafting	Developing	Implementing
Leading change thru Insightfulness	Crafting Solutions thru Innovativeness	Designing Systems thru Inclusiveness	Building Relationships thru Connectedness
Determine context	Understand opportunities	Determine requirements	Understand participants
Understand reality	Examine challenges	Identify entities	Relate to individuals
Use one's insights	Determine solution set	Develop value networks	Link people
Set direction	Assess technologies	Select extended enterprise	Recognize their efforts
Explore possibilities	Revamp technologies	Determine contributors	Reward contributors
Examine challenges	Design products/services	Create linkages	Communicate results
Lay the foundation	Develop processes	Engage people	Empower people
Inspire people	Determine networks	Produce solutions	Provide solutions
Consider options	Craft solutions	Deliver solutions	Support solutions
Aspirations	Solutions	Value Creation	Value Networks

Figure 3.1 General model for leading change.

The model is intended to be a framework of the critical elements and not a process flow diagram. It is based on cutting-edge leadership concepts and strategic innovations. While there are parallels to the strategic management process, the focus is on the critical elements that strategic leaders have to think about and incorporate in their perspectives and actions for leading change. The essential aspects of the model are identified at the top. Strategic leaders engage in strategizing, crafting, developing, and implementing. The strategizing element follows the strategic management constructs as discussed in my book, *Enterprise-wide Strategic Management: Achieving Sustainable Success through Leadership, Strategies and Value Creation.*[22] The pivotal element of the model involves crafting solutions though innovativeness. Solutions are the socioeconomic outcomes that create value and produce financial rewards for companies and their extended enterprise. Solutions incorporate a set of attributes that contribute to customer and stakeholder satisfaction and success. Customers and stakeholders want the total package of expected outcomes, i.e., they want the best solutions. The solution set is that total package of products, services, technologies and processes that provide benefits and value. For example, in the early days of mainframe computers IBM was very successful because it provided the whole solution, not just the machine (hardware). It ensured that customers had the complete package of goods and services from the hardware to the software, from installation to maintenance services, and from the operations to the emergency management and recovery. It made sure that customers would be able to achieve their goals and fulfill their needs. IBM ensured that its systems were integrated with those of the logistical supporters so that repair parts could be delivered within hours. The solution set also includes the benefits provided by the value networks of the value systems and extended enterprise, especially the products and services from providers of complementary products and services of the related industries.

Designing the system that supports solutions is also a critical factor for leading change. Embedding the system aspects into the solution set involves the integration of the organization and the entire extended enterprise. Success comes from the whole, not the pieces. For instance, automobiles without fuel or highways are worthless. Success requires a complete value system to produce the total effects and necessary outcomes. It comes from strategic leaders who have the courage and dedication to ensure that the strategies, solutions, and systems are on the cutting edge. It comes from insights and creativity that focus on technologies, products, processes, systems and business models, among numerous other aspects. It also involves having a unique perspective that ties together the solutions and systems required for success.

Building relationships is also a crucial element that is broad and open-ended. Having systems in place does not assure success unless strategic leaders build solid relationships with the key participants and recipients of the solutions. It is difficult to fully articulate how to build relationships with people; however, the critical underpinnings are honesty, trust, respect, and responsiveness. Connecting with customers, stakeholders, employees, and all of the others is more easily achieved when strategic leaders are open, transparent, accountable and trustworthy. Relationships are built on trust and ongoing commitments. And it takes FSL to assure enduring success. The best solutions, systems, structures, and relationships require the full commitment and support of strategic leaders.

Strategic leaders become successful when the other people are successful. The most important rewards are the realizations that the organization is achieving sustainable success and that people across the full spectrum of reality are successful. These rewards are intangible and are usually self-realized. In the grand scheme, the most difficult recognition to gain is one's own inner feeling of self-worth from enduring accomplishments that benefit other people.

Leading change and sustaining success involve ongoing spiraling cycles of insights, imagination, innovations, actions, and interactions. Figure 3.2 provides a sense of the effects. It is not a sequential or stepwise process in which strategic leaders can complete the elements and then move on to something else. It is more like an outwardly directed spiral that gets bigger as one leads change; one that constantly revisits the critical elements at higher levels of sophistication. It also involves the ongoing search for more exciting ways to achieve valuable ends and to continuously realize better and better outcomes. It is based on the recognitions that there are no end points and that FSL is a way of thinking, behaving, living, succeeding and enjoying. Strategic leaders engage in insightfulness and creativity to pursue higher levels of solutions and successes for contributors and recipients, and to seek new ways to provide the value and

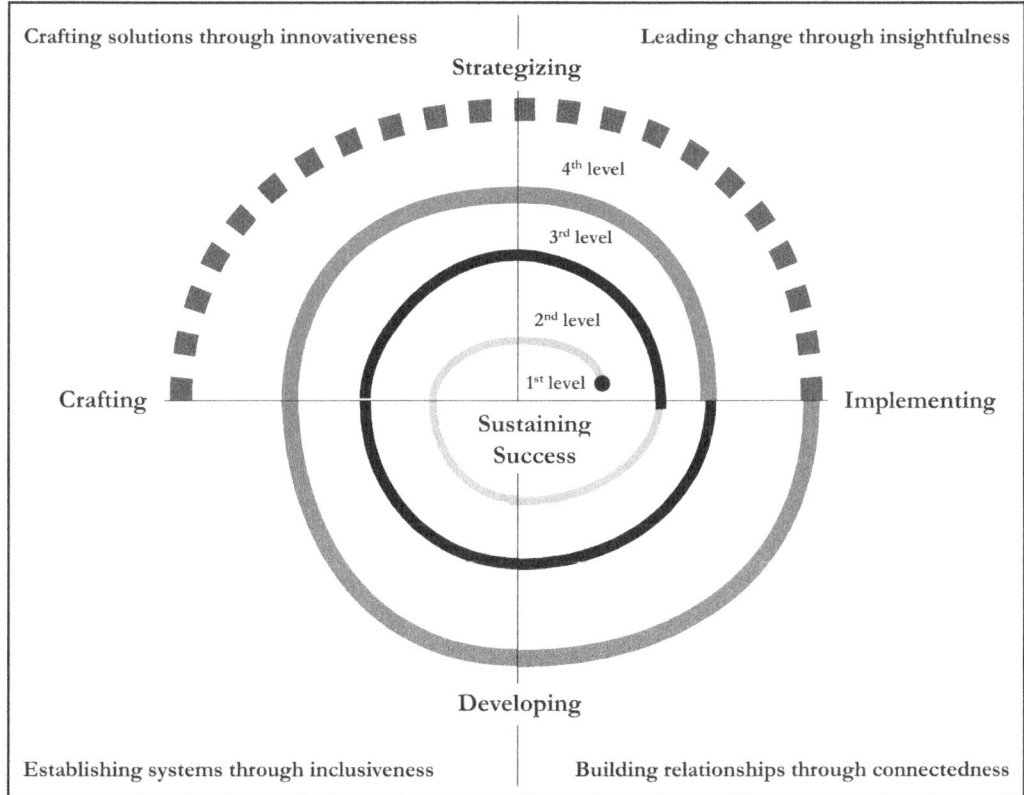

Figure 3.2 Leading change and sustaining success.

benefits of the solutions to everyone, including those who have not had the opportunities to participate previously.

The general model incorporates several iterations of the elements. Sustaining success accelerates the outcomes from the existing level to the next one. It represents the ongoing pursuit of perfection and the never-ending struggle to translate insights into realities, turn negatives into positives and convert positives into successes.

Reflections

FSL involves having exciting aspirations for the long term and robust systems and structures for designing, developing, and delivering solutions and creating sustainable success that resonate in the markets, across the broader business environment, and within the organization. FSL transcends the other management constructs in creating extraordinary value and achieving enduring outcomes through the integrated efforts and the contributions of people across the full spectrum of contributors and recipients. FSL is about engaging people to reach out beyond who they are and what they think they can accomplish to become everything that they can be. It involves enriching people through learning, knowledge, empowerment and relationships.

Leading change is one of the most important responsibilities of strategic leaders. While leading change can be mapped out as a process, it is more of a framework or general model about inspiring people in the organization and across the extended enterprise to create a new and more exciting reality. Leading change is an essential element of FSL. The concepts are broad and open-ended requiring great insights and imagination on the part of strategic leaders in exploring, contemplating, assessing, understanding, and taking advantage of the opportunities and challenges. The global business environment is full of thrilling new possibilities that did not existing a decade ago. The changes are not only moving an incredible speed, but the rate of change is accelerating to new levels of advancements, sophistication, and complexities.

Strategic leaders are the master builders. They use all of the means and mechanisms available to understand what has to be done, and then they set out to make the changes and realize the proper outcomes. The main perspectives herein include leading change, crafting the best solutions, developing the systems, building enduring relationships, and sustaining success for all over the course of time. They represent an ongoing self-reinforcing continuum that creates social, economic and environmental outcomes that benefit people. FSL engages people for the benefit of people, and it protects and provides for people so that they are enriched through success. Strategic leaders are successful when all contributors and recipients are successful. And, they produce positive outcomes, not flowery statements. The next three chapters focus on solutions, systems and relationships.

Notes

1. United Nations Human Settlements Programme, *The State of the World's Cities 2004/2005: Globalization and Urban Culture* (London, UK: Earthscan, 2004, p63).

2. C. K. Prahalad, *The Fortune at the Bottom of the Pyramid: Eradicating Poverty through Profits* (Upper Saddle River, NJ: Wharton School Publishing, 2005).
3. Allen Hammond, William Kramer, Robert Katz, Julia Tran, and Courtland Walker, *The Next 4 Billion: Market Size and Strategy at the Base of the Pyramid* (Washington, D.C.: World Resources Institute and International Finance Corporation, 2007).
4. Stuart Hart, *Capitalism at the Crossroads: The Unlimited Business Opportunities in Solving the World's Most Difficult Problems* (Upper Saddle River, NJ: Wharton School Publishing, 2005, pp107-133).
5. Joseph A. Schumpeter, *Capitalism, Socialism and Democracy* (New York: NY: HarperPenennial, 1942, 1975, pp81-86).
6. Peter Dicken, *Global Shift: Mapping the Changing Contours of the World Economy, Sixth Edition* (New York, NY: The Guilford Press, 201, pp78-79).
7. Economists are typically interested in the economic implications of technological change. They may also explore the duration of cycles to determine what the time frames are. While these are important questions, the notion of a fixed cycle assumes the past provides some indications about what will happen in the future. Theoretical strategists want to understand the conditions and trends so that the future implications become clearer and decision making is based on a solid foundation. K-wave theory may not a reliable predictor of future outcomes. It is a broad generalization of past events with somewhat arbitrary time frames. It is also questionable whether the rate of change (say fifty years) is constant.
8. Marconi got credit for the initial applications of transcontinental radio, but it was Nikola Tesla who invented many of the underlying technologies that made radio possible.
9. J. R. R. Tolkien, *The Lord of the Rings* (Boston, MA: Houghton Mifflin Company, 1954, pp259-260).
10. Note that sustainable development and sustainable solution are defined and discussed in the previous chapter.
11. David L. Rainey, *Sustainable Business Development: Inventing the Future through Strategy, Innovation and Leadership* (Cambridge, UK: Cambridge University Press, 2006, p20).
12. Christopher Meyer, *Fast Cycle Time: How to Align Purpose, Strategy and Structure for Speed* (New York, NY: Free Press, 1993, p9).
13. Id.
14. Daryl R. Conner, *Managing at the Speed of Change: How Resilient Managers Succeed and Prosper Where Others Fail* (New York, NY: Villard Books, 1992, p12).
15. Id, p13.
16. John P. Kotter, *Leading Change* (Boston, MA: Harvard Business School Press, 1996, p21).
17. www.nucor-sheetmills.com/smgw/smgw.nsf_our_story_ivers. Mini mills use electric arc furnace technology to produce steel products from recycled metal.
18. Pepper was President from 1985 to 1995, CEO from 1995 to 1999 and Chairman from 2000 2002.
19. John Pepper, *What really Matters: Service Leadership, People and Values* (New Haven, CT: Yale University Press, 2007, p20)
20. Geoff Colvin, "How to be a Great Leader," Fortune, October 1, 2007, p98.
21. Corey Hajim, "The Top Companies for Leaders," Fortune, October 1, 2007, p116.
22. David L. Rainey, *Enterprise-wide Strategic Management: Achieving Success through Leadership, Strategies and Value Creation* (Cambridge, UK: Cambridge University Press, 2010, pp358-424).

References

Conner, Daryl R. (1992) *Managing at the Speed of Change: How Resilient Managers Succeed and Prosper Where Others Fail.* New York, NY: Villard Books.

Dicken, Peter (2011) *Global Shift: Mapping the Changing Contours of the World Economy, Sixth Edition.* New York, NY: The Guilford Press.

Hammond, Allen William Kramer, Robert Katz, Julia Tran, and Courtland Walker (2007) *The Next 4 Billion: Market Size and Strategy at the Base of the Pyramid.* Washington, D.C.: World Resources Institute and International Finance Corporation.

Hart, Stuart (2005) *Capitalism at the Crossroads: The Unlimited Business Opportunities in Solving the World's Most Difficult Problems.* Upper Saddle River, NJ: Wharton School Publishing.

Kotter, John P. (1996) *Leading Change.* Boston, MA: Harvard Business School Press.

Meyer, Christopher (1993) *Fast Cycle Time: How to Align Purpose, Strategy a*nd Structure for Speed. New York, NY: Free Press.

Pepper, John (2007) *What Really Matters: Service Leadership, People and Values.* New Haven, CT: Yale University Press.

Prahalad, C. K. (2005) *The Fortune at the Bottom of the Pyramid: Eradicating Poverty through Profits.* Upper Saddle River, NJ: Wharton School Publishing.

Rainey, David L. (2010) *Enterprise-wide Strategic Management: Achieving Success through Leadership, Strategies and Value Creation.* Cambridge, UK: Cambridge University Press.

Rainey, David L. (2006) *Sustainable Business Development: Inventing the Future through Strategy, Innovation and Leadership.* Cambridge, UK: Cambridge University Press.

Schumpeter, Joseph A. (1942) *Capitalism, Socialism and Democracy.* New York: NY: HarperPenennial.

Tolkien, J. R. R. (1954) *The Lord of the Rings.* Boston, MA: Houghton Mifflin Company.

United Nations Human Settlements Programme (2004) *The State of the World's Cities 2004/2005: Globalization and Urban Culture.* London, UK: Earthscan.

4

Crafting Solutions through Innovativeness

Introduction

The solution is one of the most elegant and critical elements of full-spectrum strategic leadership (FSL). The focus of business enterprises is on solutions. Solutions are more complicated than products and services because they have to be exceptionally innovative, inclusive, and interconnected as well as having highly desirable value propositions and exceptional attributes. Solutions involve the complete array of technologies, products, services, related systems, and contributions of and interactions with the organization and the entities of extended enterprise. Solutions create value and allow people enjoy positive outcomes. While there are good and bad products, there can only be good solutions since bad solutions are not solutions at all.

Strategic leaders are the architects in crafting, developing, and delivering solutions. Crafting outstanding solutions requires strategic leaders who seek dramatic improvements and innovative ways of achieving successful outcomes even in situations that are perceived to be problematic or in ones with incredible difficulties. While solutions may solve problems, the underpinnings of solutions focus on avoiding problems in the first place. Historically, problem solving was one of the fundamental management functions. It is still used extensively. However, the focus is usually on the problems, not the solutions and on resolving difficulties, but not on eliminating their causes. The inherent difficulties with the old methodologies usually involve strategic leaders making trade-offs in which existing problems are often resolved, while creating new ones, whether foreseen or not. For instance, leaded gasoline, which was first developed by the Ethyl Corporation in circa 1925, overcame the power limitations of the internal combustion engine during the late 1920s, but it created hazardous air quality problems that lasted decades into the future until leaded gasoline was phased out in the developed countries in the 1980s.[1]

Problem solving involves relatively simple approaches using linear thinking and processes. The typical process includes describing the problem(s), analyzing the situation(s), determining the implications, developing and evaluating alternatives, and selecting and implementing the fixes. While it is sensible and straightforward, there are many potential pitfalls. One of the most significant is dealing with symptoms instead of the real problems. For instance, strategic leaders may determine that profitability is declining because prices and margins are eroding. They blame the problems on the competitive situation. They intensify marketing and try to counter the actions of the key competitors. However, the underlying causes may be product-related and not due to the actions of competitors. In reality, the products are no longer on the cutting edge, or they are not in synch with customer expectations. Customers are finding better, more up-to-date solutions elsewhere.

The basic flaw of most problem-solving methods is that they are usually limited and narrow in scope. The perceived strength of the typical method is often its most profound weakness. Problem solving is simple and examines the primary forces and/or direct factors affecting the situation(s) in the immediate or near term. While problem-solving techniques might explore the causes and the effects associated with the direct situation, the crux of the matter often involves just solving the problem(s). In the broader context of the business world, causes and effects are usually multifaceted and the interactions are extremely complicated, as discussed in the previous chapters. Simple approaches for solving complex problems often result in short-term fixes and long-term tribulations. Making tradeoffs often results in trading the old problems for new ones.

Solutions address the needs, expectations, mandates, and requirements of the individuals and entities that contribute to positive results and those that obtain the desired outcomes. They are answers to the broad questions, issues, difficulties, concerns, and problems pertaining to producing valuable and desirable outcomes and achieving sustainable success. They are based on strategic innovations, management systems, extended enterprises, and the intricate relationships among all of the participants. Solutions generally endure over time. While this is not to suggest that solutions have to be perfect, it does mean that solutions are innovative and holistic, providing a wide array of outstanding benefits and exceptional outcomes for people across space and time. The totality of the solution is the solution set; it is the sum of all of the elements, parts, components, processes, products, technologies, services, systems, and structures that make the solution possible.

Innovativeness involves creating extraordinary value through FSL, strategic direction, proactive strategies, strategic innovations, and sustainable solutions. It involves strategic leaders and other decision makers creating the best solutions possible by considering and assessing all dimensions, all contributors and recipients, all inputs and outputs, and all effects and impacts. It involves engaging all entities and individuals in the organization and across the extended enterprise in creating new solutions based on the concepts, principles and practices of FSL. Strategic leaders are the prime movers for developing solutions and achieving the desired outcomes. In crafting solutions, they are not necessarily the inventors or the designers of the solutions, but they set the stage and ensure that the solutions are of the kind, quality, and fit that are required and expected.

This chapter includes the following main topics:

- General perspectives pertaining to solutions
- The solution development process

General Perspectives Pertaining to Solutions

The solution set and its primary elements

People in the market spaces and the business environment around the world want the best solutions possible; ones that are rich with benefits and devoid of negative aspects. Customers do not just want products and services, they desire great solutions that provide ongoing benefits and exceed their expectations. For instance, do people really want to buy and own air conditioners? They are heavy, noisy, expensive to operate, and not very aesthetic. People do purchase such products because they want the end results, the comfort derived. They want to escape from the realities of hot and uncomfortable summer weather. They want the solution and are willing to pay the price and accept the burdens that go with it. However, any potential new solution using different technologies, products, processes, etc. may become the preferred solution if it has more positives and fewer negatives.

A solution set consists of products and services, related systems and processes, structures, and relationships in combinations with complementary products and services and systems of the extended enterprise that are integrated into a whole. Products tend to be relatively simple constructs because they are made of tangible and intangible elements that have identifiable parts and components. The product is an essential part and a definable subsystem within the solution set. A solution set is similar to a molecule with its own unique physical and chemical characteristics. It has its own attributes and can be viewed as a whole entity rather than just pieces or parts. Using the analogy, protons, neutrons and electrons are generally perceived as building blocks out of which atoms and molecules are constructed. It takes combinations of atoms to build molecules and then build them into materials and products.

Figure 4.1 depicts what a solution set is generally comprised of. It shows the solution set in terms of the full spectrum of inputs and outputs necessary for creating sustainable solutions. Most importantly, FSL through value creation, insightfulness, innovativeness, inclusiveness, and connectedness provides the overarching aspects for developing a solution set that ultimately produces the sustainable solution.

92 ▪ Full-Spectrum Strategic Leadership

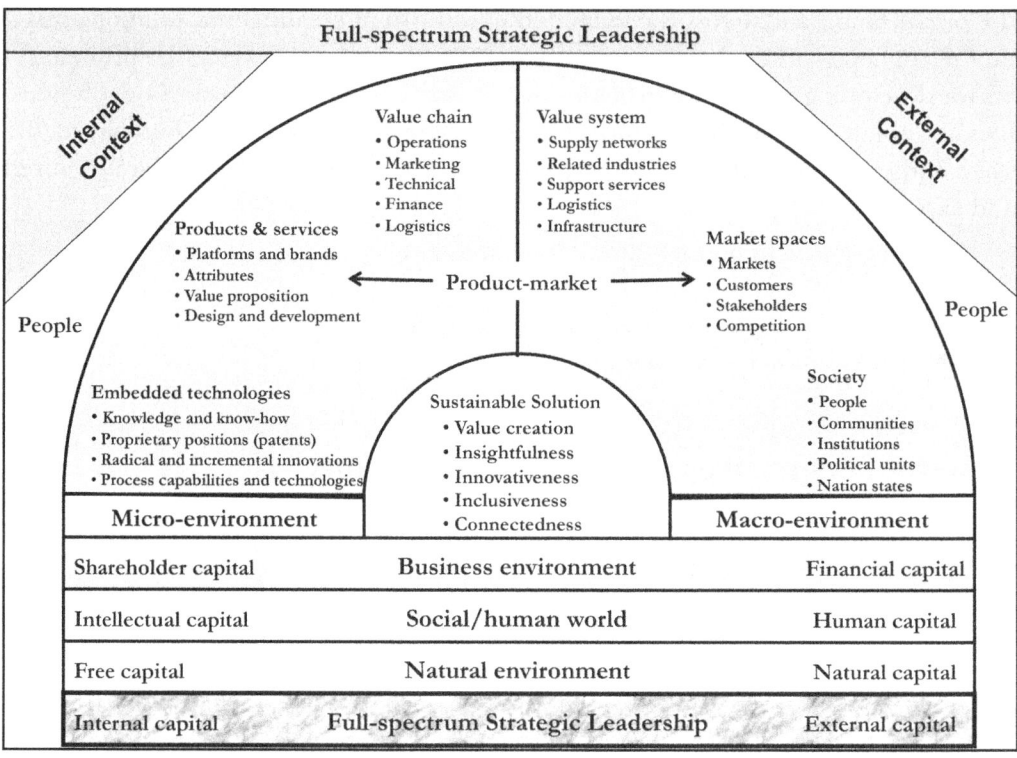

Figure 4.1 The solution set for a sustainable solution.

The solution set starts with insights, imagination, and innovativeness. Solutions are the full integration of all of the elements and entities that are necessary for providing a complete package to meet needs, wants, and expectations. Solutions involve building solid relationships among all of the players who are connected through real and virtual mechanisms. Technologies and information flow play vital roles in ensuring that solutions are effective and valuable. Solutions must create value for the participants and recipients. Without value creation that is based on win-win situations, there is no solution, especially in the long term. Fraudulent and unbalanced quasi-solutions tend to be unstable and generally do not succeed in the long term. A quasi-solution is incomplete and provides only some of the salient factors; the ones generally that the producer decides to provide and the ones that favor his or her positions. The other required elements are typically left to someone else's discretion or not provided at all. For example, if one party obtains all of the benefits and the other parties suffer or lose, then over time the other parties will quit, create conflicts or chaos, or find some other ways to realize their fair share of the results and rewards.

Context is always critical for having the right perspectives on what is necessary and appropriate. The business environment and market spaces (external context) provide a broad sense of what is important and what is required. As discussed in Chapters 2 and 3, strategic leaders must explore the whole business environment. In doing so, successful strategic leaders are more likely to discover new ways and means for understanding the needs and expectations and creating sustainable solutions. Within the external context, the main focus is often on market spaces where customers need better solutions or are looking for new ones that are not presently available. Market spaces include markets with existing customers and non-markets with latent customers. They include markets and customers that are often satisfied with the products and services being offered, but they are still looking for better solutions in the long term. In the short term, many customers may accept the bad with the good until other options become available. Market spaces also include stakeholders and competitors. Both are often perceived to be negative in most situations. Stakeholders often raise questions and issues and articulate concerns about the negative aspects of the company and its products and services. Competitors are viewed as adversaries, since they steal away customers and market share. Conventional theories focus on trying to reduce the potential impacts of stakeholders and competitors. However, from a solution perspective, they may provide insights about what the solution set should be or has to be. They may provide valuable inputs that strategic leaders can use to craft better solutions.

The product-market connection is one of the most important. It portrays the direct linkage between products and services and markets and customers. In conventional theories, products and markets are definitive and have primary elements. The typical product or service has positive attributes that provide benefits for customers; ones that are intended to meet their needs and expectations. Attributes can be tangible aspects like the physical product and intangible aspects such as the esteem or the pleasure one gets in owning the product or using the service. For example, the chemicals in P&G's Crest toothpaste that prevent disease provide tangible benefits, while the delight a BMW owner experiences in showing off his new 4-Series is an intangible. Moreover, every product or service has negative aspects that customers usually have to tolerate until better outcomes are developed. The negative aspects include the limitations of the product and the inherent downsides, etc. like defects, burdens, harms, and unwanted impacts. Some of the negative elements are difficult, if not impossible, to eliminate, such as the dangers associated with electricity. Some have negative aspects that could be reduced or eliminated, if the designers and developers made better choices or decisions, such as using non-toxic substances and clean technologies instead of polluting ones.

Many standard products are incomplete. They require additional ingredients and/or considerations to be solutions. Often customers have to seek out other ways on their own to complete the package. For instance, there are automobiles that are designed to use hydrogen, but there are very few sources of hydrogen fuel, at least in the U.S. It might be useful to have hydrogen-based automobiles, but they are of little value unless hydrogen fuel is readily available and affordable. Without complementary products, supporting value delivery systems, and an integrated infrastructure, the solution is usually incomplete. While strategic leaders do not have to provide all of the elements of solutions from their companies, they have to assure that solutions are complete and that customers can easily obtain and use the solution. For example, Hewlett Packard (HP) is a leading producer of personal computers (PCs) and printers. HP's products provide significant value for its customers, but the PCs would not be solutions without software from Microsoft, Norton, etc.

Non-markets and latent customers are those areas in which solutions are not being provided or where efforts are extremely weak or marginal. In such areas there are needs and wants but a dearth of solutions. The non-market spaces are often made up of emerging markets with many latent customers, but most of the people have marginal incomes. Non-markets are segments that made up of people who cannot afford the prevailing products and services. There are enormous market opportunities around the world, but most of the existing products and services are not solutions for the people involved, especially those in the poorest countries. For instance, people in the developing countries in Sub-Saharan Africa need basic products to improve their living conditions and health care. However, most of the high quality products from the large global corporations are not suited for the local conditions and patterns of use. Most of the prevailing products may be too large, too expensive, require too much support, take too many resources and energy, and do not fit the realities of the local conditions. They may have many wonderful attributes and work well, but in many of the emerging markets the support systems and structures may not be readily available or economically feasible. For example, standard clothes washers sold in the developed countries require an infrastructure of electricity, clean water, maintenance services, and space in the household. They are generally expensive and are not easily shared with neighbors, friends, and relatives. In many emerging markets, the price of a washing machine would have to be significant lower and they would have to fit the prevailing conditions like being mechanical devices rather than having electric motors. The answers lie in identifying the requirements for satisfying the needs and wants from the views and realities of the indigenous people and providing them with solutions that fit their specific needs and requirements.

Most products and services are designed and produced based on the driving forces in the business environment, which makes sense. However, strategic leaders have to be careful; such thinking is limited since once the new products and services become fully articulated and turned into realities in the markets, *countervailing forces* often appear shortly thereafter—ones that were not apparent or may not have even existed before the new products and services made their entry. Countervailing forces are ones that develop as the unresolved issues and impacts of products and services become apparent or significant. For instance, few people understood the negative side of chlorofluorocarbons (CFCs) until they were widely used and they enjoyed significant market success as refrigerants and solvents. CFCs were eventually phased out because stakeholder groups took aggressive actions to eliminate their use after the risks of ozone depletion were discovered and validated. Today, ethanol is perceived to be a renewable fuel and a positive contributor for solving energy problems. However, if ethanol production dramatically increases the prices of food products and reduces the availability of corn, which is the main feedstock for ethanol production in the U.S., then there may be reactions from food producers and consumers. The countervailing forces may change the viability of the products and services and make the ventures less sustainable. Dealing with stakeholder issues and concerns and eliminating the potential negative impacts lead to more successful solutions. The sooner such forces are recognized and dealt with, the better the expected outcomes become.

Understanding competitors and fitting them into the solution set from a product-market perspective provide better choices for customers. Certain competitors may decide to offer products and services that complement the company's positions, allowing the company's strategic leaders to focus on what they do best. For instance, even with Microsoft's power and capabilities, it works with other software companies to develop a broader array of complementary products and services for customers. Microsoft is usually able to select the most lucrative options, allowing would-be competitors to offer the other product forms.

Most existing and new products are designed based on the developers' research and development (R&D), their perceptions of the markets and customers, and the organization's capabilities and related product lines. Alternatively, solutions are framed based on external context and are driven by the realities of the business environment and the perceptions and realities of customers and market spaces. In simple terms, solutions are the domain of the external context and in most situations products and services are the domain of the internal context. Solutions necessitate a broader, holistic mindset to understand the whole business environment and the embedded opportunities. W. Chan Kim and Renee Mauborgne in their book, *Blue Ocean Strategy: How to Create Uncontested Market Space and Make Competition Irrelevant,* examine how strategic leader can discover new ways of achieving success; ones that are less prone to engaging in rivalry and are focused more on creating unique solutions.[2] Blue Ocean refers to markets that are built on positive buyer-seller relationships with win-win value propositions that have distinctive attributes, especially ones that are difficult to emulate. For instance, Nestlé is developing new solutions for customers in Africa where people do not have access to many quality products, especially ones that are designed from their perspectives. Nestlé's strategic leaders plan to invest about one-third of their R&D funds on such initiatives because most of its existing markets in the developed countries are mature with little room for significant growth.[3]

Sustainable solutions have unique attributes that are extremely hard to imitate and are based on a broad array of the capabilities and resources of the organization, its value systems, and extended enterprise. While it may be easy to duplicate one's products and services, it is very difficult to copy comprehensive solutions that are integrated within the value delivery systems and the complex web of supporting networks. Solutions are more comprehensive and are developed based on the insights and innovativeness of the strategic leaders and the organization.

Value creation and the solution set

Value creation and the value proposition are the underpinnings of solutions. Solutions have outstanding combinations of value creation and value delivery expressed and supported using the value system and the extended enterprise. Sustainable solutions incorporate the essential elements that provide customers, stakeholders and society with the tangibles and intangibles they desire—ones that are necessary to produce enduring outcomes and success. Strategic leader create new or enhanced value through innovativeness. Some of the primary means are new ventures, new-to-the-world technologies, innovative products, and enhanced processes. These innovations may focus on transitions and incremental changes to the prevailing business situation or transformations and radical changes to create more exciting realities. Regardless, the overarching approach is to move the solutions toward more ideal outcomes.[4]

Value creation involves developing innovative solutions with greater benefits, fewer deficiencies, and reduced impacts, i.e., the best possible solutions that maximize gains and minimize losses. Innovations that result in less value or worse situations are not really innovations at all. They are simply ineffective changes that do not contribute to the greater good. For example, marketing executives might repackage their products to appear to be more attractive, but with no real improvements. Such changes are only cosmetic and they are generally a waste of money. Instead of improving value they reduce it because the money invested does not result in real gains. This is especially the case when the changes simply focus on the glitz and glamour of the products.

Value creation involves designing, developing, and producing the best solutions possible to fit the needs, wants, expectations, and/or the requirements of the markets spaces and the business environment.[5] Value creation is the result of the contributions of the organization and the value chains of the extended enterprise that are integrated into economic usefulness, social benefits, environmental protection, and company profits and cash flow; it is the culmination of the tangible and intangible benefits made, in which the processes and activities fulfill the needs, requirements, and expectations of the driving forces and turn opportunities into valuable and sustainable outcomes.[6] Value creation also involves building enduring relationships with people. It involves people to people exchanges of goods, money, information, and intangibles like connectedness and friendship. Enduring relationships depend on trust and honesty.[7] Value creation is an objective function. It requires evidence to support the premises that the new solutions created and delivered actually contribute to enhanced value and successful outcomes. The more evidence that can be provided, the more likely it is that the premises are believable and the solutions are acceptable.

Historically, strategic leaders and functional managers concentrated on the positive side when engaged in strategizing and developing products and services. They sought the best combination of benefits as they made trade-offs in accepting negative aspects. Many wonderful new products had flaws because the decision makers were willing to accept the negatives. Indeed, for much of the twentieth century, the prevailing theory was to make trade-offs in design and development of products and services. They provided many great attributes, but the outcomes created numerous problems because designers and decision makers often failed to mitigate the negatives. The examples are countless. The typical sport utility vehicle (SUV) is a good case in point. It is big and roomy, stylish, comfortable, full of electronic gadgets, and fast. But, there are numerous defects or harms such as causing air pollution, generating noise, consuming a lot of fuel, having safety problems, and incurring high ownership expenses. It is not just large durable goods that have such problems. Many small, consumable products, like household chemicals, exhibit many downsides, defects, etc. as well. Such chemicals may provide good cleaning outcomes, but some of them leave hazardous residues, which are dangerous for children and poisonous to the natural environment. While consumers may not think about all of the impacts, the negatives of such products never disappear; they just take on different forms and move to other locations.

Arnoldo Hax and Dean Wilde II discuss in their book, *the delta project: discovering new sources of profitability in networked economy,* three distinctive ways for strategic leaders to use Hax and Wilde's Delta Model to achieve success—"best product, total customer solutions, and system lock-in."[8] The best product approach is similar to the traditional views focusing on products and services, except that the main consideration is on providing the best ones possible. It involves many management approaches used over the last several decades concentrating on developing and designing products with excellence benefits. The total customer solutions approach involves ensuring that customers enjoy superior results and creating solid customer relationships. It requires strategic leaders to make more holistic decisions about all aspects of what the customer expects and to ensure that the solutions provide them. The system lock-in approach involves integrating all contributors, especially "complementors" (related industries), to deliver the full value. The intent is to lock-in customers and supporters and lock-out competitors through proprietary approaches.[9] While the notion of integrating all of the contributors makes strategic sense, one has to be careful about the notion of lock-in. People accept and use a given solution because they are happy with it and it provides the best option. But, very few things last forever. As discussed in the previous chapter, leading change and providing solutions are unending efforts and accomplishments, in which strategic leaders have to reinvent and reshape all of the elements periodically. There are few lock-ins, which is good from everyone's perspective. Lock-ins stifle creativity. For example, Henry Ford was exceptionally well satisfied with his creation, the Model T, and he believed that customers would continue to buy his product. But, by the late 1920s the business world changed. Ford, the great innovator, forgot to continue to innovate and General Motor's more innovative Chevrolet became the market share leader. On the other hand, the late Steve Jobs and Apple Inc. enjoyed many successes like the iPhone, iPod, iTunes and iPads. Jobs knew that innovation is essential for success and that Apple must continue to be innovative and create new solutions, lest it will be eventually surpassed.

The solution set is the full complement of the elements that make up the solution. Table 4.1 depicts the key elements of the solution set.[10] The elements identified are not comprehensive. The ones listed are intended to provide guidance as strategic leaders contemplate what their solutions should encompass, how the contributors and recipients are connected, and how they can become successful. It is important to note that many of the elements that are listed as internal or external dimensions might apply to the other category as well. Given that strategic leaders select their own solution sets based on external context, each strategic leader has to decide upon the best configuration. This is particularly important since solutions are intended to be unique.

The solution set represents the freedom to create the best outcomes. It requires the proper context, the right designs and developments, outstanding deployments, and exceptional connections and relationships. It involves the best solutions, systems,

TABLE 4.1 Selected Elements and Aspects of the Solution Set

Categories	Primary	Support system	Contributors	Recipients
Internal Dimensions				
Elements	Technologies	Operating system	Partners	Customers
	Products	Value chain	Allies	Stakeholders
	Services	Value networks	Employees	Shareholders
	Brands	Extended enterprise	Complementors	Society
Positives (enhancing, improving, changing)	Benefits	Durability	Knowledge	Value
	Performance	Maintainability	Experience	Success
	Functionality	Stability	Effectiveness	Satisfaction
	Ease of use	Manufacturability	Efficiency	Compatibility
	Quality	Marketability	Productivity	Applicability
	Reliability	Ergonomics	Responsiveness	Maintainability
	Affordability	Accountability	Accepted standards	Serviceability
	Openness	Reportability	Practices	Longevity
	Trustworthiness	Sustainability	Rewards	Aesthetics
Negatives (resolving, reducing, eliminating)	High costs	Inadequacies	Liabilities	Failures
	Risks	Breakdowns	Mistakes	Premature losses
	Vulnerabilities	Stoppages	Accidents	Inconveniences
	Uncertainties	Vulnerabilities	Spills/releases	Problems
	Defects	Waste streams	Health concerns	Take-backs
	Burdens	Compliance issues	Safety issues	Accidents
	Inconveniences	Hazards	Injuries/harms	Monetary losses
	Failures	Problems	Blunders	Unhappiness
External Dimensions				
Elements	Other technologies	Value system	Supply networks	Customers
	Related products	Enterprise	Related industries	Stakeholders
	Related services	Business world	Infrastructure	Society
Positives (enhancing, improving, changing)	Creativity	Networks	Completeness	Awareness
	Enhancements	Linkages	Flexibility	Acceptance
	Value-added	Relationships	Adaptability	Availability
	Support services	Alignment	Capacity	Suitability
	Communications	Logistics	Best behaviors	Connectedness
Negatives (resolving, reducing, eliminating)	Impacts	Depletion	Selfishness	Nuisances
	Disconnections	Destruction	Lack of attention	Obstacles
	Difficulties	Degradation	Dishonesty	End-of life disposal
	Barriers	Disruptions	Deception	Waste handling
	Impediments	Waste management	Coercion	Health and safety

processes and relationships; ones that provide extraordinary outcomes that lead to enduring success, but not necessarily lock-in positions per se. People should continue to be able to select the solutions they want and need—the ones that are the best available. A solution in the real world is always evolving as the requirements of the business world change and new expectations develop; it is temporal as well as physical and psychological.

Strategic leaders navigate through all of the elements and usually orchestrate the internal dimensions through product and process developments and technological innovations. The most important elements are the primary attributes of products and services. The support system elements define some of key factors for producing and delivering the solutions to customers who are among the primary recipients of the solutions. Key contributors are the leaders, managers, professionals, and employees of the organizations and the direct partners and allies who provide knowledge, experience, know-how, and numerous other facets, some of which are listed in Table 4.1. The latter include consultants, contract lawyers, advisors, etc. Recipients are the prime motive, i.e., the customers who need and want all of the attributes that fulfill their needs and expectations. It is their perceptions about value, the benefits, satisfaction and success that really matters in most cases. Overall success should be measured from the views of the recipients and the contributors alike.

The notion of innovativeness of the whole solution is reinforced by improving the positives and resolving, reducing, and/or eliminating the negatives. This is a critical distinction, especially in a business world full of advanced, state-of-the-art, high quality, low-cost products and services. The level of sophistication on the positive side is usually high, yet the same cannot always be said on the negative side. While good gains have been made over the last several decades, there are still incredible opportunities to make even more dramatic advancements. Reducing costs, lowing risks, and uncertainties, and eliminating defects and burdens are primary areas in which great gains can be made. Recipients do not want to deal with inconveniences, problems, and extra costs. They expect workable and enduring solutions. On the other hand, contributors want to avoid wastes streams, mistakes, accidents, and unexpected adverse events that increase costs and create liabilities. The negative aspects are enhanced when risks, vulnerabilities and failures are reduced and when managing wastes and regulatory compliance are under control and improving.

From an internal perspective, there are enormous opportunities to reduce or eliminate negative aspects. Negative impacts, difficulties, and impediments, wherever they are in the extended enterprise, hurt everyone. Eliminating problems, disconnections, and barriers makes doing business easier, simpler and less expensive. Over the last decade, most strategic leaders have come to understand the true cost of the negative aspects, especially product defects. It has been estimated that negative side may cost between more than ten percent of revenues, especially if the negative aspects are not addressed properly and cured. For example, the total cost of Toyota's product problems with brakes a few years ago is expected to cost billions of dollars. The costs of recalls and fixing defects have direct effects on the bottom line and future sales. The drive toward six-sigma quality and methods is a manifestation that good is not good enough. Progress has to be relentless and enduring. Like the internal organization, the support systems of the extended enterprise have many broad-based difficulties like degradation, depletion, destruction, disruptions, and waste streams. Strategic leaders have to ensure that improvements are made in all of these areas. They are explored in more detail in the next chapter. The focus is on the requirements of the value systems and the extended enterprise. This includes the related and complementary technologies, products, and processes to complete the solution. They include enhancements, value-added nuances, support services, and a myriad of additional aspects. The key for external aspects is the integration of the networks, relationships, and linkages into a fully aligned value delivery system that provides the means and mechanisms to get the solutions to the recipients. This also includes the role of primary logistics in getting the goods through production and distribution and reverse logistics in getting the end-of-life products and materials to be reused, recycled, and/or refurbished. Moreover, the external dimensions help build awareness and acceptance of the solution in the business world. This could include competitors who may contribute to these ends by their actions in promoting market development and the overall stability of the social and economic forces. Competition may reinforce the dominant technologies and can keep potential threats of substitutes and emerging technologies out of the picture. External contributors are central for providing the whole solution and allowing room for change and flexibility.

The logic of the solution is ultimately based on the perceptions and realities of the people who are the beneficiaries of the solution. If they are not enriched and made successful, then the solution is less than what is necessary and changes must be made. Strategic leaders are responsible for ensuring that the solutions are as complete as possible and that contributors have the flexibility and adaptability to be in concert with changes and new demands. This pertains to both the internal and the external dimensions. External contributors must play central roles in the development, production and delivery of the solutions. They must be aligned with the philosophies and principles of the primary producers and providers. It is incumbent upon strategic leaders of the company to ensure that the contributors, regardless of their position within the enterprise, have the same ethical and moral persuasion.

The Solution Development Process

Perspectives about the process and the key elements

Many of the underlying aspects of what solutions have to be were articulated by several of the leading quality experts over the last three decades. These experts helped develop the underpinnings of total quality management (TQM), six-sigma techniques, and lean practices along with many of the underlying principles of contemporary leadership and management.[11] W. Edwards Deming, who was a world renowned quality and leadership guru, suggested that most difficulties are attributable to the management system. He emphasized that it is management's responsibility to ensure that conformance is measured in terms of external perspectives and that business leaders must focus on making significant transitions and transformations and on learning how to change.[12] Deming advocated using customers' perspectives when creating value. He stated:[13]

> It will not suffice to have customers that are merely satisfied. An unhappy customer will switch. Unfortunately, a satisfied customer may also switch, on the theory that he could not lose much, and might gain. Profit in business comes from repeat customers, customers that boast about your product and service [solutions], and that brings friends with them [based on solid relationships]. Fully allocated costs may well show that profit in a transaction with a customer that comes back voluntarily [sustainable success] may be 10 times the profit realized from a customer that responds to advertising and other forms of persuasion.

J. M. Juran, a quality guru, also suggested that most problems and defects are attributable to the management system.[14] He developed the concept of fitness for use, advocating that solutions are dependent upon the applications of the product or service. This is obviously a good connection to the concept of a solution herein. Products and services are not answers in themselves; they have to be linked to customers and markets. This perspective begets the contemporary term: product-market. Products are linked with the market segments they serve. It is the whole enterprise that creates the total solution. Phillip Crosby, another quality guru, argued that the goal is the pursuit of zero defects and continuous improvement. This reinforces the concept of a sustainable solution.

Astute strategic leaders realize that they must become more sophisticated and provide great solutions. Solutions encompass all of what is needed, wanted, and expected today. While there are always realities that have to be understood and dealt with, strategic leaders should be mindful of all aspects of the desired solutions because in the future there may be new technologies and new ways of achieving the desired ends. For instance, a generation ago video phones were thought to be impossible due to the limited bandwidth available. However, new technologies in a number of areas including cell phones, fiber optics, and digital cameras have made the impossible a reality.

Solutions are multifaceted, including external- and internal-driven parameters. The external world defines what is desirable in very broad terms (specifications) and the internal context creates substance and reality. The former focuses on the general aspects of the solution and what it has to be and do, while the latter focuses on the specifics including how it can be created and how it has to function. The external context is about "the what" and the internal context is about "the how."

The great success of Pan American World Airways (Pan Am) during its early years is an example of how insights lead to solutions and how solutions are created and developed through insights, imagination, and innovativeness; ones that are based on a broad value system and on the enduring relationships with people. Pan Am was founded in 1927 by Major Henry "Hap" Arnold and his partners and investors.[15] In the same year, Juan Trippe formed Aviation Corporation of America (ACA), which was backed by William Rockefeller, C. V. Whitney, and several others. Later in 1927, the Atlantic, Gulf and Caribbean Airways was launched by Richard Hoyt. In mid-1928, the three companies merged using ACA as the parent with an operating unit called Pan American Airways, Inc. Trippe became the strategic leader of Pan Am, while Hoyt served as president of ACA. Pan Am had lucrative U.S. airmail contracts to fly mail to international destinations. These government contracts provided the financial means for Trippe to expand Pan Am's airline services to Central and South America. Based on his financial successes, Trippe launched flights to Europe in 1937. The basic aircrafts were the Sikorsky S-42 flying boats that Pan Am leaders called Clippers after the fast American sailings ships of the nineteenth century. It was a clever use of terminology and a psychological enhancement, since many Americans had great respect for the accomplishments of courageous sailors of the past who facilitated trade with Europe and Asia. As Trippe extended his reach into the Pacific (Japan, China, and Hong Kong), he eventually decided to follow the shipping routes. Using the Boeing 314, the long trips were accomplished by island hopping across the Pacific with such stopping points as Honolulu, Midway Island, Guam, and Manila. Trippe's genius was that he knew customers wanted safe flights and comfortable and restful stop-over points. He orchestrated the building of hotels and restaurants in the far-flung locations along the routes to his customers' final destinations. He realized that the solution was more than planes, pilots, routes, and destinations. Trippe understood that people wanted and expected the best solution for their international travel needs, not just an airline with passenger service. He led changes in the industry and enhanced the total customer experience by providing all of the necessary related services. Trippe had the insights to know that air travel would grow rapidly if the means and mechanisms were available and if the travel was safe and reasonably pleasant. He established integrated systems to meet the customers' requirements. He created solid relationships with foreign governments to secure landing rights and partnered with a number of other airlines to support the needs of his customers within the countries of their destination.

Trippe continued to be an innovator and early adapter. After World War II, Pan Am continued to upgrade its capabilities with new aircraft like the Boeing 377 and the Douglas DC6. Pan Am owned the InterContinental Hotel chain. It provided automated reservation services and even had helicopter services. Trippe was one of the first airline executives to buy jet aircraft in the United States. For example, he (Pan Am) was the inaugural customer of the Boeing 747. However, Trippe had many detractors who believed that he was too aggressive. He engaged in many battles with his adversaries, especially with Howard Hughes of Trans World Airline. He had numerous difficulties with the U.S. Government as well. But Trippe generally prevailed in such adverse situations. He was a master at managing both the positives and the negatives. Unfortunately, after Trippe retired his predecessors were unable to follow in his footsteps. The succeeding strategic leaders were unable to handle the changing business environment, especially after the airline industry was deregulated in the 1980s. With all of its great strategic innovations, Pan Am declined and went out of business in 1991.

Strategic leaders have to think about what the solution has to be instead of thinking about what the products and services are. Strategic leaders at many large corporations who have common ways of thinking often have difficulties changing their perspectives; they often lack out-of-the-box thinking. Their mindsets are often fixed on standard methods and practices that are based on years of experience. In many situations, they are functioning on what they learned decades earlier and have not taken the time to adapt to new ways of thinking or operating. One always has to reflect on theories and practices that were relevant in the past, but some may no longer be appropriate.

Solutions incorporate many internal and external ingredients dealing with:

- The needs, wants, and expectations of market segments, customers and stakeholder groups.
- The broad elements of the extended enterprise, including the roles and contributions of supply networks and related industries (complementors).

- Societal concerns and attitudes about the business environment and the broader social, economic, and environmental effects, impacts, and implications.
- Laws, regulations, rules, and standards pertaining to the solution and the related systems.
- The economic viability and stability of the solutions and the risks and uncertainties.
- Embedded technologies from both within the industry and from other sectors and the expected changes, potential turbulence, and the associated risks.
- The internal elements of the value delivery system.

The shift in emphasis from the more limited scope of products and services to the broader perspectives of solutions is critically important in today's more demanding world. It has profound consequences for both the strategic leaders who adapt such strategic thinking and for those who do not. Great strategic leaders decide how to create innovative solutions; the laggards contemplate how they can stay close enough to the competition without making big changes or taking risks. Moreover, the laggards often simply try to emulate the products and services of the market leaders or simply continue to leverage what they have, but they usually fail to make sufficient progress because their forms of the solutions are incomplete. For example, it may be easy to copy Toyota's successful product lines, but it takes getting to another level of sophistication to duplicate Toyota's integrated management systems, its Toyota Production System, and its customer loyalty.

Theoretically, there are no generic solutions; each is tailor-made to fit the specific circumstances of the business situation and market applications based on the strategic decisions made by the company. For instance, two companies may have identical products that they are trying to market. Their product forms and specifications may be the same, but the companies often have very different configurations, value systems, and relationships with customers, stakeholders, and constituents; therefore, they most likely will have different solutions. For example, in the early 1970s, Forrest Brewing Co. (FBC) of New Bedford, Massachusetts introduced Gablinger's Beer, a 99-calorie beer, that "doesn't fill you up" before Miller Lite took essentially the same formula and created one of the most successful new product introductions in U.S. business history. The main difference between the two companies was Gablinger's Beer was sold as a "diet beer," while Miller went after the heavy beer drinkers with its famous "great taste, less filling" theme. The product form was the same, but Miller's solution was radically different. FBC failed miserably with its product, whereas Miller's solution fit the market space exactly; thus, becoming one of the greatest new product success stories of the last century.

The question of starting point is most relevant when creating a process, but it is almost impossible to generalize when discussing solutions because there many pathways to success. Context sets the stage. Since each situation is different, examining context is usually the initial step. Moreover, since it is highly desirable that strategic leaders create their own unique solutions, strategic leaders have to determine the effectiveness of their technological capabilities and how long their present technologies and products will endure. Figure 4.2 depicts a general flow of the solution development framework/process. It includes the perspectives mapped out in Figure 4.1.

The elements outlined are the most important ones that are central in developing solutions. The lists in each of the steps (categories) are not intended to be comprehensive but indicate what strategic leaders might consider. Each strategic leader has to determine whether to enhance existing positions, create entirely new ones, or make one of the myriad of choices in between. The approach has to be flexible since each situation is different.

Context as previously stated is most often the most appropriate starting point. External context provides the driving forces for the solution and defines the opportunities and challenges. It focuses on what is desired, needed, and/or expected. It includes the mandates of governments, the external standards that have to be adhered to, and the overall specifications of the solution from the perspectives of the external

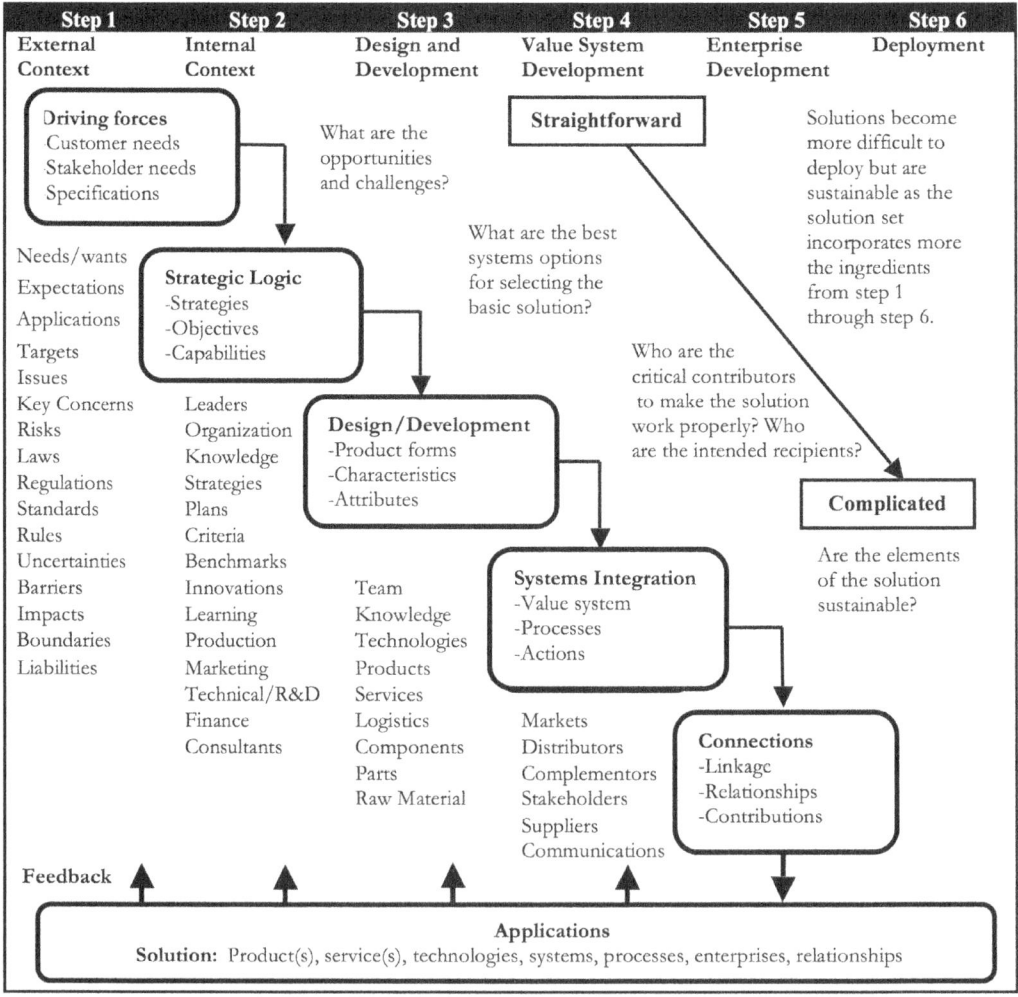

Figure 4.2 Key elements of the solution development process [16]

entities and individuals. Establishing external context requires considerable research and analysis to determine the key concerns, issues, needs, and expected outcomes. Moreover, it often involves understanding complicated forces of the business environment and determining the interactions in the market spaces. Customer expectations are dynamic and good solutions today may be obsolete tomorrow. Likewise, powerful competitors may fade into oblivion, while emerging competitors rise to center stage.

Internal context is critical as well. While the internal context in Figure 4.2 appears to be dependent upon inputs from external context, the time delay between first step and the second one should be relatively short, almost insignificant. The second step is the domain of the strategic leaders and the senior managers within the organization. Most of the determinations can be done in parallel or closely aligned with each other. Strategic leaders create the atmosphere and realities that support and produce changes and solutions. People therefore are among the most critical contributors for crafting solutions. It is their innovativeness that leads to great results. Internal context involves setting and reaffirming the strategic logic and fit of the solution(s). It is based on the strategizing and the setting of objectives and plans by strategic leaders.

Strategic leaders often have to determine whether to concentrate on enhancing and exploiting the current positions by changing existing products and services into solutions, to explore new opportunities and challenges, to invent new-to-the-world solutions, or to employ all three. Generally the right answer usually involves doing as much as possible as quickly as possible given the rapidity of change in the business world. While there are studies suggesting that exploiting present capabilities and being conservative produce better results, strategic leaders have to be careful interpreting such findings. First and foremost, the business world of the past moved more slowly than today. The fact that giant companies were historically more successful exploiting existing product lines and capabilities does not automatically mean that such approaches will lead to success in the future. Being too conservative in a fast-paced world may simply allow others to catch up and pass the organization. Moreover, there are thousands of stories of leading corporations like Pan Am, US Steel, RCA, A&P and AT&T, whose successes depended on strategic innovations, yet when they stopped being innovative they ran into many difficulties and declined.[17] There are also many examples of strategic leaders at companies like GM that exploited the present and sacrificed their long-term position. They made trade-offs. They focused on the obvious and failed to use their imagination and glean insights about the big changes going on in the world. Moreover, one's success based on the prevailing products and services may continue for ten or more years, as was Kodak's situation after the initial developments of digital cameras, but eventually the forces of change overtake one's superior positions and make them irrelevant. Relying on existing product-market conditions and the related information and data may lead to faulty conclusions. The product-market conditions may support the prevailing product lines until there is a tipping point that eradicates the underlying assumptions. For example, American automobile manufacturers made a lot of money selling SUVs in the 1990s. They continued to do so even after the price of petroleum increased dramatically in early 2000s. Earlier successes often lead to entrenched positions and decline.

Strategic leaders often put too much emphasis on the known product-market conditions, not enough on the potential opportunities and unknown challenges that require internal improvements and dramatic changes. The former is supported by statistical information and analysis, while the latter requires insights, intuition, and innovativeness. In general, it may appear to be less risky when one is making decisions based on solid information and data. However, such thinking often skews decision making toward the near term rather than a balanced perspective of both the short term and the long term. Few strategic leaders in the automobile industry would have contemplated the collapse of the financial markets in 2007 and the dramatic decline in demand for automobiles.

Near-term results that are positive often portray the wrong sense of destiny, since products are much easier to develop and track than solutions, especially products using existing technologies and ingredients. Incremental product innovations may flow from inception to reality within months, or a year or two, and achieve financial success quickly with good intensity during the first few years. On the other hand, because of the requirements for creating new technologies, developing more extensive value systems, and building connections with markets, solutions may take much longer to become realities, but the gains may be monumental. Moreover, it can be argued that the more unique the solution is, the more likely it can be expected to endure and grow profits and cash flow at substantial rates. For instance, if a new or revised product is introduced in "year 1" and grows in revenues and profits at a constant rate of ten per cent per year and a new solution is introduced in "year 3" and increases at twenty percent per year, then it takes until "year 6" before the solution is deemed to be better than the product from a financial point of view. This hypothetical example has many assumptions including that first-year results are identical, which is used here to illustrate the points on a comparative basis. Moreover, it assumes that both endure, but it is more likely that solutions will endure longer because they are designed to be unique and are more inclusive of the whole enterprise. Table 4.2 presents the hypothetical numbers with the product being the basis of comparison.

Incremental product innovations tend to exhibit favorable outcomes in the short term because they usually have a time advantage. The more comprehensive solutions, especially via radical technological innovations, tend to take longer to develop and are usually disadvantaged when analyzed in the near term. The example above indicates that the product approach and the solution approach are essentially equivalent in "years 5 and 6." If one were to analyze the situation anytime during the first five years, he or she would come to the conclusion that the product approach is superior.

TABLE 4.2 Hypothetical Example of the Results of Two Different Growth Rates

Year	1	2	3	4	5	6	7	8	9	10	11	12	Sum
Product	1.00	1.10	1.21	1.33	1.46	1.61	1.77	1.95	2.14	2.36	2.60	2.86	21.39
Solution			1.00	1.20	1.44	1.73	2.07	2.49	2.99	3.58	4.30	5.16	25.96
Difference	1.00	1.10	0.21	0.13	0.02	(0.12)	(0.30)	(0.54)	(0.85)	(1.22)	(1.70)	(2.30)	(4.57)

TABLE 4.3 Hypothetical Example of the Results Based on Ten-Year Life

Year	1	2	3	4	5	6	7	8	9	10	11	12	Sum
Product	1.00	1.10	1.21	1.33	1.46	1.61	1.77	1.95	2.14	2.36			15.93
Solution			1.00	1.20	1.44	1.73	2.07	2.49	2.99	3.58	4.30	5.16	25.96
Difference	1.00	1.10	0.21	0.13	0.02	(0.12)	(0.30)	(0.54)	(0.85)	(1.22)	(4.30)	(5.16)	(10.03)

However, if the growth rates are indeed significantly different as suggested, then in the long term the one with the better growth rate is the better choice. Factual information and data and valid analysis can produce faulty conclusions if strategic leaders are not careful in thinking about timing and the long-term implications. Moreover, in the real world inferior products and services are often swept from the markets as superior solutions are usually preferred by customers. Table 4.3 provides a sense of how the outcomes might change if the product has a ten year life span in the market and it is replaced by a competitor's solution.

The development of Intel is a good example of strategic leaders focusing on solutions. Robert Noyce and Gordon Moore founded Intel in 1968. Moore is famous for Moore's Law that suggested new technologies or new platforms had to be two times better than the previous ones.[18] This great insight was translated by Andy Grove into providing solutions instead of producing products. Grove was the director of operations, responsible for product development and manufacturing. He established the perspective that it was the whole system that produced extraordinary results and not just technologies and products. Grove's favorite saying was: "Only the Paranoid Survive." It expressed his passion for doing everything possible to stay ahead of the competition. He suggested three rules:[19]

> One, don't differentiate without a difference. Don't introduce improvements whose only purpose is to give you an advantage over your competitor without giving your customer a substantial advantage...

> Two, in this hypercompetitive horizontal world, opportunity knocks when technology breakthrough or fundamental change comes your way. Grab it. The first mover and only the first mover, the company that acts while the others dither, has the true opportunity to gain over its competitors—and time advantage in business is the surest way to gain market share. Conversely, people who try to fight the wave of a new technology lose in spite of their best efforts because they waste valuable time... [good is not good enough]

> Three, price for what the market will bear, price for volume, then work like the devil on your costs so that you can make money at that price. This will lead you to achieve economies of scale in which large investments that are necessary can be effective and productive and will make sense because, by being a large-volume supplier, you can spread and recoup those costs.

Strategic leaders of today have to be extremely careful about relying too much on historical data and experiences, especially for technologies and products that are a decade or more old. Today's business world is moving at incredible speed and change is the norm. Many of the historical ways of thinking, strategizing, and taking actions have changed, especially since the dramatic expansion of the Internet, circa 1994-1996. It is a new world with billions of people involved in the economic and social forces and the business situations are more open-ended with many more opportunities and numerous challenges.

Solutions spring from both external and internal contexts that are ever changing and full of wonderful possibilities. Observed through the insightfulness and innovativeness of strategic leaders who have the understanding and capabilities to shape possibilities into new realities, changing context makes exciting alternatives available in creating the best solutions given external forces and internal strategic logic. Strategic leaders have to think in terms of improving what they have and they must also create new-to-the-world solutions as well. It is usually not an either-or perspective, but all of the above. Again, Grove's insights are helpful:[20]

> When the environment changes in such a way as to render the old skills and strengths [and technologies] less relevant, we almost instinctively cling to our past. We refuse to acknowledge changes around us, almost like a child who doesn't like what he is seeing so he closes his eyes... We close our eyes and are willing to work harder...

Grove called this phenomenon "the inertia of success." In many industries and markets, change is slow. Strategic leaders are often caught off guard because they believe there is a status quo. They assume that the prevailing conditions will continue well in the future, especially if their strengths and positions are well suited for the prevailing market conditions.

The design and development of the solution

The third critical step is determining what the solutions must embody and contribute. One thing that strategic leaders have to ascertain is the effectiveness of their technological capabilities, and they must answer the related question of how long their present technologies and products can endure. Strategic leaders have to think about what the solutions have to be as well as what the products and services are. This requires a mindset shift from focusing on developing and deploying products and services to seeking the best solutions possible.

Strategic leaders have to be creative and have to shape their positions in the business world based on their insights, imagination, and knowledge. They need to be more entrepreneurial. Entrepreneurs instinctively know that they must engage in inventing solutions and orchestrating change mechanisms. In start-up companies, the senior leaders know that they do not have the capabilities and resources to do everything, so they depend on external partners and supporters to complete what is necessary to develop the solution set. Regardless, strategic leaders should focus on what has to be done to develop unique solutions and gain sustainable advantages. This involves crafting strategies and action plans for the design and development of the solutions. The solution set is based on descriptive, analytical, and structural understanding and inclusion of the needs, opportunities, threats, requirements, specifications, and information flows for determining, developing, demonstrating, and delivering solutions. The solution set examines all of the options to obtain the best choices for inputs and outputs. Each solution has a solution set that defines what it is and how it is created and deployed. The solution set provides: (1) a clear perspective of the purpose and fit of the solution; (2) well-articulated means and mechanisms for the creation of new technologies, new products, new processes, and new management constructs, if necessary; (3) a comprehensive framework for crafting, validating, and executing the solution; (4) a clear view of the interrelationships between the key contributors and recipients; and (5) a systematic approach for achieving and measuring results. It attempts to minimize mistakes and oversights by understanding all of the implications and potential impacts. With sufficient assessment of the inputs and outputs, strategic leaders can make good decisions and create the best possible solutions.

The solution set often has front-end elements that focus on product development and technological innovation. If the existing technologies are to underpin the solution, then the early steps involve the new product development (NPD) process using integrated product development (IPD) methodology. NPD typically involves incremental changes to existing products and product platforms.[21] These focus on: (1) market opportunities, customer wants and needs, product attributes, product and process specifications, marketing requirements, and technology issues; (2) the interrelated effects of customers, consumers, stakeholders, regulatory agencies, and competitors; and (3) the use of the extended enterprise and the internal functions to craft the best solution. IPD provides a management framework that allows strategic leaders to make a rapid assessment of the feasibility of a new product opportunity and to quickly decide on appropriate action plans. The NPD process includes idea generation, concept development and selection, program definition, design and development, validation, and commercialization.[22] It is based on an architecture that enables strategic leaders, product managers, and NPD teams to make quick determinations about the acceptability of a new product candidate, to review the expected requirements and results, and to forge an effective game plan for the design, development, and validation of the new product focusing on market acceptance and outstanding performance

The NPD process provides managers and practitioners with a clear and comprehensive view of their roles and responsibilities and the key elements of the process. The process allows managers to develop real-time approaches for handling product, production, and marketing issues; and external situations, market needs and the myriad of potential issues. The overarching objective is to quickly transform new product ideas and concepts into new products and market realities or to address other opportunities if the ideas and concepts do not lead to success. The central challenge in the NPD process is an understanding and articulation of current and future market and customer needs and requirements. It is essential that NPD is linked with making improvements in the value chain, the value system, and the extended enterprise. These elements are discussed in the next section in which the perspective moves toward the solution.

Technological innovations often involve the invention of new technologies and the creation of new knowledge. Radical new solutions are based on innovative technologies that are near the state-of-the-art. They are usually based on proprietary positions that are protected by patents and/or trade secrets, i.e., intellectual property (IP). Radical technological innovations generally offer better possibilities for obtaining unique solutions, since new-to-the-world technologies are more difficult to duplicate without the knowledge and scientific know-how, the intellectual capital, and the proper validation(s) to assure success. IP often prevents others from enjoying the benefits of the technological breakthroughs for some period of time, perhaps as long as ten to twenty years.

The selection of effective development programs depends on the capabilities, skills, knowledge, desires, and resources of the corporation. The underpinnings include requirements, mandates, and standards of the business environment and the existing technologies, products, and processes. Program selection includes methods, processes, and analytical techniques that link technological innovation, product development, and process improvement to the objectives and strategies of the enterprise.

Solution in the context of the development of the value system and the enterprise

The solution set includes the selection and inclusion of the primary elements of the value chain, value system, and the extended enterprise. It includes the internal elements of product development, production, marketing, logistics, and finance and the external elements of the value system and enterprise, especially the contributions of supply networks and related industries, and the pathways to customers' success. It explores the implications of the primary inputs such as products and services, and explores the applications of the solutions and the complementary products and services that are essential for the solutions to function properly and provide satisfaction and success.

The value chain generally provides the internal mechanisms (functions) necessary to make the solutions valuable and beneficial. Manufacturing is typically viewed to be the central requirement for producing the products and having sufficient inventory available. Production may also include delivering the information and other software necessary for proper use of the products. Operations may include the support service for installation and repair and maintenance. The value chain includes the marketing efforts to build awareness and create acceptance. It also includes the management of distribution channels and the logistics to get the products and services to the customers. Logistics and transportation are necessary get products to customers either directly or through channels. They are also necessary for taking back defective goods and delivering replacement parts. Finance provides cash flow to pay the bills and it controls the flow of money.

The value delivery system includes the direct involvement of the external contributors and recipients. It includes the inputs to the producer's operations and the primary outputs to one's customers. It also includes support linkages with complementary products, the interactions by stakeholders, and the external infrastructure.

Combined they offer the means and mechanisms to complete the requirements to create the solution.

Strategic leaders are the primary decision makers. They orchestrate the development of the elements of value system and extended enterprise that contribute to producing the necessary outcomes that make solutions real. They choose what is to be included in the value chain, the parts of the internal management systems, and what is to be done by others, i.e., part of the value system. Of course, competition also plays a role in determining how the solution plays out in the business world and the results obtained. However, the company's strategic leaders are the people who decide the parameters as they relate to one's own enterprise.

The development includes identifying all salient requirements necessary to make the solution whole. This is followed by determining what is to be done in-house (value chain) and what is to be done by others (value system and the extended enterprise). In the complex world of the twenty-first century, mapping out all of the elements and determining who is to do what elements is a daunting task. It can be done systematically by expanding outward from the value chain to incorporate all of the players in the extended enterprise. After each contributor is identified or determined, then its roles and responsibilities have to be structured according to whether it is a direct or indirect participant and how it fits into the value system or the extended enterprise.

Direct contributors like suppliers and distributors have less freedom to act on their own and their actions may have to be specified to fit the requirements of the solution. They provide important parts of the solution and their contributions often must be orchestrated to a significant degree. If they are unable to contribute to the solution in an appropriate fashion, they should be replaced or their roles modified. On the other hand, for those contributors whose roles are independent of direct control, it is incumbent upon the strategic leaders to build or enhance the relationships with such entities so that positive outcomes are obtained. Most of the entities of the extended enterprise involve independent or semi-independent relationships. The contributions of related industries (complementors) are a primary example. They may be key contributors, but they are usually engaged in their own enterprises and may only have tangential interests in supporting the solution unless it has identifiable benefits for them. For example, Symantec Corporation (Norton) provides virus protection for PCs that is essential for their proper functioning, but its contributions are based on its business model and not those of the PC manufacturers.

Upon defining what the key contributors do and the benefits derived, it is essential that each is integrated into the solution set to the extent possible. While there are often only limited actions that can be taken to incorporate independent entities, simply knowing about the importance of such contributors and their contributions help strategic leaders shape the solution set. In such situations strategic leaders have to ensure that the solution set is complete. Creating formal or informal partnerships, alliances, and other such arrangements is an effective way to align the strategies and actions of the outside contributors to complete the salient aspects of the solution set.

The creation and construction of Disneyland and Disney World are good examples of the requisite interactions and interrelationships of a solution set. Walt Disney was one of the most successful entrepreneurs in U.S. history. He had the insights and imagination to create leisure experiences, which helped people to escape from the challenges and difficulties of everyday life. Leveraging the great success of his cartoon characters and films, especially Steamboat Willie (the main character was renamed Mickey Mouse) which was first released in November 1928, Disney worked tirelessly to upgrade his short cartoon clips into full feature movies. From the earliest days of his ventures, Disney understood that people wanted solutions, not just products or services. He spared no expense in creating the best outcomes with the highest quality possible. For instance, the movie Fantasia almost bankrupted the company in 1940, but Disney made it the best of its kind. Disney continued to elevate his films from low-end shorts to full length mainstream movies. He realized that people went to the movies during the 1930s and 1940s to bring excitement and joy into their lives. They wanted comfort and out-of-the-ordinary entertainment. At the time many movie theaters were among the only air-conditioned buildings, thus providing additional benefits of escaping the heat during hot summer days. Disney knew that the solution involved the whole experience and the residual effects of feeling wonderful after the end of the movie. He understood that success was not based only on producing products that would generate short-term profits, but on creating IP that would endure for decades. Moreover, he linked his enterprises together. Success in the movies led to successes in other ventures. He leveraged his movie properties to produce television programs and theme parks in the 1950s and 1960s. And his subsequent ventures reinforced the successes of his movies making characters, like Mickey Mouse and Donald Duck, great attractions.

His theme parks were great successes based on the whole Disney enterprise; first in California with Disneyland and then in Florida with Disney World. In both situations, Disney decided what he wanted to include as part of his value chain and what he would let others do to support the solutions for his customers. Disney was not always perfect. In a few situations he did not have the full picture in mind, i.e., the total solution when he made some of the earlier decisions. For example, in building Disneyland he failed to acquire enough land for future expansion and a lot of the long-term opportunities were lost to others who built hotels and restaurants adjacent to his theme park. He made sure that would not happen in Florida. When he decided to build Disney World, Disney purchase significantly more land than necessary to keep potential competitors or challengers far from his establishment. Having land, buildings, and IP were not sufficient to create the total solution at Disney World. There were insufficient people in the local area (Orlando, FL) to generate the cash flow necessary to ensure that such a grandiose theme park would be successful. Disney knew that quasi-solutions with just products and services (theme parks) were inadequate without the contributions from many other entities and participants. Most of the potential customers, especially those living in the cities in the Northeast, Midwest, Northwest, Europe, and Japan, had to travel great distances to get to Orlando. Disney needed travel agents to spread the word and encourage people to go to Disney World. So, Disney built relationships with the airlines, especially Delta Airlines, to make flights more available and affordable. Disney also ensured that rental cars were available and affordable. And the story goes on. Disney created an extended enterprise that reached around the world.

The great genius of Walt Disney and his brother Roy, who handled the business side of the enterprises, included a dedication to designing and developing the complete package, structuring the means and mechanisms for the total solution, deploying it efficiently and effectively, and providing the best possible outcomes at the highest quality. They understood that value creation and value delivery are the essential ingredients in achieving success, not just having low cost structures or making money. Making one's customers successful, and in this example happy and excited, were also keys to success. Moreover, Disney realized that families were the dominant customer-type and that providing children with defect-free experiences would result in repeat visits and outstanding word of mouth endorsements. Well-satisfied customers would pull other customers toward Disney's incredible solutions; ones that leveraged all of the assets and capabilities of the company.

Since the passing of the Disney brothers, the company has continued to enjoy the benefits of their contributions. Moreover, the company has even leveraged the contributions of its seeming competitors in the Orlando area. Orlando is now one of the largest tourist attractions in the world. People go there to visit numerous theme parks including Disney World, SeaWorld, and Universal Studios. While Disney has to share some of the cash flow with its competitors, the overall number of visitors to central Florida has expanded dramatically, enhancing the rewards for all of the contributors to Orlando enterprises.

Deployment of the solution

Deployment is a critical element of the solution process, because without applications and use a solution is just a theoretical concept without contributions, improvements, and rewards. Similar to the constructs of strategic planning and strategy formulation, unless there are actions and outcomes through implementation and execution, the upstream planning activities are meaningless and do not create value. Strategies create value when they are implemented and executed properly. The same is true about solutions. They have to be deployed properly to realize the gains and benefits and achieve positive outcomes. Deployment involves delivering value to customers, stakeholders, and society.

Value delivery is the conversion of inputs into more valuable outputs that are economically viable, socially beneficial, and appropriate in terms of the driving forces, strategic logic, and the specifications of the solution. Value delivery involves the expression of solutions in the realities of the world. It involves actions and transactions as materials and energy are converted into parts, components, and goods that become end products purchased by customers who exchange their valuable resources to acquire the solutions necessary to satisfy their objectives, needs and desires.

Deployment necessitates an integrated approach for producing, delivering, and supporting solutions. This also includes the complementary products and services of the associated related industries. From an internal perspective, deployment generally involves operations management that integrates the elements of the solutions into a comprehensive framework, in which the elements can be implemented on a concurrent basis. The key attributes include customer-derived value, speed, flexibility, high quality, reliability, cost-effectiveness, and effective utilization of scarce resources.

The principal aims are to create and deliver solutions that meet or exceed customer needs and expectations, maximize the performance of the management system and enterprise, and minimize the negative impacts on the external business environment.[23] Value delivery involves all of the processes for effectively managing the flow of materials and finished goods, information and relationships from the origins of the supply networks to end-of-life considerations using a systems perspective to achieve a high level of performance.

In the conventional sense, deployment involves the diffusion of the solution into the market spaces and society. Solutions are delivered through actions and transactions that are sustained over time through connections between the upstream and downstream entities of the extended enterprises and the relationships between the parties and people thereof.[24] The elements include creating awareness in the market spaces and business world about the solutions and their elements. People have to receive information about the solutions and accept that they are viable and beneficial. Unlike the traditional marketing approaches that focus on persuasion, effective deployment depends on communicating the whole story in the most forthcoming ways that convince people that the solution is of the kind and quality that they seek. Moreover, strategic leaders ensure that the evidence provided is validated and the claims are honest and open to scrutiny.

Solutions are intended for well-defined customers and specific markets segments. Thus, there are potential users who should not engage in the use of a particular solution for various reasons. For example, potential users may be too young, as in case of alcohol. They may not have sufficient knowledge and capabilities, as in the case of driving a car without a license, and they may not understand the negative elements, as in the use of asbestos. There are thousands of other examples, too numerous to specify. It is incumbent among strategic leaders to assure that the right people are the intended users of the solutions and they are the ones that have access to them. The whole notion of a solution relies on having the best solution set, the best systems, the best structure(s), and the best relationships. It involves minimizing risks and potential liabilities by avoiding the unknown traps that turn great successes in dismal failures. For example, Toyota's difficulties in 2010 with inputs from suppliers of brakes have resulted in recalls and a loss of prestige and market capitalization.[25]

Deployment involves paying attention to external context as the solution becomes more widely available. Again, strategic leaders have to be mindful that countervailing forces may develop in response to the deployment of the solution. These are generally forces that were either latent or ones that did not exist prior to the introduction of the solution. While solutions are intended to be holistic and inclusive of all forces and considerations, there is always the potential for negative reactions. Strategic leaders often examine the competitors for counter actions, but these are to be expected. Countervailing forces are mainly ones that are exhibited in the market spaces or the business environment, usually by stakeholders who may have been left out of the loop or who have positions that were not originally contemplated. They may be individuals or groups who oppose the solution on ethical or environmental grounds. Such situations often result in negative views when the strategic leaders believed they would receive positive ones. For example, Shell Oil touted its approaches pertaining to sustainability. While Shell has received some good feedback, it also has detractors who believe Shell's approach is simply a marketing campaign. This example does not suggest that Shell Oil has failed to develop new solutions or that it is not genuine in its strategies to develop sustainable technologies, but it does indicate that strategic leaders have to be mindful of the potential for reactions and countervailing forces.

Reflections

Solutions are based on context and developed for the benefits of recipients. They are made possible through understanding what is desirable based on insights and imagination and by aligning the contributions of the whole enterprise toward positive ends. Strategic leaders use their innovativeness and that of the organizations and enterprises to create solutions that are difficult to duplicate and that incorporate the essential elements for success. Innovativeness is about creating extraordinary value and developing outstanding solutions that enrich customers and stakeholders, in particular, and the whole enterprise and society.

Solutions are based on the intellectual capital, capabilities, resources, and strategic positions of the whole enterprise, not just the internal dimensions of the business units. Strategic leaders focus their attention on creating and delivering the best solutions and providing customers and stakeholders with the success they desire. The focus is also on ensuring stability and creating an environment of well-being and success across the full spectrum of the enterprise. Crafting solutions through innovativeness is a continuum. It is based on the reality that as the world becomes more complicated entities and strategic leaders must become more sophisticated. FSL embraces realities and creates more value and better solutions through cutting-edge leadership and management.

Notes

1. The Ethyl Corporation was a joint venture between General Motors and Standard Oil of New Jersey.
2. W. Chan Kim and Renee Mauborgne, *Blue Ocean Strategy: How to Create Uncontested Market Space and Make Competition Irrelevant* (Boston, MA: Harvard Business School Press, 2005, pp186-187).
3. The Nestlé commitment to Africa, March 2005. www. Nestlé.com.
4. David L Rainey, *Sustainable Business Development: Inventing the Future through Strategies, Innovation and Leadership* (Cambridge, UK: Cambridge University Press, 2006, pp176-179).
5. Id.

6. David L Rainey, *Enterprise-wide Strategic Management: Achieving Sustainable Success through Leadership, Strategies and Value Creation* (Cambridge, UK: Cambridge University Press, 2010, pp45-49).
7. Id.
8. Arnoldo Hax and Dean Wilde II, *the delta project: discovering new sources of profitability in networked economy* (New York, NY: PALGRAVE, 2001, p11). Arnoldo Hax is the Alfred P. Sloan Professor of Management at MIT. Dean Wilde II is founder and chairman of Dean and Company.
9. Id, pp10-11
10. David L Rainey, *Sustainable Business Development: Inventing the Future through Strategies, Innovation and Leadership*, p178.
11. TQM is based on a systematic, integrated, consistent methodology involving the entire organization and its enterprise. It emphasizes customer satisfaction in the broadest sense and strives for continuous improvement in every aspect of the system. TQM emphasizes not only correcting defects but preventing them in the first place. Defects and variations to customer specifications are seen as losses and the primary objective is to eliminate losses and waste.
12. W. Edwards Deming, *Out of the Crisis* (Cambridge MA: MIT Press, 1982, 1986, 2000, ppix-x)
13. Id, p141.
14. J. M. Juran, *Managerial Breakthrough* (New York, NY: McGraw-Hill, 1964).
15. Hap Arnold became a five star general during World War II and was head of the Eighth Air Force, which was responsible for the strategic bombing of Nazi Germany.
16. David L Rainey, *Product Innovation: Leading Change through Integrated Product Development* (Cambridge, UK: Cambridge University Press, 2005, p580). The graphic is an adaptation of a sophisticated process for designing and developing state-of-the-art new products.
17. US Steel was a market share leader in the US steel industry; Radio Corporation of America (RCA) was a leader in radio and television; Atlantic & Pacific Tea Company (A&P) was a leader in food retailing in the 1950s; and American Telegraph & Telephone Company (AT&T) was a leaders in telecommunications.
18. Id, pp136-137.
19. Andrew S. Grove, *Only the Paranoid Survive: How to Exploit The Crisis Points That Challenge Every Company and Career* (New York: NY: Currency and Doubleday, 1996, pp51-52).
20. Id, p127.
21. Id, pp5-49.
22. Id, p10.
23. David L Rainey, *Enterprise-wide Strategic Management: Achieving Sustainable Success through Leadership, Strategies and Value Creation*, pp23-49.
24. Id.
25. Problems at Toyota, JAL taint Japan Inc's image. http://news yahoo.com/s/ap/20100131/ap_on_bi_ge/as_battered_japn_inc

References

Deming, W. Edwards (1982) *Out of the Crisis.* Cambridge MA: MIT Press.

Grove, Andrew S. (1996) *Only the Paranoid Survive: How to Exploit The Crisis Points That Challenge Every Company and Career.* New York: NY: Currency and Doubleday.

Hax, Arnoldo and Dean Wilde II (2001) *the delta project: discovering new sources of profitability in networked economy.* New York, NY: PALGRAVE.

Juran, J. M. (1964) *Managerial Breakthrough.* New York, NY: McGraw-Hill.

Kim, W. Chan and Renee Mauborgne (2005) *Blue Ocean Strategy: How to Create Uncontested Market Space and Make Competition Irrelevant.* Boston, MA: Harvard Business School Press.

Rainey, David L (2010) *Enterprise-wide Strategic Management: Achieving Sustainable Success through Leadership, Strategies and Value Creation.* Cambridge, UK: Cambridge University Press.

Rainey, David L (2006) *Sustainable Business Development: Inventing the Future through Strategies, Innovation and Leadership.* Cambridge, UK: Cambridge University Press.

Rainey, David L (2005) *Product Innovation: Leading Change through Integrated Product Development.* Cambridge, UK: Cambridge University Press.

5

Shaping Systems through Inclusiveness

Introduction

Creating an inclusive and effective management system is one of the most important elements of leading change and sustaining success. In Chapter 1, some of the most important management systems and constructs were presented. The value chain and value system were introduced and detailed. Further discussions on value delivery were included in the previous chapter as well. The discussions served as an overview of what "systems thinking" involves and how systems have evolved over the last fifty years. Today, most global corporations and small and medium size enterprises (SMEs) have elaborate management systems that provide strategic leaders, operational management, professionals, and practitioners with the processes and connections they need to manage their organizations and enterprises. Yet, many of the management systems that strategic leaders use may not be adequate for handling the complex forces and requirements for achieving success. Contemporary management systems have to be more sophisticated, far-reaching, and dynamic.

Strategic leaders form, shape, and implement the management systems and constructs that are used to drive systemic change and provide sustainable solutions. In sophisticated global corporations, strategic leaders have embedded management systems that link the strategic aspects of the company and business units with the external business environment and the operational aspects of the value systems and value chains. Each lower level is really a subset of the previous level and linked to the whole enterprise. The overall framework provides a holistic business model of the management system(s) and how they relate to each other on a horizontal level across the enterprise as well as the vertical structure of the hierarchical relationships of the organization.

System integration is a critical element for achieving sustainable success as businesses depend more and more on the capabilities and resources of their extended enterprises for realizing opportunities, achieving outstanding performance, eliminating difficulties and vulnerabilities, and creating true value. The rapidity of change has shifted the emphasis from mainly focusing on the capital assets, physical resources and core competencies to developing and deploying the intellectual capital and capabilities of the embedded management system and the whole business enterprise. While internal competencies may have driven decision making during the twentieth century, external context and the connections and contributions of all of the entities in the business enterprise are the critical factors that drive decision making and actions. Today, sophisticated corporations and SMEs are integrated and interconnected with the external entities and use all of their capabilities and contributions to create powerful strategic positions that outperform customer and stakeholder expectations and exceed the power of their competitors. In this context, strategic leaders have to embrace full-spectrum strategic leadership (FSL) and use cutting-edge management constructs and techniques.

This chapter presents several management constructs for developing, enhancing, and deploying management systems. It is intended to provide strategic leaders the key elements for establishing and using management systems. This chapter includes the following main topics:

- Cutting-edge leadership and management constructs
- Selected perspectives about management systems and inclusiveness

Cutting-Edge Leadership and Management Constructs

The embedded management system

The embedded management system is a multi-tiered management system that includes all levels of leadership and management within a business organization that are strategically and operationally integrated. The intent is the creation of a cohesive organizational force that connects all of the leaders, managers, and employees so that everyone is moving in the same direction and acting in unison. It necessitates interactive relationships between all of the contributors and recipients across the business enterprise. Strategic leaders provide direction, guidance, resources, and oversight. They ensure that the strategies, solutions, systems, processes, and activities at the operating level meet the corporate and business unit objectives and fulfill all of the mandates, requirements, and expectations. Operational responsibilities are delegated to lower-level management, functional managers, and supervisors who are empowered to achieve the desired outcomes. Strategic leaders maintain overall control and provide oversight. The relationships are built on contributions, cooperation, coordination, and communication. Trust is an essential element for having solid relationships. Inclusiveness is the glue. The embedded management system includes:

- Corporate level (C-level): Corporate strategic management focusing on the strategic direction and strategic positions related to the business environment and the markets spaces.
- Strategic business unit (SBU) level: Business unit management focusing on developing and implementing business strategies and actions for leading change and transitioning and transforming the SBUs into more capable and successful entities.
- Operating level: Operating or value delivery management focusing on serving the markets, satisfying customers and stakeholders, providing solutions, executing strategies, and achieving the desired performance and results.

C-level strategic leaders are the corporate officers and strategic leaders responsible for the whole company and its strategic direction, governance, performance, and sustainable success. SBU strategic leaders are responsible for their assigned business units, divisions, or subsidiaries. They craft, develop, and implement the strategies, actions, alignments, and linkages between the strategic management of the SBUs and the core operating level at the base of the embedded management system. They lead and achieve outcomes based on the direction, commands, and control of the corporate level. SBU leaders fulfill missions, strategic roles, and specific responsibilities. Strategic leaders focus mainly on the future of the organization and its management constructs and on ensuring success. From an FSL perspective, the SBU level is the integrating element between corporate executives and the managers and supervisors of the operations and functional areas. The operating level management focuses on the present and near term and on realizing objectives, performing the requisite activities and exceeding requirements.

Functional managers concentrate on the existing conditions, mandates, requirements, and expectations in terms of the markets, production, product innovation, finance, and the overall organization. They focus on inputs, conversion processes, outputs, and results. Operating level managers and supervisors use management constructs that produce positive outcomes and the expected performance through well-defined processes. The basic management constructs for managing the operating level focus on the resources deployed and the organizational capabilities engaged in converting inputs into outputs.

Designing and establishing management systems is one of the primary and most critical responsibilities of strategic leaders. In most situations, the management systems exist in some form. There are generally the strategic management system and an operating system. The former involves the corporate and business unit levels and the latter involves the functional areas. In addition, there may be several other management systems, especially at the operating level dealing with specific areas like quality management, environment, health and safety (EH&S) management, risk management, energy management, and lean production.

Strategic leaders and functional managers make incremental improvements to the existing systems to enhance value creation and value delivery. Incremental improvements typically address the needs and expectations articulated by the external entities of the value system. They involve transitions to an improved state. These are generally responses and modifications to short-term pressures from customers, stakeholders, and competitors or concerted efforts to stay ahead of change. Most of the requisite improvements are readily apparent because the forces of change within the business environment and market spaces are well known to the strategic leaders and managers, and astute strategic leaders and managers respond accordingly. For instance, marketing managers generally provide information, insights, analyses, and determinations about customer needs. Technical managers understand the advantages and disadvantages of the current technologies and products and have a sense of the opportunities and pressing needs for improvements. Finance managers determine the relationship between risks and rewards and calculate the benefits of proposed investments using financial models and theories (discounted cash flow and internal rate of return). Production supervisors discern the organization's capabilities to meet the operating requirements. Making simple improvements and affecting transitions in the operating management system are the desired choices because they tend to have a natural fit with the prevailing situation(s); i.e., the actions are logical. They are typically good answers as long as the dominant technologies and product designs do not change significantly. Moreover, the business environment has to be stable with relatively few major changes so that the customers and stakeholders continue to want and/or accept the existing solutions and outcomes provided.

Periodically, depending on the rate of change in the business environment, strategic leaders have to make transformations to the existing management system(s), especially when external pressures and turbulence dictate new requirements or ways for value creation and value delivery. Transformations are more far-reaching and difficult than management constructs to understand, create, develop, institute and manage. They are driven by external forces that are outside of the normal purview of the SBUs and operating systems. Transformations involve the strategic elements based on new phenomena that cannot be addressed incrementally or piecewise. Such revolutionary changes are less prevalent than evolutionary changes, but they are more profound. They typically occur when the business environment becomes turbulent and less predictable with high levels of uncertainties due to huge changes in the social, political, economic, and/or technological forces. For instance, if the technological forces are driven by disruptive technologies, especially new-to-the-world ones, then strategic leaders have to engage in transformations to stay ahead or abreast of the changes in the business environment and market spaces. Transformations focus on creating, developing, and deploying new solutions, new systems, and new means and mechanisms for leading organizations and their business enterprises. They include inventing and developing new technologies and products, creating new knowledge, developing new competencies and capabilities, and crafting innovative management systems. For example, in the age of digital cell phones, strategic leaders at Motorola had to reinvent its related business units to be able to compete in the global landscape of digital technology. The old ways were obsolete and even the inventor of the cell phone had to reinvent itself to stay at the cutting edge, otherwise it would have become irrelevant. Transformations are based on the insightfulness, imagination, and strategic actions of strategic leaders who want their companies and SBUs to exceed expectations and to outperform peers and competitors in the global struggles to achieve extraordinary performance and sustainable success. Astute strategic leaders preempt the driving forces and institute strategic innovations before others do so and become more sophisticated in their endeavors.

Business model innovation is one of the most important ways to make such transformations in the management systems of the whole company or the SBUs. Business models delineate how the element of the systems and the extended enterprise are constructed and linked to provide and deliver the best solutions. Business model innovation is discussed in more detail in Chapter 8.

The essential constructs pertaining to systems thinking

Successful strategic leaders use a myriad of cutting-edge leadership and management constructs that facilitate how to develop and/or exploit opportunities for achieving success. Some of the most important ones are: (1) employing FSL; (2) creating vision and strategic direction; (3) leading change, inspiring people, and building unique relationships; (4) creating value and positives outcomes through solutions, systems, operations, and value networks; (5) improving the knowledge, skills, and capabilities of the organization and developing fully integrated enterprises; and (6) instituting and applying far-reaching and sophisticated constructs like sustainable business development (SBD) and corporate social responsibility (CSR). Figure 5.1 depicts the networks of cutting-edge leadership and management constructs pertaining to systems integration and inclusiveness.

They include more conventional management constructs like strategic management, quantitative methods, financial management, risk management, supply networks, logistics, customer relationship management, lean business practices, and international competitiveness. They are interrelated and essential for achieving sustainable success. The end game is sustainable success.

The underpinnings include external context, philosophies, principles, values, openness, transparency, accountability, qualities, leadership development, and dual-sided perspectives. The focus is not on managing, but on leading change through strategic thinking, strategies, insightfulness, innovativeness, solutions, systems integration, inclusiveness, people, relationships and sustainable success. In particular, FSL is about leading the organization through vision, insights, imagination, conviction, courage, and fortitude as discussed in Chapter 1.

The primary constructs and main considerations discussed herein are:

- *Strategic leadership:* Leading change, creating value, inspiring people, making people successful, and creating solutions. It includes using the foundations of strategic leadership and FSL to create a better world.

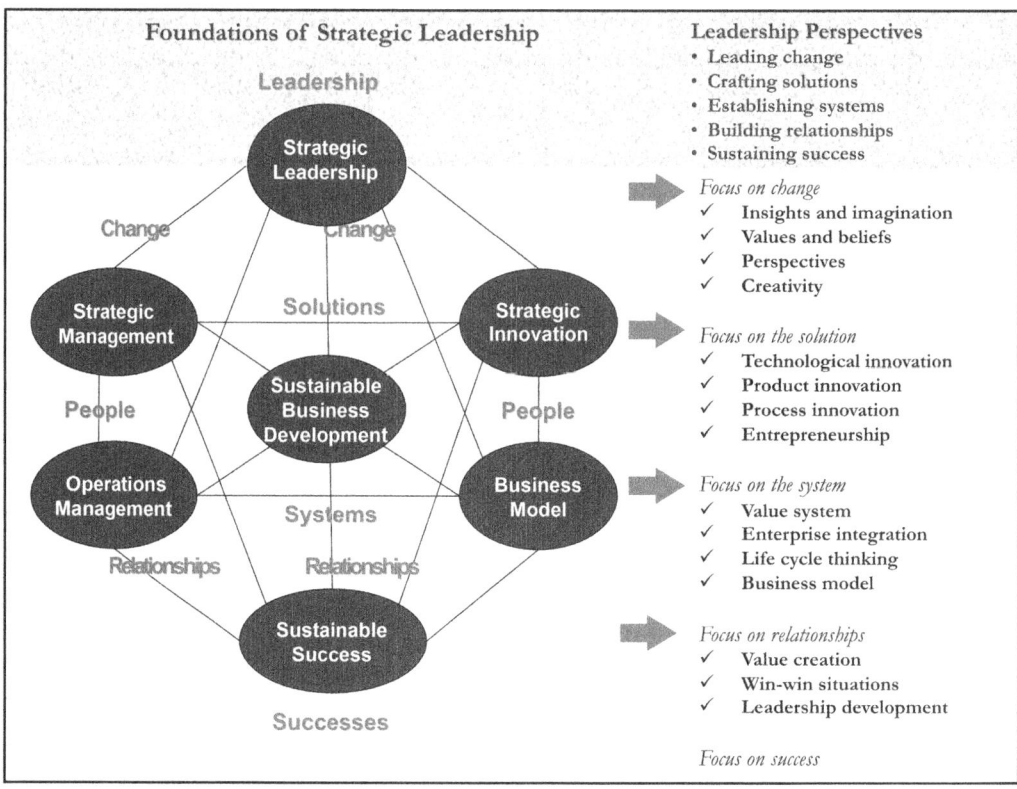

Figure 5.1 Cutting-edge leadership and management constructs for systems integration.

- *Sustainable business development:* Making dramatic improves and positive changes to the full scope of solutions, systems, relationships, and linkages with the supply networks, customers, stakeholders, and support service providers and eliminating the negative effects and impacts.
- *Strategic management:* Identifying and managing the needs and requirements of the business environment, analyzing and understanding markets, customers, stakeholders, opportunities, and challenges, and formulating and implementing strategies and actions.
- *Strategic innovation:* Acquiring the new knowledge, capabilities, and resources, creating new technologies, products, processes, and businesses, and exploiting the capabilities and resources of the organization to produce superior solutions and to deliver exceptional value and outcomes.
- *Operations management:* Creating and managing the operating systems, linking the extended enterprise with its partners and alliances, and ensuring that the performance meets or exceeds the expectations of all contributors and recipients.
- *Business model:* Creating a holistic and unique framework of the SBU and the extended enterprise based on the full scope of all of the critical entities that are necessary to create and provide the solutions. An effective business

model integrates all of the forces and entities that are driving change and providing opportunities for success.
- ***Sustainable success:*** Envisioning what the corporation and/or business unit has to be or what it has to do to achieve ongoing success. It includes creating a realistic vision for the future, leading change to realize the implicit and explicit solutions, transforming the systems and structures to implement necessary actions, and measuring ongoing results.

The embedded elements mean that the cutting-edge management constructs like FSL, enterprise-wide strategic management (ESM), SBD, strategic innovation, and business model innovation are interrelated and work in unison, as depicted in Figure 5.1 It also means that strategic responsibilities such as CSR, ethics, accountability, customer and stakeholder responsiveness, and shareholder and employee rewards are critical parts and key considerations of each of the management constructs.

FSL implies that incumbents are multidisciplinary leaders, generalists, strategists, multi-specialists, and visionaries who have the knowledge and skills to understand and manage companies, business units, enterprises, organizations, and the inherent elements therein. They are leaders who can analyze issues, problems, opportunities, and challenges, make the appropriate strategic decisions, take the proper actions and obtain appropriate outcomes. It implies that they have the courage and moral fortitude to lead and inspire people and take care of them. Strategic leaders have an expressed duty of care for their businesses and what they touch. FSL is about being competent, prepared, committed, and courageous in leading and managing all aspects of sophisticated business organizations and their systems. It is not about being a master manipulator of finance or a clever marketing type, but about being a person who is multi-talented, holistic in thought, people-oriented, in-touch with reality, and willing to walk the talk.

ESM includes strategic thinking, high-level strategic management, strategic business planning, change management, risk management, decision-making, and the integration of the full spectrum of the business reality based on spatial and temporal perspectives.[1] This includes strategic perspectives pertaining to the natural environment, the social/human world, and the business environment with all of the social, economic, technological, environmental, market, and competitive considerations and implications. Strategic management includes strategic direction, strategic formulation and implementation, and governance of the company. This also includes SBUs, their strategic management systems, and the value systems with their operations and processes. ESM involves a holistic view that transforms last century's supply-and-demand thinking into a more sophisticated strategic management framework. Ultimately, ESM focuses on how strategic leaders create sustainable solutions that are based on the ethics and values, perspectives of the entire business enterprise, and solid relationships with people. It goes beyond just meeting the needs and expectations of producers and customers.

SBD is at the center because it directly links all of the management constructs. The interrelated entities of the networks involved form a holistic system in which leaders, people, strategy, solutions, systems, and relationships are essential elements for achieving sustainable success. SBD is the linchpin that provides the underlying logic and guiding force for ensuring that outcomes are balanced and that they meet the expectations of all of the social, economic, ethical, technological, and environmental dimensions.[2]

Strategic innovation involves the creation and development of new or enhanced solutions and systems. It includes integrated product development, technological innovation, technological entrepreneurship, radical innovation, value innovation and business model innovation. They involve creating extraordinary value through research and development (R&D), and technology and product developments and deployments. Technology and product developments play vital roles in developing solutions to social, economic, environmental, and market-related problems and in discovering and developing new opportunities. They provide the means and mechanisms to fundamentally change the enterprise in its quest for achieving excellence and extraordinary results. Strategic innovation implies positive developments and dramatic improvements, not simply changes for the sake of change. As previously discussed, most marketing schemes and product changes are not innovations at all but simply a repackaging of the old versions to make them appear to be better. Technology is a complex array of the art, science, engineering, devices, methods, and know-how applied in a beneficial manner to create and affect solutions. It can take the form of products and processes (hardware and software) used to create solutions. The view of technology has expanded beyond what is embodied within the products and processes to include the constructs for creating beneficial outcomes. The Internet is the prime example. It is a multifaceted integration of far-flung computers, servers, telecommunications devices and software to create networks, information storage and retrieval systems, and protocols that require the cooperation, support and management of diverse corporations and other organizations on a worldwide basis. These topics are discussed in more detail in Chapter 7.

Operations management on an extended enterprise basis involves how the organization can maximize value creation and its operational positions through knowledge, intellectual capital, competencies, capabilities and resources, and leveraging those of its allies, strategic partners and value networks. It starts with the whole and works down to the particular. It is more expansive than conventional operations management models. It involves creating value through the integration of the entire enterprise and building positive and enduring relationships with all of the participants.

A business model is a conceptual combination of entities and patterns of interrelationships and interfaces that are linked together in formal and informal arrangements based on mutually acceptable and value-producing propositions that are guided by the strategies and actions of the entities and people involved. A business model is a more definitive form of a strategic management framework that generally pertains to strategy implementation. The concept of a business model has gained wider acceptance in recent years by strategic leaders through application and practice. While a business model may be viewed as a mental model of how a business implements its strategies and engages in its business affairs, mental models often lack real world validation that is crucial for developing a true business model. A mental model may be viewed as a management construct that requires ongoing development and demonstration in the real world before it can become a fully articulated business model. A true business model reflects reality, and strategic leaders use it to lead change and manage business enterprises in the real world. One of the most important factors for truly creating a business model is the inclusion of all of the essential entities and elements and how they interact with each other to assure successful outcomes, i.e., inclusiveness. For instance, a financial or revenue model is not a true business model because it only considers the economic aspects; business models are holistic. A real-world business model is a company's or SBU's unique way of combining internal and external dimensions into a fully articulated, coherent, and collaborative management framework that stretches from the origins of the raw materials to the ends of the applications of the solutions provided by the producer/provider and its contributors with all of their positive and negative effects, implications, and impacts. It is defined by the scope of the enterprise and the boundaries thereof, and the relationships and contributions between the parties. It is also defined by the solutions and the actions of the organization and those of the value networks that support, enhance, and contribute to the positives and that mitigate the negatives.

Sustainable success is a multifaceted management construct that focuses both on radically improving the social, economic, technological, and environmental benefits and on significantly decreasing the cost structures and eliminating hidden defects, burdens and impacts. While most companies have historically concentrated on creating or improving management systems, technologies, products, services and processes, sustainable success requires strategic thinking beyond just the tangible realities of today by exploring the best means and mechanisms for assuring success in the future. While it is always difficult to define what the long term is, generally most strategic leaders have to explore the possibilities ten to twenty years in the future and be confident that their enterprises will continue to be successful. Sustainable success involves realizing the vision, the business objectives, the "lifestyle" of the enterprise and extraordinary performance, and ensuring the well-being of the whole business enterprise and all of the contributors and recipients thereof.

Cutting-edge leadership and management constructs are about the whole enterprise and all of the systems and processes that make the solutions possible. The total solution is derived by integrating all of the essential elements into a comprehensive value system based on the philosophical underpinnings of SBD and CSR from the strategic point of view and on effective and efficient operations management from the practical perspectives. It also requires a unique business model that ties together the solutions and systems. Embedding the system aspects into the solution set involves the integration of the entire extended enterprise and organization. Success comes from the whole, not the pieces. For instance, an electric coffee maker without electricity is worthless. The great challenge for strategic leaders is to design and develop the best solutions, to create the most appropriate and compelling systems possible, and to build enduring relationships across the extended enterprise(s). And, they must engage in strategic innovation to transform today's reality into tomorrow's successes.

Framing the Management Systems

Holistic perspectives in system design and development

Like most management constructs, systems thinking and system design are based on external context first, followed by developing and linking the internal elements. The external context includes the driving forces of change. Embedded within these driving forces are the opportunities and challenges for strategic leaders to realize their dreams and aspirations, to exceed customer, stakeholder and shareholder requirements and expectations, and to outperform their peers and competitors. While paying attention to threats and vulnerabilities is a valid concern, threats and vulnerabilities are often the results of inaction or the failure to be decisive, rather than the result of preordained situations. Threats can be opportunities if strategic leaders act on them from positive perspectives. Vulnerabilities are potential harms that may overcome the well-being of the business unit or enterprise, but they are usually due to the lack of insights and understandings about how the driving forces of change impact the investments, positions, and capabilities of the company and/or business units. Even wholesale changes to the underlying knowledge and technological underpinnings can be viewed as opportunities if strategic leaders take positive actions to move quickly into the new directions. The concept of destruction-creation suggests that most change mechanisms are coated with potential strategic advantages as well as negative implications. For example, corporate leaders at Honda during the mid-1990s had the insights to view the potential for rapid increases in petroleum prices as a way to gain market share and enhanced market positions if Honda focused on new solutions based on more fuel-efficient automobiles. Quite apropos, Honda called the new product, the Insight. The strategic leaders acted decisively and created hybrid drive technologies during a period when petroleum prices were low and were not considered to be a strategic issue by most of Honda's competitors, except Toyota.

Management systems are formal constructs for connecting the internal processes of the organization with the external dimensions. The traditional approach has been to link the internal functional areas and/or departments and their processes with the external entities and their interfaces with the business units. While such approaches simplify how management deals with reality, it is technically the opposite of what the real world expects, especially customers and stakeholders. The latter expect businesses to respond to their needs and expectations and to provide the best solutions possible through systems and structures that are based on the perceptions and realities of the external aspects. The external context and the perspectives of the people therein drive the design and development of the internal systems and processes.

Figure 5.2 depicts a simplified framework of a SBU's management system from an external perspective.[3] The cutting-edge framework is presented in a non-conventional, but more accurate approach of showing the elements of the business environment at the top and the business unit aspects at the bottom. It shows the market spaces at the center of the framework, which corresponds to the importance of markets and customers when creating a management system and a business model. After all, markets and

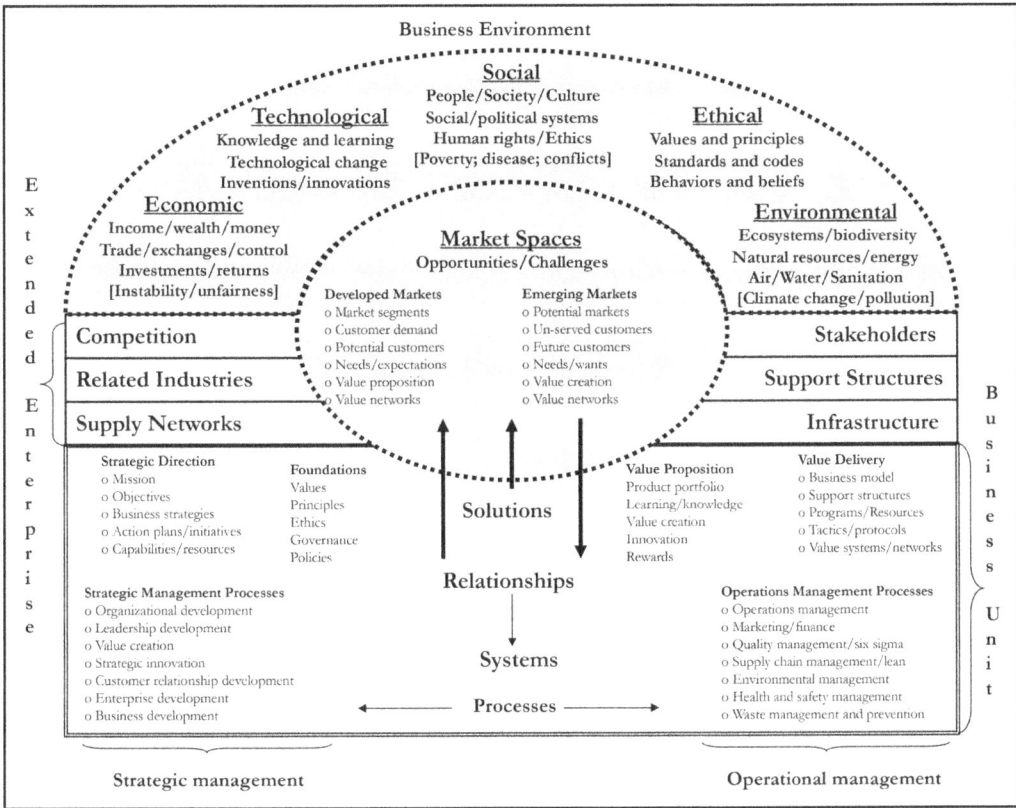

Figure 5.2 Framework of a business unit's system based on an external perspective.

customers are the critical factors for achieving success. They are the focus of strategy formulation and implementation and the critical driving forces and factors for the operating systems.

The framework is underpinned by an integrated perspective of the social, economic, and environmental aspects with the addition of the ethical and technological ones. The three former ones are often referred to as the "*triple bottom line*" (TBL) as John Elkington, founder of Sustainability in the UK, describes in his book on the TBL.[4] Elkington's insights about the TBL are profound, but they generally examined as separate elements. In the context of ESM, SBD and CSR, the next extension of the notion is the *Integrated Top of the Line*. This is a more holistic perspective that includes discovering, designing, developing, demonstrating, and delivering the means and mechanisms to be in synch with all of the elements of the business environment and market spaces and to achieve comprehensive outcomes and exceed all expectations. The social, economic, and environmental aspects should be considered in unison. They are the primary factors in determining strategies, solutions and systems, not secondary or tangential ones. Moreover, it is imperative that the ethical and technological aspects be included and integrated into the grand view of the present reality and the prospects for the future, since both are essential elements for creating and delivering solutions.

Generally, the best overall time horizon is to use fifteen years, plus or minus five years. The center of the framework is the market spaces that exist or may exist within a reasonable time horizon.[5] Market spaces include the well-established markets for the prevailing products and services and the emerging markets in developing countries. The latter includes the people who have marginal incomes and few financial resources. There are billions of people around the world who may become valuable customers over the next ten to twenty years as their incomes rise, especially people in China, India and Brazil. Assuming that the middle-class people of the world are the key driver for the consumption of products from businesses, the pressure on resources is expected to increase dramatically over the next decade. Homi Kharas and Geoffrey Gertz of the Wolfensohn Center for Development at Brookings estimate that the global middle class is expected to increase from 1.8 billion in 2009 to 3.25 billion in 2020.[6] They suggest:[7]

> Today, 1.8 billion people in the world are middle class, or 28 percent of the global population. About half of these people live in developed economies, with another fifth found in Brazil, Russia, India, and China—the so-called emerging BRIC economies. Less than 2 percent of the world's population is rich by our definition; a significant majority, 70 percent, is poor.
>
> Our scenario shows that over the coming twenty years the world evolves from being mostly poor to mostly middle class. 2022 marks the first year more people in the world are middle class than poor. By 2030, 5 billion people—nearly two thirds of global population—could be middle class.

Sophisticated strategic leaders think about the market spaces based on what can be, not just what the current demand is. There are profound changes going on, and astute strategic leaders examine reality from the broadest and most inclusive perspectives possible. They think out of the box and they are the architects of the solutions and systems. One of the best examples of making dramatic change is the success of Walmart during its early years. Sam Walton established his enterprise to serve the needs of the common person by making quality products more affordable. Rather than focusing on people with high disposable incomes, Walton concentrated on low-income customers with marginal funds. Moreover, in pricing products he asked the counterintuitive question: how low can Walmart's margins be and still make a reasonable profit? His competitors generally asked: how high can the margins be and we can still sell the products? Walton's instincts and insights served him well. Whereas people at the bottom of the economic ladder have limited financial resources, there are huge numbers of such people. And, such people in the past often paid the highest prices for their goods because they typically purchased products at small stores in small quantities. Walton understood that if Walmart had low prices, it would attract the vast majority of such people. Moreover, customers would seek out the stores with the best value for their money. While the Walmart story is complex, and the company has evolved significantly from the days of Walton, his underlying philosophies of fairness, balance and value have contributed to the growth of one of the world's largest enterprises.

Most conventional value systems and business models focus on the established markets and producing revenues and profits. Customers with disposable income are viewed as the sources of revenues and cash flows, and the market factors are well known and are assumed to be stable. Such markets are usually sub-divided into discrete market segments that are characterized in terms of demographics, customer demand, expected needs and wants, and competition, among other salient factors. Customer expectations are generally well established and the market conditions and trends are readily determined through analysis of the proliferation of data and information. Moreover, the value proposition for any given solution is generally articulated by both the customers and the providers of the solutions. It provides a sense of what is expected and expresses how valuable the solutions really are. There should be few, if any, missing key ingredients and customers should be typically satisfied with the basic aspects of the solutions. This is not to suggest that improvements are unnecessary or undesired, nor does it suggest that perfection has been obtained. Customers always want more value and fewer problems, but the overall conditions and trends are generally stable, and the associated management systems accommodate the requirements and fulfill the requisite expectations of the markets and customers. Of course, there are exceptions to the norm, especially during recessions when demand often drops significantly.

Emerging markets, especially in developing countries, are much more difficult to characterize properly. They are often fragmented with ill-defined conditions and trends. The market potential is often unclear and there is generally a lack of understanding and characterization of the market segments and their potential. Market demand is typically low or nonexistent, but the needs of the indigenous population, especially people at the bottom of the economic pyramid (BOP), are enormous.[8] Typically, there is a lack of information and data about the market potential and customer needs. Conventional marketing approaches are often inadequate because the situations in most emerging markets are much different than those in which standard marketing concepts were designed and developed. Moreover, marketing professionals are handicapped when using conventional approaches in emerging markets because most their underlying assumptions are invalid. For instance, marketing professionals often assume that people are able to receive messages through the media; therefore, they prepare marketing campaigns using conventional means and mechanisms like television, radio, newspapers, etc. However, in many developing countries the media reaches only a small minority of the population—the social and economic elites or those living in the capital city. There are numerous other concerns and problems. The value propositions are often fuzzy and difficult to interpret, and it is not exactly clear what is necessary to achieve success. Moreover, it is often hard to determine what the barriers and limitations are and what has to be done to craft appropriate solutions and create the right systems. It may be almost impossible for people to get to the established markets, the distribution channels and retail outlets, if they exist.

In both major categories, the extended enterprise is critical for developing the elements for the solutions and establishing the complete system for execution. The related industries (complementary products) of the extended enterprise are among the most crucial when determining what the systems aspects have to be. If the related industries provide some of the requisite ingredients for the complete solution, then the design of the management systems (value system in particular) can either provide the ingredients or have customers to rely on the related industries. For instance, it may be impossible for the producers of cell phone companies to provide the connections and services. In other cases, producers provide some of the hardware and depend on others to provide the installation services. For example, companies like Carrier Corporation often engage contractors as partners to provide some or all of the installation requirements. Solutions are the answers to the needs, wants and expectations. They go beyond the simple one-way links with customers and stakeholders through selling and delivering just products and services. They are combinations of the contributions of the entities of the value delivery system and the management system of the business unit(s).

The pivotal connections are the relationships between the parties. They are essential for ensuring success and what makes success possible. Moreover, solid relationships make the connections sustainable and unique. It may be easy to copy or duplicate products, but it is almost impossible to emulate relationships without having all of the tangible and intangible ingredients and emotional elements cemented together. Relationships with people and entities tie the systems with the markets and the extended enterprise.

System design and development is predicated on the solutions and the relationships among the contributors and recipients and how the value systems are connected. The next section provides some of the essential aspects systems design. The next chapter discusses some salient aspects about building relationships from the perspectives of strategic leaders.

Forming the management systems

From the highest levels of strategic leadership to the operational management, one of the most critical functions of a strategic leader is to determine the essential elements and processes of the management systems and how to integrate them into a comprehensive and well functioning system. In complex organizations, the systems are the means and mechanisms for the implementation of missions and strategies and the execution of the actions plans and activities. Strategic leaders are the architects of the management systems and the primary decision makers who establish what is to be done, how it is to be accomplished and who is responsible for the required outcomes. They form the big picture and lay out the requisite processes for achieving the desired results. The details are usually left to the persons who are directly involved in the execution.

In the ideal case, there should be one comprehensive, fully integrated management system including the strategic, operational, and functional levels with all special requirements fully integrated within the embedded system. Alternatively, as in the case of many organizations, there may be two distinct management systems; one focusing on the strategic management aspects and the other focusing on the operational and functional areas. In reality, most companies today have multiple management systems. While there is nothing inherently wrong with having numerous management systems or sub-systems, such approaches may cause fragmentation and management difficulties associated with systems integration. In certain cases, strategic leaders may believe that they are improving the focus on the specific areas by having a distinct system dedicated to a given area, such as quality management and environmental, health and safety management, but they may enhance outcomes in the selected areas at the expense of sub-optimizing others or the whole. It is often easy to make improvements in selected areas if senior management pays more attention or provides more resources to them. The improvements may justify the approaches, but in many situations someone or some other area suffers, resulting in new problems and subsequent compromises. It is imperative that strategic leaders ensure that all areas and requirements are fulfilled and successful. It is the whole that is critical for success, with attention provided to the parts and details in an integrated way. Moreover, strategic leaders must ensure that no one falls into the *either-or trap*. It involves making decisions in which only two options are presented and the decision makers have to select one. In many cases, both of the choices are based on compromises, and the end results are usually less than optimal from a systems point of view. The either-or choices may be the extremes or near the mid-point. Rather than trying to resolve all of the challenges, the choice often results in compromises in which no one is happy. For instance, in the old business world of the twentieth century, one of the most famous either-or traps was the dilemma between quality and costs. Many strategic leaders believed that high quality resulted in high costs and low costs would entail low quality. Strategic leaders were seemingly forced to decide what to focus on: quality or costs. They often took the either-or decisions rather than finding solutions that provided all of the attributes.

The strategic management process includes strategy formulation and implementation, organizational and leadership development, value creation, strategic innovation, customer relationship development, enterprise development, and business development. Each area focuses on critical strategic aspects that are crucial for long-term success. Strategy formulation involves analytical activities and strategic planning necessary to develop new or revised mission statements, formulate new business objectives and strategies, and decide upon the action plans and initiatives that set the stage for strategic implementation. Strategic implementation is the downstream side of the strategic management process that focuses on converting business strategies into high-level programs, desired outcomes, and sustainable success through systems, organizational structure, program design and development, and resource allocations.

Customer relationships management is one of the most critical requirements involving building connections and relationships with customers. This topic is cover in more detail in the next chapter. Customer and stakeholder success is essential if strategic leaders want to assure their own enduring success. It is often easy to obtain success in the present through concentrated efforts focused on short-term financial results, but unless there are commensurate rewards distributed to all of the contributors and recipients, especially customers, such situations tend to be unsustainable.

Establishing high-level processes that link the business unit with the entities of the extended enterprise is also a pivotal responsibility of strategic leaders. Such processes are situation-dependent and have to be based on the specifics involved. Nevertheless, it is critical that strategic leaders create the means and mechanisms to ensure the management systems are effectively tied to the all internal and external contributors and recipients.

Processes facilitate the flow of activities and map out what needs to be done so that there is a high degree of assurance that the proper actions are being carried out and the requisite outcomes are achieved. Processes are horizontal constructs that link activities and actions for converting inputs into outputs in a systematic way. They are most important when the activities tend to be repetitive and there are well established ways of executing the processes based on experience and optimization. However, processes are not always prescribed in detail and they usually have a high degree of flexibility and adaptability depending on the situation.

Process design and development

Process design and development involves the relentless pursuit of continuous improvements and/or dramatic outcomes with a focus on total satisfaction and sustainable success for customers, stakeholders, suppliers, distributors, employees, other contributors, recipients, and shareholders. This requires dedicated, committed and knowledgeable strategic leaders across the organization. Systems and process design and development focus on:

- Improving the effectiveness of the corporation and satisfying its constituencies.
- Identifying, analyzing and exploiting opportunities to realize the potential of the organization through innovative solutions.
- Creating and sustaining value across the enterprise.
- Developing solutions and the creative capabilities of the people.
- Instituting best processes and practices.
- Realizing the desired outcomes and extraordinary financial performance.
- Evaluating outcomes and improving ongoing performance.

Success is based on critical thinking and a predilection for action, especially focusing on being the best at creating outstanding solutions and developing systems for execution. It derives from the ongoing, never-ending quest for excellence.

Strategic processes run the gamut from selecting new businesses, developing new technologies, and creating new products to developing new leaders, enhancing organizational capabilities, and assuring the proper allocation of resources. They are based on the concepts of leading change through insightfulness and imagination, using innovativeness in designing and developing solutions, creating systems that are inclusive and building relationships through connectedness. They also are based on ensuring openness in communications, creating harmony between business endeavors, human activities, and the natural world, and creating extraordinary value for everyone on balanced perspective of social, economic and environmental considerations.

Strategic leaders have to have the knowledge and capabilities to orchestrate the design and development of new or improved processes for proactively inventing the future of the organization. They provide the intellectual contributions and the guidelines for crating the strategic processes. They may be the architects, but are not the necessarily the designers and developers. They have a cadre of senior professionals who provide the design mechanisms and the details. Philosophically, it is beneficial to get broad participation to enrich the outcomes and to obtain input and consensus from the very people who are expected to participate in the process executions.

The most critical elements of the strategic processes involve how to discover, understand and exploit opportunities; how to deal with challenges and risks; how to develop, build and enhance customer and stakeholder relationships; and ultimately, how to improve corporate reputation, image, and performance. Relationship development and management involves being in synch with constituencies and creating trust with customers and stakeholders. The challenges include how to exceed customer and stakeholder expectations using cutting edge solutions to differentiate the reputation and image of the organization and to build a sustain position for the future.

The operating system is critical because ultimately great insights, strategies, and solutions have to be converted into outcomes that benefit external recipients and contributors. The operating system links the internal capabilities and resources with the external needs and expectations to realize the dreams and objectives of all of the parties. The type of operating systems is a function of the realities that the organization faces. The general approach is to ensure the integration of the internal functional areas and/or operating processes to ensure that the solutions are produced and delivered at the highest levels of quality, integrity and value, among numerous other attributes.

Operations management processes involve effectively managing the flow of materials, energy, information, and finished goods, and the relationships from suppliers through distribution channels to customers using systematic approaches for achieving outstanding performance. Strategic leaders provide the guidelines and insights, but generally they should let the operating managers and practitioners design and develop the operations. The design of the processes includes organizing the key inputs of plans, people, resources, and information, analyzing the requirements, managing the flow activities, obtaining results, and evaluating performance. The basic approach is to convert inputs into valuable outputs through value-adding processes that lead to sustainable success. The focus is on creating value streams and networks that are strategically and operationally aligned and functioning effectively over time so that negative consequences are minimized and positive benefits and implications endure over time.

Operations management processes are intended to be couched in the real world and grounded in the realities of do-ability. They depend on the capabilities, skills, knowledge, desires, and resources of the organizations and the abilities of the people therein to perform. The most important operations processes relate to the overall operating system(s). They involve the inner workings of the operating system, how activities are initiated and performed, and what results are expected to be achieved. While creating the operating system tends to be a joint effort between strategic leaders and operating/functional management, the decisions pertaining to the architecture tend to be high-level and the specifics dealing with the flow of processes and activities tend to be the domain of the operating managers. There are however many variants.

Reflections

Improving the systems integration is a powerful way to enhance solutions and to preempt market requirements and competitive positions. Inclusiveness is particularly effective when superior proprietary management systems and processes are developed that exceed prevailing mainstream approaches. The perspectives include building superior systems, integrating the operations, enhancing intellectual capital, building new capabilities, and expanding reach with customers and supply networks. As discussed throughout the book, some of the most advantageous and fruitful ways to obtain superior positions is to eliminate economic and environmental wastes and mitigate risks and negative impacts. Economic wastes—the non-valued added activities that cost money without the incipient benefits—reduce value and increases costs. Environmental wastes cost money, result in unfavorable impacts, cause operations to be more difficult and time consuming to manage, and make the business unit more susceptible to unexpected problems and higher business risks as well as negative comments and reactions by customers and stakeholders. Implicitly, people across all spectrums desire better products and services that are more affordable and sustainable. Everyone wants to enjoy well-being, personal and professional success, and live in a better world with less pollution, wastes. Shaping systems through inclusiveness means going beyond what is expected or normal; this includes going beyond the 'triple bottom line."

Market success is about customer success and value creation, not just about engaging competitors and winning battles. Sustainable success in market spaces involves creating extraordinary value for customers, stakeholders, shareholders, and related entities. Business success is about economic and social gains and positive outcomes, not myopically about destroying competitors. Great success can be achieved by focusing on the needs, wants and expectations of the markets and providing the best possible solutions.

Notes

1. David L Rainey, *Enterprise-wide Strategic Management: Achieving Sustainable Success through Leadership, Strategies and Value Creation* (Cambridge, UK: Cambridge University Press, 2010, pp16-67).
2. David L Rainey, *Sustainable Business Development: Inventing the Future through Strategy, Innovation, and Leadership* (Cambridge, UK: Cambridge University Press, 2006, pp13-64
3. Id, p160.
4. John Elkington, *Cannibals with Forks: The Triple Bottom line of Sustainable Development* (Oxford, UK: Chapstone Publishing, 1997, pp2, 109-111).
5. The notion of a reasonable time horizon is always difficult to precisely determine. It is dependent upon the rate of change in the markets and economies involved. In fast-paced industries like electronics a reasonable time horizon may be five years. In slower paced situations it may be ten to twenty years. It is a complex question because if the selected time horizon is too long, the view becomes muddled and clarity is lost. On the other hand, if it is too short, exciting opportunities and potential challenges and vulnerabilities may be missed.
6. Homi Kharas and Geoffrey Gertz, "The new Global Middle Class: A Cross-Over from West to East," the Wolfensohn Center for Development at Brookings, 2010, p5.
7. Id. The Brookings Institute analysis from 2010 uses the World Bank 2005 PPP figures which probably understate China's PPP GDP by 27% versus updated Penn World numbers and India's

by 13%. Correcting the PPP GDP figures would mean more people in China and India are middle class already and more will become middle class.
8. C. K. Prahalad, *The Fortune at the Bottom of the Pyramid: Eradicating Poverty through Profits* (Upper Saddle River, NJ: Wharton School Publishing, 2005).

References

Elkington, John (1997) *Cannibals with Forks: The Triple Bottom line of Sustainable Development.* Oxford, UK: Chapstone Publishing.

Prahalad, C. K. (2005) *The Fortune at the Bottom of the Pyramid: Eradicating Poverty through Profits.* Upper Saddle River, NJ: Wharton School Publishing.

Rainey, David L (2010) *Enterprise-wide Strategic Management: Achieving Sustainable Success through Leadership, Strategies and Value Creation.* Cambridge, UK: Cambridge University Press.

Rainey, David L (2006) *Sustainable Business Development: Inventing the Future through Strategy, Innovation, and Leadership.* Cambridge, UK: Cambridge University Press.

6

Building Relationships through Connectedness

Introduction

Strategic leaders are responsible for building sustainable relationships with the essential contributors of the organization across the enterprise and with the recipients in the market spaces and business environment. While leading change often implies disrupting the prevailing situations and radically altering or modifying solutions and systems as discussed in the previous two chapters, astute strategic leaders realize the necessity for assuring connectedness and stability within the complexities of change. As the business world expands and becomes more diverse due to the increasing numbers of actual and potential participants, connectedness among the entities and individuals is one of the most critical factors for achieving and sustaining success. Connectedness implies that there are solid links, communications, and personal contacts between the parties and individuals, and that the contacts and linkages are based on enduring interfaces and relationships.

Relationships are the cement that connects people, the elements of value system, and the extended enterprises to realize exceptional performance and extraordinary outcomes that benefit the contributors and the recipients. Strategic leaders have to be the lynch pins for building relationships and connecting the people who engage in developing, producing, delivering, supporting and using solutions. Building relationships with supply networks, partners, allies, and supporting entities on the upstream side of the extended enterprise tends to reinforce and stabilize the value created over time and facilitates the transitions and/or transformations to the higher levels of sophistication that are necessary for continued success. While the systems, solutions, products and services, processes, components, and parts thereof may dramatically change or even be replaced over time, building solid relationships among the contributors and recipients is an effective mechanism for developing and maintaining predictable and fruitful situations and outcomes. Building relationships is one of the most important elements of full-spectrum strategic leadership (FSL).

Providing and marketing products and services for customers and satisfying them are relatively simple activities that are often transient. Most marketing organizations are successful for even extended periods of time until better products are created and offered by someone else, motivating customers to switch their buying behaviors to the more effective and often more affordable solution(s). Occasionally, well-positioned companies like Toyota with its brake-related problems do not take aggressive enough actions to correct problems and lose momentum, causing their market leadership to slip a little because of a mistake or two. Mistakes and blunders alienate customers and stakeholders, forcing them to seek other options and make other choices, especially after better options become available. This is particularly the situation when the strategic leaders are not forthright in disclosures about negative aspects. Furthermore, companies often fail to consider the customers' costs and inconveniences associated with defects and other problems. People may tolerate certain difficulties related to technologies and products, but they are usually less forgiving when they learn that the strategic leaders were not diligent in addressing difficulties, especially when the strategic leaders are trying to minimize their costs and expenses. Too often the leading companies, even ones with outstanding performance and reputations, rest on their laurels allowing peers and competitors to pass them. The problems are often exacerbated when the market leaders change their business philosophies from ensuring the best solutions to being number one in the markets or in profitability. The eventual outcomes are often the opposite of what the strategic leaders intended. Instead of being the "king of the hill," they lose ground in the markets as competitors provide better solutions and/or develop better relationships. Customers are rarely totally satisfied and are never locked-in.

Lacking proactive attention, trying to maintain the status quo, having many unresolved mistakes, and tolerating many defects often lead to severe consequences. Such difficulties are made worse by the lack of true connections and poor relationships with customers and stakeholders or due to the abuse of strategic power when one has the upper hand. Abused customers and stakeholders do not like being mistreated, but often they can only take revenge after the power structures change. Such blunders are made worse by the arrogance and self-interest on the part of the companies or their strategic leaders. Arrogant strategic leaders and their successors often do not perceive the lack of solid relationships, poor connections, and/or inappropriate actions as the causes or reasons for their problems. For instance, many companies charge excessive prices if they can do so during the times when customers have few options; however, most customers remember such situations, and when circumstances change they often retaliate by avoiding the companies using such one-sided tactics. Since the causes and effects usually do not occur within the same time frame, strategic leaders fail to realize that it was their decisions and actions during earlier periods that led to the customers taking adverse actions in the future. For example, it took about twenty to thirty years into the post-World War II period before international competitors made significant inroads into the U.S. automobile market. During the early times, customers had to choose from the product offerings of the Big Three. With limited real options and choices, customers were disadvantaged and the market leader generally set the terms and conditions. However, since the late 1970s and early 1980s customers had many more choices as international companies entered the U.S. market. The Big Three might have been in better strategic positions if decades earlier the strategic leaders had been more effective in building lasting relationships with customers and stakeholders. Mistakes happen, but blunders can be avoided by thinking about the long term, building relationships, and providing the best solutions and systems possible.

Many strategic leaders fail to build true relationships because they rely on indirect mechanisms and entities to communicate and interact with customers and stakeholders. They spend money on advertising and various forms of communications to get the messages out, but they do not make personal efforts to build connections. The messages may be effective in the short term and the targeted customers may buy the promoted products and services. However, such mechanisms are fairly weak in establishing links with the intended audiences and creating enduring connections with people. A related difficulty involves depending solely on surrogates like dealers and intermediaries in the distribution and retail channels to build relationships with customers. Value networks can be effective entities in the process for getting goods and service to the intended recipients, but they may not always be instrumental in creating as much value as they could or should. Such agents can provide valuable support in enhancing customers' experiences and outcomes, but great care has to be used to ensure that there are solid and enduring relationships between the producers (the principal) and the end customers and users of the solutions. Unless the producers create direct links with the end customers and ensure that all agents are acting appropriately and responsibly, the value networks on the downstream side may become linear or single sided. The relationships are more often illusionary than real, at least from the recipients' perspectives. Moreover, the connections may not be enduring since there are often very few, if any, ongoing actions and positive outcomes. Think about an individual buying an automobile who is misled about the attributes of the product. Given the weak connections with the actual producer other than its brochures and marketing campaigns, the customer has to rely on the producer's agent, the car dealer. If the transaction results in dissatisfaction, everyone in the process is blamed even though the producer may not be culpable and it was the inappropriate actions of the agent that caused the problems. It is incumbent upon the producer's strategic leaders to ensure that all actions are carried out in a positive and forthright manner. They must act as fiduciaries for all involved. They must audit processes and provide oversight to ensure proper outcomes. Again, FSL provides the right philosophies and approaches.

Building relationships with customers and stakeholders is one of the most effective ways for sustaining success. Success is often predicated on the basis of people-to-people connections. It usually requires interactions and direct communications at the customer interface level. The closer one is to the people involved in the actual transactions and exchanges, the greater are the opportunities to make contributions to achieve positive outcomes and success and the more likely that success continues. While this is a theoretical perspective, it makes intuitive sense and can be substantiated by the experiences of strategic leaders who follow such concepts.

Strategic leaders have to build relationships with a myriad of other external entities and individuals. This includes government leaders, social and community leaders, labor unions, the media, and leaders of non-governmental organizations (NGOs). The reputation and goodwill of the company and its SBUs are among its most valuable assets. Strategic leaders have the duty to protect, enhance, and expand these significant intangible assets. The perceived value and trustworthiness of the company are often based on what external entities and individuals believe to be true about the company. This is especially the situation with shareholders and the investment communities.

Employees and external contributors are generally more responsive and committed when they believe that they are part of the whole and not subservient to the whims and dictates of the strategic leaders. Strategic leaders are not superior to other people in the organization as discussed in Chapter 1; they simply have higher levels of authority, responsibilities, and duties. Such responsibilities include setting the moral tone, establishing or reinforcing the principles and values of the company, determining strategic direction, promulgating corporate policies, standards and decision criteria, and recognizing and rewarding achievements. The list goes on. Strategic leaders are the individuals who set the stage and ensure that employees and shareholders are well taken care of. It is their duty to protect people and the well-being of the whole and each individual.

This chapter includes the following main topics:

- Considering the critical underpinnings in building relationships
- Establishing relationships with external entities and individuals
- Reinforcing internal relationships with employees and peers
- Sustaining beneficial relationships through connectedness

The Critical Underpinnings in Building Relationships

General perspectives about relationships

Strategic leaders depend on people and relationships to achieve their objectives and to execute strategies and solutions. People are the contributors and recipients of the success of the company, from shareholders and employees to customers and society. Success means higher stock prices and greater wealth for shareholders, superior solutions for customers and stakeholders, enhanced recognition and rewards for employees, and better outcomes for society. One of the most important ways for making improvements for everyone is to develop and sustain positive relationships with all of the essential people related to and part of the business enterprise. This includes the direct and indirect relationships with employees and labor organizations, customers and stakeholders, suppliers and distributors, partners and allies, government officials and politicians, NGOs and issue leaders, local and regional communities, financial groups and investors, media organizations and reporters, and a long list of people who touch the corporation and are touched by it.

Strategic leaders have the high-level roles in building positive relationships with all of the above. They have to think about how to create, build, integrate, and maintain the complex sets of strategic connections and interfaces into cohesive dialogues and long-term relationships among the entities and individuals that support each other. While lower-level leaders and operations management concentrate on the transactional, operational, and financial implications of the business relationships, strategic leaders concentrate their perspectives and efforts on the strategic linkages, interactions, and communications, especially those pertaining to strategic direction, strategic innovations, business integration, performance, and oversight. They have the overarching obligations to protect the reputation and goodwill of the company and to ensure that all of the business connections are in harmony, are in keeping with legal and ethical mandates, and are economically and financially stable and rewarding.

Strategic leaders have to focus on the totality of the relationships based on the organization and extended enterprise. They are the purveyors of truths, integrity, factual evidence, and corporate (social, economic, ethical, technological, and environmental) responsibilities. They should be enthusiastic proponents of honesty, fair dealing, and sustainable outcomes since they are linked with the people who have important roles in determining business value and for ensuing that shareholder value is enhanced and sustained.

In an era of corporate failures and government bailouts, strategic leaders have to be diligent in building and preserving trust and ensuring that corporate and personal ambitions and achievements are holistic, positive, and balanced. Despite recent changes in business philosophies and the movements toward more openness and inclusiveness in overall corporate behaviors, actions, and communications, especially due to companies embracing sustainable business development (SBD) and corporate social responsibility (CSR), criticism and skepticism are still prevalent across many markets, communities, governments, NGOs, other stakeholders, and investors. Powerful rhetoric and good intentions do not necessarily resonant with people unless they are supported by effective strategies, proactive actions, and sustainable outcomes. Walking the talk implies that actions speak louder than words. It also means providing compelling evidence that intentions are followed by commitments and positive actions. Compelling actions are much more concrete than philosophical perspectives, eloquent vision statements, and well intentioned objectives. People measure success on the basis of outcomes in the real world, not in terms of intentions or plans.

Strategic leaders have the most influence in setting the standards for building relationships, and ensuring that corporate behaviors are positive and fulfilling for everyone involved. Dr. Henry Cloud, a clinical psychologist and author of *Integrity*, describes the most important qualities of people-related behaviors that strategic leaders have to exhibit in transforming their companies and business units into sustainable entities. He identifies six qualities of character that bring about fruitful relationships and achievement:[1]

1. Creates and maintains trust
2. Is able to see and face reality
3. Works in a way that brings results
4. Embraces negative realities and solves them
5. Cause growth and increase
6. Achieves transcendence and meaningful life

Creating trust is an essential element of building relationships. People conduct business and accept outcomes (products and services) from companies and business leaders they trust. Trustworthiness is the pivotal quality of great companies and great strategic leaders when building relationships. Dealing with reality is critical for establishing the proper agenda for creating real value and building relationships. Strategic leaders must possess the ambition to take on great efforts to create success across the broad spectrum of their reach. This is critical for creating a solid corporate image and outstanding reputation. Success is based on sustaining outcomes over time. Growth and making money are the result of investments, strategic innovations, proper leadership, leading change, and positive outcomes. Profits are usually lagging indicators of past successes, while investments and achievements are the precursors to future success. The former aspects are derivatives of the latter ones. They are resultants of good decisions, behaviors and actions. Strategic leaders seek improvements and developments through people to discover growth and new opportunities.

In the context of FSL, transcendence means preempting expectations, enriching the quality of life, enhancing human well-being, and protecting the natural environment. Strategic leaders have to prove their integrity through actions and outcomes, not just expressing grandiose speeches, platitudes, or wonderful sounding marketing messages. In a world full of information, especially through the Internet, reality is more easily determined and the lack of integrity is more quickly discovered. Moreover, trustworthiness and truthfulness are two qualities that all strategic leaders can enjoy and expand upon regardless of their innate talents and physical characteristics.

Narrow versus broad-based relationships

During the last century, strategic leaders of many large corporations kept most relationships at arm's length. They engaged the people in external organizations and employees within the organization on narrow fronts. The points of contacts tended to be formal and well articulated, especially with outside entities like suppliers, distributors, and partners. There were well-established modes of communications and most transactions and activities were expected to follow the prescribed protocols. The lines of communications mirrored the formal lines within the organization, especially those of vertically integrated corporation. Figure 6.1 provides a characterization of the conventional protocol for business relationships based on the point-of-contact concept.

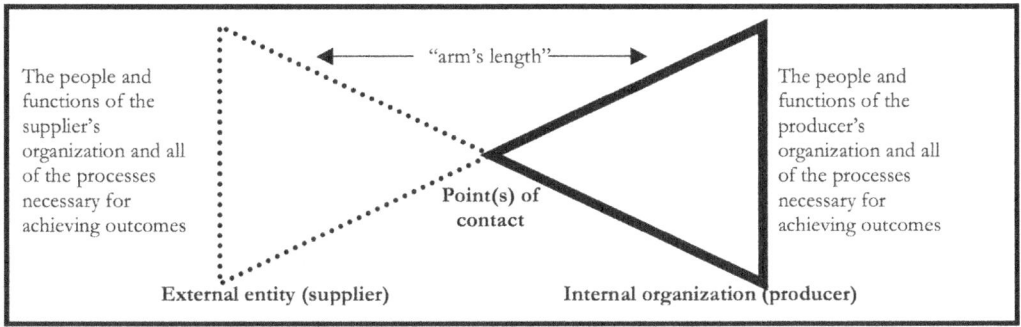

Figure 6.1 Conventional relationship protocol based on single point of contact.

In certain situations there may be several points of contact, but the overall number tended to be low and the graphic portrays the old realities fairly well, especially in a hierarchical organization. While the portrayed concept is a simplification of the actual complexities involved in communicating with external entities, it does provide a profound sense of the essence of such concepts and what arm's length implies. There are advantages and disadvantages of such thinking and methods. The main advantage is control over the processes and activities, since information and decisions are fed directly to and from the contact person(s). Only the properly designated persons are allowed to communicate and most communications are vetted by senior management before being released. Other perceived advantages include limiting unintended disclosures, orchestrating outcomes through power and influences, and using only knowledgeable, well-trained, and fully competent leaders and/or professionals to affect communications and dialogues. The main disadvantages involve the limited number of contact points between the entities and people, the restricted exchanges of knowledge and information, and the inability to build lasting relationships among the people on both sides. Even in those cases in which solid relationships were established, the number of people involved and the breadth of relationships were constricted. While the individuals at the point of contact might establish very positive relationships with his or her contacts, the quality of the connections was often low, and the enduring aspects were typically transient. Exchanges and transactions were often impersonal and lacking in long-term significance. For instance, if each side had a primary contact person who engaged in all of the discussions and exchanges for his or her company, this seemingly optimal situation (due to the efficiencies of having only one or a few people engaged) often degenerated into suboptimal outcomes, especially if or when one of the individuals left the scene because of a job change, retirement, or other normal events and reasons. The goodwill established between the individuals would dissipate and the new people would have to start anew to build the relationships.

Conversely, inclusiveness and connectedness involve many more direct contacts among a broad array of participants and much richer perspectives for enhancing and sustaining the critical relationships between and among the contributors and the recipients across the enterprise. The broader level of contacts as depicted in Figure 6.2 theoretically results in more opportunities for increased knowledge, sharing of the

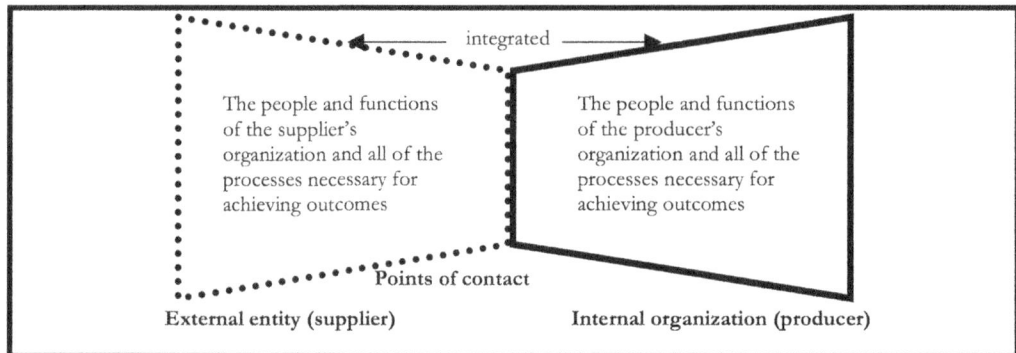

Figure 6.2 Enhanced relationship protocol based on multiple points of contacts.

information and know-how, and a better understanding of the underlying views and perceptions of the other participants. The most important advantage is the building of numerous solid relationships across a wide spectrum of the company and its extended enterprises. While such approaches do not solve all of the inherent difficulties when people communicate and work together, they do provide a greater awareness of the perceptions and understandings that others may have and how those things influence their decisions and behaviors.

The multiple points of contacts are more complicated and required more interactions and oversight by strategic leaders from a high-level perspective, but they also provide a greater degree of empowerment and flexibility for those engaged in the implementation and execution of strategies and actions. Moreover, strategic leaders can concentrate on enhancing the relationships among the people involved and spend less time on the actual exchanges and interactions between the participants. Obviously, participants have to be competent, knowledgeable, and possess the capabilities to contribute on a broader front. The advantages of such approaches include having trained professionals who can adapt to situations as they unfold and greater interactions with the people within the organization and with external parties. Education and training are requirements for assuring that participants function properly in such situations. The main concern is that employees who are viewed as acting on behalf of the organization may make statements or take actions that are not valid nor in keeping with the philosophies, principles and approaches of the company. They may make mistakes.

The enhanced relationship protocol changes the dynamics of the interactions from sterile, almost automated approaches based on "mechanical" processes to human-related interfaces and more contemplative exchanges that are based on many more variables, factors, and people. Good people acting in a forthright and professional manner can usually outperform fixed protocols and procedures that govern interactions between people and business entities. This is especially the case when people understand the underpinnings, strategic logic, and the intentions of the organization and follow the principles of FSL.

Strategic leaders have to decide what mechanisms to take and what are the most beneficial approaches given their situation. Like many aspects of FSL, there are few prescriptive approaches; moreover, it is not an either-or situation. The conventional approaches are most suitable in business situations requiring exacting controls and precise outcomes with little latitude in behaviors. These usually pertain to companies and organizations engaged in businesses and activities with high risks that have severe consequences if anyone operates outside of the generally accepted practices. For instance, operating a petroleum refinery or a chemical plant with dangerous substances necessitates stringent protocols, strictly controlled processes, and mandated requirements. The people have to be well-trained, very competent, and follow policies and procedures exactly. On the other hand, open-ended approaches are more appropriate in situations where adaptability, agility, and flexibility are highly desirable. This is often the case when teams of people from various disciplines or companies are collaborating in joint research and development projects to create new-to-the-world technologies. It is difficult for strategic leaders to specify in great detail how such people are to engage and communicate with each other. Generally, exchanges have to take place across a broad spectrum of the participants, and it is rare when a few people from the various organizations can act as the spokespersons or contact points for their organization.

The discussions in this section are intended to facilitate creative thinking about the further options and how strategic leaders can encourage relationship building within their organization and between their businesses, external entities, and individuals. There are many hybrid approaches that can be employed to enhance relationship building.

Building Mutually Beneficial External Relationships

High-level external relationships

Strategic leaders have the high-level responsibilities for building relationships with leaders of other corporations, governments, NGOs, and the public in general. While there are incredible numbers of external entities and individuals that fit into this category, strategic leaders have to initially determine what are the most crucial or requisite relationships and map out how they are going to accomplish their ends. Most strategic leaders have a sense of what the critical relationships are or have to be by knowing the strategies, objectives, and operations of their businesses and the driving forces of the business environment. They base their views on the long-term associations and connections between organizations and business engagements. Moreover, strategic leaders might use the broad external-based agendas such as social and economic problems, global issues like climate change, the need for industry standards, public policy debates, and the overall common good as areas that they must be engaged in to build relationships with other key leaders.

Strategic leaders often build relationships with government officials and elected leaders, and they often participate in the discussions pertaining to public policy and the development of laws and regulations. They have to be good citizens in resolving some of the broad social, ethical, economic, technological, and environmental problems that may disrupt stability and business prospects. Such engagements should address the well-being of society and the overall social good as well as the more specific objectives of the businesses. Building strategic relationships takes considerable time and effort and requires commitments for making positive improvements. It is difficult to prescribe how strategic leaders actually develop such relationships. It often requires highly individualized thinking and methods and personalized interactions.

Building external relationships pertains more to leadership than management. It requires the skills, knowledge, experience, good judgment, and wisdom based on the individual's personal characteristics, personality and good will to orchestrate the desirable outcomes. Solid relationships are constructed on the strategic leader's perspectives on openness, honesty, and trust. Relationships are often fragile and can be easily lost if strategic leaders and other participants are less than honest, consistent, and forthright. Strategic leaders form high-level relationships for numerous reasons, from simply ensuring good governance to providing for sustainable success. There may be altruistic reasons as well as more materialistic ones. Some of the broader, non-specific reasons include:[2]

- Preserving the social, economic, ethical, technological, and environmental stability of the business world, social and political life; and protecting the natural environment.
- Understanding external context and knowing what is expected before it is required.
- Participating in the development of public policy, global management methods, and industry standards; and identifying opportunities for significant changes that promote sustainable success.
- Increasing connectedness to reduce the vulnerabilities associated with uncertainties, globalization, and change and to improve capabilities and knowledge required for building for the future.
- Promoting ethical behaviors across businesses, governments, and social interactions.
- Providing mechanisms to enhance linkages with shareholders and organizations that provide information, analysis and/or control over corporate ownership.

Good governance and social and economic stability are among the most compelling reasons. Strategic leaders depend on the external context to provide opportunities and to mitigate the potential for adverse events or phenomena. Everyone shares in the responsibilities to make the world a better place to the extent possible and to ensure that serious economic problems, catastrophic diseases, and other forms of social and economic harms are reduced or eliminated. These efforts require collaboration among all leaders, each playing a part to create and deliver the best solutions. They benefit the company directly by ensuring that opportunities are enhanced and that vulnerabilities are reduced.

In Chapter 3, the concept of insightfulness was discussed. If strategic leaders desire a rich and open view of the realities of the world, they need to examine the world from the perspectives and perceptions of many other types of leaders. Strategic leaders need to spend a significant amount of their time garnering ideas and concepts from the external social and natural worlds, not just from their industry or served markets. Many different types of insights can be gleaned from leaders in unrelated areas who have diverse perspectives and dissimilar responsibilities. Building relationships with such leaders provides astute strategic leaders with alternate ways of understanding opportunities and challenges that their more isolated or stereotypical peers may not contemplate. Such insights open the doors to innovations and new solutions. The broader context provides a richer sense of the realities and new ways to create unique solutions and obtain more sustainable advantages.

Strategic leaders may engage in high-level contacts on an international basis. They must stay abreast of changes occurring in other industries, markets, and countries that are not generally part of their primary strategic domains. With globalization there are very few isolated situations or events. For instance, the growing economic power of China is putting pressure on the availability and pricing of many of the raw materials used in various industries from oil to strategic metals and other commodities. As an aside, China passed Japan in 2010 to become the world's second-largest economy, behind the United States.[3] Building international relationships should be based on the broad agendas that are important for business dealings and international affairs.

Broad participation with other businesses, governments, and societies allows strategic leaders to help set the agendas rather than being subject to agendas established by others. Strategic leaders often complain about restrictive regulations, but the complexities caused by regulations are sometimes the fault of business leaders who were not proactive in establishing the cures for the difficulties or by being antagonistic instead of collaborative in establishing proactive standards and codes of conduct.

The participation of strategic leaders is critical in the development of the acceptable standards pertaining to business practices and how solutions are applied in the markets and in society. Enlightened strategic leaders understand the need for ethical and legal mandates and rules of the road, because such standards reduce the probability of deviant behaviors. Moreover, they know that deviant behaviors by a few of their peers, whether criminal or not, affect all businesses and exert social and political pressures on government officials to take action. While some business leaders prefer to have governments determine the standards through directives and regulations under the assumption that they "level the playing field," smart strategic leaders realize that it is in the best interests of most organizations to collaborate in setting the standards for proper behaviors, appropriate actions and acceptable practices. Developing and providing effective communications using the concept of FSL are responsibilities of the strategic leaders.

Relationships with upstream entities and people

Historically, strategic leaders had poor relationships with the main contributors in the supply networks. The conventional approach of arm's length transactions limited the connections between the producer and their main suppliers and distributors. The producer's approach was usually based on using suppliers against each other to obtain the most favorable prices and terms and conditions when establishing contracts and on trying to secure and maintain economic advantages during the contract period. Such approaches were believed to be very effective, especially if the producer (the decision maker) had significant power over suppliers and distributors. If the contract was a single transaction, then most strategic leaders tried to maximize their outcomes at the expense of the entities in the supply networks. While this is a broad generalization, and there are many exceptions to such practices in the past and present, it is fair to say that most situations tended to be adversarial rather than being supported by mutually beneficial methods and outcomes. Producers realized economic gains in the short term, but their relationships with supply networks often suffered and long-term objectives and outcomes were less optimal as upstream entities learned how to improve their positions and gain more economic power. As producers squeezed the profit margins of their supply networks, the latter fought back by squeezing the potential outcomes—quality, delivery, and support. For instance, a supplier might marginalize the outcomes by just meeting the specifications of the contract instead of providing increased benefits at relatively small costs.

Today, sophisticated companies understand the need for the successful integration of their value systems with those of their supply networks to produce seamless flows of goods and services and all of the tangible and intangible attributes from the origins of the raw materials to the finished products. Such systems require solid relationships between the entities and people therein to assure that the proper functioning of the integrated system and the stability of the processes and outcomes over time. Short-term benefits and financial gains by any entity may be counterproductive unless all of the entities are able to obtain their short-term and long-term objectives as well.

Creating an integrated system without developing solid relationships between the entities may result in short-term advantages that increase cash flows and profits, but they may not be sustainable if there is a lack of coordination, collaboration, and trust. It may be somewhat easy to detail the elements of an integrated system and how the elements of the system and the processes thereof are suppose to work; however, it is often much more difficult to harmonize the interfaces and interactions between the entities and to synchronize the behaviors and outcomes of the people involved. While integrating the systems is a critical step toward achieving success, great outcomes may not be realized unless the relationships between the people and the organizations are friendly, mutually beneficial, and enduring. It requires strategic leaders within each of the entities to trust their counterparts and all of the interconnected participants based on positive relationships.

Questions persist about how to create such relationships. Strategic leaders of the producers have to be assured that their supply networks are acting in the best interest of the producers and the extended enterprises. In many ways, the producers (the principals) are often the most vulnerable to difficulties, poor performance, and bad behaviors wherever they may be upstream in the extended enterprise. Producers, especially large global corporations, are well known to most people in the markets and business environment, usually have good reputations and powerful brands that have to be protected; ones that can be easily damaged by adverse situations, negative behaviors, and poor outcomes regardless of where they occur within the extended enterprise. They usually have branded products and services that are the most visible in the eyes of customers and stakeholders. Moreover, producers are on the receiving ends of the contributions of the upstream entities and any problems, difficulties and delays impact them directly.

Upstream entities include not only the direct suppliers and distributors, but the suppliers of suppliers and their suppliers upstream in the supply networks. Producers must establish relationships with those entities as well, either directly or through their direct suppliers and distributors. While the actual approaches may vary considerable depending on circumstances, it is imperative that producers of end products have knowledge about all of the upstream activities and maintain connections with the leaders involved. While this can involve incredible numbers of entities, strategic leaders must ensure that the upstream entities are acting responsibly and that there are not any actions or omissions that would be inappropriate or illegal. There numerous examples where all of the entities in the enterprise are tarnished by the misdeeds of one or a few of the entities in the supply networks. For instance, in the growing and harvesting of cocoa beans in West Africa there were abuses related to the exploitation of labor. Such problems often arrive at the doorsteps of the major food producers and marketers. The strategic leaders at Nestlé had to take decisive actions and instituted programs and codes of conduct to mitigate such problems through audits, oversight, and by working with international organizations like the United Nations and the International Cocoa Organization in London.[4] Moreover, the company's leaders worked with suppliers and farmers to assure stability, fair prices for commodities, and an adequate return for farmers.[5] Strategic leaders of the large corporations are the prime players who are often in the best positions for assuring that their extended enterprises are behaving and functioning properly. It is a huge responsibility that is virtually impossible to execute reactively. Strategic leaders must proactively build solid relationships with the other entities and leaders and employ only those entities and people known to be dependable and honest; ones that have proven their trustworthiness. The upfront investment of time and effort in ensuring that the right contributors have been selected and are performing properly, that they have the correct philosophies and principles, and that there are solid relationships among the participants is more effective than using oversight to assure proper actions over time. Moreover, the former tends to be proactive, while the latter is reactive. But in the real world effective strategic leaders have to do it all. They may use trust and proactive actions but also verify results using tools like audits to ensure that everyone is performing in accordance with expectations. In a world of instantaneous communications, there is little room for misdeeds, and it takes the whole enterprise to build and keep great reputations.

Relationships with downstream entities and people

Downstream relationships are among the most critical for succeeding. Customers are usually difficult to attract and it is time consuming and expensive to gain their awareness, acceptance, and confidence. While there are numerous situations of exchanges that are expected to occur only once or very infrequently, most businesses and their strategic leaders depend on ongoing relationships. Most business situations require repeat contacts and transactions with customers that have to endure over time. To ensure that customers repeat their purchases, producers have to assure that each repetitive situation is equal to, if not better than, the previous ones. Positive exchanges necessitate having positive relationships between the customers and the producers. Thus, it is incumbent upon strategic leaders to view building relationships as a key factor for achieving sustainable success.

Strategic leaders in some of the largest global corporations that have dramatically improved their products and services often wonder why their market successes still lag behind their efforts and investments in making improvements. Often the answers lie in the past due to a legacy of poor behaviors and unresponsive approaches, especially with customers and stakeholders. The companies may have been unfriendly and unconcerned about the defects that were built into the older products. The companies' failures related to unresolved problems and the lack of regard for the economic losses that customers suffered linger for years. In the short term, customers may have to accept the inactions or the limited scale of the initiatives by companies unless there are government-backed recalls. The companies may win the skirmishes by avoiding spending money on the corrective actions, but they often lose in the long term as customers eventually find better solutions from other companies. Moreover, there is a tendency of the affected customers to avoid buying products and services from such companies, especially ones that caused them significant harm, regardless of the great improvements that have been made. For example, the American automobile companies have made significant improvements in the quality and reliabilities of their products, yet they are still unable to realize significant gains in market share. The problem may be that previous strategic leaders failed to support relationships with customers. Decades ago, customers in the U.S. automobile market were often single-minded in their purchase patterns. They were a "Ford-owner," a Chevy-owner," etc. Those ways of thinking on the part of customers have evaporated because the strategic leaders during earlier times were often not mindful of enhancing their side of the relationships. While the strategic leaders of today cannot undo the past, and many of the problems were created by one's predecessors, strategic leaders can reach out to rebuild cordial relationships with customers and re-establish a rapport with their customers. But, it takes time.

The insights from the previous three chapters indicate that focusing on products and services is inferior to crafting solutions and establishing effective and efficient systems for their development and deployment. However, such cutting-edge approaches are incomplete unless strategic leaders in particular go out of the way to build solid relationships with customers and stakeholders. Moreover, strategic leaders have to connect with the business leaders in the related industries that provide important contributions to the overall solutions.

In consumer markets, it is not possible for strategic leaders to make direct connections with the millions of customers who use or might use the company's solutions. Such seemingly unattainable outcomes can be positively affected through more open and forthright communications in the various forms of dialogues with customers and stakeholders. While high-level executives often perform poorly in advertisements or other types of marketing communications, the difficulties may be due to the single-sided aspects of the messages. The executives are often unconnected and may not be believable, especially when articulating canned messages that tell only the positive implications. They may be more effective if they simply espouse the reasons for their positions and talk candidly about their solutions from the customers' perspectives. Rather than just trying to sell products and services, it may be more beneficial for everyone if the strategic leaders simply try to forge linkages with the customers and stakeholders. Strategic leaders should focus on building confidence and acceptance. Such connections are more powerful than the elaborate marketing campaigns trying to convince people about how wonderful the products are. Single-sided messages that provide only the glitz and glamour are often rejected by customers and potential customers because they see through the illusions.

Strategic leaders have the duty to establish trust with external entities and individuals. In many situations the relationships can be developed using virtual mechanisms to convey the messages. But there must be a sense of reality and commitment on the part of the strategic leaders. Regardless of the means and mechanisms used, it is imperative that open and honest communications continue over time. Strategic leaders cannot be effective by communicating with customers just once or once a year. Communications have to be continuous. With the Internet it is relatively easy to open dialogues with people that can endure. Many corporations use social media such as twitter and Facebook to establish these direct connections with customers. While some strategic leaders may view ongoing dialogues and communications as expensive, in reality such efforts may be inexpensive and more effective than the money spent on television advertising, which tends to be one way and single-sided. Strategic leaders also have to develop relationships with industrial customers and stakeholders and promote the greater good of their industry or business.

Reinforcing Internal Relationships

Overarching perspectives and themes pertaining to internal relationships

Strategic leaders are the front-line fiduciaries with the responsibility to ensure that the internal relationships are robust, with everyone supporting the strategic direction of the company and the strategies and objectives of the business units. They are not servants to the organizations, nor are they superiors in the traditional sense. During most of the early twentieth century, executives and strategic leaders were viewed as superiors, and the employees were the subordinates. This line of thinking was based on the concepts used by military leaders who had command and control over their troops. While such approaches may be necessary and appropriate for military units, they are often less effective and even disruptive in business settings. Strategic leaders have special duties and responsibilities to lead the organization and ensure that it can achieve its ends and desired outcomes. Ultimately, strategic leaders orchestrate change through people and have the overarching responsibilities to develop people, provide them with the resources necessary for success, and to recognize and reward performance and accomplishments.

While some high-level strategic leaders believe that their positions and authority entitle them to be automatically accepted by the organization, there are counter-views, especially in some of the large global corporations headquartered in the European Union (EU). The modern concept suggests strategic leaders have to earn the confidence of the organization through positive actions, good relationships, and superior results. The concept is called authenticated leadership, in which strategic leaders obtain the consent of the organization after they have shown that they are capable of leading the organization based on the best interests of its shareholders, employees, customers, stakeholders, and other constituents.[6] While this concept may seem to be overly complex and difficult to define and measure, it does make intuitive sense. Given that strategic leaders require the whole organization to help formulate and implement strategies and to actually execute the action plans, they must have a solid rapport with the lower-level leaders, managers, professionals, supervisors, and employees. They have to build the relationships that enhance dialogues across the organization and facilitate the execution of the plans and actions. Such relationships tend to eliminate the "us versus them" mentality and the chasm that often exists between strategic leaders and the rest of the organization. Bill George, former chairman and chief executive officer (CEO) of Medtronic, advocates "authentic leadership" in his book on that subject. George suggests that:[7]

> Authentic leaders genuinely desire to serve others through their leadership. They are more interested in empowering the people they lead to make a difference than in power, money or prestige for themselves. They are guided by qualities of the heart, by passion and compassion, as they are by qualities of the mind.

Strategic leaders may have special positions and roles within their organizations, but they are not a distinctive caste that deserves special or even extraordinary attention, perks, recognition, and rewards. To the contrary, they have the responsibilities to build an organization and relationships within it so that everyone is respected and those who deserve recognition and rewards are so acknowledged. They have the extraordinary duty to make others successful and to subordinate their personal goals to those of the organization. They are not necessarily superiors in their relationships with other people within the organization; they have higher-level duties that have to be performed for the greater good and the enduring success of the whole. The notion of superior is usually determined by circumstances, not just by positions. For instance, the design team for a new product like the Boeing 787 Dreamliner may have more critical players to Boeing's success than many of Boeing's strategic leaders who are engaged in administrative duties that are important, but routine.

Strategic leaders have to participate in establishing policies and rule making and be guided by them. It is difficult to build trust and commitment across the organization when strategic leaders set themselves apart from the organization by not adhering to the very policies and practices that they have developed for the general good of that organization. For instance, if financial challenges cause annual increases in employee salary to be frozen or to be minuscule, then one would assume that such policies would also apply to the strategic leaders as well. However, there are many examples of strategic leaders taking large increases in compensation when the rest of the organization is asked to "tighten its belt" and forego increases because the company has to save money. There are many examples of strategic leaders who decimated the ranks of the organization under the guise of right sizing the organization and improving profitability, and then they took personal rewards (millions of dollars, Euros, yen, etc.) at the end of the year because of their good work. Please note that these comments are not to suggest that companies do not have to occasionally take dramatic actions if financial conditions warrant such actions. If economic pressures require that strategic leaders make adjustments for the greater good and survival of the organization, then strategic leaders have a duty to do so. It is also appropriate to reward strategic leaders in various ways for rectifying negative situations or turning around negative performance, but such rewards should be reasonable/be proportional to others. The organization depends on strategic leaders doing what is right from the top down, bottom up and across the organization. One positive example is Bill Ford Jr., former CEO of Ford Motor Company. Bill Ford volunteered to forgo new compensation until the company achieved sustainable profitability. He tried to restore the confidence and credibility of Ford's leadership and the company's fortunes.[8]

The actual mechanisms that executives use to build relationships are varied and often depend on the past or prevailing situations. There are no simple answers; however, openness and engagement help to create the right atmosphere for connecting the parties and individuals. People desire dialogue and seek empowerment. They want to be linked to the whole strategic management process, not just the implementation or day-to-day activities with no voice. They want to know why as well as knowing what to do. Such strategic thinking is akin to the success achieved by many companies using integrated product development, in which participants are concurrently engaged from the first step of the process to the end of the new product development and the commercialization of the product or service. Strategic leaders need to engage more of the organization in the whole experience. They should allow people to participate in open dialogues that solicit input, share information, debate issues, and find common ground. Moreover, strategic leaders should explain the logic of the choices that have to be made as well as discuss the opportunities and challenges that have to be addressed. However, there is no end point; building relationships with employees is a continuum. While some strategic leaders may believe that they do not have the time to engage people, such efforts are often time savers in the long term since people may become more active and engaged thereafter.

Many strategic leaders realize that the implementation and execution of strategic plans are difficult and troublesome. Such difficulties are understandable, since in many organizations formulating strategies is done by a relatively small number of executives, strategic leaders, and professionals with excellent relationships among the participants. On the other hand, implementation and execution within the broader organization are often fraught with difficulties and the possibility of failure because the strategic leaders do not focus on creating positive relationships with the people and fail to prepare the organization for what is necessary. Implementation and execution depend on many people having the knowledge, commitment, and incentives to participate in achieving the desired outcomes. These elements must be incorporated from the start of the process, at the formulation stage, not just at the beginning of the implementation stage.

Employees do not serve the strategic leaders, but the greater good of their organizations. Strategic leaders are not at the top of the organization, but are the architects, integrators, and purveyors of success. They have a duty to build lasting relationships with employees. Most people in the organization want to be part of the solutions and achieve sustainable success. However, they often realize early on that they are viewed as tangential to the processes, rather than being pivotal to the outcomes. Strategic leaders can make a significant difference in achieving greater performance and success by being inclusive and building strong relationships with the employees.

The increasing importance of internal connections

Building relationships with internal contributors does not have to be nor should be at the extremes. The old view of superior to subordinate in which lower-level people are the workers and the high-level leaders are the only decision makers is inconsistent with fast-paced changes in today's business world. Strategic leaders cannot make all of the decisions and, even if they could, the processes would be too slow to meet the demands of an interactive and fast-paced world. Moreover, strategic leaders do not have all of the insights and creative thoughts. Most situations require flexibility and the capability to move quickly; therefore, it is not possible to prescribe constructs that fit every situation.

There may be situations in which formality and rigid structures are necessary to assure safety and control. Ensuring the safety of airplanes and operation of nuclear power plants are examples of demanding situations that require robust systems and structures often dominated by command and control style leadership. Please note that the focus herein is on perspectives about strategic leadership and not about styles and personal approaches. Conversely, being too loose may not lead to appropriate results either. While there has been much discussion over the last several decades about being the servant leader, the truth may be that strategic leaders are neither bosses nor servants. They must exhibit characteristics that are dependent on the situations they face and the strategic needs of the organization. While there are numerous styles and ways to carry out one's roles and responsibilities, there is not a preordained approach that is suitable for all seasons and occasions; it is not at the extremes or even the golden mean. Strategic leaders have to determine what is appropriate in their settings and make adjustments as situations change.

Dealing with people in the organization takes confidence, courage, conviction, and commitment. People want to be engaged and supportive. Even in those situations in which employees may be seen to be resisting change, there may be legitimate business and not personal reasons for doing so. If decisions are handed down based on the older "superior-subordinate" theories, employees may be confused and unconnected to what has to be done and how to do it. The big problems are often the lack of information, inadequate dialogues, and poor resource allocations. Employees may not have the proper means and mechanisms to do the job.

Generally, conventional leadership and management constructs pertaining to organizational relationships worked fairly well in very stable and slow-paced business environment. Moreover, they work well when most people are engaged in internal processes like manufacturing or managing the financial accounts, i.e., work that is routine and repetitive. Such people are often isolated from the demands of the real world. This is not to say that their roles and responsibilities are simple, easy, or unimportant, just that in most such situations their roles are well defined and do not change dramatically day to day. If the rate of change is low and the implications of change are minimal, then the status quo is well established; i.e., internal connections can be more procedural than personal.

Internal relationships based on person-to-person connections become much more important and even critical as the rate of change increases; the pace moves from slow changes to rapid and even turbulent. Moreover, the newness of innovations and technological advancements may move from incremental to radical and possibly breakthrough changes. Thus, the complexity of the situation is often the key factor. Simple changes typically involve products and services and the functional elements that are well understood and relatively easy to accommodate. As changes become more complicated, they generally involve the whole value system and even the whole extended enterprise. Complexity generally requires more adaptability of the organizations and enterprises and often a shift in how people think and respond. Old ways have to be modified or replaced, and new means and mechanisms have to be adapted. In many situations, existing core competencies become irrelevant, and rapid learning is required to meet the challenges of the new order.

Figure 6.3 depicts the geometric expansion of three of the most important factors: the rate of change, the extent of the changes, and the newness of the changes. As an organization progresses from the center which represents the prevailing situation (the norm), leading change becomes more demanding, and it becomes more important to be connected through personal and professional relationships between the contributors.

The inner box represents the normal focus on functional areas in a slow-paced world with mostly incremental changes. While there may be exceptional demands on people within an organization like achieving six-sigma quality and lean production, most of the requirements and advancements are well-planned and executed within the existing competencies, knowledge, and relationships. As the demands increase

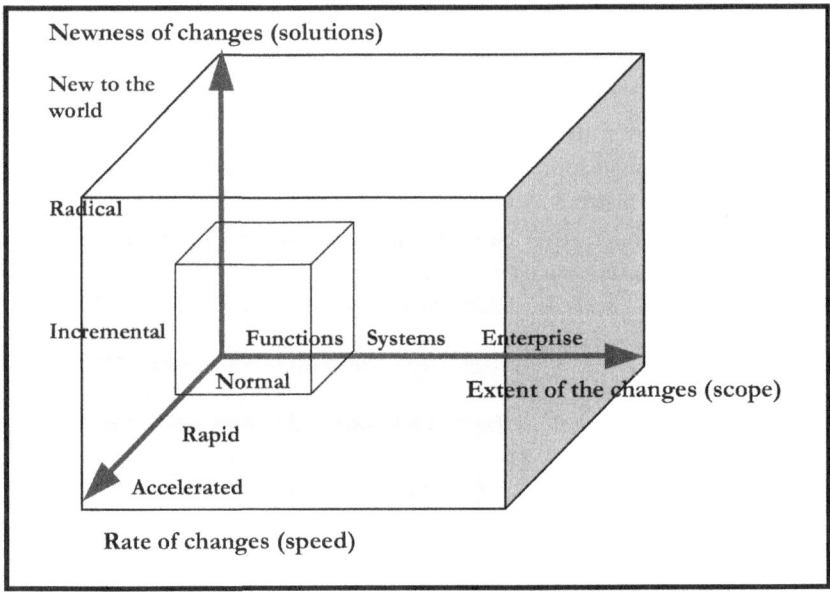

Figure 6.3 Critical factors affecting internal relationships.

in the business environment and leading change becomes more critical, the rate of change becomes more rapid, the newness of the change become more radical, and the extent of the change mechanisms reach out to the whole system and beyond. In such situations the relationships among the people and with strategic leadership have to be even more profound, interconnected, and collaborative. It becomes more imperative to have a totally connected organization and enterprise as the rate of change increases and the changes result in the need for new solutions and new systems and structures. As the rate of change becomes even more demanding and/or turbulent and new-to-the-world solutions become more prevalent, strategic leaders have to think outside-of-the-box about how to be more effective in linking all of the participants and contributors to achieve enduring success even before the needs and expectations are fully apparent. They have to build relationships up and down the organizations connecting all of the people through well-articulated processes and comprehensive systems that marshal the capabilities and resources toward productive and valuable ends.

Connecting the people within the organization and the extended enterprise is a task that strategic leaders often fail to do effectively. As suggested in the perspectives above, if the pace is slow, the changes are small and the focus is on functional aspects, then the old trickle down approaches of the top-down management styles of the past might work, or at least there may be sufficient time to make them work. However, in a fast-paced world there is little time to establish relationships with the key contributors and recipients after it becomes apparent that such actions are absolutely necessary. They have to be established as part of the organizational culture in which people respond to each other through respect and regard for what has to be done and the important roles each contributor has and not because of command and control. It is easier to lead than to push or pull people.

Strategic leaders who put themselves at the top and subordinate everyone else at the bottom are most likely going to fail or cause their organizations to decline in the long term. They may be able to command people to do things, but eventually they become overwhelmed by all of the decisions they have to make without the insights and collaboration of the managers, employees, and all of the other contributors across the full spectrum of leadership. Moreover, in most organizations there are simply too many required decisions, actions, and activities, and it is virtually impossible for high-level leaders to make all of the commands necessary to affect the solutions. It is also impossible to monitor all of the outcomes and check on all of the people.

Sustainable success is driven by people. Strategic leaders need the support and commitment of the people to achieve the goals and objectives and to continue to make progress across time. Unless the organization and enterprise are cohesive and integrated, they are less likely to succeed. In a business world in which intellectual capital and knowledge are primary factors for realizing outcomes, strategic leaders are more like the world-renowned orchestra conductor who recognizes that he or she is at the forefront but not the most knowledgeable or capable participant in any of the sections. He or she has to depend on and support the individuals of the orchestra. The conductor facilitates the developments of the players and ensures the integration of the whole to achieve the harmony necessary for the audience to appreciate a great performance. The conductor lets each person become the best he or she can be and makes sure that the players work together so that everyone enjoys success. Great conductors know that they will be rewarded with acclaim and remuneration, so they go out of their way to provide recognition and rewards for the players and their contributions.

Strategic leaders of today are the architects, conductors, and multifaceted specialists. They are the developers, the integrators, and the team leaders. They share the respect, recognition, and rewards that are achieved. Dividing respect and recognition into many parts has similar effects as dividing one's love amongst family and friends. (Love can be subdivided endless times without diminishing the effects and outcomes.) Moreover, the more they are spread across the organization and enterprise, the more that is available to be shared.

Rewards and recognition are often viewed to be the culmination of the cycle of leading change, but they are really the beginning, the middle, and the end in a never-ending reality of empowering, encouraging, and enriching the professional and personal lives of the people involved, and they are the catalysts that make leading change possible. They make the impossible possible through the efforts of the people and the dedication of the strategic leaders who are selfless in their determination to orchestrate sustainable success.

Sustaining Relationships through Connectedness

Sustaining business success, not just profits, requires building trust, creating value, and delivering positive outcomes. Having a solid reputation and being respectful are essential for achieving sustainable success. Contemporary leaders and managers often focus on marketing campaigns and strategic communications as the key mechanisms for creating positive outcomes. While conventional marketing and high-level communications may be essential for success in a competitive world, often the outcomes do not fully meet expectations, and corporations attempt to convince people that they do. Moreover, the relationships between producers/sellers and customers and stakeholders are often strained due to the difficulties associated with previous transactions or the lack of full disclosures about products, processes and services. Customers are reluctant to repeat mistakes. The traditional corporate response often involves increasing marketing expenditures to overwhelm the market segments with positive messages.

Conventional approaches may be effective in the short term, but often masks reality. Poor products and services often become liabilities rather than assets. They typically lead to problems and dissatisfaction, which cost time and money to fix and require additional marketing expenditures to neutralize. It becomes a vicious circle. While it is important to recognize that every product or service has positive and negative effects and impacts, it is also important to realize that problems do not result solely from poor design, production, and sales. In many cases, they are caused by faulty relationships.

Building trust requires a balanced message using straight talk. It means conveying the full story to customers and stakeholders so that they can make appropriate decisions. Customers and stakeholders must be apprised of the negative effects, impacts, and consequences of products, processes, and services as well as their benefits and advantages. Building awareness, gaining acceptance, and providing solutions are critical for developing enduring relationships with customers and stakeholders. As discussed in Chapter 4, people want solutions. Building relationships through connectedness necessitates providing enhanced solutions with more positives attributes and fewer negative impacts. Mostly importantly, leaders and managers have to ensure that dramatic improvements and exciting new developments are ongoing. Table 6.1 provides a summary of some of the critical attributes and impacts.

The categories are provided to facilitate strategizing how to achieve the elements. In many situations, it may not be possible to exact identify what is short term and what

TABLE 6.1 Categories of Short- and Long-Term Effects (attributes and impacts)[9]

	Short-term Effects (immediate)	Long-term Effects (enduring)
Positive Attributes (Improve/Increase)	I. Features; functionality; benefits; quality; ease of use; affordability; utility; desirability; status; satisfaction; advantages; strengths; economics; awareness; acceptance; use; competitive advantage; bottom line	IIA. Value; quality; reliability; longevity; responsiveness; stewardship; brand recognition and loyalty; trust; integrity; ethics; transparency; social responsibility; environmental protection; corporate reputation
Negative Impacts (Reduce/Eliminate)	III. Defects; burdens; safety concerns; spills; accidents; taxes; insurance; waste streams; energy consumption, pre-mature failure; hidden costs	IV. Liabilities; life cycle costs and considerations; end-of-life considerations; externalities; depletion; degradation; disruption; destruction

is long term. The distinction involves how long it takes to develop or manage the effects. The following provides some additional comments about the categories:[10]

> Category I contains the elements of conventional marketing [approaches] which focus on the short-term qualities and attributes that excite customers and elicit interest. The elements include the features, functions, and benefits of the products and services that resonate positively with customers. They address the desirability, level of satisfaction, advantages, and applications. The marketing messages usually attempt to create awareness, encourage trial, promote acceptance, and sustain use. When claims are valid and substantiated, such marketing approaches fit generally accepted practices and regulatory mandates. However, if marketers are not careful, competitors can leverage the goodwill that is developed about the products. They can try to imitate the products and messages.

> Category II includes the long-term effects of the product and process elements that are more difficult to imitate. They include intangible elements that are more difficult to emulate because they are dependent on the broader management system and corporate principles and practices. They include the long-term benefits of the products and enduring effects that are critical for sustaining success. The most power of these elements are value, quality, reliability, longevity and responsiveness. The goals are to instill trust and build brand recognition and loyalty. These enhance business and corporate positions for the long term.

> Category II also focuses on customer and stakeholder relationships. The approach is to build broader and more enduring relationships based on ethical practices, social responsibility, transparency and environmental protection. These elements expand the reach of the communications to the large communities and covey more thorough messages. The goals are to connote total satisfaction and build corporate reputation for sustainable success.

> Category III focuses on the negative side and includes the short-term negative effects associated with the unintended problems and difficulties. They include defects, burdens, safety concerns, accidents, and others. They also include costs associated with mitigating the negative side, like insurance, taxes, and penalties. These elements reduce the value of the products and services and cause customers to pay more or enjoy less.

> Category IV focuses on the long-term issues including liabilities, life cycle costs, and end-of-life considerations. It also includes the costs, effects, and impacts of externalities, depletion, degradation, disruption and destruction. This category provides a more inclusive perspective of the social, economic and environmental concerns and impacts.

Today, business leaders, managers, and practitioners have to develop and deliver outstanding solutions and achieve positive outcomes in the short term and secure sustainable success for the long term. There are many opportunities and numerous challenges. Most of the methods, constructs, and practices of the last century are no longer adequate. Leaders and managers have to envision bold and innovative ways to connect with people, especially customers and stakeholders. Developing more sophisticated management constructs that integrate the whole system and focus on sustainable solutions presents exciting approaches for connecting with people and exceeding their expectations.

Twenty-first century constructs have expanded the perspectives of how to strategize and implement solutions and systems and how to build relationships across the extended enterprise. In my book, *Enterprise-wide Strategic Management: Achieving Sustainable Success through Leadership, Strategies, and Value Creation,* the strategic aspects of the whole enterprise is discussed. They involve a broader management mindset that realizes the critical importance of the external contributors and recipients as well as the internal participants (employees). This is a fundamental shift in strategic thinking from more passive views like compliance and legal responsibilities based on being good and not breaking the laws to the more dynamic perspectives of corporate social responsibility (CSR), sustainable development, and strategic innovations for actively creating new value, solving old problems, and achieving fair and appropriate outcomes for everyone. Sustainable development and strategic innovation involve making dramatic changes, revolutionary developments, and significant improvements that have positive and typically clean outcome(s) with respect to customers, stakeholders, and the organization. The new thinking implies that strategic leaders have an implicit duty to create the best solutions and mitigate negative aspects to the extent possible. Developing clean technologies and producing a lean enterprise go a long way toward realizing these outcomes. Strategic innovations are discussed in the next chapter.

Leaders and managers have to concentrate on satisfying all of the expectations, requirements, and mandates of the business world. They include markets, customers, stakeholders, supply networks, related industries, infrastructure, and competition. The broadest perspectives involve the well-being of society and the general social, ethical, economic, technological, and environmental considerations. Building relationships and being connected involve understanding and dealing with context, and one's perspectives on context should always start with the external dimensions. It is the external business environment that drives change and provides true opportunities and exciting challenges. Achieving success involves holistic thinking and strategic insights about the business environment and how leaders and managers can improve, develop, expand, transition, and transform their companies, business units, and extended enterprises. Leaders and managers apply experiences, knowledge, and insights about the use of strategic positions, intellectual capital, competencies, capabilities, and resources, and the potential to leverage and/or influence those same attributes of their strategic partners, allies, and value networks to create extraordinary opportunities and outcomes. They also use imagination and insights to visualize what the corporation and its position in the business world could be or should be instead of what it is.

Cutting-edge corporations need highly competent, innovative, and technologically sophisticated leaders and managers who have the mindset, insights, and imagination to think broadly and to create new landscapes for meeting the needs and dreams of customers, stakeholders, employees, shareholders, and society. Moreover, such leaders and managers must extend their reach beyond the traditional perspectives of the corporation and take responsibility for the corporation's direct and indirect effects and impacts on the extended enterprise, market spaces, and business environment. The power, strategic position, and success of a company and its business units are determined by the contributions and performance of all of the players, direct and indirect. Outcomes are the sum of all of the contributions: from the conception and development of the technologies and products, the generation of new product ideas, the origin of the materials, and the conversion of inputs into products and services—to the delivery of outputs to customers, their applications, and the final disposition of the residuals. Leaders and managers must ensure that the specialized capabilities, knowledge, and advantages of the contributors are leveraged to produce desired value-added outcomes.

Reflections

The heart and soul of an organization and the extended enterprise rest with the people therein. Strategic leaders must focus on people, both externally and internally. Customers and stakeholders are the recipients of the solutions. They are generally the reasons for businesses to exist. Building solid relationships with customers and stakeholders is a key to success. It goes beyond simply providing satisfaction. It requires building enduring relationships with people and making them successful.

Building relationships involve exciting new ways of strategic thinking and leading change. It involves developing, empowering, and enriching people to become more than they are, to facilitate their well-being and development, and to enhance their probability to enjoy success. The business world has changed dramatically over the last several decades; it is more complex and more demanding. Moreover, it is changing at incredible speeds, requiring strategic leaders of today to stay ahead of those changes and to outpace expectations. No longer can strategic leaders simply respond to changes in the business environment as they occur; they must orchestrate change and become the architects of the future. Strategic leaders have to adapt new ways of thinking and leading if they are to be successful in the more complex and turbulent world of the 21st century. They have to be completely connected to all they embrace. Success is dependent on having positive relationships up and down the value systems and within the organization.

Notes

1. Henry Cloud, *Integrity: the courage to meet the demands of reality* (New York, NY: HarperCollins Publishers, 2006, pxii).
2. David L Rainey, *Enterprise-wide Strategic Management: Achieving Sustainable Success through Leadership, Strategies and Value Creation* (Cambridge, UK: Cambridge University Press, 2010, p473).
3. David Barboza, "China has passed Japan to become the second largest economy," *New York Times,* August 15, 2010.
4. The Nestle Sustainability Report, 2002, p15.
5. Id.
6. Based on a discussion with Ton Boon von Ochssee, Ambassador for Sustainable Development, Ministry of Foreign Affairs, The Netherlands at the Conference Board's session on Sustainable Development, June 21, 2006 in Washington, D.C.
7. Bill George, *Authentic Leadership: Rediscovering the Secrets to Creating Lasting Value* (San Francisco, CA: Jossey-Bass, 2003, p12).
8. Ford Motor Company, Form 8-K-Item 5.02 states that on May 11, 2005 the Compensation Committee of Ford's Board of Directors agreed to amend Mr. Ford's compensation arrangement such that Mr. Ford will forego any new compensation until such time as the Committee and M. Ford determine that the Company's Automotive sector has achieved sustainable profitability.
9. David L Rainey, *Sustainable Business Development: Inventing the Future through Strategy, Innovation, and Leadership* (Cambridge, UK: Cambridge University Press, 2006, p295).
10. Id. P295-296.

References

Burns, T. and G. M. Stalker (1961) *The Management of Innovation.* London, UK: Tavistock.

George, Bill (2003) *Authentic Leadership: Rediscovering the Secrets to Creating Lasting Value.* San Francisco, CA: Jossey-Bass.

Rainey, David L. (2010) *Enterprise-wide Strategic Management: Achieving Sustainable Success through Leadership, Strategies and Value Creation.* Cambridge, UK: Cambridge University Press.

Rainey, David L. (2010) *Sustainable Business Development: Inventing the Future through Strategy, Innovation, and Leadership.* Cambridge, UK: Cambridge University Press.

7

High-Level Strategic Innovations

Introduction

Strategic innovations involve developing new knowledge and core capabilities and creating new technologies, products, services, and processes that allow the company to lead change and to outpace its peers and competitors. The focus is on opportunities and challenges as the company seeks to discover, develop, and establish innovative ways for achieving success while at the same time eliminating limitations and barriers. Success depends on the relentless pursuit of innovativeness that requires strategic thinking, proactive strategies, compelling actions, and profound outcomes. It is the never-ending journey toward excellence based on the realization that such pursuits involve global perspectives, out-of-the-box thinking, tireless efforts, and innumerable actions.

High-level strategic innovations involve realizing the strategic direction, corporate goals, and the grand strategies using internal (organic) developments in the forms of new solutions, systems and structures, and external investments in starting new ventures and in acquiring and dramatically improving other companies, business units, operations, and product lines (brands). Strategic innovations focus on creating new or dramatically enhanced businesses and/or significantly improved strategic positions. They are based the external context (needs, wants and expectations), internal context (capabilities, resources, and direction), and the knowledge, experience, learning, and creativity of the strategic leaders and organization. The principal aims are to realize the vision, improve the prospects for the future, obtain sustainable competitive advantages, and sustain success; they also include creating new businesses to supplement or replace existing ones.

Strategic leaders are the sponsors and directors of high-level strategic innovations. They use their insights about the business environment and their imaginations about how the company can develop, build, expand, and improve its strategic and operational positions. Strategic innovations improve the value proposition for customers, stakeholders, and the organization and result in new and/or enhanced solutions and value systems. While the actual management constructs and methods depend on the types of strategic innovations, i.e., research & development (R&D), radical technologies, new-to-the-world products and processes, new business models, or new ventures, most strategic innovations have common characteristics. Such innovations involve how to create unique solutions and systems for making huge advancements and even radical changes in positions, performance, and outcomes. They are generally about making quantum leaps forward and becoming more capable and sophisticated.

High-level strategic innovations may include technological innovations and new product developments (NPD), but these areas are generally the domain of lower levels of the organization. These types of innovations may rise to be high-level if they affect the whole corporation, require significant investments, involve company-wide efforts, and/or have significant risks. For example, Airbus spent more than ten billion Euros on the development program for the A380 Super Plane. The high-level strategic program represented a huge financial commitment and a large risk for the whole company. Obviously, such a NPD program is a high-level strategic innovation. High-level strategic innovations that focus on social, economic, environmental, technological, and market-related considerations, opportunities, and challenges are typically corporate initiatives as well. If successful, they provide the ways to change the business enterprise.

Strategic innovations involve leading change across the whole enterprise and not just within the organization. Strategic leaders have to lead the strategic innovations and initiate *high-level development programs* (HDPs) at rates greater than the general rate of improvements of their peers and competitors. While strategic leaders have many concerns and engage in many developments including the financial status (bottom line) of their companies, they must invest their time and efforts on discovering opportunities and exploiting them.

Full-spectrum strategic leadership (FSL) necessitates highly competent, innovative, and technologically sophisticated strategic leaders. Such leaders must think broadly to create new landscapes for exceeding the needs and dreams of all customers, stakeholders, shareholders and society. Strategic innovations are usually on the cutting edge; therefore, strategic leaders and managers have to employ FSL as discussed throughout this book. The chapter includes the following main topics:

- Developing a sense of the most critical factors affecting strategic innovation
- Outlining the elements pertaining to strategic innovation

Critical Factors Involving Strategic Innovations

Overview

In the broadest sense, organic strategic innovations are generally game changing new-to-the-world products, radical new technologies, innovative management constructs, and business model innovations. They are usually based on the strategic planning and corporate initiatives that are directly tied to the vision and strategic direction of the company. They involve a complex array of action plans and HDPs that are intended to result in transitions and/or transformations of the company or a significant portion of it, i.e., a strategic business unit (SBU). While they may include incremental improvements that are developed and implemented by the strategic leaders of the business units, the general schemes involve radical changes that focus on the future well-being of the company and how it expects to realize its objectives and fulfill the strategies. Strategic innovations are generally intended to obtain strategic advantages that last for five or so years. Strategic innovations are the domain of the strategic leaders in the pursuit of long-tem success.

Figure 7.1 shows the main categories of strategic innovations and their relationships with respect to strategies, solutions, systems, and structures. Cutting-edge management constructs are also depicted; they are innovative ways instituting strategic methods and techniques like six-sigma management. Most management constructs usually address specific topical areas like quality management, environment, health

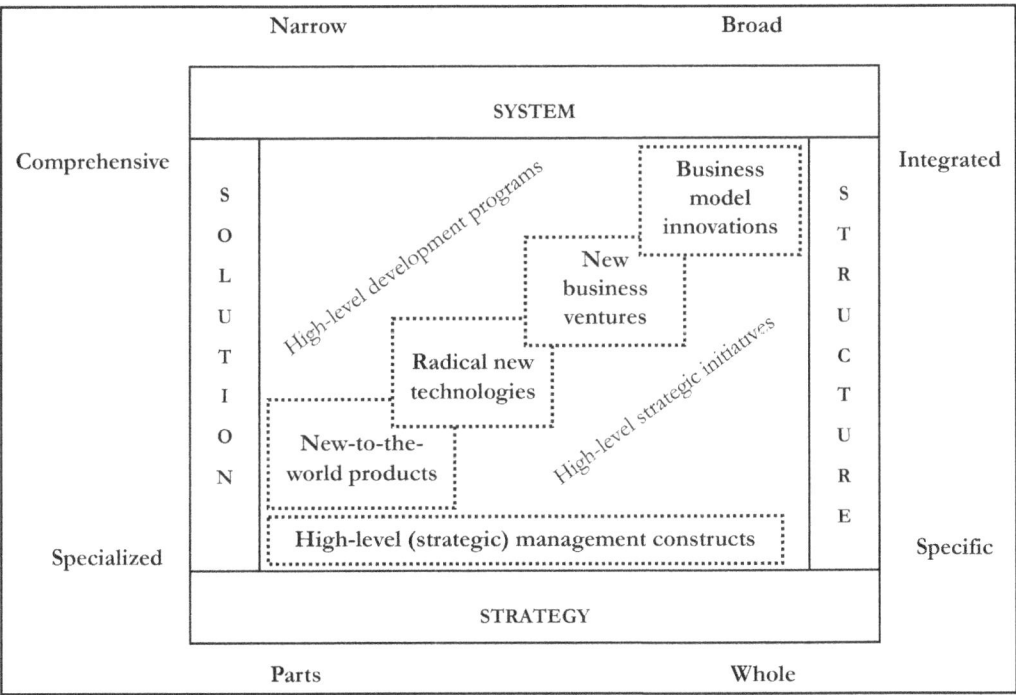

Figure 7.1 The hierarchy of organic strategic innovations.

and safety management, and lean practices, but cutting-edge ones involve corporate strategic management and SBU leadership perspectives.

The most prevalent strategic innovations are HDPs to develop new-to-the-world products like 3-D televisions and electric vehicles. They generally offer enhanced solutions, but are typically based on the established systems and structures of the company. Such strategic innovations are mainly in the realm of dramatic improvements to the solutions provided by the company; ones based on the corporate strategies. While such innovations are powerful, they may or may not be game changers. They offer additional competitive advantages and result in substantial improvements in positive financial or market outcomes. If the enhanced solutions are based on combining existing technologies, the durability of the advantages may be relatively low, especially if the intellectual capital cannot be well protected. The main concern is that most of time the enhanced advantages are replicated by other companies within the near term, say two or three years.

Radical new technologies often provide strategic advantages that last at least five or more years, especially if the new technologies are protected with patents and/or trade secrets. New-to-the-world technologies represent breakthroughs in how solutions are developed and provided. They are not only game changers, but also provide new fields of endeavors that produce significant new outcomes. For example, Toyota's hybrid drive technology gives the company numerous ways to achieve success; selling desirable fuel-efficient products (the Prius), obtaining royalty payments from competitors, and making competitors follow its strategies rather than having to follow theirs. The more comprehensive the new solution is, especially if it is based on new-to-the-world technologies and integrated into the systems and structures of the organization, the more likely the solution will endure and produce competitive advantages and extraordinary value creation.

New business ventures are innovative ways to break out of the prevailing situations. New ventures include start-ups within the company and new SBUs that are usually forms of related or unrelated diversification. New ventures generally involve developing distinct new businesses that are significantly different from the prevailing strategic positions of the company. The general focus is on emerging market spaces or untapped market potential. They involve the development of new strategic management and operating systems, and they require a considerable amount of new learning and additional innovations. Such new ventures may become separate business units with their own strategic leadership and management system(s). They have strategic leaders that develop business strategies, business plans, and business models. Starting new ventures requires entrepreneurial leadership involving creating the systems and structures and leading people.

Creating or reinventing a business model, often referred to as business model innovation, is one of the most difficult challenges facing strategic leaders. While corporate and SBU leaders do not have to actually select a new business model very often, they should always be thinking about the adequacy of the present one and how well it fits reality. The concept of a business model has gained significance in recent years because of the prominence of companies like Toyota, Dell Inc., Southwest Airlines (SWA) and Walmart; companies whose success is often attributed to their unique business models. With these models, the strategic leaders at these companies used their innovativeness to set themselves apart from the competition.

Toyota developed its Toyota Production System (TPS) in 1949 to create a manufacturing (operating) system that could compete against General Motors (GM), Ford Motor Company (FMC) and Chrysler Corporation in an era when the so-called "Big Three" of the U.S. dominated the automobile industry. The cost structures of automobile production usually depend on market size, economies of scale, and a company's market positions. GM and FMC had excellent markets shares and used their extensive production volumes to exploit the advantages of mass production. Immediately following World War II (WWII), Toyota had limited capacity and insufficient volume to use mass production. Moreover, most Japanese consumers could not afford automobiles, so the demand for any size or type of vehicle was very low and economies of scale were unattainable. Therefore, Toyota had to create a new system for producing cost effective vehicles a few at a time. TPS was based on the principles of just-in-time manufacturing, lean operations and the pursuit of efficiency and effectiveness.[1] TPS allowed Toyota to achieve low cost production based on rapid transitions from one model to another without incurring delays or idle time.

Dell was a minuscule start-up in 1984 that grew into the giant of the personal computer (PC) industry. Dell is famous for its original business model in which customer orders triggered the production process and suppliers furnished parts and components on an as-needed basis. Dell's business model eliminated the need for forecasting what customers might buy and producing inventory in expectation of customers, since Dell only produced and delivered PCs based on customer specifications and orders. Moreover, customers paid in advance and suppliers received payment after shipments; therefore, cash flow was generally positive. While Dell changed its business model during the last decade to reflect the new realities in the PC industry, Dell was able to take global market share leadership in the early 2000, and it is still one of the top three PC companies with 11.6% share.[2]

SWA is a regional carrier in the U.S. that concentrates on point-to-point routes with no frills and a single type of aircraft, the Boeing 737. Its business model is predicated on simplicity and low-cost service. Almost every element of its operating system is designed to be as uncomplicated as possible given the complexities for ensuring safety, maintaining rigorous standards, achieving high quality, meeting government regulations, and keeping customers happy. SWA often selects routes with limited competition and uncongested airports. It tries to avoid the typical problems like delays at the largest airports.

Walmart has become the largest retailer in the world through the relentless pursuit of low-cost, efficient, and integrated operations, and effective purchasing power based on direct relationships with suppliers. It manages every detail to cut costs and eliminate inefficiencies. It has linked its value delivery system and retail operations from the suppliers to customers via an integrated information technology system and logistical scheme that allows it to know what is required, when the products are needed, from whom goods are expected, and how to get the products efficiently to the right location at the right time.

Characterizing how corporations select their strategic management framework or management constructs is difficult and one of the most complicated challenges. As mentioned about sustainable success, there are not precise ways to measure how corporations are expected to succeed over the long term. A long history does not guarantee future success. The size of assets or revenues does not always provide a good indication about long-term success. Some of the biggest corporations are among the most vulnerable.

Theoretical considerations pertaining to strategic innovations

A very stable business environment generally means that business conditions and trends are changing slowly and that most of the needs, expectations, requirements, and mandates of customers and stakeholders are being satisfied. The primary attention is typically on existing markets and their potential for growth and development. The typical business strategies involve providing enhanced solutions through existing and new products using current technologies and leveraging resources and capabilities. Strategic analysis typically concentrates on market conditions and trends and on customer requirements and expectations. The prime motivations in such situations are to obtain dominant product positions and to achieve strategic, market, and financial successes. Financial performance and results are often the key determinants. The aim is not just to enhance one's strategic position but also to maintain the stability and not to disrupt market positions with radical changes. The generally accepted ways of achieving positive outcomes and ensuring stability include quality management, continuous improvement, and incremental innovations. Of course, there are exceptions like Apple, Inc.'s preemptive move in bringing a new product like iPad to the market.

As the business environment becomes more turbulent, astute strategic leaders have to think more about strategic innovations that create new solutions and significantly improved systems and structures. It is not good enough just to formulate product-market strategies and implement them or to employ incremental innovations like new products or processes. A turbulent business environment typically involves rapid changes in market conditions, trends, and requirements with high degrees of uncertainty and vulnerability. In more turbulent situations, the prevailing products and services may not satisfy customers and stakeholders. They may be insufficient to obtain competitive advantages. Existing products, services, processes, practices, and perspectives have to be examined and often replaced. New solutions may be necessary to meet the customer needs and desires. Opportunities and threats have to be identified and managed. New market spaces or new market requirements become the driving forces of change, providing both great opportunities and serious threats. The requisite solutions often have to go beyond evolutionary innovations. Strategic leaders may be forced to abandon the old ways and create new ways for realizing success.

Radical innovations are often the right response for turbulent conditions as well as for achieving significant strategic advantages based on creating new-to-the-world technologies. New-to-the-world technologies and products become the strategic necessities for assuring that the company's solutions are in concert with the new realities. R&D is often crucial for discovering, developing, demonstrating, and delivering breakthrough technologies for realizing the opportunities and/or negating the potential threats. Such technologies are referred to as breakthroughs if they are game changers or disruptive, if they have the potential to significantly change the essence of competition, market conditions or industry structure, and most importantly if they render many of the existing assets, resources, capabilities, products, and processes obsolete and even worthless.

Disruptive technologies as characterized by Clayton Christensen, world renowned professor at Harvard Business School (HBS), have the potential to change everything, destroying the prevailing case and creating a new one.[3] In a turbulent environment, disruptive, radical innovations are necessary to stay ahead of the demands and requirements of the future. Radical innovations, if successful, convert opportunities into powerful strategic positions for the future; they may also eliminate the threats by preempting the strategies and actions of competitors. Indeed, radical innovations involve changing the products, the technologies, and the business models. Moreover, the change mechanisms affect the core competencies and capabilities of the organization and enterprise and the means and mechanisms for implementing and executing strategies. The organizations so affected have to develop new capabilities and competencies often quickly and create new systems, structures, processes, and business models.

Radical changes in the business environment as discussed in Chapter 3 require emboldened approaches for sustaining success. Most strategic leaders embrace strategic innovations, but the real question usually pertains to how far they are willing to go. Figure 7.2 depicts the essential differences between incremental innovations and those involving radical change based on strategic innovations. Strategic leaders are often timid and risk-adverse; they tend to rely on simple product innovations to keep pace with change. However, simply improving old products may be a waste of time and money if the customers and the stakeholders want dramatic changes. For instance, in an era of rising fuel prices, customers want significant improvements in energy efficiencies, not just marginal improvements like ten percent – they want dramatic innovations. Moreover, in turbulent times, customers demand more value; better efficiency, reliability, and affordability.

A major challenge in selecting the proper approaches is that many strategic leaders perceive incremental innovations to be low risks and radical innovations to be high risks. In reality, the answer is not that simple: neither is automatically low-risk or high-risk; it depends on context. In situations with radical changes in the business environment, especially if there are significant technological advancements in the scientific, academic, and research communities, holding firm with the prevailing dominant technologies may result in high-risk positions. For instance, the dramatic impacts of new-to-the-world technologies like digital technologies in telecommunications made investments in product improvements based on the old analog technologies very risky. In most cases, such

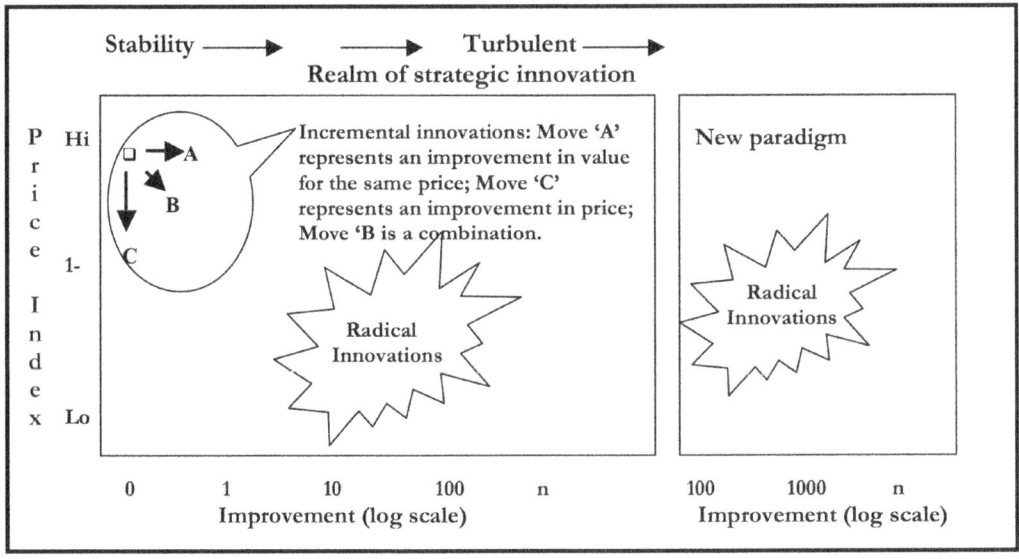

Figure 7.2 Theoretical view of incremental and radical innovations[4]

incremental improvements simply resulted in slightly better products that were still deficient and in most cases obsolete. On the other hand, proactive strategic investments into new-to-the-world technologies often produced cutting-edge strategic positions with huge competitive advantages. Radical innovations may even lead to a new paradigm that makes the existing business situations irrelevant. For example, the introduction of the Boeing 707 made the existing propeller planes immediately obsolete for the commercial airlines. The jet age in air transportation transformed almost everything from the gates to the mechanics. An even more compelling story is the transformation in movie-making in 1929 from silent pictures to "talkies." Most of the actors of the silent film era were unable to perform in the new paradigm because the new competencies included having a powerful or at least an appropriate voice to match the images. The filming changed, the cameras changed and even the movie houses changed.

Think about Intel's incredible success with its strategic investments into microprocessor technologies over the last thirty years. In 1985, Gordon Moore who was the chief executive officer (CEO) at the time and Andrew Grove who became the subsequent CEO decided to get out of memory chips because Intel was unable to justify the investments in the HDPs required to compete with the Japanese competitors.[5] Moore and Grove concentrated their efforts on microprocessor technologies that involved radical innovations. Moore's view of making dramatic technological advancements that were at least two times better than the previous technology propelled Intel into the lead and allowed it to stay there. Moore's Law involved an implicit understanding of the degree of innovation that is necessary to lead change and keep ahead of competition. Moreover, during his tenure as CEO Grove concentrated on making 10X changes in technologies, ensuring that Intel was significantly ahead of customer demands and competitor's responses. Grove was instrumental in integrating suppliers and providers of complementary products and services into Intel's value delivery system.[6] He understood that the whole system had to support the company's strategic direction and that strategic innovations had to lead to profound transitions and transformations, otherwise there was a high risk of becoming non-competitive and even irrelevant.

The main strategic questions involve how to lead change and continuously stay ahead of changes in the business environment. The underlying theory is that it is better to lead than to follow in today's complex and turbulent business world, especially if you can set the technological and business-related standards, the acceptable behaviors, and the desired and dominant solutions.

The strategic logic for leading change through strategic innovations

The strategic logic for leading change is embedded in the complexities of the global business environment. Change is ever-present and relentless. There are always numerous opportunities, challenges, problems, difficulties, risks, and vulnerabilities facing the strategic leaders of any organization causing changes or requiring solutions. Historically, the rate of changes in the business environment was relatively slow, the context was fairly narrow, and most of strategic actions taken by peers and competitors were modest improvements pertaining to the prevailing situations. While there were radical innovations like the transistor, the microprocessor, the PC, the digital camera, etc. their effects were initially manifested in the highly specialized market segments like commercial goods and luxury products. The long-term effects and implications often took many years, if not decades to filter down to the mainstream market segments, i.e., consumers segments focusing on affordable products. Given that the business environment was relatively slow and stable, the pressure on strategic leaders for most of the last century was to grow and expand within the context of their served market segments, to make incremental improvements, and to achieve the targeted outcomes and the related financial performance. While this is a simplification of the many different challenges during the twentieth century, including the Depression, WWII, and the Oil Crises of the 1970s, it can be said that the norm was fairly predictable and most changes were based on the prevailing situation, i.e., usually not radical or disruptive changes.

During those times, most strategic leaders rarely had to think beyond their existing business case; stability was assumed to be the norm.[7] As with any situation there were always undesirable aspects, concerns, difficulties, and problems. Strategic leaders at all levels had to examine their domains to determine the favorable and unfavorable aspects, the advantages and disadvantages, and their strengths and weaknesses. Based on their strategic analysis, astute strategic leaders would find the problems and solve them. *Problem solving* was a mainstream perspective and mechanism. Moreover, in the context of slow change problem solving and continuous improvement were usually meaningful, since such techniques provided relevant outcomes for a considerable time, say five years. And, in many cases, the strategic leaders and the senior professionals who engaged in problem solving became the heroes of the day if and when they solved the problem(s).

Problem-solving approaches seemingly made good sense because problems are undesirable and often inhibited market, operational, and financial performance. Moreover, many of the problems were self-evident and it was easy for most of the strategic leaders to identify the main problems and know what approaches were necessary to solve them. This is not to say that solving problems was not without trials and tribulations or that it was always easy, but the context was narrow and the time frame usually focused on the immediate or short term. For example, during the oil crises of the 1970s or even today's energy situations, the problems were or are often stated in terms of finding more sources of crude oil and expanding production capabilities. While such problems require sophisticated technologies and methods, the strategists and implementers know what they are seeking, they understand the methodologies for discovering, refining, and producing more oil, they realize that the economics are favorable, and they know that the related investments are usually positively rewarded. However, the scope of the search is narrow and the potential solutions typically lead to a temporary reprieve but not necessarily to ways out of the morass. In reality, many problem solving techniques result in temporary outcomes that simply buy more time, but they do not involve real solutions because the underlying causes continue to exist.

Problem solving techniques may provide reasonable outcomes in a slow-paced and stable business environment. Incremental innovations and continuous improvements are often adequate to maintain one's strategic and market positions and financial successes in such situations. While there are always vulnerabilities to unexpected events and radical changes, a stable business environment tends to favor innovations and improvements that are based on the prevailing technologies, products, and processes rather than revolutionary changes and discontinuous innovations. The reasons are obvious; corporations and industries have significant investments in their prevailing positions from product portfolios and dominant technologies to the production and operating systems, internal capabilities, and core competencies. Based on this line of thinking, the overwhelming business perspectives of most strategic leaders and professionals are to serve existing customers, protect their assets, recover their investments, and obtain appropriate returns. While there are usually ongoing developments into new technologies, the mix of innovations and investments is typically skewed toward the incremental, i.e., not strategic innovations.

In today's business world, the business case for major strategic innovations follows two main pathways among a number of others. One is to lead change and to be proactive, staying ahead of the driving forces in the business environment and extended enterprise, i.e., to be or become the change agent. The other involves creating a new paradigm based on the changes occurring in the business environment and market spaces. Both involve FSL and cutting-edge means and mechanisms. They are based on a realization that the business world today is more complex and turbulent and that change is ever-present; there is no such thing as the status quo. They are also based on the premises that strategic leaders and their companies either are making significant advancements and progress toward better solutions, fully integrated systems and sustainable success, or they are falling behind market expectations and becoming less competitive and successful. If the latter happens, strategic leaders and their companies may eventually become irrelevant players and fade from the scene. Markets are generally changing, growing, and becoming more demanding and more diffuse. Market spaces in the rapidly industrializing countries (RICs) are opening and expanding, existing markets and customers in developed countries expect more for less, and demand worldwide is becoming more fragmented. Social changes are impacting behaviors, desires, and expectations. People want the best solutions possible, not just the old products and services that have many negatives associated with them. Environmental concerns like climate change and resource depletion are critical issues that are central to developing new solutions. The key questions are: do real strategic leaders want to lead or are they just followers; and how does a true strategic lead? Given the global pressures, it is clear that strategic leaders have to become more sophisticated, and they have to be on the cutting edge. They have to lead and develop the means and mechanisms to exhibit proactive leadership.

Strategic logic suggests that leading change is relevant regardless of the levels of stability and turbulence in the business environment. It is proactive and recognizes that today's difficulties and problems are barriers and limitations to success and that simple problem solving is both inadequate and not enduring. Typical problem solving approaches simply delay the inevitable. For instance, what kinds of continuous improvements to film-based cameras or cathode ray tube televisions could have saved those technologies from the advancements in digital cameras and LCD TVs, respectively? The best answer for dealing with concerns, difficulties, and problems is to tackle them head on, eliminate the root causes, and discover innovative ways to create sustainable outcomes. And the best approaches in addressing such situations are to expand the context for analysis and decision making. This means examining the broader aspects of the business world using multifaceted thinking and innovative approaches.

Effective strategic leaders delve into the realms of the broad perspectives and future context. They seek ways to develop unique solutions and create effective systems that represent significant changes to the existing situations. They win by making the old battles irrelevant and of little consequence. Rather than problem solving, they embrace the notion of *puzzle solving*. While problems involve specific concerns, difficulties, or the like that are narrow in scope, puzzles are contextual situations with perplexing conditions and trends that are very broad in scope and multifaceted in their nature. Puzzle solving requires ingenuity, research, careful study, and due considerations for inventing the right solutions and outcomes. It involves sophisticated strategic thinking about all of the opportunities and possibilities. It clearly involves out-of-the-box thinking, not simply following the mainstream or what the other strategic leaders have done or are doing. Puzzling solving is more complex because strategic leaders have many more variables to understand, manage, and resolve before making decisions. It involves the realms of the many unknowns and uncertainties. Yet, it may not be any more risky than the risks associated with traditional problem solving approaches, since the underlying purpose is to expose the causes of problems and difficulties and to eliminate them. Think about the billions of dollars lost by companies like Bear Stearns, Merrill Lynch, and Citigroup whose corporate leaders believed they were engaged in conventional business practices when they invested into sub-prime mortgages. They believed that they were dealing with the problems associated with mortgage investments. Instead of following the norm and industry-related practices, such strategic leaders could have explored what instruments people really needed when buying real estate while simultaneously ensuring the risks involved from everyone's perspectives were reasonable and balanced in the short term and the long term. Specifically, the needs of the clients were the main considerations that required due diligence and being righteous.

Puzzle solving requires insights about what the prevailing situations and opportunities really are and imagination about what the business environment and market spaces could be and how to take advantage of the possibilities. Just like toy puzzles, there is a solution that is contained within the domain of the puzzle if one has the tenacity and commitment to put the pieces together properly. The answers are found in the whole, not the pieces. However, unlike toy puzzles in which there is a single solution, there are usually many solutions in the real world of business that can be created through strategic innovations and the integration of the whole enterprise. Puzzle solving often leads to new approaches or even paradigm changes that offer unique positions that are difficult for others to emulate. In the context of puzzle solving, strategic leaders have to engage every aspect of the organization and extended enterprise to create new solutions, form integrated systems, establish value networks, and organizational structures and build the requisite relationships. The outcomes have to be comprehensive and complete from every dimension. Focusing on customers, markets, and/or competition at the expense of the other critical dimensions may lead to an incomplete solution with gaps; it is akin to completing the middle of a toy puzzle and saying that the picture is finished. It provides a sense of what the complete picture is, but there are often critical elements (information) on the edges that may provide the greatest perspectives and outcomes.

Strategic leaders have the implicit responsibilities to set the stage and orchestrate what the future may hold for their organizations and enterprises. It is important to remember that there is no end point and that creativity, imagination, insights, and innovations involve a continuum. As the business world evolves and becomes more complex and difficult to manage within the existing paradigm, it may be time to think about new ways of creating desired outcomes (the solutions), integrating the elements (the systems), organizing the people (the structures) and connecting them together (the relationships).

FSL also involves going beyond the norms of the business world and inventing a new reality. Strategic leaders have to be more sophisticated, confident, competent, and courageous. They may have to create the new paradigm, referred to as *paradigm illuminating*. It involves the next higher level for leading change. While creating a new business paradigm is rare, it becomes necessary when the old notions and constructs no longer fit reality. The term paradigm has been used in science to connote what is normal and generally accepted by a community of practitioners. Thomas S. Kuhn (1922–1996), a science historian, used "paradigm" in the following senses:[8]

> On one hand, [the paradigm] stands for the entire constellation of beliefs, values, techniques, and so on shared by members of a given [scientific, academic, business, etc.] com-

munity. On the other hand, it denotes one sort of element in that constellation, the puzzle-solutions which, employed as models or examples, can replace explicit rules as the basis for the solution of the remaining puzzles of normal science.

Kuhn's work pertained mostly to scientific methodologies, but the logic applies to business as well. Some of the major paradigm changes or transformations in science include the shift from a geocentric to a heliocentric world then to the Newtonian view and more recently to Einstein's view based on the theories of relativity. While knowledge is always imperfect and there are gaps in articulating all of the elements of a paradigm, a given paradigm tends to be supported by the communities of scholars and practitioners until it is proven to be incorrect or does not meet the needs of real-world situations. For instance, the geocentric view worked fairly well as long as most of humankind's efforts focused on local agriculture and village life. Moreover, Newtonian mechanics are still relevant even though relativity and quantum mechanics are much more comprehensive and explain reality better, since our world involves very slow speeds in comparison to the relativistic world going at the speed of light, and it is on a much large scale than the atomic and sub-atomic world of the quantum dimensions. Thus, Newtonian physics provides a reasonable explanation of the physical world.

From a business perspective, some of the major paradigm shifts have been mechanization via the industrial revolution, the production of interchangeable parts introduced at the Springfield (Massachusetts) Armory in the 1850s, Henry Ford's mass production and assembly during the early twentieth century, and total quality management (TQM) and Toyota's lean production system. While there are numerous other paradigm shifts involving other factors like the technological changes from analog to digital and the financial innovations of the limited liability corporation and the extension of consumer credit, true paradigm shifts in the business world are difficult to articulate precisely and often take many years to come into full bloom. Making such determinations is especially difficult in the fast paced world of the twenty-first century in which continuous changes are the norm, and it is difficult to sort out what are the true implications and impacts of technological advancements and market dynamics from the perspective of a paradigm change. It often takes a decade or so before a majority of the scholars and practitioners to fully realize that a profound change has occurred. Moreover, many leaders and professionals try hold steadfast in the old paradigm because it is the basis of their knowledge, experiences, capabilities, power, and positions. They are unwilling or unable to accept and adapt to the new paradigm because they are entrenched in the old ways. They cannot change their basic makeup or organizations in terms of mindset, philosophies, culture, belief system, and decision making processes. For instance, it took the American automobile companies approximately thirty years before they adapted TQM and Toyota's just-in-time manufacturing philosophies and methods. In many cases, it is the new companies and business leaders that accept the new paradigm as they become the new market share leaders and star performers in the business world. The laggards eventually exit the scene as their strategies, actions, and efforts fail to succeed because they are out of synch with reality.

Paradigm illuminating construct involves proactive strategies and approaches for understanding the new realities and staying ahead of the new needs, requirements, and expectations, i.e., being on the cutting edge. It involves the recognition that the business world is changing every day and that businesses and strategic leaders must make dramatic, if not revolutionary, changes in how they do business and what business arenas they engage in. It is more open-ended than most management constructs and models, since it is impossible to specify how to create the new paradigm. Moreover, as Kuhn suggested, most of the paradigm changes involve the elements and not the whole constellation. Business model innovation as discussed in the next chapter represents some of the most important ways for making paradigm-illuminating changes on a large scale.

The Main Elements of Strategic Innovation

Value innovation: the underpinning of strategic innovation

Value innovation focuses on tying the solutions, systems, structures, the extended enterprise and the business environment together. It is a highly interactive approach for discovering, creating, developing, and implementing new solutions and systems through strategic innovations. It involves open-ended and proactive ways to satisfy existing or latent needs and wants and to develop and use innovative constructs. It requires out-of-the-box strategic thinking about the prevailing strategic logic of the business and its extended enterprise and what they could be or should be. In particular, it involves reaching out to potential customers, market spaces and people that are not currently being served or even addressed.

Value innovation focuses on multiple means and mechanisms to break down barriers and open up opportunities for creating and delivering new solutions to the underlying difficulties, limitations, constraints and challenges. It focuses on opportunities to enrich the social and economic well-being of people and to ensure that the natural environment is protected and sustained. Value innovation can be viewed as the critical element that makes strategic innovations dynamic and vibrant. Value innovation includes many, if not most, of the mechanisms for making transitions and transformations to cutting-edge leadership and management. It runs the gamut from transitions like process and product innovation to radical transformations like sustainable business development (SBD) and new business paradigms. SBD is all encompassing. It extends from the beginnings of the supply networks to end-of-life considerations. It involves eliminating wastes, defects and impacts from all aspects of the enterprise and moving toward more ideal solutions. It is the ongoing strategic perspective to create new value, to share the riches of the world with more people and at the same time to ensure that the wealth created is enhanced and protected for future generations.

Value innovation is driven by the realities of the business world, the richness of the opportunities, and the vision and strategic direction orchestrated by the strategic leaders. It often necessitates building new business models or radically redefining and reinvigorating the existing ones. In such situations, value innovation and the existing business model merge to create the new strategic logic for the corporation and its

SBUs and to become the next business model platform for ensuring enduring success. Indeed, value innovation is one of the essential elements of business model innovation. Just as technologies may be viewed in terms of platforms that require ongoing development, business models require periodic developments that lead to higher levels of sophistications and achievements. For example, Intel used the Pentium platform for more a decade to enhance its technological capabilities and enjoy ongoing success. However, Intel's strategic leaders continued to develop new platforms to keep its microprocessor technologies on the cutting edge. Likewise, strategic leaders have to reinvent the strategic logic and business models they use to stay ahead of changes in the business environment and outpace the needs and expectations of customers and the contributors of the extended enterprise. These changes also work to minimize the negative influences and impacts of competitors and other antagonists of the organization. Strategic leaders have to become first movers or fast followers.

Value innovation is a fundamental underpinning of strategic innovations, i.e., to create extraordinary value for customers, markets, stakeholders, shareholders, and all of the internal and external contributors; value that exceeds their needs and expectations. Such approaches are intended to create broad opportunities for growth and success through strategies, systems, structures, and solutions that focus on the economic and social drivers and not those opportunities just based on the competitive forces. It reverses conventional strategic management thinking about how to achieve business success from using narrow perspectives developed in an era when producers and production were the essence of business models to today's realities in which the focus is on the total solutions, integrated systems, the whole extended enterprise, and enterprise-wide strategic management (ESM). FSL, ESM, great solutions and powerful value delivery systems make competitors less important, if not irrelevant. W. Chan Kim and Renee Mauborgne in their acclaimed Harvard Business Review article, "Value Innovation: The Strategic Logic of High Growth," describe how companies can be make quantum leaps in value and profitable growth as they make competitors irrelevant by transcending market boundaries. They articulate what new market space is:[9]

> Value innovators often cross boundaries. They think in terms of the total solution buyers seek, and they try to overcome the chief compromises their industry forces customers to make.

Kim and Mauborgne use examples of companies that expanded the traditional definition of their businesses and created new models and approaches for satisfying customers. Their examples include Virgin Atlantic, an airline that changed trans-Atlantic air travel by making it more affordable, and CNN, the TV network that changed reporting the news by increasing the scope and depth of the coverage. While each of these stories have some side effects, the original was to focus on new spaces. Value innovation focuses on discovering new market spaces, finding new opportunities in existing market segments, determining new customer and stakeholders needs, and creating new ways of developing and delivering solutions. Strategic leaders can accomplish such outcomes through inventions, radical innovations, enterprise-wide integration, and leading change, among many other constructs. It requires proactive strategic leaders who are willing and able to understand the true needs and expectations of the business environment, to think holistically about the solutions, to drive innovations from the perspectives of the external entities, and to frame the business model from the basis of the extended enterprise(s) and value system(s). This means redefining the business platform(s) in terms of the total solution and not just products and services or industry structure; and to examine the whole value delivery system in terms of who has to be served and what the requisite outcomes must be. Moreover, it requires thinking about all of the market spaces, geographically and demographically, to find the best opportunities to create value and provide the best total solutions. Outstanding value innovation involves ongoing efforts to create better and better solutions that go beyond continuous improvements. It moves the business paradigm to a higher level of thinking, strategizing and taking action. It moves the solutions toward the ideal.

Corporate research and development and corporate entrepreneurship

R&D in most large corporations is typically divided into the fundamental areas being explored and developed. Corporate R&D usually involves centralized programs that pertain to new-to-the-world technologies, significant technological developments, and dramatic improvements to technology platforms. Typically, such programs involve the technology or product domains that go beyond the existing missions or operations of the business units, or they represent revolutionary changes that are outside of the current capabilities of the existing SBUs and their product portfolios. Such R&D programs often result in new business ventures. R&D programs that focus on the existing product lines are usually the domain of the strategic leaders of the business units.

R&D involves large investments of time and money that do usually not produce near-term rewards. Funding them involves huge financial risks and strategic leaders often have difficulty financially justifying the investments in R&D programs, especially during the early phases, since it often takes five to ten years or more to obtain the desired outcomes and positive cash flows. Moreover, high-level R&D programs usually involve developing and commercializing new-to-the-world technologies, products, and businesses that are disruptive to the current portfolios of the technologies and products at the SBU levels. Lower-level management may not be inclined to engage in such R&D programs, knowing that they may cause stresses within their organizations and even may cause their current operations to become less important and in some cases to be closed or sold off. SBU leaders may prefer exploiting current products rather than seeking better alternatives, especially when they have specific missions that they are responsible for and are compensated based on the short-term performance.

Clearly, the easiest way to determine what fits into high-level R&D, particularly at the corporate level, and what is in the domain of the SBUs is to examine what strategic perspectives and whose goals are driving the decision making processes. For corporate R&D, the focus should be on the vision and strategic direction of the corporation and not the missions of the existing business units. The most crucial corporate R&D programs involve advanced HDPs for new technologies and new-to-the-world products; ones that may even require new business ventures and/or new business models. They necessitate acquiring new capabilities and resources that are usually beyond those of the business units. Moreover, in the context of SBD, the radical new technologies should embrace the criteria for clean technologies that eliminate the negative aspects of the prevailing technologies. While the development of new technologies involves corporate R&D management, the development of the new business venture requires creating the technology, then translating it into a commercial reality via corporate technological entrepreneurship (CTE).

CTE focuses on the concepts, skills, know-how, information, mindset, processes, and actions that are relevant for entrepreneurs and strategic leaders who are starting new corporate ventures based on new-to-the-world technologies. It involves developing complex new SBUs within a large global corporation from its corporate R&D or acquired technologies. CTE includes establishing a strategic framework for developing new ventures, screening strategic options and selecting the most viable approaches. CTE includes developing a business plan, analyzing and determining valuation, securing sources of financing, structuring the arrangement, and obtaining the resources and capabilities for development and deployment. It also includes developing the business model, determining the methods and techniques for solving difficulties, and implementing the business plan. The creation, development, and deployment of radical and clean technologies often change the entire nature of the business model; the business practices, the management systems and processes, and the relationships in the organization may all require innovative changes or enhancements. They may require improving the effectiveness and applications of knowledge and the transformation to richer levels of technological sophistication and organizational learning.

Radical innovation

Radical innovation requires a more open-ended strategic management mindset. The approach should be entrepreneurial and creative. The strategic leaders involved in radical innovations have to be aggressive and tolerate failures as well as demanding successes. They have to conceive, discover, and analyze opportunities through the intellectual capital and capacity of the organization and turn opportunities into realities. The critical leadership perspectives involve determining why certain opportunities are important; analyzing the advantages and disadvantages of the possibilities; developing the means and mechanisms to exploit the most advantageous options; designing and developing the technologies, products, and processes (the solutions); determining how to measure success and validate outcomes; and implementing programs.

The most crucial consideration is usually the people. How does the organization acquire the talent and knowledge necessary to engage in radical innovations, especially people who have the mindset and inclination to engage in complex and open-ended HDPs and new ventures? The critical part is identifying the essential qualities and characteristics required. Managing radical innovations incorporates multiple disciplines within the organization and relies on a strategic management framework for mapping the way from inception to completion. For the more involved and complicated new-to-the-world technology and new product development programs, the organization typically uses program management methodology or a combination of program management and project management. The combination approach might be used for the less complicated programs, especially ones that are similar to successful programs of the past.

Radical innovations are highly dependent on the nature of the business environment. Again, context is critical. The starting point is assessing the business environment and the market spaces as they relate to changes and determining how the core capabilities and resources of the organization and enterprise fit the needs and requirements for the future. The focus of the former is on opportunities and threats, while the latter focuses on strengths and weaknesses. But astute strategic leaders have to exhibit care not to base decisions on the internal dimension (core competencies and strengths) but on the external ones (opportunities and challenges). The external forces usually drive the requisite strategic innovations. Some of the key drivers are:

- Changing business environment and market spaces.
- Rapidly changing customer and stakeholder expectations.
- Intense competitive pressures from world-class companies or emerging competitors.
- New mandates from governments and other stakeholder organizations.
- Dynamic technological changes and/or innovations.
- Enhanced capabilities and offerings from suppliers and related industries.

Strategic leaders use radical innovation to transition and/or transform their corporations. They convince people across the organization and extended enterprise that the vision and strategic direction necessitate new initiatives and actions to realize the aspirations. Visionary strategic leaders set the tone. Strategic leaders link the development programs with the corporate strategies, objectives and action plans. They set the agenda, the policies and the aims, and they provide the means and mechanisms. They allow for risk taking and even failures to occur.

Effective strategic leaders persuade people that the radical (strategic) innovations are imperative and that the notion of maintaining the status quo is illusionary, since the external world is changing dramatically and accelerating forward with new opportunities and challenges. While radical innovations are perceived to be risky, trying the retard change is often more risky and even fool-hardy. Strategic leaders in many different industries lost their preemptive positions over time simply because they failed to keep pace with or ahead of change. For example, AT&T was the premier telephone provider in the world for most of the twentieth century. Within two decades (1980s and 1990s) corporate leaders lost AT&T's incredible strategic positions as they tried to understand and deal with the enormous industry changes, from the development of cell phones to the rise of new competitors.

Most importantly, strategic leaders establish the front-end framework for radical innovations to assure the requisite programs are developed and implemented. The framework provides a clear map pertaining how new technology and products programs are initiated by the corporation. Radical innovations involve revolutionary changes. The requisite strategies and actions necessitate creating new realities that are

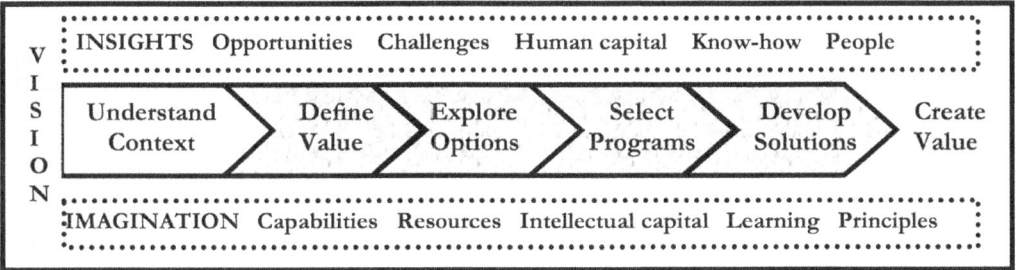

Figure 7.3 The front-end of the radical innovation framework.

superior to the prevailing ones. Figure 7.3 provides a sense of the essential elements of the framework.

Radical innovations invoke the new world of tomorrow. Since radical innovations usually take considerable time to identify, define, assess, select, verify, and develop, the focus is on creating new value and achieving long-term success. Based on the strategic direction, strategic leaders use their insights and imagination to understand context. While this is similar to perspectives discussed in previous chapters, the key to success is the full integration of the external aspects, like opportunities, challenges, human capital, and know-how that is in the public domain, with the internal capabilities, resources, intellectual capital, learning, and principles. The approach is dynamic, involving iterations. For instance, if the new opportunities are outside of the realm of the company's capabilities, then the strategic leaders have to determine how to acquire the learning and knowledge necessary to proceed.

Understanding context allows strategic leaders to define what value can be created and what the value proposition is. It is crucial to determine what creates value before options are considered. People expect the best value possible. Any proposed solutions must be capable of exceeding customer expectations, achieving world-class standards, meeting government mandates, and achieving corporate goals. The required specifications include superior performance, high quality, exceptional customer benefits, high value, low unit cost, and rapid development time or speed to commercialization. Providing exceptional customer benefits means providing an entire package of benefits; customers want solutions, not just products. Performance is a fundamental requirement. It is the ability to deliver what the customers and stakeholders want, need, and expect. But, performance is also relative. It is measured in terms of the cost (the investment) to the customer. Quality is a fundamental as well that relates to the perceived value provided by the solution. Total perceived quality is the customer's view of the experienced quality. Experienced quality is a time-dependent measure. Providing high value is a key to success.

Strategic leaders must explore many options when determining what radical innovations they plan to invest into, if any. The more options strategic leaders have, the more power they have in selecting the right programs. A significant challenge is to ensure that designs and selections have been validated using real-world information and data. During each step of the process, present and future customer and stakeholder needs and wants must be understood and articulated and then used as the basis for making key decisions about the features and benefits. The strategic innovation process begins and ends with a strategic perspective of the organization's vision, mission, objectives, and strategies and covers the all of the technical, marketing, production, and financial decisions that have to be made to be successful. These methods allow management to establish the information and data necessary to make informed decisions and to validate those decisions and outcomes. Success depends on people and their abilities and skills. Building a knowledge-based, adaptive, and creative organization is the crux for achieving superior results.

Reflections

Strategic innovations require exceptional intelligence for determining what is necessary and appropriate in the business environment and market spaces. Indeed, strategic innovations depend on the causes and effects of change and their implications. They necessitate having a full understanding and broad perspectives on future possibilities and options for businesses. Strategic innovations focus on dramatic improvements and radical developments to existing positions by creating new solutions, capabilities, systems and processes within an organization and across the extended enterprise. This involves strategically aligning capabilities and resources from cradle to grave.

Unbridled strategic innovations may lead to difficulties, especially when new segments or areas are not as viable as existing ones. For example, Google expanded into the Pacific Rim with less success than it has had in the U.S. It had difficulty dealing with the bureaucratic requirements in China. In such cases, strategic leaders have to ensure that they perform due diligence via a thorough strategic analysis as they expand into unfamiliar territory. Companies generally have a mix of strategic innovations, with some more successful than others. Companies can get into trouble when they expand without developing the requisite capabilities and resources or strategic perspectives. The integration and synchronization of the efforts and the development of the requisite knowledge, capabilities and resources are crucial for achieving success.

Strategic innovations include developing the new technologies and products and all of the requisite systems and structures. R&D organizations in such situations have to be mobile and adaptive and focus on building relationships with customers and market entities so that the value created is captured over the long term.

Notes

1. Yasuhiro Monden, *Toyota Management System: Linking the Seven Key Functional Areas* (Portland, OR: Productivity Press, 1993, p165).
2. http://www.bgr.com/2011/10/12/gartner-global-pc-shipments-jump-just-3-in-q3-2011/
3. Clayton Christensen, *The Innovator's Dilemma, When New Technologies Cause Great Firms to Fail* (Boston, MA: Harvard Business School Press, 1997, p61-76).
4. David L. Rainey, *Product Innovation: Leading Change through Integrated Product Development* (Cambridge, UK: Cambridge University Press, 2005, p308). The graphic is an adaptation that has been simplified.
5. Andrew S. Grove, *Only the Paranoid Survive* (New York, NY: Currency/Doubleday, 1996, p89).

6. Id, pp55-77.
7. Stability implies that the business environment and markets are steady, cyclical or growing or declining at relatively low rates (±10%); demand is predictable; dominant technologies form the basis for most products, and there are relatively few alternatives; economic and political underpinnings are well-understood and are stable; industry structure and participants are known, and there are predictable patterns of behaviors.
8. Thomas S. Kuhn, *The Structure of Scientific Revolution,* 3rd edition (Chicago, IL: University of Chicago Press, 1962, 1996, p175).
9. W. Chan Kim and Renee Mauborgne, "Value Innovation: The Strategic logic of High Growth," *Harvard Business Review,* January-February 1997, p107.

References

Christensen, Clayton (1997) *The Innovator's Dilemma, When New Technologies Cause Great Firms to Fail.* Boston, MA: Harvard Business School Press.

Grove, Andrew S. (1996) *Only the Paranoid Survive.* New York, NY: Currency/Doubleday.

Kuhn, Thomas S. (1962) The Structure of Scientific Revolution, 3rd Edition. Chicago, IL: University of Chicago Press.

Monden, Yasuhiro (1993) *Toyota Management System: Linking the Seven Key Functional Areas.* Portland, OR: Productivity Press.

Rainey, David L. (2005) *Product Innovation: Leading Change through Integrated Product Development.* Cambridge, UK: Cambridge University Press.

8

Business Model Innovation

Introduction

A cutting-edge business model of a company or a strategic business unit (SBU) is its unique way of combining the internal and external dimensions into a fully articulated framework for implementing and executing strategies, action plans, and operations and achieving desired outcomes. It includes the operating systems, value delivery systems and extended enterprise(s) that are integrated into a comprehensive, coherent, and collaborative arrangement that stretches from the origins of the raw materials to the applications of the solutions and end-of-life considerations. It is defined by the scope and boundaries of the business environment, the connections between the parties and the selected time horizon. It is also defined by the visions, missions, strategies, actions, solutions, systems, structures, and relationships of the organization and those of the value networks that support and enhance the positives and mitigate the negatives.

A business model is the conceptual combination of entities, interrelationships, patterns of interfaces, interactions, and the expected flow of activities between the contributors, recipients, and related constituents. The entities are linked together in formal and informal means and mechanisms based on the value propositions, value creations, and value delivery systems that are guided by the strategic direction, strategy formulation and implementation, operations, actions, and all of the people involved. A cutting-edge business model is more comprehensive than the internal management system(s), value systems, and the prevailing management constructs, and it includes the full scope of all of the critical entities that are necessary to create, develop, demonstrate, and deliver solutions and sustain success. It includes the means and mechanisms to achieve desired outcomes. Business models have gained wider acceptance through applications during the last decade.

The concept of a business model runs the gamut from simple versions that only describe how revenues and profits are generated to cutting-edge business models that are inclusive of all of the key perspectives and dimensions. Gray Hamel's business concept innovation as discussed in Chapter 1 is an example of a more sophisticated version developed over the last decade. Full-spectrum leadership (FSL) and being on the cutting edge require an even more sophisticated business model that incorporates all of the essential elements into a holistic framework for achieving sustainable success.

A business model provides an enhanced understanding of how everything is linked, what the explicit and implicit roles and responsibilities of the supporting entities are, and how they contribute to outcomes and success. Most companies have an implicit or explicit business model. A company's business model generally evolves over time as the strategic leaders reach higher levels of maturity, formality, and sophistication, especially as they become global corporations. Small and medium size enterprises (SMEs) usually have a general framework, but their business models focus on the primary factors that directly affect the company. It can be argued that start-up companies and new ventures generally have a sense of what their business model is that helps them understand and manage their businesses, but such schemes are often their business concept(s) and business plan(s) that are seedlings requiring time and loving care to mature. They often just have the vestiges of true business models that only provide the big picture. However, many start-up companies fail to update their business concepts as they grow, and the early version becomes hopelessly outdated.

Business model innovation (BMI), its development, and the associated elements and innovations are crucial for achieving extraordinary performance and success. The discussions in this chapter focus on how FSL and cutting-edge management constructs like enterprise-wide strategic management (ESM) lay the framework for BMI. The focus is on how companies or SBUs create and deliver value and how they implement their strategies and execute action plans through the elements of a business model. BMI involves creating a mental model of what could be; it also involves the design, development, demonstration and deployment of the business model. BMI is intended to be in concert with and reflect reality to the extent possible. BMI discussed herein pertains to sophisticated companies that are innovative, inclusive and connected. This chapter examines the following topics:

- Reflections on the underpinnings of business model innovation
- Discussions pertaining to business model constructs

Business Model Innovation

Underpinnings

Business models provide a comprehensive understanding of the business environment, the market spaces, the extended enterprise, and the organization and how the company or its SBU integrates all of the entities and elements into solutions, value delivery systems, subsystems, and structures. The discussions herein focus on how sophisticated strategic leaders and their organizations develop and deploy business models. Today, cutting-edge companies are transitioning from simpler management frameworks to fully-articulated business models that define who they are, what they do, how they do it, and where they are going.

Business models articulate how the company or SBUs and their extended enterprise intend to interact, what the interdependences are, how the entities are suppose to interface and work together, and what outcomes are desired and expected. They are the critical ESM constructs for linking the external dimensions with the internal ones. They define the direct and indirect roles and responsibilities of the company and its SBUs, especially those that the strategic leaders have the freedom to decide upon how to lead and manage. For instance, if there are laws and regulations covering certain business functions and activities, then the company or SBU must do what is mandated; i.e., there are no degrees of freedom in selecting whether to do it or not, nor in deciding what has to be done. They must comply with the regulations; ones that specify exactly what must be done. On the other hand, strategic leaders may have the freedom to add or eliminate certain functions, actions, activities, and requirements depending on the external realities and perceptions, especially what is expected by their customers, stakeholders, and constituents. These include the capabilities of the organization and the ability of the extended enterprise to provide value producing outcomes. Generally, all of the critical requirements and functions have to be provided, but there are degrees of freedom about exactly what is necessary and who is in the best position to provide the requisite outcomes. For instance, pumping gasoline into customers' automobiles is one of the last steps in the long chain of processes and activities from obtaining crude oil, refining products, and distributing fuel to storing it at a gas station, marketing it, and transferring it to the customer's fuel tank. While gas station owners have certain options about how to provide their customers with the products, most stations allow customers to pump their own gasoline. Most customers prefer the "do-it-yourself" approach when buying gasoline because they want to save time and avoid the added expense of full service. Such practices are generally accepted in most developed countries like the U.S. (except Oregon and New Jersey). Essentially, the business model involves what has to be done, what the actions and activities are, and who is going to do what activities.

Theoretically, a business model maps out how everything is to be configured, provided, linked, accomplished, and managed. It should also include contingences for non-routine or unexpected events, especially ones that are undesirable but have a reasonable probability of occurring. For instance, there should be an emergency deployment plan for spills, accidents, disasters, and other potential catastrophes.

In the old days of vertically integrated companies, business models were somewhat superfluous since the internal value chains and/or organizational structure defined the roles, responsibilities, relationships, and the required actions, processes, tasks, and activities. If there was a business model, it was embedded within the organizational structure. However, over the last half-century most global corporations have changed from vertically integrated structures into horizontal management systems. Those management systems are generally described as the value chain(s) (operating system) and value system with the extended enterprise as discussed in Chapter 1. With a broader scope that is more reliant on external entities, business models have become more important and even critical for achieving success as most companies now have a much more complicated management challenges in assuring that solutions are complete and are of the kind and quality people expect. As more and more businesses outsourced non-essential support services and even critical functions and activities, their value systems have become broader, more elaborate, interrelated, and interdependent for developing, producing, and delivering solutions. They are also more complicated and more vulnerable to changes in the business environment or failures of supporting entities to do what is expected.

In this context, business models link and integrate the internal (strategic and operational) management systems with the external dimensions and the value networks that contribute to the solutions provided. Business models apply not only to supply networks and related industries, i.e., contributors, but to customers and stakeholders, i.e., recipients, as well. In this context, customers may be both recipients of the solutions and providers of some of the required elements of the business model that are essential ingredients for providing solutions. For instance, most of the major airlines allow customers to carry certain luggage into the passenger section of the aircraft. This option reduces the activities required for handling customer baggage and enhances customer satisfaction because many customers do not want to wait for baggage retrieval after the plane arrives, or they want to be confident that their luggage was put on the plane.

Many strategic leaders often view the increasing complexity of the strategic management systems (SMSs) and their business models as undesirable, worrisome, and something to be simplified, if possible. However, if the business environment and the market spaces are complex and are becoming even more complicated over time, then strategic leaders need to develop cutting-edge business models that are sophisticated enough to mirror reality and provide management and employees with the means and mechanisms to be successful. Moreover, managing complexity can be a competitive advantage. It is theoretically more desirable to handle complexity at the strategic levels of the organization where there is sufficient intellectual capital and capacity to handle and resolve challenges and create new solutions rather than at the operating level where people are generally engaged in the prevailing day-to-day tasks that usually take precedence.

Many companies and their SBUs use simple business models to reflect on the opportunities and challenges of their enterprises and to establish the processes for managing the most important roles and responsibilities. Such approaches have followed the general philosophies and theories of the past to keep it simple. Whereas such business models are easy to understand and apply, they often lack the refinements necessary to articulate what has to be done and who is responsible for doing and accomplishing the actions and activities across the enterprise. With simplicity there may be many missing pieces that lead to confusion, incomplete solutions, missed opportunities, and added risks and vulnerabilities. The more sophisticated the business model is, the more likely it can provide extraordinary value creation, unique solutions, outstanding value delivery, and exceptional outcomes. Moreover, simple models are more easily copied by others, whereas the more elaborate business models are exceedingly more difficult to replicate. eBay and Google are good examples of companies having great success via their business models. Their successes are derived not only from their portfolio of affordable, efficient, and reliable services, but from their unique management systems and the effective use of the extended enterprise. Their value delivery systems are well linked with the supply networks and provide customers with solutions that satisfy not only their immediate needs, but their long-term desires as well.

A skeleton of a business model framework

The purpose of a business model is to incorporate and integrate all of the appropriate and necessary elements for creating, developing, producing, and delivering solutions using a holistic management system from the origins of creative design and the upstream processes and activities to the downstream applications and interests of customers and stakeholders and end-of-life considerations. While there are corporate business models like those of Southwest Airlines (SWA) and Amazon.com, generally business models are developed at the SBU level where there are distinct elements that pertain to markets spaces and the related extended enterprise. For global corporations like Canon, General Electric, United Technologies Corporation, IBM, Nestlé, Siemens, and Unilever, it is virtually impossible to develop a single business model framework that fits all of their SBUs. The enormity of scope and variations of missions, strategies, actions, and responsibilities are so large that a single business model would serve little purpose. Indeed, occasionally corporate leaders of large corporations create problems when they try to impose a single business model or common management constructs for all of the disparate business units.

The business model articulates what the whole enterprise has to do, including the upstream elements that support the development, production, and delivery of the solutions; the internal management system(s) for designing, producing, marketing and communicating the solutions; and the downstream elements involving the customers, applications, stakeholders, complementary products, and end-of-life considerations. It also includes elements that are not traditionally considered part of the value system. Such elements include the extended enterprise considerations pertaining to the infrastructure and competition as discussed throughout the book. The business model presents a complete picture of the external and internal workings that create valuable outcomes and deliver the resultant value to the recipients. Business models tie strategic formulation and implementation with the functional strategies and execution.

The business model framework goes beyond a representation of reality. From a systems perspective, it explores the portfolio of existing solutions, principally products, technologies, services, processes, materials, etc. and determines how they are linked into a super system that creates and delivers the value and solutions of the company or SBU. Strategic leaders and their organizations and enterprises are not expected to perform all of the requirements, but they should ensure that all of the expected requirements are fulfilled. This is especially the case for external ones.

Business models are the shared creation of the corporate leaders, SBU leaders, strategists, functional managers, and professional staffs. High-level strategic leaders are the principal architects of the business model and should tailor it to the realities of the SBU, the expected changes over time, and the existing and enhanced capabilities and resources of the organization and its extended enterprise. At the SBU level, the business model must also reflect the strategic direction and values of the corporation. Theoretically, business models are intended to set the business unit apart from all of the other entities engaged in the industry or market spaces. The uniqueness of one's business model is often the critical difference that facilitates success. It should allow strategic leaders to create value and mitigate risks in ways that make it difficult, if not impossible for others to copy. For example, SWA has a very effective business model that incorporates point-to-point routes using a single type of plane flying between non-congested airports. Its value proposition is based on responsiveness, low fares, and no-frills service. The major airlines like Delta Airline and United Airline find it difficult to copy the SWA business model because they have already gone beyond the point where they can create a similar approach. They have tremendous fixed assets or lease arrangements for various types of Boeing and Airbus planes with cost structures that can only be absorbed by a more extensive, yet often less profitable value chain and value system. They are forced to service major airports with extensive congestion and delays because they need the large numbers of customers. Moreover, the major airports have many more airlines serving them; thus, there is intense competition and less flexibility in determining many of the sub-elements of the value chain and value system, especially pricing and support.

A business model is an extension of the strategic logic of strategic management, the operating systems, and an organizational structure focusing on the implementation of strategies and action plans. However, a business model that includes only the management systems and organizational structure is narrow, focusing mostly on the internal elements. A true business model, especially one that fits sophisticated global corporations and their SBUs, must include all of the requisite external entities and necessary actions as well.

The cutting-edge business model type discussed herein is referred to an enterprise-wide business model (EBM) that incorporates and integrates twelve main elements and numerous sub-elements; ones that have tangible and intangible aspects. Each of the elements is important in its own way. All of the elements must operate in unison to affect the implementation and execution of the business strategies, solutions, systems, and structures. However, there may be situations in which one or more of the elements may take precedence or are more critical than the others. The main elements of EBM are:

- *Value drivers* are the driving forces in the business environment and market spaces that induce change and present opportunities and challenges for creating value and positive outcomes for businesses, society, and people.

Value drivers are the critical components that have profound effects on what is required and how success is realized and sustained.

- *Value proposition* is the characterization of all of the benefits, positive effects, and knowledge provided by all of the contributors in terms of the investments, costs, efforts, defects, and burdens associated with the situation.
- *Values* are core principles and beliefs of the organization and the related entities and the proper behaviors and attitudes they exhibit. The most important principles include honesty, integrity, ethics, fairness, and social responsibility. Beliefs are the personal values, morals, and ethical codes used by leaders in making decisions that are wise, equitable, and sound.
- *Vision* is the high-level aspirations and perspectives that encapsulate the desired translation of external driving forces, opportunities, challenges, and the internal capabilities and learning into new realities for the company, its business units, and their extended enterprises. It describes the strategic direction and how a sustainable entity expects to realize its desired future. It is generally understood that the vision may take years, even decades to realize.
- *Value configuration* includes the assets, physical endowments, capabilities, and resources available for achieving results. It includes the strategic positions, cost structures, and expected outcomes. It also includes the key contributors and practitioners.
- *Value innovation* involves the transformation or transition of the strategic positions of the business unit and the extended enterprise into more desirable realities and outcomes. It is based on the strategies and actions plans, capabilities and resources, and intellectual and financial capital. The focus is on new solutions and ways of achieving success through strategic innovations.
- *Value creation* involves the means and mechanisms to create valuable solutions with greater benefits, improved cost structures, fewer deficiencies, and reduced impacts. It is about creating the best possible solutions for customers, stakeholders, and society; solutions that maximize benefits and gains (positives) and minimize failures and losses (negatives).
- *Value development* includes the actual programs and activities used to design and develop new technologies, products, and processes. This includes collaborative development programs with the entities of the value networks.
- *Value chain* includes operating system involving the design, development, production, sale, marketing, and delivery of the organization's solutions. It includes the technologies, products, services, brands, knowledge, and support functions.
- *Value system*—the primary dimensions of the upstream contributors such supply networks and the downstream customers, stakeholders and competitors. It is the primary entities of the extended enterprise for meeting or exceeding the driving forces of the business environment and market spaces.
- *Value networks* include all of the interrelated entities in the extended enterprise that contribute to value creation and the sustainable success. They include all of the partnerships, alliances, supply networks, and customer and

stakeholder relationships used to discover, visualize, create, produce, and deliver value. Value networks also include links with other related and unrelated enterprises and/or networks.

- *Value deployment* includes the means and mechanisms used to implement and execute. It includes the tools, techniques, and methods to achieve outcomes. It involves processes, activities, and applications. Most importantly, it includes performance evaluation and the techniques to determine how the business model is functioning.

A business model is a living construct that is evolving and improving, i.e., the notion of business model innovation. It is a portrayal of what people do and how they do it. It focuses on entities, leaders, contributors, and recipients, and their relationships, roles and responsibilities, insights, creations, actions, and outcomes. Great care has to be exhibited when describing and mapping out the elements of a business model because the underlying premise is that each business model is a unique construct that fits the company or business unit. Theoretically, there are no generic business models. A business model construct is intended to be non-linear. Value drivers, vision, value creation, value delivery system and all of the others interact with each other on a real-time basis. Figure 8.1 provides a framework of the elements and an overview of how the components are linked and interrelated. FSL is at the center of the business model

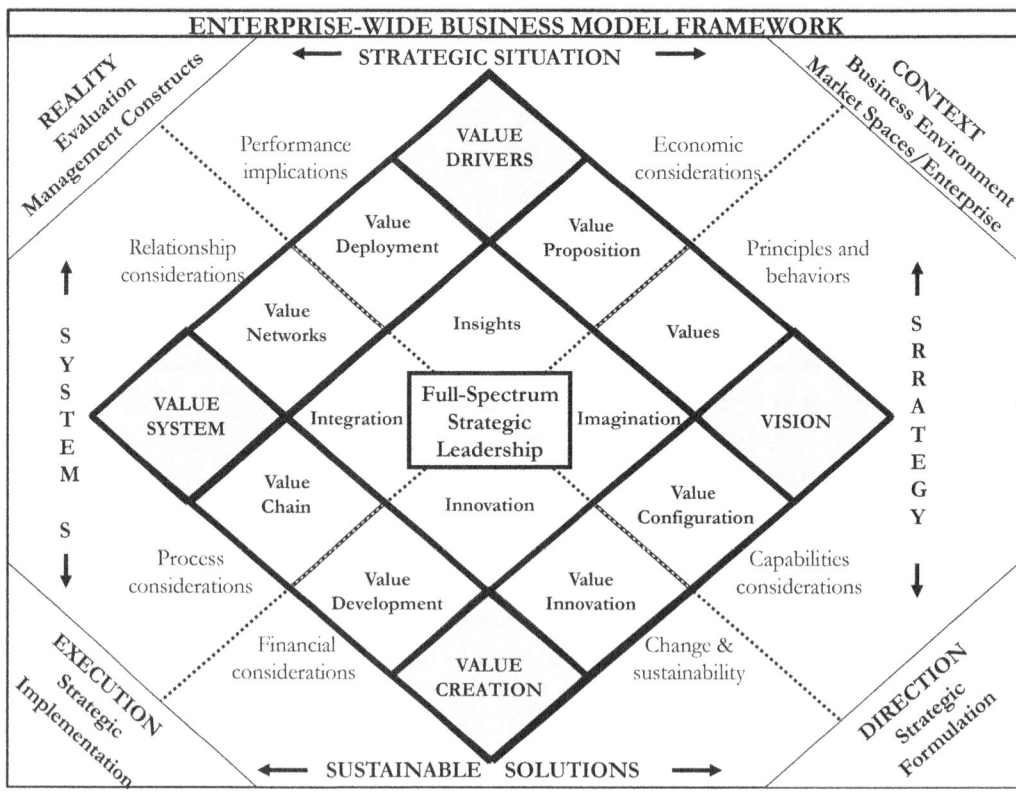

Figure 8.1 Enterprise-wide business model framework.

since it is cutting-edge strategic leadership that makes everything within the business domain work.

The EBM framework provides a sense of the main elements but not necessarily how they should be integrated to form a unique business model or what the scope should be or has to be. Moreover, the actual connections between the elements are usually dependent on context and the prevailing situation(s). There is no precise starting point or process to follow. For instance, one might assume that the corporate vision is a logical beginning, since it sets the stage for strategic direction. However, great visionary strategic leaders with outstanding imagination do not operate in a vacuum. They obtain insights from the external context in which they live. Therefore, it can be argued that the trigger point is the value drivers as shown in Figure 8.1.

In reality, all components operate concurrently in real time. Each element interacts with all of the others and there is a web of such interactions that provide the ingredients for the business model and decision making. Thus, strategic leaders can choose where they wish to start or they can concurrently develop all of the elements. Like many models, the approaches are iterative; one starts where one has the most confidence and builds the model from that point forward. As an aside, it is similar to writing a book. One creates a theme and develops an outline. That is followed by writing the chapters and detailing the content. But, it is rare when an author is so precise in the development that he or she does not have to go back and edit the chapters for consistency and flow among other necessities (language and grammar among them). After several edits the book may submitted for peer review to validate the content and the acceptability of the concepts. There may be several other edits before the document is ready for publication. Some authors, especially novelists, write the last chapter first and then develop the content to fit the ending.

The overarching perspective of a business model is to maximize the value of the company, the business units and the extended enterprise through maximizing value added and minimizing vulnerabilities and risks that results in extraordinary financial, market, and strategic successes. Value maximization of the whole enterprise is achieved through powerful solutions with superior positives and significantly reduced negatives. The elements are or can be arranged in arrays. The EBM framework as depicted in Figure 8.1 has a sense of elegance, since the elements can be rotated to suit one's purpose without changing the perspectives. The overarching arrays are:

- **Value drivers** with value proposition and value deployment. They are related to the *strategic situation*. The general theme involves obtaining insights and developing outcomes that fit reality and the future needs and expectations.
- **Vision** with values and value configuration. They are related to *strategy* and strategic direction. The general theme involves using the insights and imagination to envision and map out how the company or business unit can construct significantly better realities and possibilities.
- **Value creation** with value innovation and value development. They are related *solutions* and strategic formulation and implementation. The general

theme involves using strategic innovations to design and develop the desired outcomes for sustaining success.
- **Value system** with value chain and value networks. They are related to *systems* and structures for strategic implementation and execution. The general theme involves linking all of the entities and participants into a fully integrated business enterprise.

The business model construct is based on the context of the prevailing and future situations. Context is defined and its implications are determined during strategic formulation. While there are many ways in which the framework might be developed, EBM generally starts with the broad elements of the external context (value drivers and the value propositions) dealing with what people want and expect. The value proposition details implicit and explicit requirements for providing successful outcomes for customers and stakeholders.

These elements are then generally followed by the narrower perspectives of values, vision and value configuration. The values and vision are often determined prior to the construction of a business model since they are key elements of the strategic management process. Again, there are many ways in which the elements of the EBM framework can be initiated. The internal elements are considered and selected based on external context, especially the driving forces of change. The underlying logic suggests that strategic leaders have to understand the external context before they can articulate a vision and strategic direction. The vision is directly tied to both the upfront aspects of strategic formulation and the downstream aspects of strategic implementation. Given an understanding of the external context, it is then appropriate to think about what the vision should be, what it means, and what is required to realize it. Therefore, it can be argued that any business model is constructed around making the vision and strategic direction real and ensuring that the means and mechanisms for achieving positive outcomes are available and executable. The vision is flanked by the values of the organization (the timeless beliefs) and the value configuration that includes the critical capabilities and resources and how they relate to the strategic direction and the value proposition(s). The internal elements of values, vision, and value configuration provide the pathways toward value creation, value innovation, and value deployment that focus on developing and making real the future prospects of the company. Ultimately the company's systems, especially through the value chain and value system, translate innovations and desires through actions into possible outcomes. This is accomplished through a myriad of management constructs via value networks and value deployment.

FSL plays a critical role in determining the framework and the specifics of the elements; one of the most important responsibilities of visionary strategic leaders; i.e., they envision, create, produce, and deliver solutions through their imagination, insights, innovations, hard work, and dedication that contribute to sustainable success. In the process of maximizing the contributed value, successful businesses generate cash flow and profits that provide new wealth for the company and its shareholders. Cash flow and profits are derivatives of vision, value creation, and value delivery. With financial success, the enterprise can reinvest into developing more strategic innovations and building more networks that provide more opportunities. Success begets success.

It is important to reiterate that strategic formulation generally precedes the design or redesign of the business model construct. For mature companies and business units, the actual flow has to be flexible. In such situations, the strategic management system and business model elements are usually well established and are generally working well. Strategic management involvement is a continuum rather than just a series of steps or a process. Strategic leaders are always engaged in strategizing and making decisions. Their business model(s) may be explicitly defined for most large corporations, but for many SMEs they are simply implicitly known and understood but generally lacking the rigors and formality of a well-articulated framework.

The Main Elements of the Enterprise-Wide Business Model Framework

Value drivers

Value drivers are the social, economic, ethical, political, technological, and environmental forces and factors that cause and lead to significant changes; ones that represent wonderful opportunities, difficult challenges, serious risks, and potential threats. The value drivers of the real world are the conditions and trends and new phenomena that are affecting change or have the potential to significantly alter the prevailing situation. They may be positive, negative, or both. There are a myriad of value drivers, from the basics of demographics, the state of economy, and consumer confidence to more profound phenomena such as technological advancements, political upheavals, and pandemics. Those in the former category tend to be more predictable and evolve over time. The latter are often wildcards that enter the scene quickly and are much more difficult to understand and manage. Moreover, they have the potential to radically upset the status quo, if there is one, and affect many of the other elements of the business model(s) in profound ways. For instance, in the automobile industry changes in the economic factors, especially the rising cost of fuel and the reduced availability of credit, have dramatically impacted the value propositions of buying and using automobiles. As automobiles become more costly to own and drive, alternate forms of transportation potentially become more attractive solutions. In the U.S. ridership in many of the large metropolitan transport systems increased by about twenty percent during 2008.

Value drivers are often the underpinnings of the economic and market forces driving strategic decision making. For instance, over the last decade outsourcing to companies in China and/or developing joint ventures with Chinese partners have been some of the most significant factors pertaining to economic development from a global perspective. Many global corporations have shifted production from their own facilities or those of indigenous suppliers to those in China or India on the basis of reducing the cost structures and improving profitability. While the results in the short term have been generally positive, the long-term prospects are more questionable. In some cases, strategic leaders have obtained short-term improvements at the expense of long-term liabilities, vulnerabilities, and new costs. The value drivers are often overwhelmed by a small number of powerful forces. Two of the most critical of these over the last decade are the interconnections of the global communication systems and the relatively low cost of global logistics. The business world is now interconnected via the Internet, global satellite systems, and fiber optics. The cost of communications and information and data exchanges is a small fraction of what was before the construction of the digital superhighways in the 1990s. The effectiveness and reliability of communications and logistics are also significantly improved. These dramatic improvements have had powerful effects on international trade and the flow and costs of goods. Products can be produced in far-flung locations and shipped to the ultimate customers without significantly increasing the final cost of goods. Low-cost logistics allow global corporations and many SMEs to take advantage of low-cost wages in developing countries without incurring countervailing higher costs in other areas like transportation and handling. However, great care must be exercised since such conditions may radically change as labor gains more power and seeks increases in compensation and better working conditions in many of the rapidly industrializing countries (RICs). There are potential countervailing forces and concerns including less control of product quality, loss of IP, threats of socialization, and growing power of stakeholders groups that advocate for better and fairer wages and improved work and living conditions.

Value drivers run the gamut from economic factors that business leaders have some experience in dealing with like inflation, interest rates, and recessions to emerging phenomena like resource depletion, climate change, and political instability. Today, there are numerous non-traditional factors from a business perspective that are playing significant roles driving change and affecting strategic decision making. They include globalization, urbanization, population migration, water scarcity, deforestation, and numerous factors, some of which were discussed in Chapters 2 and 3. Strategic leaders have to include and be prepared to handle all of the forces.

In today's business world, astute strategic leaders have to have a much broader view of reality and a better understanding the real world as they interface with the plethora of driver forces facing their corporations and business units. Moreover, customers and stakeholders, especially those in the markets in the developed countries, want and expect complete solutions from social, economic, technological, and environmental perspectives. They are usually not as willing as the predecessors were to make trade-offs. They want to live in a cleaner and safer world. They want leaders of all persuasions to eliminate problems and the underlying causes. For instance, many people believe that the state of the natural environment is a critical factor related to economic and social stability and their well-being. It may be irrelevant that corporate leaders think that climate change and other environmental issues are not significant concerns if most of their customers and stakeholders expect business leaders to help find solutions and take appropriate actions. Understanding and dealing with the broader context is not only a fundamental responsibility, they are the means for obtaining more opportunities and developing new ways to provide unique solutions; ones that people desire based on all of the value drivers.

Astute strategic leaders seek an in-depth understanding of the value drivers so that they can develop and deploy the next wave of strategies and solutions. They stand out because they view the big challenges as great opportunities. Opportunities lead to new strategic innovations and enhanced outcomes. Astute strategic leaders grasp seize upon innovative solutions where others perceive just the problems. They understand that value drivers provide insights about what the corporate vision should be or has to be. The cycle is never ending as value drivers provide additional insights about the vision, which invokes one's imagination about value creation that presents new means and mechanisms for the value chain and value system. These perspectives form the basis for why value drivers are viewed as positives even though some of the value drivers are negatives.

Thomas Kuhn, the great science historian, observed that reformulations of scientific thinking and radical innovations depend upon both theory and practical approaches. In discussing paradigm change he concluded:[1]

> They [scientists] were working both with fact and theory, and their work produced not simply new information but a more precise paradigm, obtained by the elimination of ambiguities that the original form with which they worked had retained. In many sciences, most normal work is of this sort.
>
> These three classes of problems—determination of the significant fact, matching facts with theory, and articulation of theory—exhaust, I think, the literature of normal science, both empirical and theoretical.

The value drivers are the critical elements in the business environment that drive change and present enormous opportunities to change the business world for the better. Facts and evidence are taken from context. Critical factors present themselves in many ways, and certain insightful facts are embedded in the ambiguities of the social and natural worlds. Dealing with the ambiguities and complexities allows visionary strategic leaders to find new theories about how to dramatically improve their prospects for obtaining the desired outcomes and achieving sustainable success. Insights and imagination lead to new visions. And visions lead to new developments and/or improvements in all of the other elements of the business model. It is the never ending quest toward perfection, with the realization that perfection is a distance dream.

Value proposition

The value proposition is one of the most critical perspectives of FSL, ESM and EBM. It sets the stage for the vision, value creation, and value delivery. The value proposition is pivotal in developing a viable business model because it is value that links all of the entities, and it is a central theme for providing solutions and articulating the systems. People want value when they acquire products and services. Moreover, they engage in transactions, exchanges and activities that result in good solutions and outcomes. People regardless of situation or circumstance want and expect valuable outcomes.

The value proposition is a relatively simple concept; people expect to obtain positive outcomes. Customers and stakeholders know that the real world is not perfect, but they expect that business solutions maximize the positives and minimize the negatives. They want the best solutions and outcomes possible that exceed their purposes and expectations. For instance, no one really wants to buy and own toothpaste per se; they want the desired outcomes: clean and healthy teeth, a fresh breath, and pleasant appearance. They want the value provided by using the products and services. True value is derived through having positive outcomes (both tangible and intangible) with a sense of well-being and avoiding negative effects like having poor health or worse.

Value maximization is one of the aims of developing and deploying a business model. The intent is to create successful situations so that everyone can maximize value to the greatest extent possible. While it is difficult to prescribe the actual flows and realizations of value for every entity or constituent within the business model, a balanced approach means that each participant receives his or her expected outcomes and benefits thereof and that the negative effects, impacts, and implications are minimal, if not eliminated altogether. Customers want valuable solutions with maximum benefits. Stakeholders usually expect positive outcomes without significant problems; governments want full compliance with laws and regulations and their protocols for product certifications. Suppliers want fair and appropriate exchanges. Related industries want positive relationships and outcomes in supporting value creation and the value delivery systems. The list goes on. Overall, people want the best solutions possible given the realities of the world. Ethical producers want to satisfy customers, stakeholders and others and at the same time achieve reasonable profitability with a minimum amount of defects and liabilities.

The value proposition can be expressed in terms of the value equation. The value equation provides a relative sense of the value proposition. Figure 8.2 depicts the general form of the value equation from an enterprise perspective.[2]

It expresses value as a ratio of the prevailing and long-term benefits derived from exchanges and actions plus the knowledge gained or learned, i.e., the positives in terms of the investments (costs) plus the negative defects and burdens. The value equation simply portrays value based on the positives and the negatives; positives add value, negatives reduce it It is generally impossible to map out all of the implications of what value means since there are always many other tangible and intangible aspects that are difficult to precisely define and measure.

	Leading effects		Lagging effects		Limiting effects
	Tangible	*Intangible*	*Tangible*	*Intangible*	
Value ≈	$\sum$Benefits		$+ \sum$Long-term	benefits	$+ \sum$Knowledge
	$\sum$Investments		$+ \sum$Defects		$+ \sum$Burdens
	Money	*Time*	*Quality*	*Liability*	

Figure 8.2 Value equation of the value proposition.

The mainstream view by most strategic leaders and professionals is the simplified version of performance (ΣBenefits) to price (ΣInvestments). Per this simple version, value is improved by increasing performance, decreasing investments (cost or price) or both. Performance is improved by enhancing the benefits, both the tangible and intangible ones. Tangible benefits are the direct outcomes that meet the needs of customers, stakeholders, or other constituents. Intangible benefits are the psychological effects. For instance, the tangible benefits of a product include the functions and features; the intangible benefits may be the status and enjoyment of owning and using the product. For most of the 20th century, the general approach was to increase performance at a rate greater than the increase in the price or cost. More recently, the prevailing approach is to increase the benefits and decrease the price or costs as well. Personal computers over the last three decades fit the notion perfectly. Their attributes have improved between ten thousand and one hundred thousand times the original devices, yet prices are significantly less than what they were in the 1980s.

The sum of the benefits represents the leading effects that are sought at inception. The leading effects are the primary benefits that are usually apparent to the producers and customers at the time of the exchanges. They are the attributes that drive customers' decision making based mostly on traditional economic perspectives. The value of the leading benefits is established by the investment of time and money to produce or acquire the benefits. Money might be viewed as the tangible aspect of the investment(s) since it represents actual resources, property, or physical goods. Time might be viewed as intangible, since it cannot be captured or stored. In many situations, time may be just as critical as money in the determination of the investment given that time can never be recovered. People are often willing to pay more for a solution in a given circumstance so that they can save time. For example, most convenience products cost more than the alternates, but the fact that they save people time make them more valuable. The leading effects are usually apparent when determining whether products, services, programs, projects, etc. are worthwhile.

Lagging effects, the long-term benefits or defects, are a little more difficult to ascertain. They are often discovered at a much later time frame. Positive lagging effects are often the benefits that were not contemplated or available at inception. For example, Microsoft has enjoyed great success with its Windows operating system because as more and more people used the same operating system interconnectivity increased dramatically, making the solution more valuable for everyone involved. Providing exactly what is desired over the long term enhances the value proposition and makes the associated solution(s) more viable and more successful. Defects are debasers in the long term. They include excessive costs involving owning and operating the devices, the quality defects, inefficiencies, unnecessary extras or frills, and negative environmental impacts; anything that does not provide value or sub-optimizes the solutions. They cost additional expenses, require extra efforts, and make the value proposition less attractive. For instance, many companies have large expenditures for warranty claims or have expensive products recalls that costs billions of dollars, Euro, yen, etc. Imagine the savings and the improvements in profitability if such expenses could be avoided.

The limiting effects are often the state of the art of humankind's knowledge on the positive side and the resultant social, economic, and environmental burdens on the negative side. The more strategic leaders know about the realities of the world, the better they are in forming the best solutions. While knowledge is a limiting effect in the sense that there are always unknowns and hidden difficulties, value is significantly enhanced by new knowledge and the reduction of the unknowns. All products and production operations have undesirable side effects. If all of the side effects are effectively determined and articulated, then the potential positive aspects can be realized through disseminating information about the proper applications and deployments. This is one of the goals of product stewardship. For instance, lead is great for radiation shielding, but it is a poison that should not be used in consumer products.

Economic and environmental burdens are the negatives that usually require money and effort but contribute nothing positive. Burdens tend to limit the viability of the solutions in the market spaces. Pollution and wastes ultimately result in stringent regulations that restrict the amount of pollution and wastes or the applications of the products and services. For instance, if air quality declines to the point at which the ambient air causes significant health problems, governments might impose restrictions on the applications of power plants, automobiles and other polluting devices. Environmental burdens include disposing of the residuals from the products or dealing with end-of-life considerations. For instance, customers may have to pay to get rid of old products like TV sets and appliances. In other cases, governments or society pays for the ills associated with the burdens and impacts. Air pollution from stationary sources and moving vehicles inflict damages on everyone. Eliminating such burdens is an obvious way for moving toward better outcomes by providing significantly improved solutions

The ultimate goal is to move toward ideality with maximum benefits and zero defects, burdens and reduced costs. Ideality is easy to understand from an external perspective. Customers obtain affordable, reliable products with no or few negative effects. Society does not suffer with problems, issues, impacts, and burdens. Producers, on the other hand, might view this approach as a zero-sum game with all of the benefits and gains going to the external dimensions. But making solutions more affordable does not mean that prices ultimately have to be zero. If all defects and burdens are eliminated, the costs of the associated corrective actions or expense elements for liabilities could be eliminated in calculating the costs and prices of the products. The price to the customer could be reduced without any negative effects on profitability. Imagine the implications! As the products and processes are improved using clean technologies, the cost per unit is reduced and volumes are increased as savings are passed on to customers. While prices may fall, profit margins may actually be higher since the total costs are lower. Indeed, the profit objective is to achieve the strategic outcomes and overall financial success and not to maximize the profit per transaction or per product. The answer for the producers is to achieve their business objectives using value-added techniques rather than traditional approaches like clever pricing strategies and fancy advertising constructs.

Values

The values and beliefs that companies and their leaders and employees hold underpin everything. They are the foundation upon which the vision, business strategies, actions, and the business model are developed and built. Unless strategic leaders are committed to solid values and beliefs that are shared by most people of good will, there is little point in mapping out a business model using the constructs herein. If greed, deception, and self-interests are at the core strategic thinking of the strategic leaders and the organization, there is little point articulating the other elements. Strategic leaders have to be the examples for their organizations and enterprises. They have to uphold the highest standards of principles and behaviors. They must convey the spirit and wholesomeness of the organization. Values include the philosophies, principles and behaviors that people share and believe in. Some of the important values are:[3]

- **Being honest and truthful**—disclosing all positive and negative factors; ensuring that others are truthful and eliminating deceptions. It takes courage to tell the whole truth; to be honest and open; organizations have to eliminate operating in the gray area.
- **Being good and using proper behaviors**—ensuring that proper behaviors are followed; ones that follow the generally acceptable practices of a society. While it is difficult to prescribe exactly what proper behaviors are given cultural differences, most people recognize and know what they are and should be. Many companies have formal codes of conduct. And there are universal norms that are appropriate regardless of the location.
- **Being ethical**—being ethical implies that the leaders adhere to the highest standards of personal behavior and professionalism in decision making and actions. Ethics are the codes and standards governing conduct and behavior in the setting or situation.
- **Being fair**—being fair means being impartial and unbiased in decisions and actions. It often pertains to how others are treated and impacted. It implies equal treatment for all. Being fair is a duty of leadership, especially in ensuring that decisions and actions are not skewed toward one's personal position and fortune or against weaker and disadvantaged people.
- **Having Integrity**—having integrity involves conviction and commitment to one's beliefs and acting in a consistent and sound manner. It involves unwavering adherence to one's values. Integrity builds trust and others rely on their trust of the leader's personal values when they decide whether to follow the leader.
- **Respecting others**—respecting others involves recognizing the contributions of other people and ensuring their views and actions are duly considered and valued. Leaders who respect others are more likely to be respected by others. It is difficult to obtain the respect of the organization if one eschews the views and contributions of other people.
- **Taking care of people**—taking care of the people is a key responsibility of leadership. Strategic leaders are responsible for the well-being of the peo-

ple and have a duty to make others successful to the extent possible. This includes ensuring that they are recognized and rewarded for their achievements and that their well-being is safeguarded.
- **Forgiving others**—forgiving or not blaming others is critical for assuring that problems and mistakes result in positive outcomes via corrective actions. While it is appropriate to find the causes of difficulties, strategic leaders should avoid affixing blame, especially when proper behaviors and well-intentioned actions are used. If problems occur, strategic leaders should fix the problems and forgive and forget in a majority of the situations.

These values are obvious and self evident. There are many others that could be listed. The business world is built on well-conceived and established values that are enjoyed across the organization and enterprise. Trustworthiness is one of the most important ingredients in being a successful strategic leader and creating a viable business model. Instilling trust is the linchpin for success. Trust is difficult to build and easy to lose. Strategic leaders who fail to follow through with their words and commitments destroy trust and loyalty among employees and lose the confidence that outsiders may have in the company.

Vision

The vision is a critical ESM element and a main element of the business model. Visionary strategic leaders play a decisive role in making the vision real as an essential element of the business model. In the context of the business model, the vision is used to articulate the why and what of the strategic direction and how everyone is expected to play a role in achieving positive outcomes and excellent performance. It provides the tenor for the organization and the extended enterprise. Most importantly, it establishes what transitions and transformations are required and what the expected outcomes have to be.

The vision makes the business model construct dynamic. It ties all elements of strategic formulation with the elements of strategic implementation and with the other elements of the business model. It helps make a company's business model unique, alive and inspirational. While many companies tend to follow similar strategies, visionary strategic leaders can set their company aside from the pack by having a powerful vision integrated into the business model to create a more positive future for their company and all of its contributors and recipients. A powerful vision focuses on sustainable solutions and success through management constructs like sustainable business development (SBD), corporate social responsibility (CSR), and strategic innovations. They seek excellence from every aspect to make everyone successful.

Value configuration

Value configuration is the people-intensive element of the business model that links the vision to the requisite innovations. It involves the intellectual capital of the organization and enterprise and the strategic thinking and imagination of the leaders to translate strategies and action plans into externally beneficial outcomes and sustainable advantages. Value configuration involves people who can start new ventures, invent new technologies, develop new products, and initiate new processes that serve existing and new markets, customers, and stakeholders through enhanced solutions. Its focus is on strategic innovations using creativity, as the pathways to improve existing solutions or to create radically new ones. Sustainable advantages in today's business environment and market spaces are derived through innovative solutions that are difficult to emulate and have many factors that require the entire enterprise.

Value configuration involves the organization structure. Table 8.1 provides a list of some of the most important sub-elements associated with value configuration. It provides a sense of the underpinnings and the implications for value creation and the value delivery systems. Moreover, the significance of each perspective is dependent on context of the company and its whole enterprise. Strategic leaders and people across the enterprise must create a sense of well-being and confidence. Value configuration includes the tangibles and intangible contributions and gains made by all of the people and processes to fulfill the needs, requirements and expectations of the driving forces and turn opportunities and vision into valuable and sustainable outcomes. It involves people to people exchanges of goods, information, and intangibles like positive feelings and friendship.

TABLE 8.1 Selected Sub-Elements of Value Configuration

Perspective	Considerations	Implications
Enhance the learning process, build capabilities	Capabilities and learning are the centerpieces of discovery; learning enhances knowledge and decreases uncertainty; learning builds intellectual capital and the ability to understand the variables and construct new solutions.	When uncertainty is high, learning is paramount for success. Learning gives new insights and understandings about what is possible and preferable. Answers are time and activity dependent. They supports strategic innovations.
Acquire and enhance knowledge	Discovery, understanding and invention are based on intellectual capital and leadership; knowledge and experience are crucial for developing state-of-the-art technologies; knowledge is acquired through observations and engagement.	Capabilities are the complex arrangements of science and art based on scientific principles, knowledge, and experience; initial failures can be considered a success if they improve knowledge and the organization's capabilities to achieve future successes.
Inspire people	People are the essential ingredient in creativity. People have to be inspired and rewarded.	People are emotional and logical. Inspiration is both self-induced and generated by short-term gains.

Value innovation

Value innovation focuses on the dynamics of change, how to exploit opportunities through new solutions, and how to create desirable ends through strategic innovations. Value innovation is about changing the very nature of doing business. Value innovation involves ensuring that the strategic positions are enhanced, that the solutions are developed and refreshed, actions are taken and improved, and that sustainable success is realized. It involves the relentless drive to embrace change and gain significantly from it. In the context of the business model, it examines the ways in which new or additional value can be created through the next generation of solutions, radical breakthroughs, and/or ways of achieving desired outcomes and success.

Value innovation engages the innovative capabilities of the company or business unit to transition and transform its reality into a higher level of sophistication. Value innovation requires not only tangible aspects like resources and development programs, but intangibles like inspiration and encouragement from FSL. Employees have to be guided, supported, and rewarded on an ongoing basis to ensure that they continue to be creative, productive and successful. It requires the personal involvement on the part of the strategic leaders who have to go beyond motivating people. They have to lead from the front, not just pushing from behind. Value innovation was discussed extensively in Chapter 7.

Value creation

Value creation focuses on the creation of sustainable solutions necessary to attain business objectives and strategies and to realize the opportunities and challenges. Solutions are broad based, multifaceted and ever changing. They emerge through strategies, actions, initiatives, programs, and outcomes. As discussed in previous chapters, solutions represent the totality of all of the products, services, complementary products, etc. They provide customers, stakeholders and constituents with the desired outcomes.

Value creation necessitates ongoing strategic innovation. It uses insights gained from reflections on reality and the understanding of the possibilities for change. It also requires investments in developing new competencies and capabilities before they become necessary or important. It is difficult to change methods, approaches and behaviors if people are not prepared for change. Resistance to change is a common reaction that comes generally from within the organization because people have not engaged in the learning processes to build new skills and capabilities. Moreover, the whole enterprise must acquire the new knowledge necessary to exploit the prevailing opportunities.

Value development

Value development is an objective function. It requires evidence to support and validate the premises that the new solutions actually contribute to successful outcomes. The greater the amount of evidence, the more likely the premises will be viewed as credible, and this will result in acceptance by the external entities and people in general, including customers and stakeholders. Customers and others receive the expected benefits of solutions and business units obtain positive rewards. Revenues, cash flow, margins, and financial returns are the derivatives of effective leadership and management and outstanding value delivery. Stakeholders question the reality of the messages and require proof of intent and action. In a world with many sources of information, value development has to be real and based on real-world factors, not just fancy messages and marketing campaigns. For example, several giant oil companies adapted the principles of SBD and made improvements to their enterprises. But, they used their initiatives as a marketing campaign before they were fully integrated with the actual processes of the companies. Customer reactions were distrustful.

Value development has to result in extraordinary and sustainable outcomes for shareholders, the investors of the financial capital, and the risk takers of the businesses. Shareholders play a vital role in the success of the enterprise through investments, and they must be rewarded accordingly. Value development drives the value chain and value delivery system. Value development focuses on people, exchanges, logistics, connections, actions and outcomes that involve real world execution. Risk mitigation is also an important part of value development, especially in areas that focus on external aspects.

Table 8.2 provides a flow of the key considerations in value development. The development of new technologies, products, and processes is the important means for strategic leaders to secure and maintain competitive advantages in a dynamic business environment. Rapid product development has evolved because customer expectations require continuous improvements in product performance. Shortening life cycles mean that new product design and improved capabilities are an ongoing requirement to maintain viable and effective products. New products have to be tailored to meet the needs of the intended market segment or reinvigorated to sustain their appeal to be in line with customer expectations. For example, personal computer product-market exploded during the 1990's via faster, more capable machines and improved software with significantly higher performance-price ratios. As newer generations became available, the cost-effectiveness of using the older equipment quickly dissipated. The evolution of the technology and products forced users to do ongoing assessment of their needs and resources and to obtain the better solutions.

Value deployment involves imperatives that are critical requirements that must be managed and accomplished regardless of the situation. They are usually the first order mandates or requirements from the external context and from corporate management and/or board of directors. They include ensuring the health and safety of people, complying with laws and regulations, providing proper governance of the company, following policies and directives, managing the financial affairs of the company, and preparing and communicating all required financial and managerial reports. Special imperatives may involve communicating with political, social and economic leaders in the country, state, province and/or community to ensure the acceptance, stability, and continuity of operations and actions. They may also include site specific requirements such as managing hazardous waste problems of the past; solving protracted labor issues, resolving tax problems and remediating contaminated sites.

TABLE 8.2 Key Considerations in Value Development

Perspective	Considerations	Implications
Understand the driving forces (Context)	Markets, stakeholders and corporations do not want technologies; they want solutions and applications to fulfill their needs.	The forces driving change make or break a solution. All driving forces, including government regulations, change over time.
Consider social, economic and environmental implications (Context)	A solution is a social and economic construct. It has to benefit people in ways that are overwhelmingly positive and cost effective. Burdens detract from the positive aspects.	Solution has to fit the social and economic realities of the business environment. People require benefits that are worthwhile. They have to be able to afford the solution.
Create value and improve the value proposition (Value)	Value is the overarching construct; Value is created through obtaining enduring benefits as well as reduced costs, defects and burdens. They make the value proposition more likely of realizing success.	The value proposition provides answers to the sustainable aspects of the new solution. If defects and burdens are reduced and benefits and performance are enhanced, the solution exhibits the potential for success.
Use imagination and insights to think about possibilities (Options)	Imagination and insights provide the foundation for creative thought; Innovations are often based on combinations of solutions that lead to new capabilities and realities.	Radical innovations are derived from the vision that involves revolutionary changes not based on the mainstream approaches. Using lessons learned from others facilitates the process and reduces trial and error.
Build new relationships (People)	Developing new-to-the-world products and technologies requires a myriad of people and know-how across the enterprise; ensure that everyone is part of the team and is respected.	New-to-the-world products and technologies require new capabilities, new knowledge, and new ways of doing thing. It takes dedicated groups of people who can work together effectively at achieve results.
Possess integrity, maintain honesty and build trust (Principles)	Provide credible evidence about the solution and its benefits, and communicate the negative aspects as well. Be honest about the technology; do not overstate or oversell its potential. Corporate reputation is often the most valuable asset. Trust is the glue of success.	Lack of integrity and honesty tends to mislead stakeholders about the viability of the technology. Effective corporations communicate problems early and resolve them before huge investments are made. If there are problems, effective leaders want to know them immediately to solve them or terminate actions.
Maintain objectivity (Principles)	Professionals should follow scientific thinking. It is important to be skeptical about observations until there is sufficient evidence to draw conclusions. All technologies have positive and negative aspects.	Maintaining objectivity is critical. People often accept too many unproven theories. Solutions should be based on objective evidence and sound methods. Discover the leading and lagging effects. See all sides of the opportunities and challenges.
Build long-term commitment (Sustain value)	Persistence is necessary for complex programs; Answers and solutions are sporadic; management and participants feed each other.	Success is a long and uneven road; difficulties and frustrations are part of the equation.

Value chain

During the early 1980s, Michael Porter developed models of the internal and external dimensions of the company or business unit as discussed in Chapter 1. The internal dimensions are referred to as the value chain. The external dimensions are called the value system. Porter's models dramatically shifted the management framework from a vertical organizational approach to a system approach with horizontal processes.[4] Porter states that:[5]

> A firm's value chain and the way it performs individual activities are a reflections of its history, its strategy, its approach to implement its strategy, and the underlying economic of the activities themselves.

The value chain includes the internal processes necessary to satisfy customer needs and expectations. The internal value chain maps out the key processes and functions of the organization. Figure 8.3 depicts the value chain of Siemens AG's Automation and Drives.

While the Siemens example follows the Porter's value chain, there are significant differences. Procurement and logistics are covered under supply chain management, which is given a primary perspective. Operations are viewed as part of product life

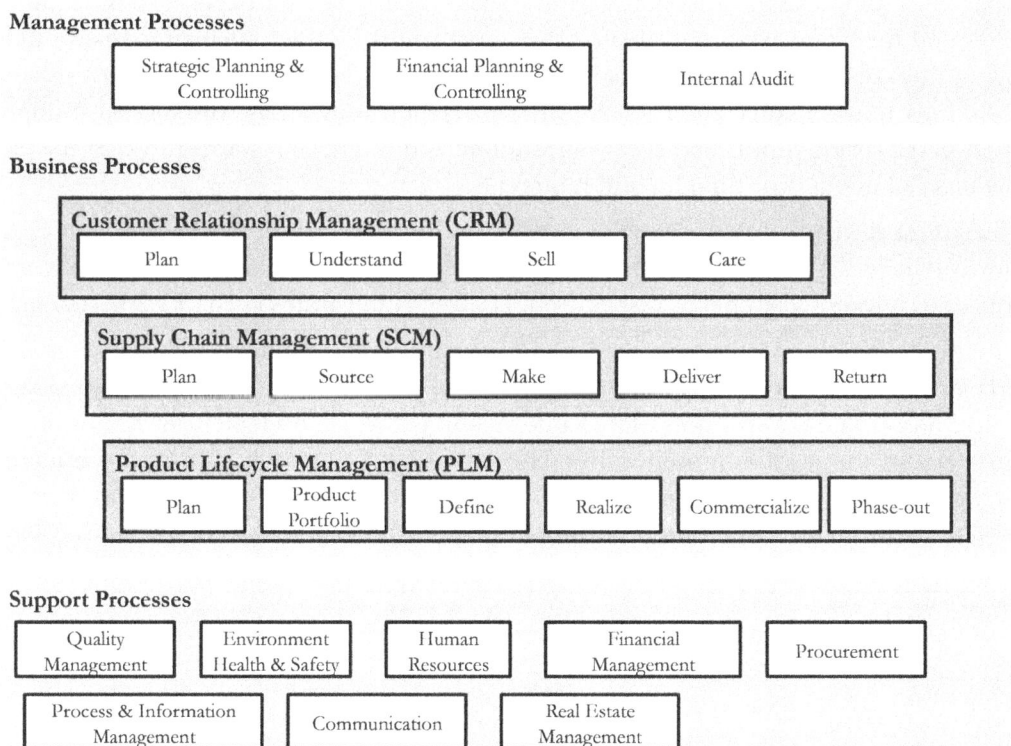

Figure 8.3 Value chain example: Siemens Automation and Drives[6]

cycle management. Marketing and sales are included under customer relationship management. The focus is on the customer and building solid relationships. Support processes include additional important processes like environment, health and safety and communications.

Value system

The value system links the elements of the value chain and the broader entities of the extend enterprise. It is the collection and combination of the value chains of the contributors and recipients of the solutions that are both internal and external to the company and/or its business units. The value system includes the upstream value chains of suppliers, suppliers of suppliers, deep into the supply chain, and the downstream value chains of distributors, customers, customers of customers, and the other supporting entities that enhance value creation and delivery. They are the primary players in the economic equations involving transactions and exchanges. The focus is on the stream of processes and activities required to produce and deliver the desirable outcomes to sustain success and satisfy people. It is the most comprehensive system which includes all appropriate and necessary internal and external dimensions.

The value system provides the means to produce outcomes that allow the entities and individuals involved in the actions and transactions to contribute to the overall objectives and desired outcomes and to realize their aims and expectations. Companies and their business units create value, organize the value systems(s), ensure that all entities play their parts, and assure that integration is achieved. Customers obtain solutions that enhance their short-term satisfaction and long-term success. Supply networks provide inputs and receive economic and financial rewards through the exchanges of goods, information and money.

Porter developed the original construct of the value system as discussed in Chapter 1. It includes the upstream and downstream value chains of suppliers and the channels and buyers (customers), respectively. Figure 8.4 illustrates Porter's value system.[7]

Establishing the value system is an important part of building a business model because it focuses on customers, the recipients of the benefits, and all of the necessary and appropriate contributors. The value system is the main element of the business model and the most comprehensive. The underlying approach is to create human-business-technological partnerships for maximum efficiency, effectiveness, productivity and performance, and for minimizing difficulties, problems and complexities. Value

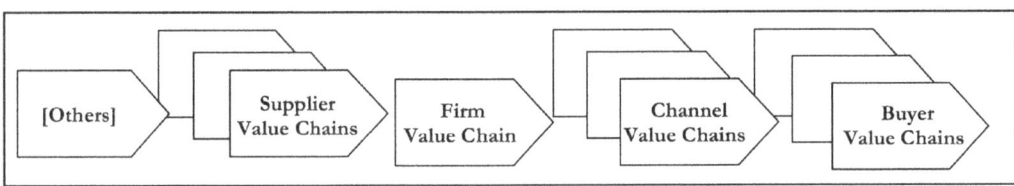

Figure 8.4 Porter's value system.

systems involve linkages between the essential economic entities based on integrated processes that have to flow smoothly as they successfully convert inputs into outputs. The processes must focus on delighting recipients and building a solid foundation that provides long-term capabilities to sustain success. This includes building new knowledge, improving processes and enhancing positions over time to realize even greater success and financial rewards.

The purpose and expectations of the value system is to produce and deliver cost-effective solutions that meet or exceed customer needs and expectations, maximize the performance of the management system, and minimize the negative impacts on the external business environment. The value delivery system involves the conversion of inputs into more valuable outputs that are economically viable and valuable and the delivery of the solutions to the intended recipients. The value system is a structured framework that provides strategic leaders, managers, and practitioners with a clear understanding of the interrelationships between elements and their impacts on the value delivered and of the realities associated with the supply networks, stakeholders, markets, customers and providers of complementary products. The intent is to dramatically reduce the time, money, and resources required to successfully bring solutions to the recipients.

The value system incorporates the primary flows to get goods to markets and the secondary flows to manage the associated waste streams. It involves all of the actions and transactions as materials and energy are converted into parts, components and goods that become end products purchased, and used by customers who exchange their valuable resources (money) to acquire the solutions necessary to satisfy their objectives, needs and desires. It also involves reverse logistics to recover, reuse and recycle residuals across the enterprise.

Figure 8.5 shows value system that is based on constructs of an EBM and the constructs in my book, *Enterprise-wide Strategic Management* (ESM).[8] It is also shown in Chapter 1.

It links the upstream and downstream elements of the value system to the internal value chain and the other element of the extended enterprise. The value system is supported by the corporate strategic management and business unit strategic management as indicated at the top of the framework. The value delivery system involves an integrated approach for sourcing, fabricating, producing, delivering, and supporting products and services. This includes the complementary products and services of associated related industries. The value system is both a strategic management and operations management construct that integrates the essential elements of the solutions into a comprehensive system, in which the elements can be carried out (executed) on a concurrent basis. The value system must be lean and agile. Shortening product life cycles and the ever changing expectations of customers and stakeholders require lean business operations and practices that focus on customer-derived value, speed, flexibility, quality, reliability, cost, and effective utilization of scarce resources.

From an execution perspective, the value system is generally the domain of functional management. Functional management uses tactics, processes and activities in

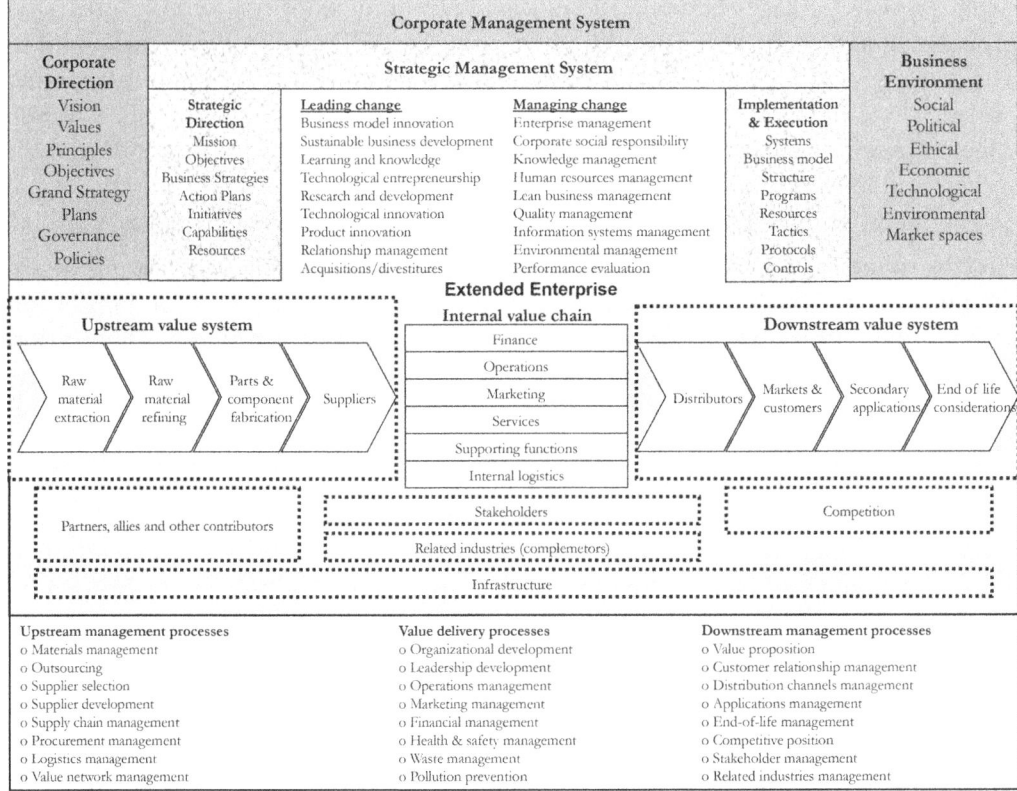

Figure 8.5 Connections of the value system based on ESM.

conjunction with the extended enterprise to produce the desired outputs that provide satisfaction to the downstream value system. The focus is on delivering the solutions based on the portfolios, brands, capabilities and resources of the organization. The value delivery system provides products and services that generate revenue, income and financial rewards. The value system includes positioning solutions in light of market realities and building flexibility into the process. Delivering the solutions involves holistic management that defines the solution based on customer and stakeholder specifications. The input from potential customers is an essential ingredient for success.

Today's value systems are more dynamic because of advanced technologies, the global expansion of the supply networks, strategic innovations, and the impacts of more stringent regulatory requirements from a multiplicity of governments among hundreds of other reasons. In recent years, many organizations have streamlined their value systems to improve customer service, reduce excess inventory in the system, cut costs from the network of suppliers, and form new relationships to facilitate interactions and communications. The value system aims at selecting and integrating the processes, methods, and tools so that management can implement innovative ways to strategically obtain results. The ability to innovate faster than external expectations is a key factor in achieving and maintaining a sustainable competitive advantage. Some of the most important factors include: assessing the financial conditions and trends of the enterprise; understanding the risks and rewards associated with decision making; knowing the impacts of actions, activities, transactions, and outcomes on working capital requirements; determining the cost structures across the enterprise; and integrating the financial considerations of the businesses.

The value system uses generally accepted accounting principles to realize the financial implications and outcomes and to prepare the financial reports. Strategic leaders have to understand the financial aspects of the business model that include cash flow statements, working capital management, financial performance measurements, cost-volume-profit relationships, cost allocation, activity based costing, time value of money and capital budgeting. This includes the analysis of the financial positions of the business unit.

Solutions require positive and enduring relationships between the upstream and downstream entities of the extended enterprises and the connections between the parties and people thereof. The relationships are reinforced by the actions of strategic leadership. Business is about people and based on people. Strategic leaders take an active interest in creating and supporting the human interactions that are essential for sustaining success. The organization also supports the relationships through positive exchanges of goods, information and goodwill. The systems provide interfaces between the parties and the processes for accomplishing the desired outcomes.

The value system is supported by and supports the value networks. Value networks include all of the other entities, relationships, and connections that contribute to value creation and delivery. These include how things are done and what is necessary to assure success.

Value networks

Value networks are the complex arrays of the entities and the interrelationships among them that generate and apply economic and social outcomes and other beneficial results through interactions and exchanges among the participants. Value networks may be tied to the value delivery system as essential contributors or recipients, or they extend beyond the value system by providing additional tangible and intangible contributions.

Value networks are dynamic and non-linear. They link the broader aspects of the business environment and the social world with the value delivery system. Value networks are people-oriented. They provide support services, create and disseminate knowledge and enrich participants through tangible and intangible exchanges. A value network involves building relationships with entities across the whole enterprise and beyond. Verna Allee provides a solid perspective on what value networks are intended to be. Allee suggests the approach involves relationships as follows:[9]

> The goal of a value network is to generate economic success or other value (benefits) for its participants. People participate in value network by converting their expertise and knowledge into tangible and intangible deliverables that have value for other members of the network. In a successful value network every actor or participant contributes and receives value

in ways that sustain both their own success and the success of the value network as a whole. Where this is not true participants withdraw... or the whole system becomes unstable and may collapse or reconfigure.

There are many great insights in Allee's view. Value networks contribute to value creation and value delivery. They involve broad contributions and knowledge that lead to solutions and positive outcomes. Everyone must contribute to success and be successful. Some of the most important contributors to value creation and value delivery are the indirect entities and agents who are acting in the broader arenas of economic, social and environmental development. For instance, the colleges and universities engaged in higher education and basic research are critical to the success of businesses. They are part of the value networks.

Value deployment

Value deployment involves the myriad of tools, techniques, and methods used to execute strategies and deploy the solutions and systems. It involves the ways in which activities are carried out. It includes the management constructs used to produce and deliver value. It involves positioning the vast arrays of capabilities and resources to accomplish the mission and carry out the strategies. It involves all of the internal and external structures and deployments that are necessary for the thousands, if not millions of actual operations and activities that flow over time. Figure 8.6 shows how value deployment flows.

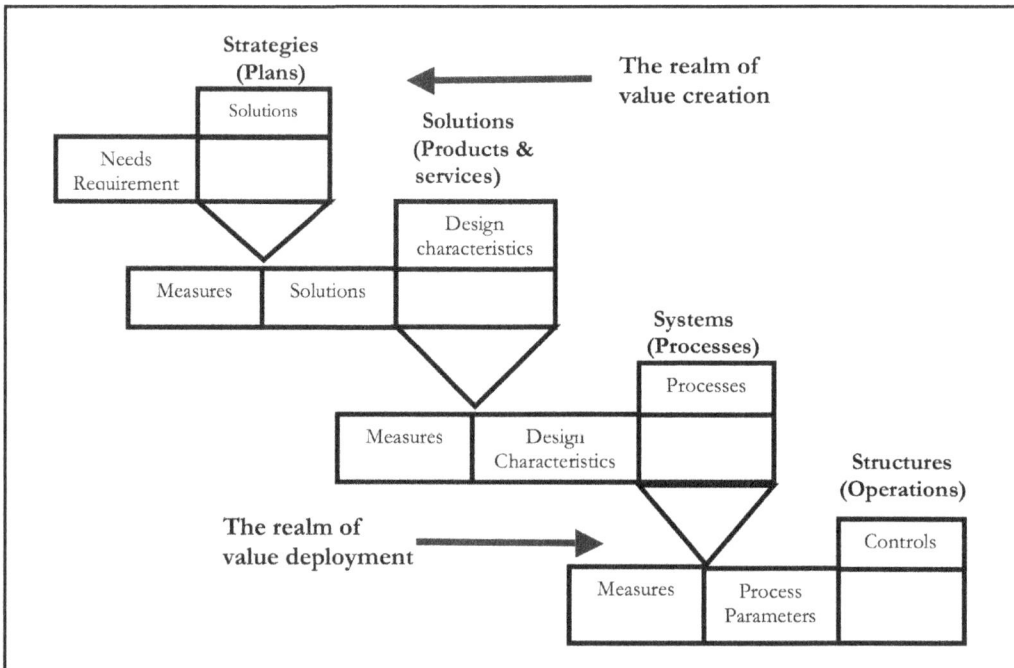

Figure 8.6 Value deployment.

From an FSL perspective, the higher levels of value deployment are addressed by corporate and business unit strategic leaders. The depth of deployment to which strategic leaders go depends on the specifics of their business environment and business situations. It is always difficult to prescribe exactly what is strategic and what is operational. Generally, strategic leaders determine the why's, the what's and the metrics. The why's involve the strategies and the logic and the what's are the needs, requirements, standards and mandates. They pertain to the external forces and the strategic direction and leadership. The primary aspects focus on external requirements like compliance with laws and regulations. The internal aspects include the means, mechanisms, and organizational linkages for getting thing done. They also include the measurements for determining how well the strategies, solution and systems are performing. Measurements provide the external check on what success has been achieved and what the new expectations are.

Companies and their strategic leaders have come under enormous pressure to optimize financial performance. The investment community and shareholders encourage corporations to focus on critical activities and subcontract low priority activities. Strategic leaders try to determine the best way to manage their processes and all of the requisite activities.

Value deployment implies that some activities are handled within the organization and some are outsourced. The key question is how to obtain the maximum value when making such decisions. Since the deployment involves are myriad of such decision making and operations management, the details of the section have to be articulated in another book. Value can be viewed as the alpha and the omega.

Reflections

Strategic leaders are responsible for designing and deploying the most effective business model. Business models are based on the integration of the whole enterprise into a seamless entity that focuses on the best solutions, using the best systems and structures to link people and create extraordinary value, and creating solid relationships that are supported by value networks and lean business processes and practices. In most situations, the changes are subtle, but the quest is relentless. Strategic leaders never stop trying or settle for being average. They seek every opportunity to make significant improvements and even radical developments. They base their decisions on the full context of the business environment and their internal capabilities and learning, yet they aspire to go beyond the realities of the world and create unique business models and outcomes that lead to strategic positions that are difficult to emulate.

Complexity increases dramatically as the basis for competitive advantages moves from products, services and operations to solutions, systems, and relationships. But, so does the ability to obtain distinctive sustainable advantages that are almost impossible to emulate. Specifics like products are more easily copied; even some of the most innovative products are copied within months by competitors. This phenomenon results in commoditization in which competitive advantages are fleeting at best and may not exist at all. However, sustainable advantages are much more likely if the basis for uniqueness is the system, the whole extended enterprise and enduring relationships. Successful companies produce great solutions, have excellent value delivery systems, provide outstanding value deployment, and build outstanding relationships with people. Visionary strategic leaders think in terms of the solutions that people want and need, not just the products and services that the businesses produce and sell. Anything that provides a greater solution, one that is better than the existing choices, has the power to change the prevailing situation.

Table 8.3 provides the key elements of EBM that link strategies, solutions, systems, and structures from the general to the specific.

While not all strategic innovations prove to be great solutions, strategic leaders who emphasize strategic innovations and better choices that fit the customers' and stakeholders' situations in better ways open the door for greater customer and stakeholder satisfaction and successes, better relationships, and sustainable success. Leading change and developing new sustainable advantages that go beyond past financial success are critical for long-term financial and business performance. Strategic leaders create an EBM that provides the right ingredients configured using means and mechanisms to assure outstanding results.

TABLE 8.3 Selected Elements Linking Strategies, Solutions, Systems, and Structures

Perspectives	Focus of the enterprise [broad/external]	Focus of the company or business unit [narrow/internal]	Focus on financial outcomes [specific/money]
Strategies	Business environment Market spaces Sustainable advantages	Vision and direction Transformations & transitions Strategic innovation	Investments/rewards Risk taking/mitigation Accountability
Solutions	Value creation Sustainable success Strategic innovations	Business integration Portfolios and brands Products & services	Cash flow Profits and margins Reporting and control
Systems	Value delivery system Value delivery Connections	Value chains and value systems Process management Operations	Exchanges Revenues and income Returns on investments
Structures	Value networks Relationships Intellectual capital	Functions & teams People (capabilities) Resources	Cost structures and costs Operating expenses Accounting
Leadership	Visionary Enterprise-wide	Strategic Operational	Financial management Money—short term

Notes

1. Thomas S. Kuhn, *The Structure of Scientific Revolution*, 3rd Edition (Chicago, IL: University of Chicago Press, 1962, 1996, p34).
2. David L. Rainey, *Enterprise-wide Strategic Management: Achieving Sustainable Success through Leadership, Strategies and Value Creation* (Cambridge, UK: Cambridge University Press, 2010, p405)
3. David L. Rainey, *Sustainable Strategic Leadership: Becoming a Successful Strategic Leader through Principles, Perspectives, and Professional Development* (Charlotte, NC: Information Age Publishing, 2013, p49).
4. Michael Porter, Competitive Advantage: Creating and Sustaining Superior Performance (New York, NY: Free Press, 1985, p33-61).
5. Id, p36.
6. Dr. Helmuth Ludwig, bei A&D SE, „Qualitäts- und Prozessinitiative bei A&D SE", Fürth, Germany, June 24, 2004.
7. Michael Porter, *Competitive Advantage: Creating and Sustaining Superior Performance,* p34.
8. David L. Rainey, *Enterprise-wide Strategic Management: Achieving Sustainable Success through Leadership, Strategies, and Value Creation* (Cambridge, UK: Cambridge University Press, 2010, p444).
9. http://www.vernaallee.com/value_networks/Understanding_Value_Networks.html

References

Kuhn, Thomas S. (1962) *The Structure of Scientific Revolution, 3rd Edition.* Chicago, IL: University of Chicago Press.

Porter, Michael (1985) *Competitive Advantage: Creating and Sustaining Superior Performance.* New York, NY: Free Press.

Rainey, David L. (2010) *Enterprise-wide Strategic Management: Achieving Sustainable Success through Leadership, Strategies and Value Creation.* Cambridge, UK: Cambridge University Press.

Rainey, David L. (2013) *Sustainable Strategic Leadership: Becoming a Successful Strategic Leader through Principles, Perspectives, and Professional Development.* Charlotte, NC: Information Age Publishing.

9

Sustainable Success and Concluding Comments

Introduction

Cutting-edge leadership and strategic management constructs tend to converge at the highest levels of organizations and enterprises. Leadership and management have certain similarities and many common elements. They both focus on context, strategic direction, decision making, and enduring success. Full-spectrum strategic leadership (FSL) pertains to the open-ended elements and intangible aspects of inspiring and engaging people. Strategic management, especially enterprise-wide strategic management (ESM), pertains to the company's strategic positions and direction, those of the strategic business units (SBUs), the governance of the company, and formulation and implementation of objectives and strategies.

FSL involves multifaceted perspectives that encompass the opportunities and challenges associated with leading organizations during the heady days of the twenty-first century. FSL covers the whole spectrum of the strategies, solutions, systems, structures, and relationships from the individuals of the organization to all of the entities of the extended enterprise. It embraces the whole and includes the needs and expectations of society and the global communities. Most importantly, it involves strategic thinking and action plans about how to create a unique business enterprise with distinctive characteristics and capabilities that are light years ahead of peers and competitors. It involves focusing on the market spaces and the business environment that produce extraordinary outcomes and sustainable success for contributors and recipients. It also involves the integration, harmonization, and synchronization of the whole enterprise;

this includes respecting and rewarding people from the top to the bottom of organization and across space and time.

ESM involves strategic thinking, high-level decision making, and taking initiatives through management systems, processes, and actions of the organization and enterprise. It involves the planning, developing, and implementing of strategies and initiatives by strategic leaders and the board of directors and engaging in the decisions and actions for realizing the strategic direction, fulfilling the mission(s) of the organization(s), and ensuring that operations are properly executed so that the desirable performance and results are obtained.

Traditional strategic management constructs involve widely-accepted approaches that are often used by strategic leaders, strategic managers, and planning professionals in crafting strategies and implementing the related action programs. Strategic management has a relatively long history of scholarly contributions and refinements that have been grounded through the decisions, actions, practices, and experiences of strategic leaders and professionals in real-world companies. While traditional strategic management constructs are not as narrow as those pertaining to generally accepted accounting practices and production, there is a sense of formality of well-defined and used constructs that many strategists and strategic planning professionals follow because they do not want to be viewed as being radicals or taking excessive risks. From their personal and professional perspectives, many senior managers often perceive out-of-the-box strategic thinking and actions as too risky, but being too timid is also very risky.

Business is about creating solutions, taking actions, and obtaining positive outcomes. It involves realizing the organization's aspirations and aims for the future and becoming the cutting-edge entity that visionary strategic leaders envision. Sustainable success is a mindset about pursuing perfection, and the ultimate but virtually impossible to realize overarching goal. It is the alpha and the omega of the objectives and outcomes. It is the never-ending progression of advancements dedicated toward creating extraordinary value for people across the full spectrum of the business enterprise. Sustainable success involves taking actions and realizing outcomes through insights, solutions, systems, and relationships with people that exceed expectations and outpace changes in the business environment and the markets spaces.

The concepts and constructs of FSL covered throughout the book reflect on how strategic leaders of today and future leaders as well can improve their prospects for leading change and sustaining success within the demanding context of global complexities, technological innovations and managerial sophistication. Unlike many of the prevailing theories about strategic leadership and strategic management that prescribe certain approaches like using power and influence when one has them, coercing people to accept your ways of doing things, or exploiting external entities and workers, the multifaceted perspectives of FSL examine the full spectrum of possibilities, reflect on the multiplicity of options, and focus on innovative ways of strategic thinking about how to create a more desirable reality in the foreseeable future. FSL involves taking on new challenges like providing solutions for people in emerging markets around the world so that they can enjoy the fruits of the knowledge of humankind and so that the business enterprise can realize its opportunities to continue achieving sustainable success. FSL is the never-ending quest toward being the best and having the best solutions possible.

This chapter covers a number of selected perspectives pertaining to strategic leaders and organizations based mainly on the constructs of sustainable success and FSL. It focuses on how strategic leaders and potential leaders can develop new ways of thinking about themselves and the people they engage that are creative, comprehensive, constructive, caring and rewarding. It also focuses on how strategic leaders can be more inclusive, innovative and connected in dealing with people and in their decision making processes.

The concluding comments reflect on some of the most critical aspects and considerations of cutting-edge leadership and management. This includes the concept that strategic leaders can become what they desire through intensive experience, learning and positive changes. Strategic leaders are not borne per se; they are educated and self-developed through personal development, professional actions, and well-rounded experiences.

This chapter includes the following main topics:

- Sustainable success and FSL as the means and the ends
- Concluding comments

Sustainable Success and FSL as the Means and the Ends

Exciting opportunities and challenges for sustainable success

Sustainable success is the all encompassing continuum. It is the singularity at the inception of a business and the enduring challenges of realizing achievements, advancements, and higher levels of sophistication. It also embodies the enduring strategic goal that propels strategic leaders and organizations into the future. Moreover, sustaining success is the guiding perspective that links the means and mechanisms for transitioning and transforming companies and business units into much more sophisticated entities over time.

Sustainable success involves moving along the pathway to the future that becomes more exciting and richer as success is built upon success, as depicted in Figure 3.2. It is akin to an outward spiral of strategic thinking, planning, and actions that continuously revisit the most important elements for achieving sustainable success, but each visitation is at a higher and more sophisticated level. The needs, requirements, and expectations at each new curve of the spiral become more and more demanding, but ones that produce and provide richer levels of well-being with greater and greater rewards. It is the ongoing journey of countless insights, innovations, interactions, and iterations that play out at increasingly higher and higher levels of sophistication. The business world is full of new and exciting opportunities and daunting challenges as the global economy unfolds. It is the duty and key responsibility of strategic leaders to assess and understand global realities and make good decisions. They strategize what actions are required and craft the requisite solutions using imagination, insightfulness, and innovativeness. They assure proper implementation through establishing systems and building relationships. Upon achieving a given level of success, they accelerate their efforts toward the next higher level of achievements and sophistication.

FSL involves strategizing, crafting, implementing, evaluating, accelerating, and sustaining. There is no end point. Sustaining implies that gains must be captured and integrated into the whole enterprise and used beneficially for obtaining the next levels. Accelerating infers that subsequent levels are more intense, more challenging, and more exciting than the previous ones; thus requiring even more intensity of actions at faster rates of change. Actions have to be increased dramatically. For instance, overall knowledge of humankind has been increasing at huge rates over the last several decades. It is believed to be doubling every ten years or so. As knowledge increases, people and organizations have to become more capable. As they become more capable, more is expected and required. Those that learn and gain knowledge, competencies, and capabilities at significantly higher rates than the norm are more likely to be successful. Those that fail to keep up fall out of synch with reality, become less relevant and may eventually fade away. This phenomenon plays out for organizations and for strategic leaders as well. No one can rest on one's strategic positions or past achievements! The challenges are immense, but the rewards can be great as well.

Figure 9.1 provides a graphical representation of the scheme. It is intended to indicate that the degree of sophistication covered by each subsequent level becomes higher and greater without an end point. While some strategic leaders might want the speed of the changes in the business world to slow down a little, it is highly desirable that the prospects for the future burn brightly and expand dramatically.

The levels of sophistication are indicative of philosophical perspectives, general positions, and main thrusts used by the strategic leaders and senior management of the organization (and operations and functional management). A given level is a representation of the overall situation and/or position related to organizational capabilities and its abilities to achieve sustainable success. A given level represents the general perspective of the company and its strategic leadership and their relative positions with respect to external context (economic, regulatory/political, environmental, social, ethical, technological, and cultural considerations) and internal context (capabilities, positions, resources knowledge, learning, etc.).

Level "1" represents the traditional narrow business perspective of *supply and demand* or *product-market* with operational management, financial matters, and economic considerations being the main dimensions. The focus is usually limited in scope with the basic tenets of the internal dimensions being production, marketing, and finance (traditional value chain) and those of the external dimensions being consumption, customers, markets, and competition (traditional value system). Such companies or business units are generally the producers and service providers that design, develop, produce, and deliver products and services for customers and clients. Their objectives are to generate revenues and make profits and to meet customers' wants and needs

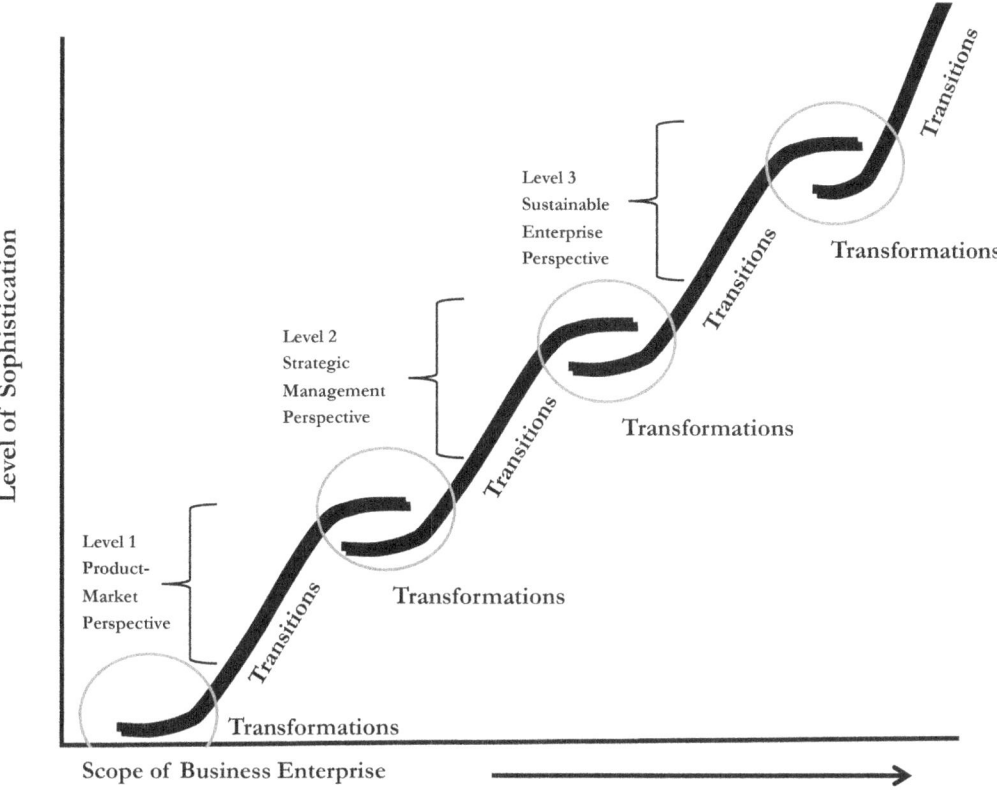

Figure 9.1 Theoretical levels of sophistication of companies/business units.

with reasonable offerings, i.e., affordable and of the kind and quality people expect. Strategic leaders provide the means and mechanisms to satisfy customer expectations, to make money, and to manage outcomes and risks. Level "1" also involves achieving compliance with all laws and regulations, including those pertaining to health and safety, the environment, labor, consumers, etc. The major objectives and initiatives are often to increase market shares, generate more revenues, and improve profitability. For instance, marketing promotion and sales efforts are often used for getting customers to buy more products and services; these methods are seemingly sensible approaches for making advancements. However, there are concerns about using such simply approaches. Increasing marketing efforts without resolving the underlying causes of problems often results in less cash flow and more frustration in the future. Many of the marketing approaches are really tactics or functional strategies that do not address the strategic management agenda, get to the essence of causality or improve sustainability. They generally address the product-market situations and short-term objectives without too much regard for the long-term implications.

Level "2" represents a slightly broader perspective of a *strategic management* or *strategic business* and the related approaches. It involves efforts used by companies and their strategic leaders to go beyond what is expected and mandated and provide more than the minimum requirements. Instead of simply meeting the basic requirements, the strategic leaders focus on exceeding needs and expectations. The internal dimensions include strategic management and operational management. The external dimensions include market, economic, technological, and environmental considerations. Level "2" involves achieving strategic success with good financial performance and outstanding market success in the short term and the near term. The most important considerations entail making strategic—not just operational or tactical—decisions and achieving strategic success through extensive planning and strategic actions. The causes of problems and difficulties are explored and corrective actions are taken. The emphasis is on prevention and risk mitigation. New solutions are developed at the strategic level and implemented at the operational level. Green initiatives are incorporated across the company, but generally not across the enterprise. Such companies move from being company-centric to market-centric.

Level "3" represents an increasing broader perspective of *sustainable enterprise.* The focus is on the whole business environment, the organization, and the extended enterprise. It takes an ESM perspective that is multidimensional, dynamic, and holistic. The scope includes the business environment and extended enterprise with all of the customers, stakeholders, supply networks, strategic partners, related industries, competition and infrastructure. The cutting-edge leadership and management constructs include FSL, ESM, sustainable business development (SBD), strategic innovations, leading change, sustainable solutions, value systems, building relationships, and business model innovation. SBD implies having value delivery system based on cradle-to-grave considerations and life cycle assessments.

The focus is on designing, developing, delivering, and validating sustainable solutions for all participants and creating the systems and structures for achieving outstanding performance and superior results. It provides a framework for ensuring that all of the essential dimensions and elements therein are covered. Indeed, a sustainable enterprise view involves a broad perspective of reality and examines reality in the context of what is and what can be done to make significant, if not, radical improvements and developments. Strategic leaders ensure that everyone is successful and that success is sustained across the enterprise and over time. Success is underpinned by creating outstanding management systems and building solid relationships.

Thinking in terms of the effects, impacts, and their consequences based on the levels of sophistication makes it easier to understand why certain organization and strategic leaders are very successful in earlier periods and then fail to keep pace with change. Certain strategic leaders of the past stopped improving and rested on their laurels believing that they had made significant achievements or that they had reached the strategic heights that they sought. However, from FSL and ESM perspectives, there are always necessities for more learning, additional improvements, and more significant strategic innovations. Ongoing efforts are required, especially in a faced-paced world with exciting emerging markets and new competitors with competitive advantages like large potential home markets, low cost production and modern facilities with high-tech equipment. The growth and developments of businesses in countries like China, India, and Brazil have the potential to radically change the global competitive landscape. Therefore, all strategic leaders have to be proactive and adapt cutting-edge leadership and management approaches if they want to succeed in a turbulent and unforgiving business world. Even if some the new competitors do not succeed, there are many others in the wings waiting to usurp the power and positions of the current global powerhouses.

FSL: The means and mechanisms for personal and organizational development

FSL is more than just strategic management because it embraces everyone and everything within the domain of the organization and the enterprise. It embraces strategic management constructs, but goes beyond strategic planning, strategic formulation and implementation, and execution. It involves having a perspective that examines the business world in all of its richness and endeavors to create the best solutions possible time and time again as the future unfolds with new opportunities and challenges. It is the relentless pursuit of the positives and sustainable success. It is also the persistent quest to eliminate the negative aspects as well.

In a business setting, FSL implies a higher level of authority and responsibility. While an individual can be a business leader based on his or her own ambitions, pursuits, and actions to promote and achieve certain desired outcomes, being a true strategic leader, one based on FSL, involves having multifaceted perspectives and pursuing the quest to achieve the best performance and outcomes and to become the best strategic leader possible. True strategic leaders inspire their organization to achieve extraordinary performance and outcomes and to reach beyond the obvious or simple. Furthermore, they ensure that the organization has the means and mechanisms to be successful.

FSL requires a mindset that envisions a more sustainable and inclusive vision for the future based on an architectural blueprint of the whole enterprise and on being on the cutting edge. It provides and enhances the capabilities and resources necessary to dramatically improve the present situation and to create a more sustainable reality in the future. It defines what is good, what is right, and what is expected.

Astute strategic leaders can use the leading change/sustainable success mindset to guide their own developments and achievements. Young leaders may not have the opportunities early in their careers to lead change to a large extent, but they can use the overarching perspectives (principles, philosophies, and concepts) of FSL to orchestrate their own personal development. They can find opportunities to excel, to learn faster than required and to outperform expectations. They can craft their own solutions that can be deployed to preempt the realities of the day. They can develop new ways and means to assure that the solutions are implemented properly. Most importantly, they can build relationships with people across the full spectrum of the enterprise that endure over time. Many aspiring young leaders often attempt to build beneficial relationships with the senior leaders who are influential and powerful. While this makes intuitive sense, it is also useful in the long term to create positive connections with people at lower levels of organizations and in other organizations.

The ability to lead often depends on having many people who are compatriots; individuals that trust and respect the person who is leading them. Leadership also depends on having people across the realities of the business environment that believe in the leader's competencies, capabilities, and honesty.

As leaders mature and gain experience, knowledge, influence and power, they can use the logic and mechanisms of the FSL to enhance their positions. They can orchestrate their own successes through imaginations and insights about what can be done instead of following the prevailing (mainstream) approaches. They can reflect on the completeness and effectiveness of the current solutions. They can work hard with others to create and implement new solutions and establish systems and the related means and mechanisms to assure success. They can build and reinforce relationships and ensure that everyone is moving the same direction and achieving good results. They can assure that success is properly distributed across the enterprise and that it is sustained. Moreover, they can realize that the pathway to the future is never ending; there is always the next level that is more challenging, more exciting, and potentially more fruitful.

The road to personal success that embraces a host of compatriots and supporters has many people pulling in the same direction. The challenges become easier and less taxing when everyone is helping and supporting common goals and the common good. On the other hand, strategic leaders that follow the road of coercion and exploitation of others for personal or professional gains usually find that the road to sustainable success is full of debris, potholes, pitfalls, and potential defeats. While some may succeed in spite of the difficulties, many fail to become what they could have been if they had embraced other people and supported them. The success stories of arrogant leaders often portray that power, coercion, and exploitation are appropriate ways to succeed. What such stories fail to show are the countless numbers of other strategic leaders who followed such dictates to their demise or how many of the arrogant leaders eventually failed in the end because they exhausted their capital and goodwill along the way.

Being successful necessitates an ongoing affinity and caring for people across the full spectrum of life. It is open-ended and difficult to truly articulate. It involves deep seated feelings about ontological good of people, the belief that one's success depends on the success of others and embracing the ongoing challenges to make the world a better place.

Sustainable success involves thinking about the possibilities, creating options for exceptional outcomes, crafting outstanding solutions, doing what is necessary in a positive way to orchestrate success, embracing people, and building enduring relationships. Ultimately, it is about producing positive outcomes, eliminating negative barriers and limitations, and accelerating everything to the next level of achievement as the driving forces of change demand more and more. It is not a process per se, but an overarching perspective about thinking, creating, connecting, embracing, doing, sustaining, and accelerating.

Concluding Comments

Great strategic leaders seek excellence for their organizations and enterprises and for the greater good of humankind. They are unselfish in their quest to succeed by ensuring that everyone involved is successful to the extent possible. Not only do great strategic leaders reach out beyond the direct responsibilities and realities of their positions, they encourage and energize everyone else to do the same. They seek rewards for the whole enterprise, not just for themselves.

As discussed throughout the book, FSL is a multifaceted construct about engaging and inspiring people across the organization and enterprise to contribute their best efforts, to embrace learning and development, to accomplish positives ends, and to lead change across the dimensions of the enterprise. It is an overarching construct that precedes and transcends those of management and administration. Strategic leaders of today must leap ahead of their peers and contemporaries and envision what they need to be or become in outperforming expectations and creating strategies, solutions, systems, and structures that exceed the mandates, requirements and expectations. Many of the significant problems that strategic leaders have today are due to the failures of their predecessors to effectively deal with the issues and challenges of their times. It is relatively easy to keep it simple in the present by transferring problems into the future. For example, numerous U.S. corporations had inadequate environmental management policies and methods during the most of the early twentieth century, especially prior to the proliferation of environmental laws and regulations of the 1970s and 1980s. In keeping things simple, the strategic leaders of the earlier periods simply created huge problems for those who followed them. They created enormous liabilities and sub-optimized future positions as they tried to optimize their own performance, thus threatening the company's sustainability and survival.

As change accelerates, strategic leaders have to prepare the pathway to the future by finding new avenues for making dramatic changes. They must use cutting-edge leadership and management constructs that resolve, if not dissolve, problems and liabilities. They must be adept at crafting whole solutions that include improving the positive aspects and eliminating the negatives. Crafting solutions involve examining the realities of the business world and the opportunities therein from every perspective. It means thinking about what is and what could be. It involves holistic thinking about the full spectrum of realities and possibilities.

Solutions have to be reinforced by having inclusive systems that provide the means and mechanisms to assure that the solutions can be developed, produced, delivered, and deployed. It is the integrated system that ensures that customers and stakeholders are satisfied and successful and that the contributors and participants are recognized, respected, rewarded and sustained.

Traditional strategic leaders often focus on two main categories of relationships that may skew their thinking and the results. They concentrate on shareholders and their short-term desires and on existing customers and their existing demands. While both aspects are understandable, appropriate, and necessary, strategic leaders must think and act beyond the obvious and include all aspects of the business environment. Success is predicated on the whole, not the parts. Success is achieved in the long term and in the short term.

Business is a people-oriented endeavor. Strategic leaders often forget that the essence of business success is based on having solid and enduring relationships with people. While customers and stakeholders are pivotal for success, there are many others who are critical for realizing the dreams, aspirations, and goals. Building relationships include all of the contributors and recipients of the enterprises from employees to related industries and partners.

Changes in the business environment and the market spaces are relentless. Strategic leaders must come to realizations about the meaning and implications of change through insightfulness and reflection, and then they must lead change to take advantage of the opportunities and challenges. Every opportunity requires a multifaceted perspective to ensure that the full potential is realized. For instance, the incredible growth of China over the last decade is perceived to be a phenomenon that is expected to continue over this century. Yet, there are already countervailing forces that may slow its growth and present insurmountable challenges. The lack of control of the use of toxic materials and the generation of hazardous wastes are examples of factors that may limit growth. Moreover, air and water pollution and their impacts on air and water quality may reach intolerable levels. While these kinds of problems caused by industrialization played out over a hundred or more years in many of the developed countries, the effects and impacts are being accelerated in many rapidly industrializing countries (RICs). Such negatives may make it impossible to continue developing at high rates of growth unless the strategic leaders involved lead change.

Moreover, the growth models used by the many government and business leaders in some of the RICs appear to be singled sided or one-dimensional, focusing on economic development at the expense of the other factors like social and environmental considerations, especially the well-being of workers and the society. In such situations, the elites (generally the upper 20% of the population and high-level government bureaucrats) may be faring very well, but a majority of the population does not enjoy economic and political freedom. They often live under uncertainty and marginal conditions. And, the conditions may become even more uncertain, less productive and more costly. There are still many locations in the world with attractive manufacturing situations where suppliers and producers can move their operations to reduce costs and expand economic benefits.

It is plausible to think that over the next fifty years most of the developing countries and emerging markets will become more capable and have the wherewithal to produce goods for their own needs and to compete on the global stage. While this does not imply that RICs like China and India will not continue to grow at significant rates, it does suggest that there will be many more contributors and recipients of global economic growth and development. This kind of economic development is expected to benefit most people as global poverty is reduced and social, economic, and environmental aspects are enhanced, hopefully resulting in less disease, fewer environmental difficulties, and increased wealth and well-being. Nevertheless, humankind is a long way from such realities, and it will take concerted efforts by leaders of all persuasions to achieve such lofty outcomes.

Globalization and sustainability are among the most critical factors facing strategic leaders wherever they may be. The national economies of the world are becoming more interconnected and more interdependent. There are few self-sufficient countries and companies. Many American and European enterprises are now dependent on suppliers in China for many of commodity-type parts, components, and even large durable products like TVs and appliances. Chinese companies depend on international markets for technologies, revenues, and cash flow. Everyone seemingly is dependent on the availability and cost of petroleum. Most people are dependent on many others for food production.

Globalization has many positive aspects including the sharing of information, the rapid exchange of goods, and generally low-cost production and distribution. Many of the old barriers to trade like tariffs and high transportation costs have been significantly reduced. Doing business on a global basis is easier and friendlier. Strategic leaders can obtain information and data about markets and customers at little cost and feel comfortable doing business in far-flung areas. Moreover, people in emerging markets are obtaining some of the means and mechanisms to eliminate the obstacles to their success and to become more productive and successful contributors.

The phenomenal rise of the Internet on a global basis is one of the most profound changes of the last quarter century. It is the all-pervasive means that has dramatically changed the lives of people and businesses. People can obtain information on anything, from anywhere. Businesses can exchange money, goods, and information without significant costs or time delays. Connectivity is a way of life. The Internet and the related technologies are expected to continue to evolve and expand, especially into developing countries. Internet protocols are some of the most significant contributors to social, economic, and technological developments in the early twenty-first century. They make doing business easier and less expensive. They provide a wealth of free information and instantaneous communications.

Access to the Internet provides some of the essential means and mechanisms for achieving success by the poor as well as the wealthy. For instance, the Internet could be of great benefit to poor farmers in isolated regions in Africa or South Asia who have crops to sell but little access to potential customers. Such farmers are usually disadvantaged because they lack information about markets and wholesale prices. They often sell to intermediaries at marginal prices because they are unaware of the true value of their products, or they do not have the ability to realize it. The intermediaries then sell to other intermediaries for the same reasons. Imagine if such farmers had access to the Internet, even if there were just one source per village, and could sell their crops using exchanges like eBay's auctions.

The business world is not only changing, the changes are accelerating. The next ten years are expected to be even more dramatic then the last ten years. Strategic leaders have to be prepared to stay ahead of the changes and to engage in novel ways of leading and managing their organizations and enterprise. The forces of change in the global economy necessitate that strategic leaders embrace being on the cutting edge and focus on the full spectrum of the business environment and extended enterprise. They must view the enormous changes as opportunities to excel and outpace peers and competitors. The economic realities have also changed dramatically with billions of new participants in the global economy, all seeking their place in the world. There are tens of thousands of global companies producing high quality cost-effective products and services.

Strategic leaders who came of age during the 1980s and 1990s, especially those in the U.S., may have a difficult time adjusting to the new realities of the global economy over the next decade or two. There will be many new powerful business entities on the world stage vying for customers and market shares. Some of the most powerful companies will be relatively new corporations from RICs. These companies are expected to have low-cost positions with other advantages like few legacy problems such as unfunded benefits for retired employees.

Some of the most significant limitations that conventional strategic leaders may have are their narrow perspectives and their steadfastness to many of the popular, but obsolete management theories of the late twentieth century. Many of them continue to try to keep things simple. They may continue focusing on just making money and think in terms of annual financial performance. But making money and financial success are the results of great strategies, solutions, systems, structures, and relationships; they are derivatives or end results of excellence, not primary mechanisms. Moreover, the focus on short-term results and financial performance at the expense of the long-term investments and sustainable success is often one the main culprits for decline. In the grand scheme of achieving sustainable success, the annual financial cycles are irrelevant. While it is understandable that strategic leaders have to ensure sound results on an annual basis, it is imperative that they do not sacrifice the future to maximize the present.

Other theories that need to be more holistic include going beyond focusing on core competencies, exploiting one's strengths and providing customer satisfaction. While such theories are not inherently wrong, they are too prescriptive and limited. Core competencies are often powerful ingredients in achieving near-term success. But as times change core competencies and capabilities have to be strengthened, augmented, and even replaced with others that better fit the new situations and circumstances. In a fast-paced world core competencies are difficult to maintain and often become irrelevant as new-to-the-world technologies and business approaches come and go. Many leadership theorists argue that strategic leaders should exploit their strengths and not worry about their weaknesses, but these theories can be deceptive. Today's strengths may become unimportant, and the areas of one's weaknesses may become critical factors for success. In the short term, focusing on one's strengths may pay dividends, but in the long term they may become barriers to success. Concentrating on customer satisfaction has similar negative aspects. It is sensible, but too narrow. Customers of all sorts want to be successful. They want quality, reliability, affordability, etc., and they expect even more. They expect the best solutions possible. True strategic leaders make stakeholders satisfied and successful as well.

Many business leaders want to be viewed as great strategic leaders. There are many ways to achieve such recognition; however, many contemporary business leaders fail to be great leaders because they are self-centered, arrogant, and often exploitive of people. While some of the most well-known business leaders of today and the recent past are touted as having achieved exceptional financial performance, it is difficult to call their achievements great if they left their organizations and enterprises in shambles or if they destroyed the lives of thousands of employees by simply making more profits instead of sustaining the well-being of the company and the people thereof. It may have been easy for such leaders to maximize the present, but what will happen to their companies five or ten years after they have departed? Business history is replete with stories of seemingly great leaders who destroyed the future of their organizations because they failed to invest into that future, especially through strategic innovations.

On a positive note, great strategic leaders usually exhibit outstanding qualities of leadership. They are honest, open, transparent, and personally accountable for their decisions and actions. They accept blame when appropriate and share the credit with contributors and participants. They take a FSL approach and ensure that they properly engage subordinates, superiors and peers alike. They are aware of the broader responsibilities to society, customers, non-customers, stakeholders, employees, and shareholders. They do not skew inputs and outputs from one extreme to the other and they ensure that outcomes are balanced and enduring.

Great strategic leaders recognize the important of sustainability and SBD. They provide great solutions that are supported by the contributions and support of the entire enterprise. The solutions are reinforced through the systems and structures that produce the complete package outcomes that people want and expect. They build enduring relationships that facilitate success. Great strategic leaders focus on people and ensure that they are successful. They know that success begets success and that short-term outcomes are meaningless unless they can be sustained and further enhanced in the future. They know that their overarching objectives are sustainable success and the well-being of the company(s) and all of the people it supports and that support it. Great strategic leaders are great because they make other people great.

FSL is the never ending desire to accomplish more and provide more beneficial outcomes for people. It is based on the recognition that good is never good enough, that the needs, wants, and expectations of tomorrow are expected to be more challenging than those of today, and that strategic leaders have to provide solutions to the myriad of problems, concerns and issues. It is also based on the multifaceted perspective that such challenges are really opportunities for excelling and creating value for everyone. Truly great strategic leaders provide solutions that maximize the positives and minimize the negatives. They embrace SBD, corporate social responsibility, sustainability, and sustainable success. Lastly, truly great leaders make the world a better place.

Glossary

Agility Agility is the ability to move quickly in new directions, and flexibility means being able to transform existing core capabilities into new ones that are in sync with new realities.

Attributes The sum of the benefits, features, and functions of a product deployed to meet the needs of customers.

Balanced scorecard According to Robert Kaplan and David Norton, an organization must use what they call a 'balanced scorecard' when making decisions. They suggest that business organizations balance their objectives by including financial considerations, customer satisfaction, organizational learning, and internal business improvement.

Benefit-cost (B/C) analysis B/C analysis or B/C equation depicts the sum of the benefits divided by the sum of the costs. It is a ratio of expected outcomes to expected costs (investments). The equation can be expressed as: $B/C = \Sigma \text{benefits (B)} \div \Sigma \text{costs (C)}$.

Bottom of the pyramid (BOP) The bottom of the pyramid includes the poorest people in the world. They live on less than $2 PPP US per day. They are often non-customers or latent customers who would like to have products and services if they were affordable and meet their conditions.

Breakthrough or disruptive technologies Breakthrough technologies are new-to-the-world technologies that change the nature of competition and provide the ability to create new types of products. It often requires the development of an infrastructure and support/related industries.

Business model A business model is a company's and/or business unit's unique way of combining the internal and external dimensions into a fully articulated framework for implementing and executing strategies and action plans and achieving desired outcomes. It includes the operating systems, value delivery systems, and extended enterprise(s) that are integrated into a comprehensive, coherent, and collaborative framework that stretches from the origins of the raw materials to the applications of the solutions and end-of-life considerations.

Business model innovation (BMI)   BMI involves the design, development, demonstration, and deployment of the business model. BMI is intended to be in concert with and reflect reality to the extent possible.

Business environment   The business environment includes the external forces impinging upon the corporation. They include the social, economic, ethical, political, technological, environmental, and market forces. It includes the external dimensions of markets, stakeholders, competition.

Capabilities   Capabilities are the strategic assets (people and resources) that translate the objectives and strategies into realities. They are the means for crafting strategies, effecting solutions, and sustaining them in the future.

Concept   A concept is a new product candidate that is fully articulated into a defined opportunity, expressed in terms of the targeted product/market and described based on its technical design aspects, marketability, manufacturability, and feasibility perspectives.

Connectedness   Connectedness implies that there are solid links of communications and personal contacts between the parties and individuals and that the contacts and linkages are based on enduring interfaces and relationships.

Construct   Constructs are the theoretical frameworks (models) used to analyze and determine strategies, systems, structures and solutions. The concept of a construct is relatively new. A construct is intended to be a representation of the dimensions and elements of business situations. It combines information, data, and experience with theoretical thinking about how to view the corporation in light of its opportunities, challenges, and constraints.

Continuous improvement   Continuous improvement is a broad concept that implies products and processes are never perfect and require ongoing improvements.

Core competencies   Core competencies are the capabilities of the organization that it uniquely possesses and are difficult for others to emulate. C.K. Prahalad and Gary Hamel define core competencies as "the collective learning in an organization."

Core capabilities   Core capabilities are the fundamental strengths and intellectual capital that an organization enjoys, but they are not necessarily unique to the organization.

Corporate management system   Corporate management is responsible for the embedded management system related to enterprise thinking, strategic direction, innovation, and product delivery. It involves creating a sophisticated business model that provides proper strategic direction and governance and guides the strategic and operating actions of the corporation.

Corporate Social Responsibility (CSR) CSR implies that corporations have a fiduciary duty to meet the needs and wants of customers and stakeholders and protect the health and safety of humankind and the natural environment. More specifically, it means taking corporate responsibility for the decisions and actions of the whole enterprise, not just those of the corporation.

Corporate strategy Corporate strategy is the pattern of decisions in a company that determines and reveals its objectives, purposes or goals; produces the principal policies and plans for achieving those goals; and defines the range of businesses the company is to pursue, the kind of economic and human organization it is or intends to be, and the nature of the economic and non-economic contribution it intends to make to its shareholders, employees, customers, and communities.

Countervailing forces Countervailing forces are ones that develop as the unresolved issues and impacts of products and services become apparent or significant. Countervailing forces often appear shortly thereafter; ones that were not apparent or may not have even existed until the new products and services made their entry.

Customers Customers are the buyers and/or users of the products and services provided by businesses. They are the direct recipients of the economic benefits of the corporation.

Distribution channels The distribution channel provides a means to reach potential customers. It consists of intermediaries, wholesalers, retailers, and/or agents who link the organization with the ultimate customer and provide the flow of information and physical products.

Dual-sided perspectives Dual-sided perspectives involve broader and more inclusive views that include satisfying and making customers successful, having an effective and integrated business enterprise, achieving success, providing positives outcomes for all contributors and recipients, and gaining new knowledge through learning and experience. Dual-sided perspectives focus on insights based on the full spectrum of realities and possibilities, balanced strategic thinking, inclusiveness, innovativeness, and thoroughness. They are holistic and multifaceted. They explore variables and parameters to the fullest extent possible.

Economic dimension The economic dimension includes the economic forces and factors and the conditions and trends of the global economy, the national economies, and economic activities in general. The economy, whether national, global, or subsets thereof, consists of the aggregation of the exchange of goods and services, the availability and use of resources, and the applications of labor and intellectual capital, land, and rents, among numerous other considerations.

Effectiveness Effectiveness involves selecting the right programs to investigate, analyze, and implement; allocating the appropriate resources to achieve the desired results; and leading the proper change mechanisms in the right direction. It is about discovering opportunities for leading change and creating solutions that eliminate underlying problems and impacts.

Effects Effects are the implications or consequences on the downstream processes, operations or customers if the failure or potential failure is not prevented or corrected. They are also the outcomes of upstream actions at some time in the future.

End-of-life (EoL) considerations EoL considerations involve producers assuming the responsibility for providing solutions for mitigating negative impacts and providing disposal of their products at the end of their useful life. Most importantly, producers are expected to build solutions to end-of-life disposal problems through creating a 'take-back' system, reuse, recycling, remanufacturing and other related initiatives.

Enterprise The enterprise is the entire organization (corporation) with all of its external relationships and linkages. It is a high-level strategic management system of the corporation and all of its strategic business units and their value delivery systems along with the all of the direct and indirect relationships with supply networks, partnerships, alliances, and other value networks.

Enterprise-wide strategic management (ESM) ESM involves the full integration of the strategic aspects of the organization and the internal functional areas with all of the external driving forces of change, the critical factors influencing the business, and the extended enterprise. ESM encompass the whole, both internal and external, and the present and the future. The power of ESM is that it is inclusive of all of the essential dimensions in managing and leading an organization and for achieving sustainable success.

Either-or trap Either-or trap involves making decisions in which only two options are presented and the decision makers have to select one. In many cases, both of the choices are based on compromises, and the end results are usually less than optimal from a systems point of view. The "either-or" choices may be the extremes or near the mid-point. Rather than trying to resolve all of the challenges, the choice often results in compromises in which no one is happy.

Ethical dimension The ethical dimension focuses on adhering to proper principles, standards, codes of conduct, and practices. The ethical dimension is based on underlying human rights and the overarching and generally accepted principles and practices that most people, cultures, and societies adhere to. It involves principles and standards of corporate behaviors that transcend laws and regulations in the cases where the laws and regulations do not adequately provide for proper behaviors and safeguards. It establishes the basis for conducting business that is respectful of the people, culture, and the natural environment.

Extended enterprise The extended enterprise includes all customers, stakeholders, supply networks, strategic partners, related industries, competition, and infrastructure.

Framework A framework is a management construct that includes the interrelated dimensions and the elements thereof and defines the boundaries and scope from a spatial and temporal perspective.

Full-spectrum Strategic Leadership (FSL) FSL is a dynamic and broad-based strategic leadership construct for leading change and sustaining success in complex business situations. FSL implies having and using a broad array of qualities, capabilities, values, attitudes, roles, responsibilities, and duties. These include having the knowledge, ability, confidence, and courage to lead change, being broad-minded, and selfless, practicing self-discipline, respecting and inspiring people, upholding the highest ethical standards, and being the architect of the organization's future. It necessitates having broad social, economic, ethical, market, technological, environmental, and organizational perspectives, crafting strategies and taking actions that are based on a holistic framework for understanding global realities and opportunities, orchestrating strategic direction, and achieving the desired outcomes.

Globalization The notion that world economies are shifting toward a borderless economic structure in which nation-states are less relevant and global corporations vie to satisfy customer demand based on standardized products and more homogenized approaches. Space and time are compressed, and geography is less of a critical factor.

High-level development program High-level development programs involve developing and deploying radical new technologies that provide strategic advantages that last at least five or more years, especially if the new technologies are protected with patents and/or trade secrets. New-to-the-world technologies represent breakthroughs in how solutions are developed and provided. They are not only game changers, but also provide new fields of endeavors that produce significant new outcomes.

Holistic management system A holistic management system incorporates the contributions of the value networks into what customers seek and expect, plus the full scope of all contributing and receiving entities. It provides a sense of what is necessary to create and develop solutions and to deliver them. The underlying philosophical aspects involve creating, developing, and deploying unique solutions and systems that generate the maximum value and benefits possible. It suggests that strategic leaders have to incorporate external value networks as essential components as well as internal capabilities and resources.

Human resource management Human resource management pertains to the policies, processes, and activities for maintaining effective management, administration, and control of the people within the organization. It is somewhat of a misnomer in the sense that people are the essence of the organization and not resources at all.

Inclusiveness   Inclusiveness is one of the fundamental aspects of sustainable business development. It is crucial for ensuring that decision-making includes all dimensions, all constituencies, and all effects and impacts, both positive and negative. Global corporations are expanding their view of the enterprise to include cradle-to-grave participants, partners, stakeholders and customers.

Infrastructure   The external infrastructure includes the Internet communications, telecommunications, energy systems, the airways, the roads, the waterways, etc. These networks and resources add value that facilitate the movement of goods, information, data, wastes, and energy to and from the supply networks. The infrastructure provides logistical support for the flow of products to customers.

Innovation   Innovation is a change or improvement that has a positive outcome(s) with respect to customers, stakeholders, and the organization.

Innovativeness   Innovativeness involves creating extraordinary value through strategic direction, proactive strategies, strategic innovations and sustainable solutions. It involves strategic leaders and other decision makers creating the best solutions possible by considering and assessing all dimensions, all contributors and recipients, all inputs and outputs, and all effects and impacts.

Insights   Insights are the perspectives and/or lessons gleaned from an assessment of the business environment or a portion thereof that lead to a broader understanding of reality and how to manage the situation and make appropriate decisions.

Insightfulness   Insightfulness involves understanding the true nature of the underlying forces of change and how to engage them. It involves discerning the most appropriate innovative solutions that provide customers, stakeholders, and all related contributors and recipients with extraordinary outcomes. Insightfulness also involves how strategic leaders can explore, develop, improve, and expand their strategic and operational positions through knowledge, intellectual capital, competencies, capabilities, and resources, and how to leverage those of their strategic partners, allies, and value networks. Insightfulness is an essential element for leading change, inventing solutions, making investments, managing risks and creating business value.

Integrated product development (IPD)   IPD is the concurrent development of new products using cross-functional teams that are aligned strategically and tactically. It is the prevailing form of product innovation. IPD is a powerful management construct that systematically links the external business environment and its needs, wants, opportunities, and challenges with the internal dimensions of the organization and its capabilities and resources to create innovative solutions based on improved products and services.

Intellectual capital/property   The intellectual capital of a corporation includes its knowledge, learning, and experience, the intellectual property (patents, trade secrets, protocols, databases), and the creative talents of the people within the organization.

Leading change   It generally involves using cutting-edge leadership and management thinking and approaches to achieve extraordinary value and to produce exceptional outcomes and sustainable success before anyone else. It is based on the concept of being ahead of the pack and proactively staying ahead over time. From a FSL perspective, it means formulating and implementing proactive strategies and actions to preempt the driving forces of change: to lead rather than follow! It involves creating new-to-the-world solutions through strategic innovations.

Management system   The management system is the integration of all of the processes and activities, the relationships and people, and the leadership and organizational capabilities, knowledge, skills, and methods. It is the modern platform for translating strategies into the structure of the organization and for developing initiatives and action plans.

Market spaces   Market spaces involve customers, non-customers, stakeholders, and competitors. They are the pivotal perspectives, since most businesses are market-oriented entities that produce and sell products and services for customers. Non-customers are people, especially those in less affluent areas and regions around the world, who would like to buy certain products and services if the right solutions were available, i.e., ones that meet the requirements of the person's circumstances, are affordable, and function with minimal support mechanisms.

Methodology   The processes, procedures, practices, and guidelines used by management and practitioners to formulate and execute strategies, programs, and action plans. It includes the methods, techniques and analyses to understand the situation(s) and to determine appropriate actions.

New product development   The overarching term used to describe the processes, programs, and practices to identify, conceptualize, design, develop, validate and commercialize new products and services. It is also the process for developing new products and processes.

New-to-the-world products   New-to-the-world products are new creations not based on previous products lines or technologies platforms. They normally are the results of technology development and new technologies derived from technological innovation.

Non-government Organizations (NGOs)   NGOs are usually voluntary, nonprofit organizations that focus on enhancing the public good or a specific sub-set including protecting the environment, promoting social justice, developing economic opportunities for the disadvantaged, and working on climate change concerns.

Organizational structure   Organizational structure defines the lines of authority and the management roles and responsibilities. It also defines the reporting relationships, the work processes, and the scope of activities.

Paradigm-illuminating   Paradigm-illuminating involves proactive approaches for understanding the new realities and staying ahead of the new needs, requirements, and expectations. It involves the recognition that the business world is changing every day and that businesses and strategic leaders must make dramatic, if not revolutionary, changes in how they do business and what business arenas they engage in. It is more open-ended than most management constructs and models, since it is impossible to specify how to create the new paradigm.

Political dimension   The political dimension deals with governance of people, the affairs of governments, and political leaders, and public policy. It is theoretically about the proper governance of civil society and the common good. Governance in this context is about the systems, structures, and management of government and public affairs. It involves making good policy decisions for the greater good of society and ensuring balance and fair treatment for all. It especially involves enacting laws and promulgating regulations to protect the well-being of people, to eliminate criminal behaviors, to control and punish deviant actions, and to provide fairness and a level playing field.

Pollution prevention (P2)   P2 represents the 'second generation' of environmental management that focused on creating an EMS to systematically deal with environmental laws and regulations and attempt to prevent pollution and waste problems before they became significant. P2 focused on pollution reduction at the source, reuse, recycling, and proper disposal of wastes.

Power factor   The power factor derives from the fact that a clean technology can be developed, produced, and deployed millions of times with little additional expense and relatively few impacts after the initial investment. The power factor is akin to the concept of leveraging physical resources and operations, especially those involving production. Whereas leveraging usually means increasing capacity utilization by ten to twenty percent, such as using the existing but underutilized productive resources for counter-seasonal products, thereby improving many aspects of the operating system through more efficient deployment of resources, the power factor involves improvements of hundreds, thousands, or millions of times more than what the previous or alternate technology could do.

Problem solving   Problem solving involves relatively simple approaches using linear thinking and processes. The typical process includes describing the problem(s), analyzing the situation(s), determining the implications, developing, and evaluating alternatives, and selecting and implementing the fixes. While it is sensible and straightforward, there are many potential pitfalls. One of the most significant is dealing with symptoms instead of the real problems.

Product (value) delivery system   The product delivery or operating system includes the marketing and production of existing products and the related services. It includes the contributions of supply networks to meet the needs and expectations of customers and stakeholders and managing EoL considerations. It focuses on near-term results and the operational requirements to meet expectations.

Product innovation   Product innovation is a broad management construct that includes the initiatives, methods, techniques and processes for making incremental changes and improvements to existing products and services. It involves making evolutionary changes to the products and products lines employing the prevailing technologies and organizational capabilities. It represents improvements for meeting the needs of customers and stakeholders.

Product portfolio   The product portfolio includes the core products, related products, services, after-market products and services, and their relationship to new products.

Puzzle-solving   Puzzle-solving requires ingenuity, research, careful study, and due considerations for inventing the right solutions and outcomes. It involves sophisticated strategic thinking about all of the opportunities and possibilities. It involves out-of-the-box thinking, not simply following the mainstream or what the other strategic leaders have done or are doing. Puzzling-solving is more complex because strategic leaders have many more variables to understand, manage, and resolve before making decisions. It involves the realms of the many unknowns and uncertainties.

Radical change   Radical change focuses on creating a new reality. It is difficult to articulate precisely the implications, but often the results lead to improvements that are 10x to 100x or more. It also involves eliminating significant barriers or burdens associated with the prevailing technologies.

Radical innovation   Radical innovation involves creating new-to-the-world technology that brings about revolutionary changes and often creates a new industry or market structures or involves dramatic changes to the existing ones. It may involve starting a whole new business unit or subset thereof, or making substantial changes to the existing strategic management system, including developing new customers, new markets, new supply networks and other related entities.

Related industries   Related industries provide complementary and support products and services that make the new product more valuable or even feasible.

Single-side perspectives   Single-sided perspectives are usually narrow and generally concentrate on the positive aspects. It contends that business leadership is rightly guided by the "economic self-interest" of capitalism; i.e., the purpose and primary objectives of corporations are to maximize profits and shareholder wealth.

Social dimension The social dimension encompasses all of the social factors pertaining to people, their human rights, and the prevailing conditions and trends. It includes demographics, people's economic circumstances, lifestyles, cultures, the makeup of local, regional and global communities, and the concerns and perceptions of stakeholders and people in general.

Solution A solution is a multifaceted concept that includes the product, the service, the underlying technology(s), and all of the tangible and intangible elements of the system that accompany it. It is temporal and psychological as well as physical.

Solution set A solution set consists of products and services, related systems and processes, structures, and relationships in combinations with complementary products and services and systems of the extended enterprise that are integrated into a whole.

Stakeholder A stakeholder is any individual or group that is directly or indirectly affected by the products, programs, processes, and/or systems, but does not directly benefit as an economic participant, such as a customer or supplier. Stakeholders include government agencies, interest groups, communities, society in general, and other constituencies.

Strategic innovations Strategic innovations are generally game changing new-to-the-world products, radical technology developments, innovative management constructs, and business model innovations. They are usually based on the strategic plans and initiatives that are directly tied to the vision and strategic direction of the company. They involve a complex array of action plans and initiatives that are intended to result in transitions and/or transformations of the company or a significant portion of it (select business units).

Strategic management Strategic management provides the direction and strategic logic for achieving sustainable success. It includes the planning and analysis of strategic business issues, opportunities, and vulnerabilities, and the selection of a vision for the future, long-term objectives, and a grand strategy for the corporation.

Supply networks Supply networks include the suppliers, suppliers of suppliers, distributors, and other entities that provide the flow of materials and finished goods, information, and relationships from the origins of the raw materials through distribution channels to customers.

Sustainability Sustainability implies that all human and business activities are carried out rates equal to or less than the Earth's natural carrying capacity to renew the resources used and naturally mitigate the waste streams generated.

Sustainable business development (SBD) SBD is a holistic management construct that includes the entire business system from the origins of the raw materials to production processes, to customer applications and to the end-of-life solutions. SBD involves making dramatic improves and positive changes to the full scope of relationships and linkages with the supply networks, customers and stakeholders, and support service providers. It also involves life cycle management about all of the effects, impacts and consequences from cradle to grave. It involves achieving sustainable outcomes that balance the performance objectives of the present with the needs of the future.

Sustainable success   Sustainable success is a multifaceted management construct that focuses both on radically improving the social, economic, technological, and environmental benefits and on significantly decreasing the cost structures and eliminating hidden defects, burdens and impacts. It is an overarching goal as well as a driving force. Sustainable success involves realizing the vision, the business objectives, the "lifestyle" of the enterprise and extraordinary performance and ensuring the well-being of the whole business enterprise and all of the contributors and recipients thereof.

Technological change   Technological change involves the driving forces of change in the business environment caused by the discovery, invention, and development of new technologies, knowledge, and mechanisms for providing solutions to customer, stakeholders, and society.

Technological innovation   Technological innovation is the systematic creation of new-to-the-world technologies that are superior to their predecessors and the improvement of existing technology portfolios. Technological innovation also occurs when improvements are made to the use and effectiveness of knowledge or when technological sophistication and organizational learning are advanced.

Technology   Technology is a complex term that includes art, science, engineering, devices, methods, and know-how that are applied in a beneficial manner.

Technology development   Research and development and/or related constructs for the invention, discovery, and development of new technology(s). It also includes enhancing technology platforms. Improving existing technologies and derivatives thereof.

Theoretical construct   A theoreticl construct is a management model that represents the real world situation or management system defining how the elements are linked together and how the responsibilities, relationships and actions are designed; and examining the spatial and temporal relationships with every constituent.

Total quality management (TQM)   TQM is a widely accepted quality management system related to the value system or operating system that incorporates quality management practices and techniques necessary for meeting customer expectations in terms of quality, reliability and responsiveness. The basic philosophy of TQM is to build quality into every product and process and to strive for continuous improvement.

Triple bottom line   A framework underpinned by an integrated perspective of the social, economic, and environmental aspects.

Value chain   The value chain links the flow of activities within the operations. It involves a more horizontal perspective on value creation within the firm. It includes the primary activities from the flow of materials and parts into the operations via inbound logistics to the actual in-house operations involving production and assembly of products or operational elements for services. It also includes the marketing and sales efforts linked with the upstream elements of operations and the downstream aspects of services and customers support.

Value creation Value creation involves moving toward ideal solutions with greater benefits, fewer deficiencies, and reduced impacts. The objective is to create the best possible solutions for customers, stakeholders, and society; solutions that maximize gains and minimize losses.

Value innovation Value innovation is an interactive approach for discovering, creating, developing, and implementing new solutions and systems through strategic innovations. It involves open-ended ways to satisfy existing and latent needs and wants and developing innovative constructs. It requires out-of-the-box strategic thinking about what could be or should be. In particular, it involves reaching out to potential customers, market spaces, and people that are not currently being served or even addressed.

Value networks Value networks are all of the interrelated entities in the enterprise that contribute to value creation and the sustainable success of the enterprise. They include all of the partnerships, alliances, supply networks, and customer and stakeholder relationships used to create value.

Value maximization Value maximization is the underlying premise of a corporation that the main objective is to maximize value for all constituents, including customer, stakeholders, shareholders, etc.

Value proposition The value proposition examines all of the benefits, positive effects, and knowledge in terms of the investments made by all of the constituents; and, similarly, all of the costs, defects, and burdens associated with the situation.

Value system The value system includes the primary dimensions of the operating system, supply networks and customers. It includes the value chains of all upstream supply networks and other contributors to value creation and delivery, and the downstream aspects related to customers and their applications. The upstream elements include parts and materials flow from raw material extraction, materials refinement, energy providers, parts fabrication, production of end products and the requisite support services. The downstream aspects include customer buying patterns and applications, reuse, and end-of-life considerations.

Vision Vision is the high-level perspective that encapsulates the desired translation of external forces, opportunities, challenges and internal capabilities into a new reality for the enterprise. It should describe how a sustainable entity meets the needs of the present and the future. Vision guides the people within the organization as well as customers, stakeholders, shareholders and other constituents, clearly stating for them why the organization exists and what it seeks to do to create an improved future.

About the Author

Dr. David L. Rainey is an internationally known author, educator, academic leader, and business consultant. He is a leading authority on sustainable development, strategic leadership, strategic management, technological innovation, product development, and energy management. He is a strategist and pragmatist working at the intersection of leadership, strategy, innovation, systems, and solutions pertaining to the opportunities and challenges in today's turbulent business environment.

Professor Rainey is Acting Dean of Rensselaer at Hartford focusing on advanced professional education for working professionals. He is a professor of practice and the former chair of the Hartford Department of the Lally School of Management at Rensselaer Polytechnic Institute. He has over forty years of experience and leadership in industry and academia. Dr. Rainey is a visiting professor at the Technical University of Munich and an associate of "the Center for the Study of Corporate Sustainability", Instituto De Estudios Para La Excelencia Competitiva in Buenos Aires, Argentina.

Professor Rainey has advised companies on developing business strategies and radical technologies in the fields of biotechnology, energy systems, fuel cells, aircraft and submarine design, hydrogen peroxide applications, cryogenic processing, bioremediation, recycling, high temperature plasma-arc furnaces, and many other technologies and products. He has consulted with more than fifty global corporations, including United Technologies Corporation, Sikorsky Aircraft, Toyota, BMW, Siemens AG, AT&T, Electric Boat Division of General Dynamics, Holnam, International Fuel Cells, Lego Systems, Pennsylvania Power & Light, Pfizer, Inc., and others. He has participated in the start-up of more than thirty entrepreneurial companies. He was a principal, owner and executive of GNA Industrial Furnaces, Inc., a systems engineering company, in Montreal, Canada that specialized in designing and producing equipment for the aluminum industry.

Dr. Rainey is the author of *Product Innovation: Leading Change through Integrated Product Development* (2005, ISBN 0-521-84275-1), *Sustainable Business Development: Inventing the Future through Strategy, Innovation and Leadership* (2006, ISBN: 0-521-86278-7) and

Enterprise-wide Strategic Management: Achieving Sustainable Success through Leadership, Strategies and Value Creation (2010, ISBN: 978-0-521-76980-8). The books are published by Cambridge University Press. His more recent books include *The Pursuit of Sustainable Leadership: Becoming a Successful Strategic Leader through Principles, Perspectives, and Professional Development* (2013, ISBN 978-1-62396-127-5), *Visionary Strategic Leadership: Sustaining Success through Strategic Direction, Corporate Management, and High-level Programs* (2014, ISBN 978-1-62396-3200) and *Full-spectrum Strategic Leadership: Being on the Cutting Edge through Innovative Solutions, Integrated Systems and Enduring Relationships* (2014) published by Information Age Publishing. His next book is *The Pursuit of Sustainability: Creating Business Value through Strategic Leadership, Holistic Perspectives and Exceptional Performance*

Dr. Rainey was President and CEO of a U.S. subsidiary of Alfa Laval AB, a Swedish multinational. He was Vice President and General Manager of the U.K.-based Wellman Engineering Corporation, a manufacturer of process equipment for the automobile, steel, aluminum, and pulp and paper industries. He began his business career at Combustion Engineering, Inc. holding successive positions as research and development engineer, project manager and manager of strategic business planning.

Dr. Rainey earned a BS in Mechanical Engineering, a MBA, and Master of Science degrees in Engineering Science and Business Management. He earned a Ph.D. in Urban and Environmental Studies from Rensselaer Polytechnic Institute.

CPSIA information can be obtained at www.ICGtesting.com
Printed in the USA
LVOW03s0341010914

401731LV00005B/148/P